IF CHRIST CAME TO CHICAGO!

It is written, My house shall be called the house of prayer;
but ye have made it a den of thieves.—*Matthew 21: 13*.

IF CHRIST CAME TO CHICAGO!

A Plea for the Union of All Who Love in the Service of All Who Suffer

"Said Christ our Lord, I will go and see
How the men, My brethren, believe in Me."
—*Lowell.*

BY

WILLIAM T. STEAD

CHICAGO
LAIRD & LEE, PUBLISHERS
1894

PRESS OF THE

EIGHT-HOUR HERALD,
CHICAGO.

ISBN
0-924772-11

Reprinted by

831 Main St. Evanston, IL 60202

Cover design by **Dorothy** Kavka, Evanston, IL.

INTRODUCTION

Among the 9,067 books about Chicago I have collected, the most treasured was the copy of *If Christ Came to Chicago*. Of all of them, it best described the life of the city, analyzed its strengths and weaknesses, and told what Chicago could and can be.

For the most part, pages of original copies of this book have now turned brittle. Still, for almost 100 years, they have fascinated readers with a hoard of details portraying the in-depth story of what Chicago was like in 1893.

And Chicago was something. It was — to borrow the title of a later book — an "exploding metropolis." It grew faster in the 19th century than any other city in the world ever had. This growth included tremendous influxes of immigrants, the erection of hundreds of thousands of miles of streets and streetcar lines, and the development of schools and churches. Along with the growth came the two by-products of civilization: culture and corruption.

If Christ Came to Chicago is about Chicago's culture and especially its corruption.

And William T. Stead was also something special. He was the most talked-about journalist of his age, having earned his reputation on the English publication *Review of Reviews,* where he was a reform-driven editor.

Stead was attracted to Chicago in 1893 not only by its reputation but also by the World's Columbian Exposition in Jackson Park that year.

He became far more interested in Chicago than the World's Fair, which was a pretentious reconstruction of ancient Rome and Greece and a genuflection toward the more imitative culture of the East Coast.

And what a study he did of the city! Few, if any reporters, writers, photographers, or novelists have ever captured the soul of Chicago as Stead did.

Stead's is a sincere book. He was one of the first of the progressives who used Chicago as a base, if not a home. He firmly believed things could be better, very much better, and it was humankind's responsibility to join the exciting flow in the upward direction of mankind.

Stead's book is remembered, however, better for its detailing of what was corrupt about Chicago in 1893 than for his plans for its improvement.

A century later, much of his descriptions are still accurate, his analysis valid, and his vision yet possible. And reading his book is still a pleasure.

William T. Stead died April 15, 1912. He went down with great dignity aboard the White Star liner *Titanic.* A fellow passenger later described his behavior in assisting others, without care for himself, as demonstrating "superhuman composure". It was as though Stead, possibly the most famous journalist of his era, chose not only the style, but also the front page itself on which to banner his exit from life.

-Kenan Heise
Fall, 1990

CONTENTS

CONTENTS—Continued.

PREFACE.

"If Christ came to Chicago!" It was under this title that, after a month's sojourn in the city, I summoned a Conference in the Central Music Hall, which was held in November, 1893. Nothing was further from my thoughts at that time than publishing a book on Chicago. The impression produced by the Conference was so remarkable that I promised to print a report of the proceedings, with an appendix, and for that purpose contracted with a firm of stenographers for a verbatim report of the speeches. The stenographers, however, failed to supply the promised report, and I returned to Chicago to see what could be done.

My second visit to Chicago occurred at a critical time. The pressure of the problem of the unemployed was beginning to be severely felt; the movement in favor of a Civic Federation, initiated at the conference at the Central Music Hall, was entering into the region of realized fact; the American Federation of Labor was about to meet in the city; the trial of Prendergast, the slayer of Carter Harrison, and of Dan Coughlin, for the murder of Dr. Cronin, were in progress; and, more important than all else, Mr. Hopkins, the rising young Democrat, was entering the field as candidate for the mayoralty, then temporarily held by Mr. Swift. For three months I was an intensely interested spectator of the rapidly unfolding drama of civic life in the great city which has already secured an all but unquestioned primacy among the capitals of the New World.

This little volume, originally projected as a mere reprint of the proceedings of a Sunday's conference, has assumed its present shape as the result of much consultation with

many of the leading citizens of Chicago, who have been
kind enough to encourage its publication.   It is based upon
the carefully collected opinions of the ablest and most
respected residents, which have been collated and compared with the opinions of other residents as able perhaps,
but who unfortunately are neither respected nor respectable.   Throughout all my work of interrogation and con-
densation I have clung to the hypothesis which forms the
keynote and the starting point of the whole: "If Christ
came to Chicago!"

I have discussed the question with ministers of all
religions and with the avowed unbelievers, with bankers and
merchant princes, with the keepers of saloons, and even
with the madames whose infamous calling has not entirely
obliterated the Divine image which is the heritage of every
child of man.   It has been a strangely interesting and most
suggestive discussion.   To men of the world, to busy administrators, to labor agitators, to the crook and to the
harlot, the question: "If He came to Chicago, what would
He think of us and of our lives?" was often strangely
unfamiliar, and sometimes provoked the most incongruous
replies.   "We take no stock in Christ in Chicago!" said
one man.   "He was all very well nineteen hundred years
ago in Judea, but what have we to do with him in civic
life in Chicago?"   Not much, it is to be feared— "'tis true,
'tis pity, and pity 'tis 'tis true."   But, although there was
sometimes a disposition to scoff at this insistence on the
presence of the Son of Man, even in the precincts of the
Board of Trade, the conception grew in power and in influence, and I often marveled to note the effect which the
thought produced even on the most hardened and vicious.
It might only be temporary, as most things are in this
transitory world, but it was well if even for a moment some
ray of Divine light should lighten the darkened soul with
a passing vision of the love of God.   For Christ, even

to those who use His name but to garnish their profane and filthy talk, still represents the most majestic and the most pathetic of all the conceptions which Man has formed of God. In the bleared eyes of the besotted drunkard, and in the dazed and despairing heart of the fallen woman, there was a recognition of the infinite love and tender sympathy which, long since, became man in order to interpret God. Christ, even to those who regarded him as a myth, is at least an accepted standard of ideal character, shining out luminous as the sun against the dark and gloomy background of human society as it is. The fascination of the popular conception of the Christ is His intense humanness. It is not as the Judge of all the earth, nor as the Second Person in the Divine Trinity, that He appeals to the common people. Christ is to them the Man of Sorrows, who was tempted in all points even as we; the Divine tramp, who said of himself, "the foxes have holes and the birds of the air have nests, but the Son of Man hath not where to lay His head;" the heretic and outcast who supped and made merry with winebibbers, who came eating and drinking, and was called a gluttonous man, a friend of publicans and sinners. Christ was and is to the common man merely his own highest self, radiant with Divine love, suffused with infinite compassion. That idea of a perfect standard of right and wrong, applied by One who has a sympathy that never fails, because based upon an understanding of all the facts, can never be forgotten without loss, or ignored without peril.

"Oh, Christ is all right!" said one poor girl on Fourth Avenue, "it is the other ones that are the devil." And she spoke a bitter truth. For He dwells in us but partially, and that which is in us without Him is carnal, earthly and devilish in sad reality. But the thought of Him recalls the ideal, and by applying that ideal to the actual circumstances of the civic life of Chicago, men realized more clearly how far short they had come of carrying out His will. To very many the conception of the Citizen Christ was so new as almost to be distasteful. To them it appeared at first almost as some strange heresy that the Son of Man could have either part or lot in such mundane institutions as municipalities and primaries. But by degrees it began to dawn upon those who pondered the matter in their hearts that the Churches, by insisting so exclusively upon the other life, have banished Him from His own world, and by the substitution of Divine Worship for Human Service have largely undone the work of the Incarnation. To re-enforce this growing sentiment, to strengthen this dawning consciousness of the reality of the Citizen Christ, this book is given to the world. Whatever value it possesses, whatever help there is in it for the citizens of Chicago, or of any other city, will depend solely upon the fidelity with which I have succeeded in expressing the mind of Christ on the subjects which it treats, and of bringing those who read its pages within the shadow of the presence of the Son of Man.

The original conception of Christ coming to Chicago reached me, like most of my religio-philosophical notions, through the poetry of James Russell Lowell. The short poem which he styled a parable always seems to me to sum up in a page the vital essence of Christ's teaching. It is as it were a new chapter of the Gospel of St. John, done into English by the American poet-seer of the nineteenth century. I quote it here as the best explanation of the title of this book.

> Said Christ our Lord, "I will go and see
> How the men, My brothers, believe in Me."
> He passed not again through the gate of birth,
> But made Himself known to the children of earth.
>
> Then said the chief priests, and rulers and kings,
> "Behold, now, the Giver of all good things;
> Go to, let us welcome with pomp and state
> Him who alone is mighty and great."

With carpets of gold the ground they spread
Wherever the Son of Man should tread,
And in palace-chambers lofty and rare
They lodged Him, and served him with kingly fare.

Great organs surged through arches dim
Their jubilant floods in praise of Him ;
And in church, and palace, and judgment-hall
He saw His image high over all.

But still, wherever His steps they led,
The Lord in sorrow bent down His head,
And from under heavy foundation stones
The Son of Mary heard bitter groans.

And in church, and palace, and judgment-hall
He marked great fissures that rent the wall,
And open wider and yet more wide
As the living foundation heaved and sighed.

"Have ye founded your thrones and altars, then,
On the bodies and souls of living men?
And think ye that building shall endure
Which shelters the noble and crushes the poor ?

"With gates of silver and bars of gold
Ye have fenced My sheep from the Father's fold ;
I have heard the dropping of their tears
In heaven these eighteen hundred years."

"O Lord and Master, not ours the guilt ;
We build but as our fathers built ;
Behold Thine images, how they stand,
Sovereign and sole, through all our land.

"Our task is hard, with sword and flame
To hold Thy earth forever the same,
And with sharp crooks of steel to keep,
Still, as Thou leftest them, Thy sheep."

Then Christ sought out an artisan,
A low-browed, stunted, haggard man ;
And a motherless girl, whose fingers thin
Pushed from her faintly want and sin.

These set He in the midst of them,
And as they drew back their garments-hem,
For fear of defilement, "Lo, here," said He,
"The images ye have made of Me."

As this poem suggested the title, so it has inspired every page in this book. The dominant idea which Lowell insisted upon is the truth which, more than any other, is needed to inspire and vivify our impotent, limp and ineffective conception of Christianity. How we believe in Christ is shown not by what we say about Him, nor by the temples which we build in His honor, nor by the hymns which we sing in His praise, but by the extent to which we succeed in restoring in man the lost image of God. The tramp is Christ's brother, the harlot is Christ's sister. These are the images which we have made of Christ. As the strength of a chain is tested by its weakest link, so the extent of our failure to save the least of these, His brethren, may be illustrated by the actual condition of those who are lost.

When once this idea is clearly and firmly grasped, when the condition of our fellow citizens is recognized as the test of the measure of our faith in Christ, the religious aspect of civic politics acquires a new and supreme importance. For the improvement of the lot of the least of these, Christ's brethren, the assistance of the municipal authority is indispensable. The law must be invoked, if only as the schoolmaster, to bring men to Christ. Before we can make men divine, we must cast out the devils who are brutalizing them out of even human semblance. But this cannot be accomplished excepting by the use of means, which can only be wielded by the City Council. Hence, as it used to be said of old time that all roads lead to Rome, so the more attentively we study the way out of our social quagmire, the more clearly will it be discerned that all roads lead to the City Hall. Thus it has come to pass that this little volume, begun with the simple object of recalling the conception of the Man Christ Jesus, has developed into an attempt to illustrate how a living faith in the Citizen Christ would lead directly to the civic and social regeneration of Chicago.

WILLIAM T. STEAD.

Commerce Club,
      Auditorium Building, Feb. 24, 1894.

IF CHRIST CAME TO CHICAGO!

PART I.—Some Images Ye Have Made of Me.

CHAPTER I.

IN HARRISON STREET POLICE STATION.

"In the name of that homeless wanderer in this desert of stone and steel, whose hopeless heart lies leaden in his bosom, whose brain grows faint for want of food — in the name of that unnecessary product of American freedom and prosperity, the American tramp, I bid you welcome to the Imperial City of the boundless West." So spoke William C. Pomeroy, Vice-President of the Trade and Labor Assembly, on behalf of the labor unions of Chicago, to the convention of the American Federation of Labor which assembled at Chicago in last December.

He but expressed in his own vivid way some of the bitterness of discontent which all men felt in Chicago last winter.

Among "the images which ye have made of Me," the tramp is one of the most unattractive, and in December he was everywhere in evidence. The approach of winter drove him from the fields to seek shelter in the towns, which were already overburdened with their own unemployed. Like the frogs in the Egyptian plague, you could not escape from the tramps, go where you would. In the city they wandered through the streets, seeking work and finding none. At night if they had failed in begging the dime which would secure them a lodging they came together in three great herds, presenting a sad spectacle of squalid misery and forlorn manhood. These nocturnal camps of the homeless nomads of civilization were all in the center of the city. Of these the most wretched was that which was pitched in Harrison Street Police Station.

The foot-sore, leg-swollen tramp who had wandered all day through the city streets, looking more or less aimlessly for work or food, sought shelter at night wherever he could find a roof to shelter him and warmth to keep the frost out of his bones. Some kenneled in empty trucks on the railway sidings, rejoicing even in a fireless retreat ; others crept into the basement of saloons, or coiled themselves up in outhouses, but the bulk of them were accommodated in the police stations, in the Pacific Garden Mission and in the City Hall. Such improvised shelters were all the appliances of civilization which Chicago in the year of the World's Fair had to offer to the homeless out-of-works.

There is something dreary and repelling about a police station even in the least criminal districts. But Harrison Street Station stands in the midst of darkest Chicago. Behind the iron bars of its underground cages are penned up night after night scores and hundreds of the most dissolute ruffians of both sexes that can be raked up in the dives of the levee.

The illuminated clock of the tower at the depot shines dimly through the frosty smoke-mist, as a kind of beacon light guiding the tramp toward his destined haven. Down Harrison Street, trailing his weary, shambling legs over the dirty snow, he crosses in succession the great arterial thoroughfares through which the city's miscellaneous tide of human life runs loud and fast, until he sees the road barred by the horizontal pole and the spot of green light which arrests traffic across the grade crossing of the railway. The bell of the locomotive rings without ceasing, keeping up its monotone as if relays of sextons were tolling for the victims who that day, as every day, had been slaughtered on the tracks. A patrol wagon full of officers and prisoners drives up to the brick building at the corner of Harrison Street and Pacific Avenue and begins to unload. The occurrence is too familiar even to attract a passing loafer. The cold and frost-keen wind makes even the well clothed shiver. The tramp hesitates no longer. He pulls open the door of the station and asks for shelter.

Harrison Street Police Station is one of the nerve centers of criminal Chicago. The novelist who had at command the life story of those who, in a single week, enter this prim brick building surrounded by iron palings, would never need to draw on his imagination for incident, character, plot, romance, crime—every ingredient he could desire is there ready to hand, in the terrible realism of life. For the station is the central cesspool whither drain the poisonous drippings of the city which has become the *cloaca maxima* of the world. Chicago is one of the most conglomerate of all cosmopolitan cities, and Harrison Street Police Station receives the scum of the criminals of Chicago. It is also the great receiving house where the police and the bailsmen and the justices temporarily pen the unfortunate women who are raided from time to time "for revenue only," of which they yield a goodly sum to the pockets of the administrators of "justice."

The cells, if they may be called such, are in the basement, half underground. They resemble the cages of wild beasts in a menagerie. There are two short corridors into which the cages open on the right and left, while the remaining corridors have only cages on one side, the other being the stone wall. The floor is of stone. In each cell there is one bench on which the first comers can sit while the others stand. An open gutter at the back provides the only sanitary accommodation. One policeman and one police matron are in command. Each of the corridors is closed by an iron barred gate.

The place is lit with gas and is warm, but the atmosphere is heavy, sometimes fetid, and the cages and corridors reek with associations of vice and crime.

Into this criminal stock pot of the city the homeless tramps were thrown to stew in their own juice together with the toughs and criminals and prostitutes, the dehumanized harvest nightly garnered by the police of the district.

It is true that the tramps were not mixed indiscriminately with the criminals. The women, for instance, were kept in their own corridor. The prisoners were in the cages behind the barred gates, the tramps slept in the corridor between the cages and the wall. There was, however, nothing to hinder the freest possible communication between the arrested men and the casual lodgers. Conversation went on freely between the tramps and the toughs and occasional interchange of papers and tobacco went on easily through the bars of the cages.

The place had a weird fascination about it. It is not a locality where a very sensitive psychic could live, for its cages have witnessed the suicide of desperate prisoners who, while the jailer's back was turned, hanged themselves to death from the bars behind which they were imprisoned. Murderers red-handed have lodged there, maniacs have battered their heads against the iron gates, for there is no strait waistcoat or padded cell in Harrison Street; women shriek and wail in hysterics, and, saddest of all, little urchins of ten and twelve who have been run in for some juvenile delinquency have found the police cell the nursery cradle of the jail. Sometimes when the Justice needs dollars, and raids are ordered in scores that the bail bonds may be paid, there are two hundred women crowded into the cells. Many of them are drunk before they come in, others get drunk after they arrive, having carefully provided for that contingency before they mounted the patrol wagon; all of them, the novice in the sporting house, as well as the hardened old harridan who drives the trade in human flesh, are herded together promiscuously with thieves and shoplifters.

They smoke, they drink, they curse, they yell obscenely, and now and then one goes into a fit of hysterical shrieking which rings through the gloomy corridors like the wail of a damned and tortured soul.

One night when I was there a French woman was brought in with her man. There had been a quarrel; her face was streaming with blood, she had been drinking and was in violent hysterics. I have seldom seen a more squalid specimen of human wretchedness. When they separated her from her companion, placing them in separate cells, she began to shriek at the top of her voice — and a shrill voice it was. She clung to the bars of the cage shrieking for Jacques, only stopping when she had to wipe away the blood that was flowing from her mouth and temple. She was shrieking and wailing with unabated energy when I left. The police matron told me that she kept it up for some time before she sank exhausted to sleep. Early in the morning she woke and at once began again the agonized cry and kept it up for two hours. Such was the music and such the companionship which were allotted to the lodgers at Harrison Street.

That was bad enough. But if the city had provided adequate accommodation for her lodgers even in this underground Inferno, there might be less to be said. Unfortunately, however, there was no accommodation other than the stone floor of the corridor and there the casuals were pigged together literally like herrings in a barrel. The corridor was some hundred feet long and ten feet broad. I shall never forget the moment when I first saw it with its occupants. From the outer iron gate to the further wall, nothing could be seen but a pavement of human bodies. The whole corridor was packed thick with this human compost. They lay " heads and tails," so that their feet and legs were intermingled. At either end some favored ones propped themselves against the wall or the gate, drowsily slumbering. The majority lay on their sides with their heads on their arms; some had taken off their coats; many had prepared their bed by spreading an old newspaper upon the stone floor; other mattress they had none, neither had they pillow, bed clothes, or opportunities for washing or for supper. The city, like a stony-hearted step-mother, provided for her children nothing but shelter, warmth and a stone bed.

The spectacle of these human beings massed together along the corridor floor, recalled vividly to my memory a picture in an old Sunday School book, representing the Caliph of Islam riding over the prostrate forms of his devoted followers. But in the Moslem there was the enthusiasm and ecstacy of self sacrifice, the joy of the disciple at being made the causeway of the Commander of the Faithful. Here there were the bodies indeed, but there was no joy of surrender, only a sullen stone-broke resignation as they bowed themselves and laid down and let the iron-shod hoofs of Laissez Faire and Political Economy trample them to the dust. It was an ugly sight.

Only once had I seen anything like it outside the picture book. It was when I was in one of the worst prisons in St. Petersburg. The officials demurred rather to let me enter, but ultimately gave way and with many apologies allowed me to see the inmates of the House of Detention, where the riffraff of the capital were herded together to await the weekly clearing which dispersed them to Siberia or to the four winds of heaven. Only in that Russian prison had I even seen men crowded together as beasts are crowded in cattle trucks. But in Russia they were more merciful than in Chicago. They at least provided a sloping wooden bed with straw pillows for their prisoners. But what Russian humanity deemed necessary even for criminals, the city of Chicago did not vouchsafe to the honest workman tramping around in search of a job.

The curious thing to a stranger was the apathetic indifference of the sufferers themselves. They made no audible or articulate complaint. Their patient endurance, their passive acquiescence in treatment against which English tramps would have blasphemed till the air was blue, was very strange. Everything that was subsequently done to improve their condition was done from the outside, and was received by them with the same apparent passivity. They did not even make a demonstration or frame an appeal.

Another remarkable thing was the apparent indifference of the better-to-do citizens, not merely the rich, but the employed working people. When, immediately after my arrival in Chicago, I ventured to tell the Trade and Labor Assembly that the workingmen of London would not tolerate the treatment to which the tramps were subjected at Harrison Street, and urged them to take action in the matter, this was the way in which a leading evening paper thought it right and safe to refer to the subject:

In this self-respecting city of the West, the "cause of humanity" stands in no need of advice from British fanatics who base an argument upon the analogy of the London pauper system. The American tramp is *sui generis.* He would not work if work were offered him. He deserves not the tear but the lash. We know how to deal with him. Mr. Stead does not. The toe of a boot by day and a cold stone floor by night—these be the leading courses in the curriculum by which we would educate into self-respect such tramps as are capable of it. The tramp is a pariah and we ought to keep him such.

It was on the eve of a contested election, but the editor, although a keen partisan, never seemed to dream that his language might be used to the detriment of his party when the polls were opened.

As a matter of fact no electoral use was made of this utterance by the other side. And as a matter of justice I should add that the same paper after a few weeks' further agitation became so strenuous in its demands for more liberal charity in dealing with these outcasts as to leave far behind it even "the maudlin sentimentalism of the Stead school of philanthropists."

The doctrine that the American tramp is a pariah and that he ought to be kept such is not often formulated so bluntly, but it embodies the underlying doctrine of the American method in dealing with the tramp. We have in England made so many failures in our attempts to deal with the sturdy vagrant that we have no pretention to teach others. But we have at least learned from our failures sufficient to see that to refuse to deal with the tramp excepting as a temporary human nuisance, to be hustled on to the neighboring town with the utmost dispatch, is the worst possible way of solving the question. For even if the tramp is the spawn of the devil, as it is constantly assumed, instead of being a son of God and brother of Christ Jesus, to persist in a practice which entails of necessity the quickest possible dissemination of the spawn aforesaid over the widest possible area of territory is of all courses the most fatal. But when anything is proposed either by way of reclamation or of redemption, there is an outcry against " pauperizing the citizen." So the work of criminalizing him goes on apace.

"Oh, he's only a bum !" was the cry which at first met all efforts to arouse a Christian sentiment in Chicago. That was supposed to settle all things. A bum was outside the pale of human sympathy. A bum was supposed to possess all the defects of human nature and none of their virtues. He was declared to be an incorrigibly idle loafer, a drunkard, a liar and a reprobate. The grim old Calvinistic doctrine of reprobation seemed to be revived expressly to make his damnation irrevocable. And yet nothing was being done to prevent the steady degradation of the honest willing worker to the level of the bum.

As a genial speaker at the Presbyterian Social Union remarked, even the most respectable of men, if compelled to tramp about for a week without change of linen or opportunity to wash, would feel he was becoming very bummy. There is of necessity, in every period of depression, a considerable number of men who are thrown out of work. These men take to the road, are driven to it because they have no means of transporting themselves from a place where there is no work to a place where work may be had. If the present system or no system goes on, they will tend irresistibly to gravitate to the bum pariah class, and the practice of massing them together in herds in Harrison Street and the City Hall accelerates the process.

Take but one instance, the impossibility of keeping clean or free from vermin under the present conditions. "You can always tell the bum," said a justice, "by his smell. There is an ancient stink about him which you can detect in a moment."

There is no greater barrier between man and man, and still more between woman and woman, than that raised by the sense of smell, with its suggestion of the presence of filth. Most people can put up more readily with a criminal than with a filthy man. But how can the willing worker or tramp keep clean when he is pigged together with a foul-smelling herd on the floor of a prison?

One night at Harrison Street I witnessed a strange Rembrandtesque scene. In the center of the corridor allotted to the tramps at Harrison Street, the men had made a bonfire of old paper. It was not quite so crowded as it had been before, and there was room in the center. They were diligently feeding the fire with shreds of paper. The blaze illuminated the dark and forbidding surroundings of the prison, casting a flickering glare upon the dirty, careworn faces that surrounded it. I asked the officer in charge whether he thought it was safe to allow a mob of men to make a bonfire on the floor of the station. "I don't blame them," said he, shortly; "I don't blame them. An old bum got in there who was literally alive with vermin. When they found it out we fired him out, but the few papers he had been lying on were lifting with lice, so that is what they are burning. And I don't blame them," he repeated : "what else could they do ? "

For one man who is so verminous that the very paper on which he lay lifted with the insects dropped from his rags, there must have been scores and hundreds more or less haunted by the unpleasant habitues of uncombed hair and unwashed bodies. Their tendency is constant to multiplication. The longer a man goes unwashed, the denser becomes the colony of parasites; and the more closely he is compelled to herd with his neighbors, the more widely does the loathsome contagion spread. Hence the willing worker, forced into contact with the idle and shiftless and worthless bum, becomes himself bummier and bummier until at last he is branded as one of the pariah class and " he must be kept such ! "

The Harrison Street Police Station, although the most conspicuous sheltering place of the outcast wanderer, held by no means the largest crowd. The Pacific Garden Mission, at Van Buren and Clark Streets, accommodated a larger number of homeless ones than the police station. The spacious hall of the mission was turned into a dormitory, where, night after night, some five or six hundred persons occupied chairs till morning. Every evening there was a religious service, after which the attendants were free to remain all night. The place was warm and orderly, and it had the advantage over Harrison Street Police Station of enabling each man to sleep by himself. But, as a Cheshire man told me, who had crossed the Atlantic many times as stoker on the transatlantic ferry boats and who had for some months past been firing steamers on Lake Michigan, it is little sleep you get unless you can lie down flat. The poor fellow's story was very simple ; he had spent three nights in the mission and four days tramping round hunting work. He was out every morning before seven, and on his feet till after nine at night always meeting with the

same response. "When you're on your feet all day," he
said, "and cannot get a lay-out at night, your legs swell
almost to the knee. You become lame and cannot even
go hunting the job no one seems able to find." He was
a stalwart, strapping fellow, who literally wept when a
little friendly help was given him. But in process of
time that man would also become a bum, unless he
could be arrested on the down grade along which he
was being hurried by no fault of his own.

The great sleeping place of the tramp, however, was
neither in Harrison Street Police Station nor in the
Pacific Garden Mission. The heart and center of Chicago
is the huge pile of masonry which reminds the visitor by
its polished granite pillars and general massive and
somber grandeur of the cathedrals and palaces of St.
Petersburg. The City Hall and Court House form
one immense building, in which all the city and
county business is transacted, both judicial and administrative. The peculiar system under which Chicago is
administered makes the City Hall, in a peculiar manner,
the center of the floating unemployed population. I have
never seen a city hall so thronged by loafers during the
day time. The politician out of a job, the office-seeker
waiting impatiently for his turn, the alderman and his
strings of hangers-on, the ex-official, the heeler, the
jobber swell the throng of those who do business
until the air in the corridors is heavy with smoke, and
the pavement is filthy with the mire of innumerable
boots and stained with the juice of the tobacco plant—for
not even the American allowance of spittoons can suffice
for the need of the citizens in their Civic Hall.
This court and reception room of the sovereign people—
where Coughlin was being tried for his life on one side,
and the multitude were being vaccinated in droves
on the other, while all the multitudinous wheels of
municipal machinery revolved between—was selected
as the chief camping-ground of the nomadic horde.

The City Hall cost five million dollars to construct.

It is the solitary municipal building of any pretensions in the city. In it are kept the city archives, the records of the courts, and all the documents relating to the registration of property and the due transaction of public business. Here is the headquarters of the best equipped and most efficient fire department in the world, and high overhead is the accumulated wealth of the public library of Chicago. In this building, crammed with invaluble documents, the seat and center of the whole civic machinery, for want of any better accommodation, there were housed night after night, through the month of December, from one to two thousand of the most miserable men in Chicago. Most of the men were penniless ; almost all of them were more or less desperate ; many of them were smoking. As they used newspapers as mattresses, the corridors were littered with paper, amid which a single lighted match might have made a blaze which might not easily have been extinguished. Yet the risk was faced perforce for want of a little care, a little forethought, and a little necessary expenditure.

The tramps were not accommodated in the Council Chamber or in any of the offices. They were allowed to occupy the spacious, well-warmed corridors, and make such shift as they could upon the flags. No one was admitted to the upper stories, but every stair up to the first landing was treated as a berth by its fortunate occupant. Less lucky lodgers had to content themselves with a lay-out in the corridor. They lay with their heads against the wall on either side, leaving open a narrow track down the center. Down this track came reporters, messengers to the fire department and other offices, followed before many nights were over by curious philanthropists, university professors, ministers of religion, and then by the representatives of the Federation of Labor, all of whom marveled much and said many bitter things about the contrasts of the great city where "Mammon holds high carnival in its gilded palaces, while little children hunger, mothers grow faint for food and die, and strong men weep for want of work.''

But after a time that narrow pathway was choked up, and even reporters could not elbow their way through the crowd; for the City Hall corridors were very warm; the midnight air was nipping keen, and when all sleeping room was filled men preferred to stand in the warm, close air, rather than shiver in the frost and snow. It seems strange, but it appears to be undisputed that the habit of allowing the homeless to shelter in the corridors of the City Hall is no new thing in Chicago. Indeed the only new thing last winter seems to have been the limitation of the area of improvised casual ward to the ground floor and the first flight of stairs. It was not till the 12th of last November that wire doors were placed on the stairs, and all access to the upper part of the building shut off. This necessary precaution was taken not in order to avoid peril by fire or pillage, but simply because the lodgers quarreled so fiercely among themselves for favorite locations that for the sake of peace and quiet they were stalled downstairs. There they were quiet enough, smoking, sleeping and doing a little talking in an undertone. But for a floating population with the reputation of the bum, the crowd was singularly quiet, patient and well behaved. In the Pacific Garden Mission the superintendent reported the presence of 500 sleepers every night had been attended by so little disturbance, that the upstairs tenants were never conscious that there was a crowd below. The officer in charge at Harrison Street declared that the genuine bum was in a greater minority than had ever been observed before. Most of his lodgers were hardworking men, honestly anxious to find work.

It was, of course, impossible to do more than sample the mass of human wretchedness thus caged up nightly in a few centers, but Professor Hourwitch, with a band of students from the university, subjected 100 of the crowd of 2,000 odd to a searching analysis. His report is

very interesting. Only ten of the 100 selected at
random from the lodgers in the City Hall belonged to
labor unions. Only two had worked for less than a
dollar a day. More than half, sixty-four out of 100,
had earned from $1 to $2 a day, twenty from $2 to $3.
Almost all classes and conditions of men were represented in the motley crowd — except millionaires. Fifty-
nine were native-born Americans, forty-one foreigners.
Of the latter the first place was taken by the Germans,
followed by the Irish and the Scotch in the order named.
Most of the men were in the prime of life, from twenty
to forty-five; only one was below twenty, and four over
fifty.   Their professions or occupations, as stated by
themselves, were as follows: Common laborers, 33; team-
sters, 6; painters, 6; waiters, 5; molders, 4; bakers, 4;
miners, 3; cooks, 3; rolling millers, 3; sailors, 3; ma-
chinists, 2; cigarmakers, 2; shoemakers, 2; carpenters,
2; wood finishers, 2; while a brickmaker, a clerk, a
glass packer, a plumber, a florist, a varnisher, a brewer,
a druggist, a glazier, a draftsman, a wood carver, a
cooper, an upholsterer, a boxmaker, a stove polisher, a
chair factory man, a steam fitter, and a salesman completed the list.

Several of the men were well educated. One was a
graduate of the University of Nebraska. Most of them
had come to Chicago from other towns seeking work,
and none of them could find it. Of all the dishearten-
ing occupations that of seeking work and finding none
is one of the worst. The curse that in the Old Book
is said to have followed the Fall is often in the New
World an unattainable boon. It was a quaint but true
conceit of Mrs. Browning's that "God in cursing
gives us better gifts, than man in blessing." But
whether malediction or benediction, work was what these
men wanted, and work was the one thing they could
not get. If they only had been horses there would
have been men eager enough to claim them to feed, to
lodge and to care for them. But, alas, they were only

men! Even then, if they had been slaves, liable to be
sold at the auction mart, and whipped to work on the
plantation, this army of 2,000 able-bodied wanderers in
the prime of life would have probably brought at least
a million dollars at the auction block. But as they had
the misfortune to be free men, free citizens of the great
republic, none would give even a nickel for their services or provide a bed in which they could shelter.

It was a composite industrial army, capable of doing
much good work if only it could but find leadership and
tools and rations. All were wanting, the first most of
all. For the loyal confidence of man in man, which is
the tap root of all true leadership, does not spring up
easily in the camps of the unemployed. The nomads of
the prairie and of the steppe have more of that element
than the nomads of civilization. Hence, if they are left
to themselves they threaten to gravitate ever downward.
From poverty and homelessness comes despondency, loss
of self-respect follows on enforced dirtiness, and the
undescribable squalor of filthy clothes. Work being
unattainable, they beg rather than starve, and if begging
fails they steal. Thus by steady inevitable forces, as of
adverse Destiny, the dislodged unit gravitates downward,
ever downward into the depths of the malebolgic pool of
our social hell. Industry, honesty, truthfulness, sobriety
are rotted out of the man, and at last the only remnant
of the soul that aspires is visible in the craving after
drink. In his cups, at least, he may drown his regrets
for a vanished past, and may indulge for some brief
moments in brighter visions of the unattainable to-
morrow. For in the utterly demoralized tramp, the only
symptom of the God within is often that very passion
for drink which, by its sore intensity, testifies to the
revolt of its victim against the injustices and abominations of the present. Yet, of him, also, let us remember
what Lowell wrote of another lost unit of the human
family :

The good Father of us all had doubtless intrusted to the keeping of this child of His certain faculties of a constructive kind; He had put in him a share of that vital force, the nicest economy of every minute atom of which is necessary to the perfect development of humanity. He had given him a brain and heart, and so had equipped his soul with the two strong wings of knowledge and love, whereby it can mount to hang its nest under the eaves of heaven. And this child, so dowered, he had intrusted to the keeping of his vicar, the State. How stands the account of that stewardship? The State, or Society (call her what you will) had taken no manner of thought of him until she saw him swept out into the street, the pitiful leavings of last night's debauch, with cigar ends, lemon parings, tobacco quids, slops, vile stenches and the whole loathsome next morning of the bar-room — an own child of the Almighty God! I remember him as he was brought in to be christened, a ruddy, rugged babe; and now there he wallows, reeking, seething — the dead corpse, not of a man but of a soul, a putrifying lump, horrible for the life that is in it. Soon the wind of heaven, that good Samaritan, parts the hair upon his forehead nor is too nice to kiss those parched, cracked lips; the morning opens upon him her eyes full of pitying sunshine, the sky yearns down to him, and there he lies fermenting. O sleep! let me not profane thy holy name by calling that stertorous unconsciousness a slumber! By and by comes along the State, God's vicar. Does she say, "My poor forlorn foster-child! Behold a force which I will make dig and plant and build for me." Not so, but—

let us hustle him out of the town and thank God we are rid of the nuisance of his presence!

But with at least fifty thousand able-bodied tramps in ordinary years patrolling the country at an estimated minimum cost of ten million dollars per annum for means of subsistence, making no estimate of the indirect damages to property and morals, it is beginning to be increasingly doubtful whether the popular expedient is paying in the long run. Of course, so long as each city or village or township bases its policy on the question of Cain, nothing can be done. But even in Russia, which so many affect to despise as semi-barbarous and inhuman, they do better than that. For there they christen their tramp a pilgrim and by brotherly kindness and generous hospitality convert every wandering brother into a means of grace.

CHAPTER II.

Christ was a man. It is therefore easier to conceive of him as a pilgrim tramp, footsore and hungry, resting his weary limbs among the bums in the police station than to conceive of his marred image in a female shape. But the woman-Christ like the child-Christ, either as the Christ of the Dolorous Way or as the redeeming and regenerating Saviour is a conception which must never be lost sight of.

The Christian Church, which for more than a thousand years has consecrated its proudest temples to the memory of the Magdalen, is a witness throughout the ages to the indestructibility of the divine element in every woman even when she has sunk so low as to make merchandise of her sex. The image of God in woman remains indefaceable even when in Lecky's words, which it is impossible to read without a shudder, she becomes "the eternal Priestess of Humanity blasted for the sins of the people." But although the publicans and harlots in His time welcomed the wandering eccentric from Nazareth, who shared their meals and sympathized with their sorrows, the conventional sentiment of this day would stand aghast at any such intermingling of the Messiah with the lost women whom He came to seek and to save.

In Chicago some people have gone even further. One of the most zealous and faithful of the saintly and devoted women who have dedicated their lives to the service of the fallen told me with a heart sore with the anguish of thwarted sympathy, that so far from her efforts being supported by the Church, they were regarded as a development not to be encouraged.

33

"It was this way," she said. "I have given myself up to this work. I visited constantly in the levee and knew most of these women as friends. Now and then I would come upon one or another girl who would long to escape from her sad life. When I found such I took them into my own house, loved them, labored with them, and I rejoice to know that several of them became happy and converted Christians. I was pleased, my pastor was pleased. The penitent Magdalens were received into the church and we were glad to see their simple faith and Christian life. But a deputation of the leading residents and church officers waited upon my pastor to protest against this kind of thing. They did not want their daughters to associate with harlots even though they were repentant. *Besides the presence of these women would lower the character of the neighborhood and the social standing of the church."

"That is incredible," I said abruptly, "to wish to close the doors of Christ's Church on the penitent Magdalen—that would be not the act of Christian but of devil!"

"It was what they did," said my friend. "Fortunately my pastor is a good Christian and he refused to yield one single jot to the pressure brought to bear upon him. But the opposition was great. The respectability of the church must not be endangered by the admission of lost women, even when they have been found and are anxiously and prayerfully seeking to enter in to the fold."

Here was a revelation indeed! Such a church may be respectable as Thurtell the murderer was declared to be respectable—because he kept a gig; but its respectability will not save it from going down, with all its conventionalities, into perdition, nor will it have far to go. For the abode of such is nigh unto the gates of Hell.

Swinburne's bitter lines came back to me as I listened to this good woman's story of some Chicago Christians and heard its confirmation from others in other churches.

Surely your race it was that He
Beholding in Gethsemane,
Bled the red bitter sweat of shame,
Knowing the name of Christian should
Mean to men evil and not good.

And assuredly in the long roll of the anti-Christian acts of the conventional church there is no blacker record than that which deals with the lost women of our streets. Nothing can exceed in revolting injustice the conventional mode of treating the weaker and the most tempted as a moral leper, while her guiltier partner occupies the highest places in the synagogue.

Justice is at least as holy a thing as charity and the injustice of the world's judgment which the church has countersigned is as loathsome as the selfish immorality of the man which it condones as a kind of offset to the Draconian severity with which it avenges the faults of the weaker sinner.

The lost women, these poor sisters of Christ Jesus, the images in which we have fashioned a womanhood first made in the image of God, are as numerous in Chicago as in any other great city. The silent vice of capitals abounds here at least to the same extent that it prevails in other cities of the million class. Where there are a million inhabitants it is probably an under estimate if it is assumed that there must be at least a thousand women who make their living, not intermittently but constantly by means of prostitution. These regulars of the army of vice constitute the solid core or nucleus of a host far more numerous of irregulars, who, either from love of license or from need of money, give way to a temptation which is always at hand. The inmates of the sporting houses, so called, are probably not one-tenth of the total number of women who regard their sex as legitimate merchandise.

Both sporting houses and "roomers" may be found in all parts of the city, but there is no section in which they are so concentrated as in the district between Harrison and Polk and between Clark and Dearborn streets. It was there in the center of the heart of Chicago that I found Maggie Darling in the house of Madame Hastings.

Madame Hastings is a familiar figure in the alsatia of more than one city. She is famous in Chicago courts as having been the defendant in the case which led to the practical ruling that the police could not arrest anyone they pleased on a warrant made out against those mythical personages, Richard Roe or John Doe. Before she contested that case, strange though it may appear to those who are unfamiliar with the Turkish methods of Chicago "justice," a policeman armed with a warrant charging Richard Roe with an offense against the law could, on the strength of that document, arrest anybody at his own sovereign will and pleasure. Mary Hastings, being raided on such a warrant, appealed to the higher court, which as was to be expected, promptly decided against the validity of the Richard Roe warrant, and Mary's name became famous in a leading case.

Apart from this excursion into the law-making region, Madame inspired some awe, if not respect, by the vengeance she wreaked upon certain police officers, who, having a grudge against her, smashed her furniture during her enforced absence from her property. She reported them to Mayor Harrison in person, and their offense being proved, three policemen and one sergeant were dismissed the force; from which it may be seen that the name and fame of Mary Hastings are as familiar to the administration as to the lawyers. Her establishment is not a very large one beside the double house of Vina Fields, which almost immediately adjoins it, and the extensive premises of Carrie Watson on Clark Street. Madame Hastings' house is rather crowded when it contains twelve girls. Madame, who is Belgian, bred and born, owns another house at 2004 Dearborn Street, and in course of a somewhat adventurous career has seen much of the seamy side of life, both married and single, in Canada and the United States. She has plied her calling in Toronto, in British Columbia, in Denver, Portland, Oregon, in San Francisco, and has a wide and varied experience with the police wherever she has wandered. In San Francisco she was in prison for six months for conduct too scandalous even for Californians. On the whole she has the greatest terror of the police of the Dominion. "When the English say you're to git, you've just got to git and that's all there is to it," she said mournfully, "you can't do anything with them; with our police it is different."

Of which there is no doubt. For as big Pat the Tarrier, the policeman, went his rounds in Fourth Avenue, he seldom failed to look in upon Madame at supper time, or indeed, at any time when he felt thirsty. Pat was one of the four custodians of law and order whom it was necessary for Madame to square. The relations between the sporting houses and the police on their beats is intimate, not to say friendly. The house is at the absolute mercy of the officer, who can ruin its business by simply keeping it under constant observation, or he can, if he pleases, have it "pulled" every day in the week if his moral sense or his desire for vengeance should so prompt. The keeper of the house, if she is to live and thrive, must make friends with the policeman, and there is usually not the least difficulty in doing so. Tariffs vary in Fourth Avenue as in Washington, but Madame had succeeded in securing virtual protection at a blackmail scale of $2.50 per officer per week with free drinks, and occasional meals whenever the "cop" felt hunger or thirst. As there were four of them on duty, two by day and two at night, and they were often thirsty, it may be taken that this police "protection" cost the house $15.00 a week or $750 a year.—an irregular license fee paid to private constables for liberty to carry on. This of course does not include the further fees levied by superior officers, the fines, the money paid to bailsmen, and other incidental expenses, which fall heavy upon the houses of ill-fame.

"Ye ould ———s," said the Tarrier, one evening, as

he marched in at the back door, " and wat kind o' soup
hev ye's today? An' shure, and pass me the whusky,
and for shame to ye, Maggie," he added, seeing one of
the girls emptying a wine glass, "for shame to ye, to
think that ye are Oirish and a drinkin' wine! It's
whusky ye should drink."

He was not an ill-natured man, was Pat, and as he sat
down and drank the whisky and tasted the soup in the
midst of the scantily attired women, his good nature
beamed on his fat face and he became confidential :

"Now, I's tellin' ye," he said. "Be shure and look
out, for I am going on another beat for the next month,
and the cops that's coming are mean divils, and if ye
don't take care it's pulled ye'll be, so look out for yourselves."

Sure enough, the next day there was a new patrolman
on the beat, and the girls were more cautious in their
hustling. The routine of the day at Madame Hastings
was monotonous enough. In the morning, just before 12,
the colored girl served cocktails to each of the women
before they got up. After they dressed, they took another
refresher, usually absinthe. At breakfast they had wine.
Then the day's work begun. The girls sat in couples
at the windows, each keeping watch in the opposite direction. If a man passed they would rap at the window
and beckon him to come in. If a policeman appeared,
even if it were their fat friend, the curtains would be
drawn and all trace of hustling would disappear. But before the officer was out of sight the girls would be there
again. They went on duty fifteen minutes at a time.
Every quarter of an hour they were relieved, until dinner
time. At five they dined, and then the evening's business began, with more drinking at intervals, all night
through, to the accompaniment of piano playing with
occasional step-dancing, and adjournments more or less
frequent, as customers were more or less plentiful. About
four or five in the morning, when they were all more or
less loaded with drink, they would close the doors and go

to sleep. Next day it would begin again, the same dull round of drink and hustling, debauch and drink. A dismal, dreary, monotonous existence broken only by quarreling and the constant excitement supplied by the police.

For a day or two the girls were discreet, but finding no harm came they relapsed a little, and "Redhead," the new policeman, saw them hustling at the window. So a warrant was sworn out at the police station and at five o'clock at night a posse of nine policemen sallied forth to "pull" Mary Hastings. The pulling of a house of this description is one of the favorite entertainments of the district. It attracts the floating and resident population as much as a first-class funeral draws the crowd in a country town. All unsuspecting the fate in store for them, the girls were preparing to sit down to dinner. Maggie was mixing the absinthe when the bell rang. Bohemian Mary—for here as elsewhere in Chicago, there are people of all nationalities under heaven—opened the door. A policeman placed his foot so the door could not be closed in his face and demanded Madame. When she came he produced his warrant and eight other officers filed into the house. Every door was guarded. There was no escape. Had there been but a few minutes warning the girls could have fled down the trap doors prepared for such an event, which led to the cellar from whence they could escape to a friendly saloon which frequently received them into its hospitable shelter. But it was too sudden. "Oh —— !" said Maggie, running up stairs, "we're pulled!" "Yes," said the officer, "and you'd better dress yourselves and make ready to go off to the station.

As Maggie was hastily putting on her dress one of the officers who had followed her to her bed-room touched her on the shoulder. "Would you mind making a date with me?" he said. The girl's appearance pleased him. "And though he was on pleasure bent," like John Gilpin, "he had a frugal mind." Policemen get their women cheap, and when you are arresting a woman she cannot haggle about terms. So Maggie said, "For sure." "Well," he said, "I am on Clark, can I meet you there some day next week?" "Certainly," she replied, "send me a message making the date and it will be all right."

By this time they were getting ready to start. Madame had thrust a roll of 300 dollar bills into her stocking. The girls, not less mindful of contingencies, had stuffed into their stockings small bottles of whisky and cigarettes and made ready to accompany their captors. There were six altogether. The housekeeper, the cook and one of the girls, a newcomer who was passed off as a servant, remained behind. Madame and her family of five stepped out amid the curious crowd which watched for the patrol wagon. "It makes a girl feel cheap," said Maggie, "let's start for the station." No sooner said than done. Bohemian Mary set off at a run followed by her cursing, panting custodian; then came the other girls, while Madame brought up the rear. It was no new thing to her. The house had been pulled only two months before and it was all in the day's work.

When they arrived at the police station they were taken down stairs and locked up all together in one of the iron barred cells. The police found a bottle of wine in a French girl's stocking and drank its contents to the immense indignation of its owner, who gave him in her own vocabulary "blue blazes." He only looked and laughed. "Here's to your health, Frenchie!" said the policman as he drank the last drop. Madame in the meantime had dispatched a trusty messenger for a bondsman and as soon as he arrived she was bailed out. The girls in the cell amused themselves with shouting and singing and cursing and drinking, while Maggie and another tested their agility by climbing like monkeys up the iron bars of their grated door.

It was more like a picnic than an imprisonment. They had drink and cigarettes and company. They

were as noisy and more lively and profane than if they
had been at home.

In about an hour Madame bailed them all out, putting
up $10 a head for their punctual appearance at the po-
lice court on Monday morning. Then the half dozen,
more drunk than when they were pulled sallied out in
triumph and resumed business as usual in the old premises as if nothing had happened.

Five or six hours afterwards, about midnight, I made
Maggie Darling's acquaintance. I had been around
several of the houses asking their keepers and their
inmates to attend my meeting at the Central Music Hall
the following day. A strange pilgrimage that was from
house to house, to discuss what Christ would think
of it, with landladies whose painted damsels in undress,
were lounging all around! At last, well on to midnight, I came to Madame Hastings. The excitement
of the "pulling" was still visible; Madame was indignant. She knew who it was that had put the "cops"
on to her and she cursed them accordingly. Maggie was flushed and somewhat forward ; both her eyes
were blacked, the result of a fight with a French inmate
of the house.

"I don't want anything," I said to Maggie. "Why
can you not talk decently once in a while? Sit down
and let us have a good talk."

Maggie looked at me half incredulously and then sat
down.

"I want you to come to my meeting tomorrow night,"
I said, "at Central Music Hall."

"Yes," she said, "what kind of a meeting is it?"

"Oh, quite a new kind of meeting," I answered. "I
am to speak on what Christ would think of all this,
and I want you know it all, to come to the meeting."

Maggie became serious ; a dreamy look came over her
face.

Then she said, " Oh, Christ ! He's all right. Its the

other ones, that's the devil." Then she stopped. "Its no use," she added, shortly.

"What's no use?" I asked, and after a time she told me the story which I repeated in brief at Central Music Hall next day.

It was a grim story; commonplace enough, and yet as tragic as life, that was told to me at midnight in that tawdry parlor. The old Jezebel flitted in and out superintending her business; the jingling piano was going in the next room where the girls were dancing, and the air was full of the reek of beer and tobacco. Maggie spoke soberly, in an undertone so that Madame might not hear what she was saying. Her narrative, which she told without any pretense or without any appeal for sympathy or for help, seemed a microcosm of the history of the human race. The whole of the story was there; from the Fall to the Redemption; from the Redemption to the Apostacy of the church, and the blighting of the hopes of mankind. I give it here as a page, soiled and grimy it may be, but nevertheless a veritable page torn from the book of life. Maggie Darling is a human document in which is recorded the ruin of one of the least of those of the brethren of Christ. It illustrates many things in our social organization, from the ruthless sacrifice of childhood, due to the lack of factory laws, to the murderous brutality of conventional Christianity, aping the morality without the heart of its Lord.

"No," said Maggie coldly. "Its no use! Don't commence no religion on me. I've had enough already. Are you a Catholic?"

"Why?" I asked. "No, I am not a Catholic."

"I'm glad," she said, "you're not a Catholic. I have no use for Catholics. Least of all for Irish Catholics. I will never go near any of them any more, and if I could do them any harm, I would travel a thousand miles to do it."

Maggie was excited and troubled. Something in the past seemed to harass her, and her language was more vigorous than can be quoted here. After a little she became more restrained, and by degrees I had her whole history.

She was born of Irish-American parents, in Boston, in 1870. Her father was a carpenter by trade. Her mother died when Maggie was a mere child. Shortly after her death the family crossed the continent to California, where her father married again. He was a drunkard, a gambler and a violent tempered man, much given to drinking, and inclined to treat his children with great brutality. Maggie, after spending a year or two in a convent school in San Francisco, left before she had learned either to read or to write, and began to make her own living, at nine years of age. She was employed in a shoe factory, where she made from $4.50 to $7 a week at piece work. There were several children of only seven years of age in the factory. These infants were employed in picking shavings. They started work at six o'clock in the morning, had half an hour for dinner, and were dismissed at five. At the factory Maggie learned to read out of the newspapers, by the aid of her companions, and when she was eleven was sufficiently smart to obtain a situation as companion and reader to an old lady, who was an invalid, at $15 a month and her board. The place was comfortable. She remained there until she was eighteen.

From that situation she went as chambermaid to a private family in Golden Gate Avenue. She was eighteen, full of vigor and gaiety. She was a brunette with long dark hair, a lively disposition, and with all the charming audacity and confidence of inexperience. She fell in love. The man was older than she and for a time she was as happy as most young people in their first dream. Of course she was going to be married. If only the marriage day would come! But there are twenty-four hours in every day, and seven days in every week. Her betrothed, not less impatient, hinted that after all they were already united, why could they not anticipate the ceremony. Did she not trust him? He swore that it was all right, that everybody did it and they would be so much more to each other.

But why repeat the oft told story? At first Maggie would not listen to the suggestion. But after a time when he pressed her and upbraided her and declared that she could not love him if she did not trust him, she went the way of many thousands, only to wake as they have done with the soft illusion dissipated by the terrible reality of motherhood drawing near, with no husband to be a father to her child. When she told him of her condition, he said that it was all right; they must get married directly. If she would leave her place and meet him next day, at the corner of a certain street, he would take her to a church and they would be married. In all trusting innocence, relying upon his word, she gave up her situation, put up such things as she could carry and went next day to the trysting place. Of course the man was not there. After waiting till heartsick she went to make inquiries; she soon discovered the fatal truth. Her lover was a married man, and he had skipped the town followed by the brother of another of his victims.

Imagine her position! She had exactly fifteen cents in her pocket. If she had gone home her father, fierce and irascible as he usually was, would have thought little of killing the daughter who had brought disgrace upon the family. She dared not return to her old situation which she had left so suddenly. She had no character from her mistress and no references. Besides in six months she would be confined. What was she to do?

Her position is one in which some thousands of young women find themselves all over the world at this very moment. She was in the position of Eve after she had eaten the forbidden fruit and had been cast out of the Garden of Eden. It is a modern version of the Fall, and as the Fall led down to destruction, so it was with Maggie Darling. She seemed to be shut up to sin. She wan-

dered about the town seeking work. Finding none all
that day she walked about in the evening. She kept
walking aimlessly on and on, until night came and she
was afraid. When it was quite dark and she found a
quiet corner she crouched upon a doorstep and tried to
sleep. What was she to do? She was lonely and miserable; every month her trouble would grow worse. Where
could she hide? She dozed off, only to awaken with a
start. No one was near; she tried to sleep again. Then
she got up and walked a little and rested again. When
morning came she was tired out and wretched. Then
she remembered the address of a girl she knew who was
living in the neighborhood. She hunted her up and was
made welcome. But her friend had no money. For one
night she sheltered her, but all her efforts to find work
were in vain.

What was to be done? On the third day she and her
friend met a man who asked them if they wanted a job.
They answered eagerly, yes. He gave them the address
of a lady who he thought could give them something to do.
They went there and found it was a house of ill-fame.
The woman took them in and told them they might
stay. Maggie hesitated. But what was she to do? She had
lost her character and her place, and she had no friends.
Here she could at least get food and shelter, and remain
till her baby was born. It seemed as if she were driven
to it. She said to herself that she could not help it, and
so it came to pass that Maggie came upon the town.

Two years she remained there, making the best of it.
Her baby fortunately died soon after it was born, and
she continued to tread the cinder path of sin alone.
This went on for three years, and then there dawned
upon her darkened life a real manifestation of redeeming
love. One day when she had a fit of the blues, a young
man came into the house. He was very young, not
more than twenty. Something in her appearance
attracted him, and when they were alone he spoke to her
so kindly that she marveled. She told him how

wretched she was, and he, treating her as if she were his own sister, encouraged her to hope for release. "Take this," he said, as he left her, giving her five dollars. "Save up all you can until you can pay off your debts and then we will get you out of this."

He came again, and yet again, always treating her in the same brotherly fashion, giving her five dollars every time, and never asking anything in return. After she had saved up sufficient store to pay off that debt to the landlady, which hangs like a millstone round the neck of the unfortunate, her young friend told her that he had talked to his mother and his sister, and that as soon as she was ready they would be delighted to take her into their home until such time as they could find her a situation. Full of delight at the unexpected deliverance, Maggie made haste to leave. The young man's mother was as good as her word. In that home she found a warm welcome, and a safe retreat. Maggie made great efforts to break off the habit of swearing, and although she every now and then would make a bad break, she made such progress that at length it was deemed safe and prudent to let her take a place as a general servant. The short stay in that Christian home had been to her as a glimpse into an opening paradise. Hope sprang up once more in the girl's breast. She would be an honest woman once again. Thus, as we have seen her reproduce the Fall, so we see the blessed work of the Redeemer. Now we have to see the way in which His people, "the other ones," as she called them, shuddering, fulfilled their trust.

Maggie went to a situation in Oakland, Alameda Co., Cal. Her new mistress was a Mrs. McD—, an Irish Catholic of very devout disposition. She was general servant at $10 a month. She worked hard, and gave every satisfaction. Even the habit of profanity seemed to have been conquered. Gradually the memory of her past life with its hideous concomitants was becoming faint and dim, when suddenly the past was brought back to her with a shock. She was serving at table when she suddenly recognized in one of the guests a man who had been a customer in the old house. She felt as if she were going to drop dead when she recognized him, but she said nothing. The "gentleman," however, was not so reticent. "Where did you get that girl from?" he asked Mr. McD—. "Get her," said Mr. McD—; "why, she's a servant in our house." "Servant," sneered her guest; "I know her. She is a —— from San Francisco."

How eternally true are Lowell's lines:

> Grim-hearted world, that look'st with Levite eyes
>   On those poor fallen by too much faith in man,
> She that upon thy freezing threshold lies,
>   Starved to more sinning by thy savage ban,
> Seeking that refuge because foulest vice,
>   More God-like than thy virtue is, whose span
> Shuts out the wretched only, is more free
> To enter Heaven than thou wilt ever be!
>
> Thou wilt not let her wash thy dainty feet
>   With such salt things as tears, or with rude hair
> Dry them, soft Pharisee, *that sitt'st at meat*
>   *With him who made her such, and speak'st him fair,*
> Leaving God's wandering lamb the while to bleat
>   Unheeded, shivering in the pitiless air:
> Thou hast made prisoned virtue show more wan
> And haggard than a vice to look upon.

But in this case it was even worse. The lamb which had sought shelter was driven back into the wilderness. Mr. McD— would not believe it, but said that he would tell his wife. Mrs. McD— at once sent for Maggie. "If only I'd been cute," said she to me when telling the story, "I would have denied it, and they would have believed me. But I thought I had broken with all that, and that I had to tell the truth. So I owned up and said yes, it was true, I had been so, but that I had reformed, and had left all that kind of life. But the old woman, d— her! she would listen to nothing. 'Faith, she would not have the disgrace of having a —— in her house!' that was all she said."

"Have you anything against me?" said Maggie.

"Have I not done your work for you ever since I came?"

"No," was the reply, "I have nothing against you, but I cannot have a person of your character in my house. You must go."

Maggie implored her to give her a chance. "You are a Catholic," she said, "will you not give me a helping hand?"

"No," was the inexorable reply. "That does not matter. I cannot have a —— in my house."

Feeling as if she were sinking in deep water, Maggie fell on her knees sobbing bitterly and begged her for the love of God to have mercy on her and at least to give her a recommendation so that she might get another place.

It was no use. "I cannot do that, for if anything went wrong I would be to blame for it."

"Well then," said Maggie, "at least give me a line saying that for the four months I had been here I have worked to your satisfaction."

"No," she said.

"The old hound!" exclaimed Maggie to me. "My God, if ever I get the chance I'll knife the old she devil. Yes, if I swing for it. What does it matter? She's blasted my life. When I saw it was all no use, I lost all heart and all hope and I gave up there and then. There's no hope for such as me. No, I had my chance and she spoiled it, God d—n her for a blasted old hypocrite. And now it is no use. No use, never any more. I have taken dope, I drink. I'm lost. I'm only a —— I shall never be anything else. I'm far worse than ever I was and am going to the devil as fast as I can. It's no use. But —— —— me to blue blazes if ever I come within a thousand miles of that old fiend if I don't knife her if I swing for it. When I think what I might have been but for her! Oh, Christ!" she cried, "What have they done with my life?"

What indeed? After the Fall the Redemption, after the Redemption the Apostacy, and now as the result, one of

The images ye have made of Me!

CHAPTER III.

WHISKY AND POLITICS.

It was in Brant Smith's saloon where I first met Farmer Jones. Brant Smith is the Democratic captain of the Ninety-first Precinct of the Hundredth Ward. Like many other Democratic captains in Chicago and in New York, he combined the political duties of leader of the precinct with the commercial calling of saloon-keeper. In his district there is no more respectable saloon than that of Brant Smith. It is a marvel. To the left and to the right of it there are saloons which are frequented by the toughest characters in Bum Street. A little further down are saloons which are merely annexes to so many houses of ill-fame, overrun with loose women who hang about in all stages of dishabille, endeavoring as best they can to attract the attention of customers who drop in for a drink or for a cigar, to their faded charms. There is nothing of all this in Brant Smith's. You may go in, as I have gone, at any hour of the day or night and you will not see any of that class of women; indeed it is a rare thing to see a woman at all either at the counter or at the billard table which occupies the most conspicuous position in the rear of the saloon.

During my stay in Chicago Brant Smith's became one of my favorite resorts, partly because of its situation—it was an oasis of cleanliness and light in the midst of a district which was decidedly tough—partly because of Brant Smith himself, who is one of the most intelligent and interesting politicians I have met in Chicago, and partly, and perhaps most of all, because Brant Smith's was the hang-out of Farmer Jones. Farmer Jones is a remarkable man. I made his acquaintance during my first visit to Chicago and renewed it when I

returned.   It was, however, not until the night on which
Mayor Hopkins was elected that I fully appreciated the
significance and the value of my new acquaintance.   I
think, on the whole, Farmer Jones had done more to
reassure my faith in the future of Chicago, and to give
me the clue to its secret than any other man in the city.
Yet when I walked along the street with Farmer Jones
on one occasion and passed a doctor who had for many
years practiced on Bum Street he deemed it his duty to
send a special messenger to warn me to take care,
as the man I was with was one of the toughest of
the toughs in the slums.   Farmer Jones' appearance at
that time, it must be admitted, was rather against him.
There was an ugly wound on his right cheek which was
partly concealed by sticking plaster, his chin was covered with the stubbly growth which indicates that the
barber is three days behind his time, his eyes were
bloodshot and restless, while for his hair,—well.   It is
said in Chicago that Mayor Hopkins was elected by the
silkstockings on the one hand and the short hairs on the
other; Farmer jones was emphatically not a silkstock-
ing dude and he was as conspicuously one of the short
hairs.   He stood about five feet ten or eleven, somewhat spare in his build, with a slight slouch and a curious amble in his gait caused by a lameness in one of
his feet.   You usually saw him with a billy-cock hat
on his head and a cigarette in his mouth, and his
clothes, to put it mildly, were somewhat the worse for
wear.

When I did my day on the streets with the broom
and shovel brigade Farmer Jones was kind enough to
accompany me.   It was from him that I had borrowed
my working clothes.   They had been lying for twelve
months in a locker in Brant Smith's saloon.   They
were pretty dilapidated, but when I was fully equipped
and I sallied forth together with Farmer Jones and took
our places in the street cleaning brigade we were as
pretty a pair as there was to be found in Chicago.   Yet

this tough denizen of the slums, with his stubbly beard and bloodshot eyes, was, by universal consent of all who knew him, one of the smartest men in politics. It was only whisky that was the matter with him, that was all. But then, it must be admitted, there is a good deal in whisky, especially when it is applied internally at pretty frequent intervals from morning till night.

The first time I met Farmer Jones I was so busy talking to Brant Smith that I did not hear much of what he had to say. But on the second occasion I well remember what he said. It was the first night of the registration for the mayoralty election, and, as was to be expected under the circumstances, Farmer Jones had celebrated the occasion by such frequent libations that it was somewhat difficult for him to maintain his equilibrium. By holding on to the counter, however, he was able to explain with some considerable triumph the number of Democrats whom he had registered that day. There was a gain on the total number and there was great joy in the saloon over the result of the first day's innings. When Farmer Jones saw me, he steadied himself for a moment by the counter and said:

"I want to talk to you, Mr. Stead. I want a long talk with you. But not now."

"Why not now?" I asked.

"I have a great deal to say to you," he continued, "but I cannot say it to-night."

"But why not?" again I asked.

"Because," he said, as he looked at me very solemnly as he swayed to and fro, with a curious owlish look in his eyes, "because, Mr. Stead, my head is rather muzzy — and my tongue — is so thick — and to tell you the truth, Mr. Stead," he said, as he gave a lurch towards me, "to tell you the truth — I am half drunk."

There could be no doubt as to his condition, although there might have been some dispute as to the fraction. But he had still enough sense to know what he was driving at. After a time I got him persuaded to endeavor to use his thickened tongue in order to explain what he wanted to say to me. He had evidently been impressed by the way in which I had spoken about the saloons at the Central Music Hall. The saloon people in Chicago have been so accustomed to receive nothing but vitriolic denunciation from every person who speaks in public on temperance or morality that they could hardly believe their ears when they found that for once they had been treated with ordinary justice.

He said, at last, "If you want to do any good in this town begin a crusade against the indecent saloons. You will do no good at all if you go against all the saloons, but you should distinguish between the decent and the indecent saloons."

"But what do you mean by an indecent saloon?"

"A saloon like this is a saloon and nothing else; but a saloon to which I could take you a few doors from this is not so much a saloon as it is the door to a house of ill-fame. There is a field where every honest man will support you. Why do you not stick to that and let us have in Chicago saloons that are saloons and not saloons that are sporting houses and gambling hells as well!"

I agreed with my friend that this was a practical policy; but he was hardly in a condition to go into details, so we adjourned the conference until a more convenient time.

That time did not come until the day of the mayoralty election. When my son and I walked over to the saloon after dinner we found Brant and his friends in a state of great jubilation. It was just after eight o'clock and sufficient number of returns had come in to show that Hopkins' election was all but assured. There was a crowd of men in the saloon. Brant, as usual, was behind the counter, as sober as a judge, while far back, in a state of complacency which often accompanies the early stages of befuddlement, sat Farmer Jones.

"Hopkins is in all right," said he to us, "there are only two more precincts to come in and his majority is over a thousand. But come," he said, "sit down and I will tell you all about it."

He led the way into the back of the saloon and setting himself against the wall placed chairs on either side of a small wooden table and proceeded to unfold the true inwardness of electioneering methods in the Ninety-first Precinct of the One Hundredth Ward in the year of our Lord 1893. It was extremely interesting, instructive and full of suggestion.

The scene of the narrative was in appropriate keeping with the nature of the story which was unfolded. The saloon was well filled with a number of men who seemed to consider that the importance of the occasion and the significance of the victory demanded continual relays of drinks. As for Farmer Jones himself, he found it necessary at intervals throughout the evening to lay in stores of hot Scotch whisky; this, he explained to me apologetically, was owing to the fact that his extremities got so very cold, he needed just a little something to keep up the circulation. Beer was the general drink, but although every now and again a free and independent citizen who had been vindicating the rights of the people by voting for Mr. Hopkins would require a little slumber after his exertion, there was no quarrelling, and there was a great deal of good nature. Outside in the street in front of the saloon a great bonfire was blazing. Some luckless garbage boxes from the back yard and all the available timber that was lying loose was pressed into service in order to celebrate the Democratic triumph. Farmer Jones took no part in building the bonfire, contenting himself with giving words of command to the gang of men who tramped backwards and forwards through the saloon, carrying fuel to the flames. Most of the men wore the white silk badges of the Democratic party, while some of them carried a card with the portrait of Hopkins in their hat. The bard of the occasion was one Brennan, an Irishman, who became so effusively hilarious as the hours stole on towards midnight, that, after having sung an indefinite number of songs, many of his own composition, and executing step dances to the music of an accordion, he insisted upon decorating me with a Hopkins card. Farmer Jones protested. He said I was a stranger and a visitor and not a naturalized citizen and that I ought not to be compelled to wear the Hopkins card, but the bard insisted; and by midnight my son and myself might have been mistaken for two of the staunchest of the Democratic citizens who had exercised their right of citizenship by returning Hopkins at the head of the poll.

"You see," said Farmer Jones, as he settled himself to his hot Scotch and looked at me through his cigarette smoke, raising his voice slightly so as to be heard over the drone of the music and the laughter that followed each verse of Bard Brennan's song, "you see we have done our part in this precinct. It is a black Republican precinct and we polled a majority of ninety for Hopkins. I took most of them to the poll myself," he said with some degree of justifiable pride. "Yes, I polled ninety votes in this precinct for Hopkins, and it did not cost me more than half a dollar a head, whereas the Republicans had to pay their men $3 each before they could get them to the poll."

This inside glimpse into the finances of voting somewhat startled me. "But," I said, "do you mean to say that the Republicans paid $3 a head for their votes? That was rather high, was it not? The Democrats in the 17oth Ward were only paying their men $2 a head."

"They paid $3 in this precinct," said he. "There was any amount of money going on Swift's side. Why, I was offered $100 myself if I would only stay at home on election day and do nothing."

"But who offered you that?"

"The Republicans, of course. They have been spending money all round. They sent me word that if I would go down to the Central Committee I should have $100 merely to stay at home. They tried that on all round. Why there was Skippen—you know Skippen, that infernal scoundrel! Why, he went round trying to bulldoze the lodging house keepers in this neighborhood. When he found that he could not frighten them by telling them he would put crape on their doors if they did not help to elect Swift, he offered them any amount of money merely to keep citizens from voting. They would not do it, not they. He had to get out of that pretty quick I tell you. Oh, Skippen, he is a son of a gun, he is!"

"What is the matter with Skippen?"

"Why, Skippen is a U. O. D."

"What in the name of mischief is a U. O. D.?" I inquired anxiously.

"Well," he said, "a U. O. D. is short for a member of the United Order of Deputies; that is the most powerful secret society which exists in America at the present time, and its object is to prevent anyone having anything in politics or anywhere else that was not born on American soil. But I reckon," said Jones, complacently, "that Skippen will not show his head in this precinct again."

"Why?" I asked.

"Do you know what we did as soon as the polls opened this morning?"

"No."

"We simply fired Skippen out of the polling booths."

"Fired him out! How did you do that?"

"We told him he had to git and he got."

"But how could you do that?"

"Don't ask any questions," he said. "They know what it is that is meant. Skippen would have been killed, that is all I can say."

"But who told him so?"

"There was no need to tell him. There is no need to say such things. They did not take long to clear out and leave us alone."

" Well," I said, " supposing he had refused ? "

" Well, we should have had to use arguments with him.
We should have convinced him, never fear. We might
have been sorry to use them but he wisely did not force
us to use them.   It reminds me," said Farmer Jones,
" of a story that used to be told about Mr. Hamlin.   He
used to travel with a circus up and down the country.
It was a habit of his always to ride ahead of his show
to make the business arrangements.   One day he was
riding along in Virginia and he came to a plantation.
He rode into the front yard where he saw an old
gentleman sitting upon a stoop.   'Stranger,' said he
'are you from the North?'   'I am,' said Mr. Hamlin, whereupon,   before he knew what was going to
happen, the old gentleman picked up a rock and flung
it at him so that it struck his head and fetched the
blood.   Thinking he had had enough of the conversation Mr. Hamlin rode away until he came to a trough
be the wayside, where he dismounted and began to wash
away the blood which was streaming down his face.
While he was so engaged a negro came riding up in hot
haste and said 'Are you de gentleman dat de colonel
threw a rock at?' 'Wall,' said Mr. Hamlin, wonder-
ing what was the matter, 'I guess I am.' 'Oh,' said
the nigger, 'I have come from the colonel, and a bery
fine gentleman he is — a bery fine gentleman indeed —
a perfect gentleman ; he wishes to apologize — he says he
is bery sorry he hit you with a rock, sah, he is bery sorry,
bery sorry indeed, sah, and he sent me to ride after you,
sah, to give you his best respects and his compliments,
and say to you, sah, that he never would have hit you
with a rock if he had had any other weapon handy !'
So," said Farmer Jones, when he had finished his story,
" Skippen understood and took the hint in good time."

" Well," said I, " when you got the polling stations
in your hands, what did you do ? "

" Voted our men, of course."

" And the negroes, how did they vote ? "

"They voted as they ought to have voted. They had to."

"But," said I, "the ballot is secret enough, how could you compel those people to vote against their will?"

"They understood, and besides" said he, "there was not a man voted in that booth that I did not know how he voted before he put his paper into the judges' hands."

"And your own men, you say it cost you half a dollar a head?"

"Well," said he, "I had not to pay more than half a dollar for any of them. My total expenses today for everything is only $45 and I voted many for a drink and some voted for quarters, but no one got more than half a dollar. You know," he said with a smile, "we have some curious experiences on polling day, and sometimes they get a laugh on a fellow. For instance, I went into a stable this afternoon and I found nine citizens who had not voted and it occurred to me that they were very thirsty. So I borrowed a pail and went into a saloon and got it filled with beer, which cost me 35 cents. I took it to the stable expecting that when they had quenched their thirst they would be capable of the exertion of going to the polls and voting for Hopkins. But it did make a fellow feel cheap when they took that pail of beer and gave it to one of the horses."

"Then you did not vote them after all?"

"Oh yes I did, but it cost me half a dollar a head."

"How did the foreigners vote?"

"I voted fifty-four Italians all in a block and I had not a cent to pay for them. You see," said he, "the Italians are great believers in Democratic principles."

I said I thought it would be rather difficult for them to know the difference between Republican and Democratic principles.

"No, you will find that they are all devoted admirers of Democratic principles and Republican institutions," he said with emphasis. "These Italians voted all right because I made them citizens. They would not have had a vote but for me. Not one of them could speak a word of English, either, what is more." Then waxing wroth as something came to his mind, he said, "We have got some judges in Chicago who need to be removed. Think of that Judge Gibbons! I took those Italians down to naturalize them as citizens—fifty-four as fine men as ever you set eyes on, all residents in this ward and all good Democrats. When I brought them in Judge Gibbons asked me if they could speak English. I said, 'No, your honor.' He asked me if I could answer for them being good citizens. I said I knew they were great believers in American institutions, and then that judge absolutely refused to naturalize them."

"What did you do?"

"I thought it was time to take a change of venue. So I went to another judge. This judge he said to me, 'Now Jones, what do you want to do with these men?' 'I want to make citizens of them.' 'Can they speak English?' 'No, not one of them.' 'Can you speak Italian?' 'Not a word.' 'Then how can you answer for them?' 'I can answer only for one.' 'Which one is that?' 'This one,' I said, 'he can speak a little French and I can speak French, and I can answer for his allegiance to American institutions. I will answer for him, and I want you to enroll him as a citizen.' The judge did so. Then that man answered for another and so on until the whole fifty-four were American citizens. I voted them to the last man for John Patrick Hopkins."

"But," I said, "Jones, I do not understand how you get hold of those fellows."

"I work 'em," he said. Then, replenishing his hot Scotch he raised his hand to about four feet above the floor, and added, meditatively. "She is just about that high, a little bit of a thing just about eight years old."

"What do you mean?"

"It was a little Italian girl helped me or I could never have done anything."

"Do explain what you mean," I said.

" Well," said he, as he lit another cigarette, " two years ago I noticed that a friend of mine who lives down the block had a bright little girl who was beginning to go to the public school. He was an Italian and a very fine man although he could not speak much English. I kept my eye on that little girl and whenever I went to see her father I always took her a pound of candies or a toy tortoise or a snake or anything of that kind, even if to do so I had to borrow a quarter. So I quite got hold of the little girl ; she thinks I am her best friend in the world and she will go anywhere with me and do anything I want. When the elections come round I just go to her with a bag of candies and we go canvassing together. She can speak both Italian and English ; so she goes with me and translates anything I have got to say. I have got great hold over the Italians here and it is all through that little girl."

Up to this point I had been more or less scandalized, but now I began to get interested — interested as a man is interested when, after a long search in a great ravelment of odds and ends and thrums and tatters, he comes upon a skein which may possibly give him a clue to the confusion. This story of the way in which Farmer Jones had roped in the Italian girl as his go-between and interpreter, so as to enable him to get hold of the non-English-speaking Italians and made them his friends and voted them for the Democratic candidate—here was something which made me inclined to cry " Eureka ! " Here at last was something like a clue to the agency which has worked this great conglomerate of rival nationalities into one homogeneous whole ; here in a low and rudimentary state, no doubt, but with vigorous vitality in it, there was the principle of human brotherhood and the recognition of human service. There was religio—a real religion— or the linking together of man to man. Which of all the churches, I wondered, would take so much trouble for so long a time merely in order to get hold of a little Italian girl to work into their organization this rough unas-

similated hunk of Italianism which Farmer Jones had
got hold of in order to strengthen the Democratic party?

Farmer Jones, however, did not see anything in it, but
was more intent upon pursuing the thread of his own
meditations.

"Stop a minute," said he, "I want to show you something." With that he disappeared. Making his way more
or less unsteadily across the saloon, he presently returned,
bringing with him a black hat through the rim of which
a jagged hole was punched near the right temple.

"You see that," said he   "Do you know what made
that?"

"No," I replied.

"A knife, and it nearly cost me my life. But it would
not have happened if I had taken a hint from my little
Italian girl. I got it from an Italian, the ungrateful
hound."

" Tell me about it. "

" You see,' said Jones, "It was that scoundrel Billerot,
the ungrateful dog! But never mind, I will be even with
him yet. It was only this year that we were having the
elections for constables. Billerot was put up for election. I did not like the fellow and voted against him
at the first ballot. We had to vote again. He came to
me and said, ' Oh, Jones, me wants two votes to be elected.
Me a good fellow, Jones, do give me your votes.' 'No,'
said I, ' I don't like you, I won't vote for you.' 'Oh, me
very good fellow,' said he, and he went on so that I had
compassion for him and, against my own judgment, I
voted for him and got him five votes. He was elected,
the son of a gun," said Jones, betaking himself to his hot
Scotch with an assiduity which made me fear that his
tongue would again become so thick as to preclude the
possibility of my receiving the end of his interesting
discourse.

"Well," said I, "what about Billerot?"

"He is an ungrateful wretch. The other day we had
a meeting of Italians in the ward for Mr. Hopkins. So

I went for my little girl to go with me to the lodging houses to get my men. Who should I find at the first lodging house but Billerot. I said to him, 'Well, Billerot, are you going to come to our meeting?' 'What meeting?' asked he, and before I could answer the little girl twitched the side of my trousers and I saw that I was in the wrong box. 'Why, Mr. Hopkins' meeting,' I said. 'Me no go, me no for Hopkins.' 'What!' I said, 'you no for Hopkins and I got you to be constable?' 'Oh, you good fellow, Jones, but me no like your alderman. Me no like Hopkins.' 'Well,' I said, 'all right. I will go and see the Italians.' 'No,' said he, 'you no go in, me no let you go in. No vote for Hopkins, me don't like your alderman.' "

"Then," said Jones to me, " you know I am rather hot tempered and I sometimes say things I ought not to say, but I cannot help it, and I just bent forward to him and said, 'Billerot, you remember there are some people in this town who are in a secret society, that killed Dr. Cronin, and they are called the Clan-na-gael ; and there are other people in this town of all manner of nationalities except Italians, and they blew up the policemen at the Haymarket ; and,' I continued, looking him full in the face, 'there is another set of men in this town and they call them the Mafia.' I had hardly got out the words when as quick as lightning he flashed out his knife and struck at me with all his force. I dodged the knife and instead of splitting my head open as he intended it went through the brim of my hat and cut open my cheek. The little girl was standing close by us, otherwise he and I were alone. The blood streamed down my face, but the moment he struck at me I grabbed my gun and began blazing at him. But he quit fast as soon as he saw he had missed me, and the blood was so much in my eyes that I could not see plainly to hit him. I went across to see some of his countrymen and they said 'Did you call him a Mafiote?' 'Indeed I did,' said I.

'Well,' said he, 'I am not suprised that he tried to knife you, for it is God's truth.'"

Jones stopped. Then he added, complacently, " I think that man's political career is ended."

"What will they do with him," I asked.

"I don't know, but no good, I reckon. No doubt he will lose his constableship next election, and there is no future for that man in Chicago."

Jones remained quiet for a time. He had told the story with a vivid realism that made it stand out like a picture by one of the Dutch masters of the interior of a tavern or a camp—a vivid little thumbnail sketch, as it were, of the realities of politics and electioneering in the first ward: the Mafiote with his knife stabbing madly at the American with his gun, whose one regret was that the blood in his eyes rendered it impossible for him to shoot his fellow citizen, and consoling himself with the thought that by his political pull he would be able to blight the Mafiote's rise in the political hierarchy of the American Republic. Here at least were realities and not theories.

After another song from Brennan, "What a genius," he said, meditatively, "what a wasted genius; that man will sing from morning till night. As long as he has his beer he never seems to tire. But here," said he, ", is another citizen who would not have voted but for me." So saying, he introduced a tall, somewhat melancholy man who was doing odd jobs about the saloon. "Here is my friend Dafton, who has been unfortunate. He has just come out of the penitentiary in Indiana, where he had been sent for two years." We made room for the gentleman at the table and soon he was quite sociable and friendly.

His story was rather a sad one. He was a teamster in good work in Chicago, whose wife had proved unfaithful to him, and feeling discouraged he had gone to work on a railway in Indiana. When there he had taken care of the swag of a fellow workman who was lying dead

drunk at a strange saloon. He got drunk himself before he could explain matters and was arrested for stealing his comrade's money. He was sent to jail for two
years. On coming out he came to Chicago but would
not have been allowed to vote but for his friend Jones.
He wrote to the chaplain of the jail in Indiana, who replied in high terms of the behavior of Dafton while in
custody. Armed with this credential Jones had been
down to the election commissioner and received from
him a certificate which entitled his friend to vote at the
election. Dafton was an interesting man, who had seen
hardship and who, in his melancholy, saturnine way, was
somehat of a mournful philosopher and a good Democrat
all the same, so he was welcomed to the fraternal bond
which united us all that night in celebrating the return
of Mr. Hopkins.

After hearing of his intervention to get Dafton his
right to vote, I said laughingly to Farmer Jones that he
seemed to be kept quite busy in the ward.

He put down his cigarette, looked at me and said
bashfully, "Well, I reckon that I get more people into
the County Hospital and more people out of the police
station than any alderman in the city. Yes, I am kept
quite busy. I think I get one man a week into the
County Hospital, and—let me see—about two and a half
every week out of the police station. That is not all,
either," he added, "I have to bury a good many of
them also."

"Bury them, what is that for?"

"Well," he said, "I know a good many Irishmen, fine
fellows, and when they die I have not the heart to let
them be buried by the county. I have got eight freehold lots in Oakwood Cemetery in my own possession,
and the ninth is nearly ready."

"What on earth have you to do with burying them?"

"Well, I have got something inside of me here," he
said, laying his hand upon his breast, "which causes me
a great deal of trouble. I cannot see a fellow creature

suffering without trying to help him if I can. When these poor fellows have died I go round to the hotels, and to my friends, and beg the money, and I have never failed yet in raising all that is necessary."

"How much is necessary?" I asked.

"I will tell you," said he. He went over item by item pretty much as follows, "There is $10 for a lot in Oak-wood Cemetery, $3 for moving the corpse from the morgue, $16 for the coffin, $5 for the shell, and I always take down four or five pall-bearers and bring them back again. I also pay $2 for an itinerant preacher to say service over the grave. Altogether it comes between $45 and $50. They are buried properly and never a doctor's knife in any of them."

"But about the County Hospital?"

"There is sometimes trouble about getting a man in. So if any of my friends need to be attended to I go with them. They know me at the hospital and they must take him in if I go with him."

"How is that?"

"Well, if they object to take him in I sit there until they do or until they send him to Dunning. It saves the man trouble and gets over a good many obstacles which are made to a man being received."

"I can understand that, but how do you get the people out of the police station?"

"Oh," he said, "that is not difficult. You see I have got a pull and anyone who has got a pull can do a great deal."

"Supposing I were your friend and had been arrested, what would you do?"

"Supposing one of my friends were locked up to-night for being drunk, I would go to the police station and see the cop who had run him in and I would tell him that I could answer for that man, that he was a good man and that he was all right."

"But supposing he was not all right?"

"Oh, but then he is all right," said Jones. "You can

not say that it would be good for a man to be locked up with thieves and criminals because he took a glass too much."

"But supposing he was a thief?"

"That would be a different matter; I would do nothing for a crook. Neither would I do anything for a man who kept on making a beast of himself. He had better go to the Bridewell. But when a good fellow gets overtaken once in a way I get him out."

"But supposing that the police will not let him out?"

"Well, then there would be nothing for it but to bail him out and see if I could not get him off the next morning. The justices know me. If I could not get him off, then I would get his fine suspended."

"What do you mean by suspended?"

"Why, suspended! It means that the fine is taken off, and you do not pay it."

"But," I said, "when a fine is imposed, is it not collected?"

"Not when it is suspended, and you can usually get your fine suspended when you have a pull. I had a little experience of my own that way."

I begged him to tell the story, and, nothing loath, he began.

"It was once when I was very discouraged. I had been employed by a corporation, and another corporation was jealous of me, and they had me fired out. I was so discouraged that I got drunk for two days. It was a very big spree, and at the end of two days I felt very bad. I thought I had had enough of it, and I wanted to be sent to the Washingtonian Home to be cured. So I went down to the police station, and asked them to lock me up and send me to the Washingtonian Home. But the cop who was there was my friend, and he said, 'Jones, I could not lock you up; I could not do such an unfriendly action to you.'"

"'But I want to be locked up.' But he said, 'I could not do it, Jones; you have not done anything.' 'Yes, I

have,' I said.   'I am drunk, and I want to be sent to the
Washingtonian Home in the morning.'   'No,' said he,
'I would not do it for a friend.'"

"'Well,' said I, 'you will have to lock me up if I
commit a crime.'"

"'But you would not commit a crime, Jones?'"

"'I will if I am driven to it.   I want to get to that
home.   I will one way if I can't 'get there another.'"

"'Oh, nonsense,' he said, and he laughed."

"I went out and I felt that it was too bad that I could
not get locked up without committing a crime, but as I
had to commit a crime I thought I might as well take it
out of the corporation which had lost me my situation.
I went down the street and stood opposite the window.
It cost $100 and I kicked my foot through it and then
took a stone and in a few minutes there was not much
left of that window.   There were two men inside the
office, but they were afraid to give me in charge, so I
marched up and down the street to a cop and gave myself
up.   I said 'I want you to arrest me for malicious injury
to propert.'   He took me to the police station.   When I
got there I said, 'Now you must take me in charge, as I
have committed a crime.'   The cop said he did not
know what to enter on the charge sheet.   I told him to
put me down 'malicious injury.'   So he took me down
to the cell and locked me up; I was very tired and I
felt as if my head were three feet long, but I got to
sleep."

"The next day I did not feel so discouraged and I did
not want to go to the Washingtonian Home any more.
When they brought me into court, who was there but
my old friend Justice Jennings.   The plate glass insurance people were there and the corporation also.   I
looked at the justice, and you know," said he with a
half bashful smile, "there is somehow or other an odd
smile on my face which comes when I cannot help it.
I no sooner stood up before the justice than my old
smile came back upon my face.   The justice said, 'What

are you doing here ?' I said, ' I have been on a drunken spree and I have done some mischief but I would like to pay for it.' The window cost $100 and I had not a red cent to pay it with. I said I would go out and collect the money if he would release me for a time. The plate glass insurance people, however, objected ; they said that it was a scandalous case and that the utmost rigor of the law must be insisted upon. So the justice went into the case. When he had heard it he fined me $7 and $1 costs. I said, ' Will you give me time to raise the money, your honor ?' 'Wait a minute,' said the justice. So I waited until the insurance man and the corporation people had gone. Then the justice said that the fine was suspended if I paid the dollar costs. A detective, a friend of mine, lent me the dollar and I paid the costs. Then I borrowed a dollar and paid the detctive back and we all had a drink together. I have not been to the Washingtonian Home yet, and now I think I had better have another hot Scotch before going home," he added.

To most people, possibly to every one who reads this chapter, such an inside glimpse of the practical working of the Democratic machine in Chicago would fill them with a feeling of despair. This, they will say, is the outcome of Democracy, the latest triumph which Republican institutions have achieved in the New World ! What a picture ! Bribery, intimidation, bull-dozing of every kind, knifing, shooting, and the whole swimming in whisky ! Yet it is from that conversation I gained a clearer view and a surer hope for the redemption of Chicago than anything I had gained from any other conversation I have had since I came to the city. Here at least I was on the bed-rock of actual fact, face to face with the stern realities of things as they are. Yet here, even in this nethermost depth, was the principle of human service, there was the recognition of human obligation, set in motion, no doubt, for party reasons, and from a desire to control votes rather than to save souls. But whatever might be the motive, the result was unmistakable. Rough and rude though it might be, the Democratic party organization, and, of course, the Republican party organization to a less extent in the same way, are nevertheless doing the work which the churches ought to do. They are stimulating a certain number of citizens to render service and discharge obligations to their fellow citizens and so are setting in motion an agency for molding into one the heterogenous elements of various races, nationalities and religions which are gathered together in Chicago. In its own imperfect manner this rough, vulgar, faulty substitute for religion is at least compelling the heeler and the bartender and the tough, whom none of the churches can reach, to recognize that fundamental principle of human brotherhood which Christ came to teach.

CHAPTER IV.

THE CHICAGOAN TRINITY.

Chicago, though one of the youngest of cities, has still a history, which begins, like that of more ancient communities, in blood. That royal purple has seldom been lacking at the beginning of things. Whether it is Cain and Abel, Romulus and Remus, or the massacre of the garrison of Fort Dearborn, the baptism of blood fails not. In the New World, as in the Old, the same rule holds true, and every visitor to the capital of the Western World is naturally taken to the historic site of the event with which the history of Chicago may be said to have begun.

On the rim of the shore of Lake Michigan, on a spot then a desolate waste of sand hills, but now crowded with palaces, stands, leafless and twigless, the trunk of an old cottonwood tree, which marks the site of the massacre of the garrison. Four score years and more have passed since the thirsty sand drank the life-blood of the victims of that Indian war, but still the gaunt witness of the fight looks down upon the altered scene. In 1812, when the British were at war with the French in Europe, our Canadian representatives were busy fighting and diplomatizing against the French and their allies on the great lakes. The Americans had struck in on their own account on the side of the French, and the British had just whipped them out of Detroit and Michigan, which had a narrow escape of becoming a Canadian province. War is war, and British and Americans fought on, each using as best it could the Indian tribes which swarmed in the unsettled country. The British made allies of Tecumseh, the great chief of the Pottawatomies, and

69

Fort Dearborn, the American outpost at Chicago, became the immediate objective of the allies after the
Americans had been driven out of Detroit and Michigan.
The officer in charge, Captain Heald, a weak incompe-
tent, decided to evacuate by arrangement with the
Indians. Whether this decision was right or wrong, he
carried it out in the worst possible way. He first summoned the Indians to a council and promised them all
the goods in the fort, including the ammunition and fire-
water, and then broke his word by throwing all the
powder and shot down a well, and emptying the liquor
into the river. The Indians, furious at this breach of
faith, waited until the little party had reached the open,
a good mile distant from the fort, when they attacked
and massacred all but twenty-five soldiers and eleven
women and children. The scene of the massacre is
marked by the venerable trunk of the cottonwood tree,
while close by the genius of a Dane has commemorated,
at the cost of a millionaire, the evacuation and the massacre, in a spirited group surmounting a pedestal with
bas-reliefs.

The sculptor by a happy inspiration has selected as
his motif the one incident of that bloody fray that
possesses other than a gory interest. While the Pottawatomies were scalping and tomahawking the pale faces,
regardless either of sex or age, Mrs. Helm, the daughter
of Mr. Kinzie, the patriarchal settler of early Chicago,
was rescued from imminent death by Black Partridge, an
Indian chief, who had long known and loved her father.
The group on the summit of the pedestal represents
Mrs. Helm desperately struggling to seize her assailant's
scalping-knife, while the splendid chief, Black Partridge,
intervenes to snatch her from her impending doom.
The surgeon who was slain is receiving his death blow
at her feet, while a frightened child weeps, scared by the
gleam of the tomahawk and the firing of the muskets.
The bas-reliefs, which are not in very much relief, tell
the story of the evacuation, the march, and the massacre,

and enable the least imaginative observer, as he looks out over the gray expanse of the lake, to picture something of the din and alarm of that bloody August day, and to recall, too, something of the elements of heroism and of humanity, which redeemed the grim tale of India war.

With the mind full of the Pottawatomies and their tomahawks, pondering upon the possibilities of latent goodness surviving in the midst of the scalp knife savagery of the redskin tribes, you tear yourself away from the traditions of Black Partridge, the Kinzies and the rest, and find yourself confronted by the palaces of millionaires. Mr. George M. Pullman's stately mansion stands in the shade of the cottonwood tree, his conservatory is erected upon the battle field, and he lives and dines and sleeps where the luckless garrison made its last rally. Prairie Avenue, which follows the line of march, is a camping ground of millionaires. Within an area of five blocks, forty of the sixty members of the Commercial Club have established their homes. Mr. Marshall Field and Mr. Philip Armour live near together on the east side of the avenue a little further south. Probably there are as many millions of dollars to the square inch of this residential district as are to be found in any equal area on the world's surface. It is the very Mecca of Mammon, the Olympus of the great gods of Chicago.

What strange instinct led these triumphant and militant chiefs of the Choctaw civilization of our time to cluster so thickly around the bloody battle field of their Pottawatomie forbears? "Methinks the place is haunted," and a subtle spell woven of dead men's bones attracts to the scene of the massacre the present representatives of a system doomed to vanish like that of the redskins before the advancing civilization of the new social era. Four score and two years have hardly passed since the braves of Tecumseh slew the children in the Dearborn baggage wagon, but the last of the Pottawatomies have long since vanished from the land over which they roamed the undisputed lords.

Long before four score years have rolled by the millionaire may be as scarce as the Pottawatomie, and mankind may look back upon the history of trusts and combines and competitions with the same feelings of amazement and compassion that we now look back upon the social system that produced Tecumseh and Black Partridge. How the change will come we may not be able to see any more than the Pottawatomies were able to foresee the value of the real estate on which Chicago was built. They parted with it in fee simple for three cents an acre, and did not even get that. But the Pottawatomie passed and the millionaire will pass and men will marvel that such things could be.

Chicago, though nominally Christian, does not concern itself particularly about the Trinity, whose nature and attributes are so carefully and precisely defined by St. Athanasius. So far as Chicago men are concerned St. Athanasius might have spared himself the trouble. They have a trinity of their own of whom they think a great deal more than they do of Father, Son and Holy Ghost. In abstruse theological dogmas, modern Chicago takes little stock. But it subscribes with both hands to any thing that is undersigned by the three Dii Majores of Prairie Avenue, Marshall Field, Philip D. Armour and George M. Pullman. These three millionaires are the real workaday deities of modern Chicago. They have the dollars and more of them than anyone else. Therefore, they of all men are most worship-worthy. They are the idols of the market place. Not that there is much of reverence in the popular homage. Chicago, like the Hindoo, is quite capable of scourging its idols once a year and throwing them into Lake Michigan. But worship in the real sense does not necessarily imply genuflections, kotowing and chin-chinning oriental fashion. You worship what you consciously or unconsciously set before yourself as the ideal toward which you aim, the model according to which you endeavor to fashion your life. That is real worship. Incense burning and prayer drill and hymn singing and sermon hearing may or may not have a close and living connection with your religion. But that which a man really worships he honestly imitates as the manifest expression of the best conception he has of the will of God.

Interpreted in that sense there is no doubt that the members of real working trinity of Chicago are Field, Armour and Pullman. The young man of Chicago has one aspiration. He would like to be as successful as they. Each of them in his own way is a beau ideal of triumphant money-making. The honors which the French paid to their Louis the XIV or the first Napoleon, which Italy paid to Michael Angelo and Raphael, or which England paid to Shakespeare or to Gladstone, Chicago pays to the supreme money-getters of their day. "Marshall Field," says one citizen, "has made $40,000,-000 in twenty years;" and all other citizens, metaphorically speaking, act as did the subjects of the Chaldean monarch when the sound of the cornet, flute, harp, sackbut and psaltery and all kinds of music summoned them to fall down and worship the golden image that Nebuchadnezzar, the king, had set up. Chicagoans, being practical, dispense with the musical instruments. The chink of the silver dollar is enough.

"As their gods were so their laws were," and as our gods are so our lives are. Millionaires are some of the images into which society has modeled human clay out of the semblance of Christ. They are specialists whose whole existence is devoted to one purpose, and that the acquisition and the accumulation of gold. Carlyle, you remember, draws a weird and ghastly picture of a man who, living solely for the gratification of his gluttonous appetite, becomes in the end merely an appendage to an enormous stomach. Millionaires have all of them a constant tendency to drivel and shrivel up into mere patent safes for the custody of their gold. Fortunately for Chicago, her millionaires have made their money, they have not inherited it. The real significance of the millionaire who works to build up his fortune will not be seen or appreciated until we have the millionaire who inherits it.

Marshall Field, the first of the greater gods in the Pantheon of the West, is a born trader. He comes of the true Yankee breed, and he has made his fortune by being quick to perceive that the day of the great store had arrived. What the Louvre and Bon Marche are in Paris, what Whiteleys and Shoolbreds are in London, Marshall Field & Co. are in Chicago. Their wholesale store is one of the sights of the city, and the guide books tell with admiration that "Richardson, the eastern architect, received $100,000 for the plans of this stupendous pile." The floor space devoted to the wholesale trade covers twelve acres; the building is 130 feet high, there are thirteen elevators and in this huge hive of industry 1800 employes are constantly employed dispatching the largest wholesale dry goods business in America. In their retail establishment on Wabash there is what is probably the perfection of business capacity directed to the facility of distribution. As the latest finishing touch to the conveniences of this gigantic bazaar, sixty pneumatic tubes, ramifying into all parts of the building, convey cash and return change with almost lightning-like rapidity. A brigade of some 3,000 men and women are employed behind the counters, and the universal testimony is that the management is far in advance of that of most dry goods stores in Chicago or elsewhere. Merit is readily recognized; promotion comes so rapidly, that the present head of the retail establishment, is still quite a young man. There is none of the scandal, such as rumor has persistently associated with other dry goods houses in Chicago and elsewhere. They do not use up extreme youth by employing juvenile cash girls, neither do they pay their female assistants rates of wages which suggest, if they do not enforce, the necessity for supplementing their earnings elsewhere.

Marshall Field & Co. is familiar as a household word throughout the city, and it is readily recognized that wherever money is required in public benefactions an appeal is seldom made to Mr. Field in vain. He and his partners were leading members of the syndicate of millionaires which ran the World's Fair, and although much has been said, and little printed, concerning the jobbery which prevailed in that select circle, there is no doubt but that they acted with a lavish munificence which contributed immensely to the success of the Exhibition. It was Mr. Marshall Field also whose bequest of a million dollars led to the establishment of the Art Palace as a permanent memorial of the great exhibition. Mr. Field therefore is undoubtedly a high class specimen of the public-spirited millionaire, and to this extent Chicago is fortunate in having him at the apex of her social system.

Regarded from the standpoint of business Marshall Field's career undoubtedly offers much that is attractive and tempting. If, in these days of competition, the man who can go one better than all his other competitors and clear the field of all other rivals is to be considered as having reached the ideal of a business man, then Marshall Field unquestionably stands near the top of the tree, if not at the very top. His partners say with pride that there is not a dollar of the forty millions he has made which is not clean money gained in legitimate commerce. That is more than can be said of a great many of the money kings of the present day. But after all this is admitted, the estimate in which the Marshall Fields and all that class are held very closely resembles that with which we regard the Hannibals, the Tamerlanes and the Napoleons of history. They loom up before the eyes of their fellow men because they have succeeded in ascending a pyramid largely composed of human bones. They represent the victor in the warfare of their time. They have gone out to battle, taking their chances as other men, and they have come out uppermost ; but for

those who have gone under even history can shed her
tributary tear.

Old residents in Chicago have told me how when each
fresh department was added to Marshall Field's stores it
was as if a cyclone had gone forth among the smaller
houses which were in the same line of business. When
Marshall Field opened any new department, say of cutlery
or hardware or millinery, jewelry, etc., or what not, he
would run it at cut rates so as to give him the command of
the field, contenting himself with the profits of the other
departments.   Against such a power, so concentrated in
turn against each detachment of the enemy, or the com-
petitor, nothing could stand.   The consumer is loath to
pay a nickel more to an old tradesman for what he can
get for a nickel less down town.   So it has come to pass
that Chicago is honeycombed from end to end with
elderly men who twenty years ago had businesses of their
own in retail stores ·by which they expected to make a
living of their own and to have a comfortable competence on which to retire in their old age.   They reckoned
without their Marshall Field, however, and others of his
class who have passed through the streets of Chicago
with much the same effect upon the smaller stores as that
which the angel of the Lord had upon the besieging
host which surrounded Jerusalem under Sennacherib.

He breathed but a breath on the camp as he passed

And the little store put up its shutters and the place
which knew it once knew it no more. All this, of course,
was legitimate business, just as the campaigns of Caesar
and Gustavus Adolphus were legitimate warfare.   Mr.
Marshall Field has no explosive bullets in his locker.
What he has done to others, others were allowed to do to
him, if they could.   All the same, although it may be necessary and inevitable, no one who knows the devastation which is wrought by each successive triumph of centralization in distribution, no one who sees
the changes which are wrought when a dozen centers of
supply are merged into one great concern, when the

store keepers become only retail clerks depending for their existence upon the caprice of their manager, can refrain from sighing that the gain should be purchased at such cost. The merging of all the distributing centers in a few great stores can only be regarded with the mixed feelings with which German patriots look back upon the unification of Germany. It was necessary, and the advantage outweighs the loss, but the process was cruel while it lasted and the ultimate gain is not yet in sight.

Marshall Field is a silent and reserved man, who very seldom commits himself to a public utterance. Even the ubiquitous interviewer seldom obtains from Mr. Field more than a succinct sentence. The ornamental as well as the oratorical part of his marvelous business he leaves to his partners. He does not give the impression to those who know him well that his immense wealth has been a source of joy and gladness which most men think can be purchased for cash down. Marshall Field, like other men, has found that the most triumphant success before the world may be accompanied with bitter disappointments, to avoid which he would have done well to have bartered many of his millions, but alas, in matters of life and death and health and home what the gods give is given, what they withhold is withheld, nor can they be tempted to change their gifts by all the wealth of Croesus.

Mr. Field probably rejoices to believe that in the conduct of his own business he has never stooped to anything which would conflict with his own idea of right and wrong. But it is not surprising that his conception of duty as a business man, and the conceptions of those who are not weighed down by his responsibilities, or hardened by the life of struggle in which a business man spends his days, do not altogether coincide. Mr. Field can hardly be said to be living up to the highest conceivable standard of social excellence. The great millionaire is currently reported, for I cannot find any public utterance of his to that effect, to look with scant sympathy upon the tentative efforts of the social reformer to shorten the hours of labor, and put an end to the curse of sweating. Neither does he acquiesce joyfully in the restrictions which the interstate railway law places upon the tyrannous strength of great trusts and corporations. Sweating, of course, he would consider to be an unavoidable evil. If it is possible to suppress it in Illinois he can still get sweated goods supplied from other states where the wage-earning class has not so much of a pull over the legislature. This may be so, but Mr. Field might consider whether it had not better be met by urging the other states to level their legislation up to the Illinois standard than to use the example of the backward legislatures in order to break down the bulwark which Illinois has erected for the protection of the sweated worker.

The second person of the Chicago trinity, Mr. Philip Armour, is probably the best of the three. Those who know him well declare that in many respects he is an ideal man of business, full of brawny common sense. He is a Scotchman, and he might have been nurtured from infancy on the Book of Proverbs, which is said to be responsible for much of the business instinct which enables the Scotch to freeze out the Jews, an achievement which entitles them to a first rank among the nations. Mr. Armour is the head of the most gigantic butchering establishment in the world. He is a kind of mythic genius presiding over the transformation of beeves and swine into extract of beef and canned meats.

He is generous and open-hearted and many stories are told of his liberality in relieving individual distress. Some of these stories may be legendary and many no doubt are apocryphal, but they all point in one direction and indicate that the lord of the packing trade is a man liberal of hand and soul who thoroughly enjoys bestowing largess upon those who are in need of his bounty. As a man of business he is methodical, industrious and untiring. No clerk is more punctual at his desk than the head of the great packing establishment which last year did nearly one hundred million dollars of business. No galley slave is more closely chained to his oar than Mr. Armour is to his desk. He is the first man to arrive at the office, between six and seven every morning, nor does he leave it till late in the afternoon, when everything has been attended to and all the innumerable questions arising in the dispatch of his world-wide business are left shipshape. Mr. Armour is one of the few men who live up to Benjamin Franklin's wise saws and eschew the use of midnight oil. " Early to bed a.id early to rise makes a man healthy, wealthy and wise," is an old saw which may be said to have fulfilled itself so far as wealth is concerned in the case of Philip Armour. He is said to be in bed every night by nine o'clock and has had his beauty sleep before midnight. He is up with the lark and by the time most of his competitors are having their breakfast he is already half through his day's work. He began this long ago when he was a young man and it has become to him a habit from which he cannot break away even if he would.

A Chicago journalist one time said to Mr. Armour, " Why do you not retire? You have made far more money than you know what to do with. Even if you slept round the clock money would still come in, more money than what you could use. Why cannot you get out of it all and leave the field to younger men? Why not give them a chance? You overshadow everything, monopolize everything in the place, and we have only one great butcher in the place of a thousand little ones. You have made your pile, why not clear out ?"

Mr. Armour listened patiently, as he always does, and answered, " Because I have no other interest in life but my business. I do not want any more money ; as you say, I have more than I want. I do not love the money ; what I do love is the getting of it, the making it. All these years of my life I have put into this work and now it is my life and I cannot give it up. What other interest can you suggest to me? I do not read, I do not take any part in politics, what can I do? But in my counting house I am in my element; there I live, and the struggle is the very breath of life to me. Besides," he added, "I think it is well for me to remain in business in order to set an example to younger men who are coming up around me."

Set an example he certainly does, an example which, so far as business habits are concerned, punctuality, dispatch, close attention to affairs, leaves nothing to be desired. But whether such a life is beneficial, that leaves the man who pursues it no other interest in the world excepting the mere struggle in the competitive arena, is a point upon which there will not be much difference of opinion. To live for only one interest, and that the struggle for victory, whether on the battle-field with the sword and cannon or in the market with the no less potent weapons of the modern capitalist, is a life that is dwarfed and deficient in most of the elements which make men truly men. They come to judge everything in the world only from the point of view of money.

Of this a curious illustration was told me in connection with Mr. Armour by Mr. Onahan. Some time ago the papers were full of their periodical fits of anxiety as to the welfare of the Pope. Leo, it seems, was declared to be profoundly uneasy in the Vatican and to be meditating seriously a flight across the sea to some retreat where he could find a shelter more to his mind than that of the Vatican. The Pope was going here, he was going there, he was going to Malta or Spain. Each correspondent had his own story and the air was filled with a babel of voices as to the future seat of the Holy See.

"What is this?" said Mr. Armour to Mr. Onahan, "what is this I see in the papers about the Pope? Do you think the Pope will leave Rome? Where do you think the Pope is going to?"

Mr. Onahan said he did not know that the Pope would

go anywhere, but if the revolution broke out in Italy he might be compelled to take refuge with some friendly power.

"Why should he not come to Chicago?" said Mr. Armour.

When Mr. Onahan told me this I was much interested, because I used to hold up the prospect of coming to Chicago before the monsignori of the Vatican as a kind of terrible looking forward to of punishment to come. When I went to Rome in 1889 one of my objects was to ascertain whether or not the Pope contemplated a flight from the Eternal City, and in that case to suggest that he had better come to London or to Chicago. Chicago was too far afield for him to go at one flight, but if the Holy See is to regain the leadership of the world which it held when the barbarians overran the Roman Empire the Italianization of the papacy must come to an end and its English-speaking era be close at hand. I well remember the shudder that passed over the Archbishop of Ephesus as that octogenarian prelate pictured himself and the Sacred College shivering in a blizzard on the shores of Lake Michigan. Such a change would undoubtedly have quickened promotion among the higher ranks of the Catholic hierarchy. I was naturally much interested in hearing that the idea of bringing the Pope to Chicago had apparently occurred simultaneously to Mr. Armour.

Mr. Onahan continued his story. "I explained to Mr. Armour," he said, "that the Pope was not a meer individual, but he was a spiritual sovereign with departments of state and that it would be impossible for him to transfer himself to Chicago as easily as if he were a Cook's tourist. He would require great administration buildings."

"I don't see that that makes any difference," said Mr. Armour. "It is all a question of money, is it not? Why could we not form a syndicate, some of us, and take up a large plot of land, as large as you like, and put up

buildings and make everything ready for the Pope so
that he could come and settle here with all his cardi-
nals and congregations, and then," said Mr. Armour,
with a twinkle in his eye, " we should make more
money by selling what was left of the land than we
spent in buying the original tract."

Here was a disillusion indeed.   I had imagined that
Mr. Armour was sharing my dreams of the future of the
papacy and of a reformed and English-speaking pope
acting as director general of the moral forces of the
world from his new throne on the shores of Lake Michigan, when, lo, the only thought at the back of Mr.
Armour's mind was the number of dollars which might
be made if the Pope were duly exploited by a Chicago
syndicate with a view to a speculation in real estate!

It is perhaps only natural for Mr. Armour to look at
political changes through financial spectacles.   The beginning of his colossal fortune was laid by the prescience
with which he was able to divine the effect which politics had on prices.   It was in the spring of 1865, when
Mr. Armour was still only a junior partner in a pig killing firm at Milwaukee, that he made his first million.
The author of that interesting volume, " The World's
Fair City," tells the story as follows :

> The price of pork was gradually rising, owing to the great demand
> created by the army, until the spring of 1865, when it was selling at
> $40 a barrel.   New York dealers became greatly excited, and believ-
> ing that it would go up still higher, bought eagerly all the pork they
> could grasp.   Mr. Armour looked upon the situation in a far different
> light.   He foresaw that the war was nearly ended and that pork, in-
> stead of rising in value, would suddenly collapse.   Mr. Armour at
> once started for New York and made a great sensation in Wall Street
> by selling pork short for $40 per barrel.   Then came the news of the
> fall of Petersburg ; a change was produced in the pork market.   Rich-
> mond was taken and the Confederate army surrendered.   Then Mr.
> Armour bought the pork for $18 that he had sold for $40 before he
> owned it.   This was his first great success in speculation ; it made
> him a millionaire.—Dean's World's Fair City, p. 353.

It would, however, be a mistake to regard Mr. Armour
as entirely immersed in his business.   Within the last two
or three years he has gained a new interest in life.   The

foundation of the Armour Institute, that magnificent technical college in which young men and young women of all classes meet together on a common footing to equip themselves for the battle of life, has been a great benefit to Mr. Armour if to no one else. It is his toy, his plaything. Dr. Gunsaulus is its president, but Mr. Armour never ceases to brood with paternal care over the institution which his liberality has brought into being. The institute is a great success, so great indeed that already the cry is for more of a similar kind. Mr. Armour endowed this institute with well nigh two million dollars, but not even that magnificent donation has been able to provide accommodation for all those who have sought it eagerly this year.

There is nothing that delights Mr. Armour more than to be able to help a promising youth who has got the capacity in him to succeed, but who finds it impossible to take advantage of the course of study provided at the institute. In such cases Mr. Armour's generosity is characterized by the delicacy and tact of a generous and sympathizing heart. Nothing is more remote from his nature than an attempt to make those who profit by his bounty feel indebted to him. Everything, indeed, is done, to make them feel that they are on a footing with the rest of the students. Not that he is indifferent to the use which is made of his benefactions; on the contrary, he keeps the sharpest lookout upon the recipients of his bounty, and if they prove unworthy their allowance is speedily stopped.

If the interest which he takes in the institute and its students is a growing interest, instead of it being, as is to be feared, somewhat of a toy of which its owner will get tired as soon as its novelty has worn off, there may be great things in store for Mr. Armour and for Chicago. But at present business is still Mr. Armour's absorbing occupation and even his beloved institute is but a subordinate consideration compared with the fierce joy and rapture of the strife which fills Mr. Armour's heart when bulls and bears are in conflict over the price of wheat or there is a speculation about the coming hog crop for the season.

In thinking of Mr. Armour, as of Mr. Field, even when we contemplate the lavish generosity with which he endows an institution which bears his name, it is difficult to forget the ruin of the small tradesmen. Mr. Armour feels no compunction, say in conducting a campaign against the butchers of Joliet, or any of other town in Illinois or elsewhere, where by the aid of preferential railway rates and his enormous wealth he is able to drive into the bankruptcy court the tradesmen who refuse to deal with Armour. But it is not surprising that the tradesmen who have fought a losing battle and have been beaten out of the field regard Mr. Armour's ascendency with feelings the reverse of pleasurable. Mr. Armour, however, would contend that he only did on a large scale what they were trying to do on a small. He kept strictly within the laws of the game and if the weaker went to the wall was that any of his lookout? Is not *viæ victis* the law all over the world?

Indirectly Mr. Armour and his class have played a very considerable part in the social revolution which is going on in Great Britain. Lady Henry Somerset lamented the other day that Armour was rendering it difficult for the small farmers on her Gloucestershire estates to obtain paying prices for their cattle, and there is no doubt that the immense development which Mr. Armour and his allies and rivals have been able to give to the American meat exporting trade has had a very powerful effect upon British politics. The rise or fall of a penny in the pound in the price of beef makes all the difference between prosperity and penury to the grazier in Ireland. The price of Irish cattle is influenced largely by the ruling prices in the Chicago market, and much of the strength of the Home Rule agrarian agitation in Ireland was due to Mr. Armour and others of the same class in facilitating the dispatch of American beef to the

English market. If many of our aristocrats are little better than splendid paupers, as one of their number recently declared, and if Home Rule is within measurable range of being obtained, these results are chiefly due to Mr. Armour and his class.

Mr. George M. Pullman, the third member of the trinity, is a man of different make. He has made the Pullman car a household word in every land for its convenience, its comfort and its luxury. Unlike Mr. Field, who is said to be a leap year politician, voting only once in four years when a president is to be elected, Mr. George M. Pullman is an active Republican politician well known in Washington, and much esteemed by party treasurers to whose campaign funds he has been a liberal contributor. Mr. George M. Pullman, in addition to many acts of private charity, is notable among the millionaires of Chicago as the man who, taking a hint from Krupp, endeavored to found a town in his own image. The town of Pullman, which was named after the author of its being, is a remarkable experiment which has achieved a very great success.

Unlike Mr. Field or Mr. Armour, Mr. Pullman has built up his fortune without resorting to the more ruthless methods of modern competition. Indeed, his career is notable as an instance of competition by high prices rather than by low. Mr. Field wiped out the retail storemen, and Mr. Armour the small butchers, by underselling them. Mr. Pullman has undersold no one. He has always succeeded, not by producing a cheaper article but by producing a dearer, but the higher priced article was so much better that Mr. Pullman succeeded in establishing a virtual monopoly of one of the most highly specialized businesses in the world. This is the more remarkable because Mr. Pullman was not originally a mechanic. He was merely a man of reflective mind, of native ingenuity and of great persistence. The inconvenience of a journey on the cars before the Pullmans were invented turned his attention to the possibility of making the sleeper as comfortable in the cars as in a hotel. The moment he set to work to realize his idea he was confronted with the fact that it could not be done " on the cheap." Nothing daunted, he decided it should be done at a high price if it could not be done at low. The first Pullman car which he constructed and put on the rails cost $18,000 to build, as against $4,000, which was the price of the ordinary sleeper. Railway men shrugged their shoulders. It was magnificent, they said, but it was not business. A palace sleeping car at $18,000 could not possibly pay. Mr. Pullman refused to be discouraged. " Let the traveling public decide," was all he asked, " run your old sleepers and the new one together; I will charge half a dollar more for a berth in the Pullman and see which holds the field." The verdict of the public was instant and decisive; everyone preferred the Pullman at the extra price, and the success of the inventive car builder was assured. He has gone on step by step, from car to car, until at the present moment he is said to have a fleet, as he calls it, of nearly 2,000 sleepers, which are operated by the Pullman Company. They have besides 58 dining cars and 650 buffet cars. Altogether the cars which the company operates number 2,573.

Other competitors have come into the field, but Mr. Pullman deserves the distinction of having placed every railway traveler under an obligation by acting as pioneer of commodious, luxurious and safe railway traveling. After building his cars in various parts, Mr. Pullman decided finally to centralize in the center of the American continent. Carrying out his decision, he naturally fixed upon Chicago as the site for his works. The Pullman Company was incorporated with a capital of $30,000,000, the quotation for which in the market to-day is twice that amount. He took up an estate of over three thousand acres round Lake Calumet, which is fourteen miles from the center of Chicago, and which was at that time far outside the city limits. There, following the example of Messrs. Krupp at Essen, he set to work to construct a model city in his own image. The car works were, of course, the center and nucleus of all. In these gigantic factories, where 14,000 employes work up 50,000,000 feet of lumber every year, and 85,000 tons of iron, they have a productive capacity of 100 miles of cars per annum. Their annual output, when they are working at full stretch, is 12,500 freight cars, 313 sleeping cars, 626 passenger cars and 939 street cars.

Mr. Pullman's ambition was to make the city which he had built an ideal community. In order to do so he proceeded in entire accordance with the dominant feeling of most wealthy Americans by ignoring absolutely the fundamental principle of American institutions. The autocrat of all the Russias could not more absolutely disbelieve in government by the people, for the people, through the people, than George Pullman. The whole city belongs to him in fee simple; its very streets were the property of the Pullman Company. Like Tammany Hall and various other effective institutions in America, not from the broad basis of the popular will, but from the apex of the presiding boss. Mr. Pullman was his own boss. He laid out the city, and made the Pullman Company the terrestrial providence of all its inhabitants. Out of a dreary, water-soaked prairie, Mr. Pullman reared high and dry foundations, upon which, with the aid of his architect and landscape engineer, he planned one of the model towns of the American continent. Here was a captain of industry acting as the city builder. With his own central thought dominating everything the city came into existence as a beautiful and harmonious whole. He achieved great results, no doubt. Before long the increment of the value of the real estate on which Pullman is built is expected to amount to as much as the whole capital of the Pullman Company. Every house in Pullman is fitted up with water and gas and the latest sanitary arrangements. Grounds have been laid out for recreation and athletics; there is a public library, school house and popular savings bank, theater, and a great general store where the retail distribution is carried on under the glass roof of a beautiful arcade building. It is a town bordered with bright beds of flowers and stretches of lawns which in summertime, at least, are green and velvety. It has its parks and its lakes, and its pleasant vistas of villas, and, in short, Pullman is a great achievement of which not only Chicago but America does well to be proud.

It was not a philanthropic, but a business experiment, and none the worse on that account. The great principle of *quid pro quo* was carried out with undeviating regularity. If every resident of Pullman had gas laid to his house, he was compelled to pay for it at the rate of $2.25 a thousand feet, although the cost of its manufacture to the Pullman Company was only 33 cents a thousand feet. Ample water supply was given, with good pressure, but of this necessary of life the Pullman Company was able to extract a handsome profit. The city of Chicago supplied the corporation with water at 4 cents a thousand gallons, which was retailed to the Pullmanites at 10 cents per thousand, making a profit large enough to enable the corporation to have all the water it wanted for its works for nothing. Thus did the business instinct of Mr. Pullman enable his right hand to wash his left, and thereby created at the very threshhold of Chicago are object lessons as to the commercial profits of municipal socialism. But between municipal socialism, representing the co-operative effort of a whole community voluntarily combining for the purpose of making the most of all monopolies of service, and the autocratic exploiting of a whole population of a city, such as is to be found in Pullman, there is a wide gulf fixed.

As a resident in the model town wrote me, Pullman was all very well as an employer, but to live and breath and have one's being in Pullman is a little bit too much. The residents in the city, he continued, " paid rent to the Pullman Company, they bought gas of the Pullman Company, they walked on streets owned in fee simple by the Pullman Company, they paid water tax to the Pullman Company. Indeed, even when they bought gingham for their wives or sugar for their tables at the arcade or the market-house, it seemed dealing with the Pullman Company. They sent their children to Pullman's school, attended Pullman's church, looked at but dared not enter Pullman's hotel with its private bar, for that was the limit. Pullman did not sell them their grog. They had to go to the settlement at the railroad crossing south of them, to Kensington, called, because of its long row of saloons, " bumtown," and given over to disorder. There the moral and spiritual disorder of Pullman was emptied, even as the physical sewage flowed out on the Pullman farm a few miles further south, for the Pullman Company also owned the sewerage system, and turned the waste into a fluid, forced through pipes and conducted underground to enrich the soil of a large farm. The lives of the workingmen were bounded on all sides by the Pullman Company; Pullman was the horizon in every direction."

All this provoked reaction and a feeling of resentment sprang up in the model city against the too paternal despotism of the city builder, and so it came to pass that the citizens by a vote annexed themselves to Chicago, of which it is now part and parcel. This was a sore blow and a great discouragement to Mr. Pullman. But no annexation can destroy his control over the town. It is still the property of the corporation of which he is the chief and controlling mind.

But in the civic life of Chicago Mr. Pullman takes no part. He may reply that he has done enough for duty and more than enough for glory in creating what is a model suburb of the city, and if every employer had done as much Chicago would have been a very different place from what it is to-day. That may be admitted, but the fact remains, so far as the administration of Chicago is concerned, Mr. Pullman is almost as much of a nonentity as Mr. Marshall Field or Mr. Philip Armour. Where Mr. Pullman can be autocrat he is willing to exert himself; but where he must be one among a multitude, although he might be if he chose *primus inter pares*, he will do nothing, no, not even although a little exertion he might do everything. He lives in Chicago. His house is one of the best built mansions on the lakeside. Compared with his lordly pleasure house the residences of Mr. Field and Mr. Armour dwindle into homely insignificance but at the City Hall we look in vain for any trace of the influence which has revolutionized the traveling accommodation of the world.

Mr. Pullman in Chicago is something like the mediatized sovereigns in Germany. He is not exactly in the sulks, but he has about as much direct influence in the city administration as the King of Hanover had in the North German Confederation when his kingdom was absorbed against the will of its monarch. Field, Armour and Pullman, these three each supremely successful in his own respective lines, each superbly generous and liberal in the matter of private benefaction, all three industrious, hard working men of business, they are in many respects not unworthy to occupy the summit of the local Olympus. They all take life seriously, perhaps a trifle too seriously. They have each fashioned for themselves and their families a luxurious home, but what have they done for the city? What have they contributed to the good government of Chicago? If Christ came to Chicago would these men of many talents be able to show a good account of their stewardship?

Let us see. What Chicago is suffering from, as a city, a want of probity, an almost total lack of ordinary business honesty in the transaction of the city's business. These men, are upright and inflexibly honest, how comes it that their honesty has no more influence in the City Hall than the sickly smile of a December sun has upon an Alpine glacier? These men are among the greatest financiers in the world, the smartest, shrewdest, brainiest men to handle dollars and cents whom the United States has provided. But the city finances are all in a snarl, the city treasury is empty, and Chicago with nearly two thousand millions of taxable property has only two hundred and fifty millions that can legally be taxed. This is but a poor showing as the net outcome of the way in which their lives have been lived. For the city is suffering from the lack of those very qualities of which the trinity have been gifted in superabundance beyond all their fellows. The spectacle is a sorry one. It reminds us of those detested regraters in famine times who stored million of quarters of wheat in their granaries and watched the people perish of sheer starvation at their gates, waiting callously until wheat reached its highest point. Is it not even worse? The speculator for a rise at least sells when the price suits, but the garnered harvest of financial experience, the ripened fruits of fifty years business management, which these men have, will perish with them. In that the city has no share.

This surely, is not an ideal condition of things. In America and the New World, under the generous stimulus of the Democratic idea, we have a right to look for something at least as good as that which is attained in the monarchical and aristocratic systems of the older world. But instead of being better the plutocratic system as it prevails even at its best in Chicago is worse than the results obtained by the aristocratic system which prevails in England and Germany. I do not for a moment mean to say that the English plutocrat is not as selfish a creature as his American brother. I am not speaking of the plutocrats so much as of the territorial aristocracy. The principle of noblesse oblige is recognized by the aristocrat as it is not by the plutocrat. The obligations of property are recognized and acted upon even by a very third rate landlord to an extent to which the ordinary holder of consols or of scrip would stand aghast. He may be a scamp, sometimes he is ; he may be dull and stupid, that he very often is; but take him as a whole there is more sense of the stewardship of wealth and responsibility of personal service among the English and German aristocrats than in the monied class either in the Old or the New World.

I suppose that in London the Duke of Westminster corresponds somewhat to Mr. Philip Armour, so far as wealth and social position is concerned. The Duke of Westminster is one of the few nobles that Mr. Philip Armour has not helped a long way towards the bankruptcy court. The Duke of Westminster does not draw his revenue from beef, or pork, or wheat, he is a ground landlord in London. Some time ago Lord Meath said to me: "You do not know how hard the Duke of Westminster works; he has hardly an afternoon or evening to himself. I went to see him a month or two ago in order to get him to take the chair at some philanthropic society. He looked over his note book and said, 'I am afraid that I have not a spare evening or afternoon which I could let you have.' "But I do not want it this week,' said Lord Meath."

" 'I am speaking for the whole of this season, " the said, turning over the leaves of his note book again; 'but I find I have one afternoon, and I ought not to have kept that back, I admit. But I have reserved that afternoon to see Clevedon.' (Clevedon is one of the Duke's country seats in the neighborhood of London.) 'I have never seen it this year,' he said, 'and I had reserved that afternoon to go and just take a look at it. But I will give that up and take your meeting.' "

That is only a little thing; nobody thought about it or talked about it. It was all in the days work of an ordinary duke.

There is a good deal of trouble in all this, but it is toil and trouble for which there is an ample reward, not merely in the security which it gives to the system that is based upon the consciousness of service rendered to the people, but also in the immense multiplicity of inter-

ests which it gives to life. The Duke of Westminster
may not be an ideal citizen, but he at least is in no danger of degenerating into a mere money-rake. He faces
life at many points and he is compelled to share it with
his fellow men. He has other interests than the perpetual scheming to anticipate a rise or fall in the price
of wheat or pork, and so it would be with every one who
did the same amount of work for his fellow men.

The ancient Greeks had a keener appreciation of the
virtue of this altruistic service than the Christian Democracy of the present century. As Frederick Harrison
has recently reminded us, in the republics of ancient
Greece the Democracy did not think it safe to rely upon
what may be called the voluntary altruism of their
wealthy neighbors. If in Athens, for instance, or in any
of the other Greek cities, a citizen had grown wealthy
and multiplied his estates, it was considered well within
the prerogative of the community to saddle that gentleman with the duty of contributing both in purse and
person for the general welfare. He says:

> At Athens, the liturgies were legal and constitutional offices, imposed
> periodically and according to a regular order, by each local community,
> on citizens rated as having a capital of more than a given amount.
> As magistrates and ministers certain men of wealth were charged with
> the cost and production of the public dramas, choruses, processions,
> games, embassies, and feasts. In times of war they were called on to
> man and arm a ship for the fleet * * * It always remained a
> *public service*, an honorary distinction, a coveted office, a duty to be
> filled by taste, skill, personal effort, and public spirit. No millionaire
> ever seems to think of giving his fellow-citizens a series of free
> musical entertainments, a historic pageant, much less a free dramatic
> performance," as did the liturgists of Greece.
> No Anarchist or Communist is working so desperately" to hurry
> on their abolition as are the rich men themselves.*

If some such institution as the Greek liturgies were
established in Chicago, it would be opposed as a tyrannical interference with the rights of the private
property and of individual freedom. But at present
no one suggests such a thing. Even the mild and tenta-

---

* "The Uses of Rich Men in a Republic," by Mr. Frederic Harrison, *Forum*,
December, 1893.

tive proposal of an income tax, now being discussed at Washington, has excited a whirlwind of indignation on the part of the wealthy classes, who are going great lengths in their efforts to persuade the masses of the people that the income tax is class legislation and therefore repugnant to American principles!

All that is asked is that, instead of setting an example before the coming generation of business men in Chicago of cynical neglect of civic duty and indifference to the responsibilities and obligations of citizenship, Messrs. Field, Armour and Pullman should do their duty to the city.

Some four years ago, when the first London County Council was about to be elected, Mr. McDougall, a chemical manufacturer in the east end of London, had arrived at a point in his business career when he could retire from the manufacture of chemicals or renew his partnership with every prospect of doubling his fortune. He was in the prime of his life and had amassed a moderate competence, not probably a hundreth part of the fortune of Mr. Field, but still enough to enable him to live comfortably until the end of his days. There was great need for eapable citizens in the London County Council, and after a long and prayerful consideration Mr. McDougal decided that his duty both to God and man demanded that he should give up his business and devote the rest of his life to the service of the city. He did so, and was elected to the County Council. For the last four years he has worked steadily in the Council for six hours a day every week in the year as hard as he formerly worked in the counting house at his chemical works. Whereas he formerly worked for himself, he now works for the city. With this result among other things:

Among the multifarious duties which the London County Council has inherited from the churches, the care of mentally afflicted is one of the greatest. The Council stands *in loco parentis* to 11,000 insane persons, who are housed in great asylums scattered round the metropolis, every one of whom absolutely depends for their daily bread upon the city authorities. Mr. McDougall, who is a humane man, was appointed to the Asylums Committee, and be dedicated to the task of alleviating the miseries of these afflicted ones all the energy of his nature. It is largely due to his exertions that the percentage of discharges has risen from forty-five per cent to fifty-two per cent. That is to say, as the direct result of the improved administration in asylums, brought about by the self-denying labors of such men as Mr. McDougall in the London County Council, from seven hundred to eight hundred lunatics were discharged cured last year, who would still have been in the asylums if the old system had prevailed and Mr. McDougall had gone on making an increased fortune in chemicals instead of dedicating the rest of his life to the service of his fellow citizens. There is ample work of a similar kind waiting to reward the genius of Mr. Field, Mr. Armour and Mr. Pullman, if they would but consecrate the remainder of their lives to the service of the city to which they owe so much.

It is not so much by the direct abuse of the power which money gives that the millionaire of to-day will be weighed in the balance and found wanting; it is not so much the sins of commission as those of omission which lie piled at his door.

Great wealth, unless greatly used, will not be left long in the administration of individual men. If it be true that the getting and hoarding absorbs the whole of the gray matter in the millionaire's brain, then we shall not have long to wait before we shall see the crystallizing of the inarticulate unrest of the suffering multitude in the conviction that there should be a division of labor, and that while the millionaire should be allowed to get his millions, the elected representatives of the Democracy should decide the way in which it should be spent and distributed. The millionaire would thus be relieved of the burden of looking after his millions, and could devote the whole of his time and energy to the more congenial task of amassing them.

No necessary work can long be left neglected, and if millionaires will not distribute their own wealth and use their great position with great souls and hearts, they will find that they will come to be regarded by the hungry and thirsty Demos much as compensation reservoirs are regarded by the inhabitants of the cities who have constructed them to replenish the stream which their thirst would otherwise drink dry. These great fortunes of $70,000,000 and $100,000,000 and $300,000,-000 will come to be regarded as the storage service upon which mankind draw in seasons of scarcity and drought. That is the use which society will make of its millionaires, if millionaires do not anticipate the inevitable by utilizing their millions. Some people imagine that the progress of Democratic Socialism will tend to discourage the accumulation of these huge fortunes; it is more likely that Demos will regard his millionaires as the cottager regards his bees. These useful insects spend the livelong summer day in collecting and hoarding up in their combs the golden plunder of a thousand flowers, but when the autum comes the bee wishes to take its rest and enjoy the fruits of its summer toil. But the result does not altogether correspond with the expectations of the bee.

The supreme test of every institution is not how does it help the few who are inside, but how does it help the million who are outside. Christ's test, "the least of these my brethren," is the one eternal test. That which does not help the common man and the common woman to make their lives human, at least, if not divine, stands marked as a brand for the burning, whither have been hurried by the inexorable destinies the noblesse of the *ancien regime*, by road of the guillotine, and the slave-holders of the South, by way of Gettysburg and Appomattox Court House.

That is what I meant when I said that the millionaire would go the way of the Pottawatomies, and as Black Partridge is remembered for his kindly and grateful rescue of the Kinzie's daughter, when all the rest of his tribe are forgotten, so it may be that the memory of the Field Museum and the Armour Institute and the Pullman city will be fragrant in the mind of men long after the last millionaire has joined the last of the Pottawatomies in the happy hunting grounds of the Summerland.

CHAPTER V.

WHO ARE THE DISREPUTABLES?

If Christ came to Chicago he would find that many of the citizens have forgotten the existence of any moral law apart from that which is embodied in the state or municipal legislation. The idea of the law of God as distinct from the statute book seems to have largely died out in the hearts of many men. In their opinion it is sufficient that their conduct is legal. If it is legal it must be right. When I was at Detroit I had a very interesting conversation with an alderman, a German who had been educated for the priesthood, but who had forsaken the sacred calling, and had become an out and out freethinker. He argued strenuously that there was no need for any other law whatever beyond the state law or the municipal ordinances; that they covered the whole area of human action, and that other law there was none. Religion, he said, was only ceremonial. If a man obeyed the state law he did his whole duty to his fellow men. The same from this sentiment has sprung the prevailing conviction, especially in commercial and political circles, that anything that does not land a man in the penitentiary is permissible. There is a wide region within which conduct may be legal but nevertheless supremely wrong, but this does not seem to have made its way into the moral consciousness of many American citizens. The law of God is exceeding broad. It is in vain with the man-made yardstick of human ordinances to endeavor to supply a substitute for this invisible, impalpable, all-pervading higher law.

It is not thirty years since in this very state of Illinois, as Governor St. John told me the other day, he was prosecuted for the great and heinous crime of giving food to a black boy under the so-called Black Act which was then on the statute book. Illinois legislative wisdom endeavoring to formulate the eternal truth and the divine law into a human statute, decreed in its wisdom that any person who fed a negro, excepting under such circumstances as were by statute provided, could be sent to the penitentiary for a minimum term of two years, with an additional fine. Governor St. John, who was the last prosecuted under this act, cleared that iniquity from the statute book. But with such evidence on every hand as to the absolute antagonism between divine law and human statutes, it is marvelous to hear good people, as well as bad, talking as if the mere compliance with written law was sufficient to justify a man in any course of iniquity which he may chose to pursue. "It is not my business to look into the questions of right or wrong; that is for the law to do," is a formula which is frequently heard in the city.

The citizen who argued this point most strenuously was a man who owned property used as a house of prostitution in the levee district. I sent him a circular calling his attention to the fact that he was guilty of an offense in allowing his premises to be so used. He first of all said that he was thoroughly convinced that some one was behind me and that there was a deal in real estate somewhere or other in connection with that circular. I assured him that there was nothing of the kind, and then we went on to discuss the question. He denied that he knew anything of the character of her tenants; then he said he was perfectly willing to let the house to a church for the purpose of a Sunday School if it would pay him as much rent as he received at present. "You see," said he, "they pay me about twice as much as I could get from anybody else."

"Well," I said, "that may be. But if they are using it for purposes of vice?"

"I have nothing to do with that," he replied. "That

is not my business, if there is anything wrong it is for the city to look after that. What I have to do is to see to it that I receive my rent."

"Without any regard as to the character of your tenants?" I asked.

"Without any regard as to the character of my tenants. Why should I look into those things? That is not my duty. If there is anything wrong with them the authorities must do their duty. I will do mine—that is to look after my rent."

" But," I said, " let us leave the question of prostitution out of the question. Supposing that these people were thieves and that they used your house for the purpose of storing their stolen goods?"

" If they would pay me $3 where I would only get $1 from honest tenants certainly I would let them have it."

" Would it not then make you a partner with the robbers?"

"No," said he, "I am simply a landlord, and my concern is with the dollar. Questions of right and wrong such as you are raising are for the city, not for me."

"Well," I said, "let us go a little further. Supposing that these were murderers and your premises were made the headquarters of a gang of thugs, who sallied forth every evening to murder the citizens and bring back their gory scalps to your house. Would you, knowing what they were, let them the house?"

" If they would pay me $3 in the place of $1 which I could get from an ordinary tenant, certainly, I would let it to them directly. I am after the dollar, as every one else is, if they would only say so. As long as I keep within the law that is enough.

Here we have asserted, in its baldest and plainest form, the working principle on which the smart man of Chicago acts. Everything that is not illegal is assumed by him to be right, no matter how dishonorable it may be, no matter how infamous it may be, or

cruel it may be; so long as it is permitted by law,
or so long as they can evade the law by any subterfuge,
they consider they are doing perfectly right. They
believe in the state; they have ceased to believe in God.
A man is considered honest, no matter how great a
scoundrel he may be, so long as he keeps within
the limits of the law. In like manner a woman is
considered respectable and of good repute, no matter
how false, vain, idle and selfish she may be so long as
she refrains from publicly advertising her loss of chastity.
A man may be a thief, all the same, even though his
plunder is legalized by an ordinance, and a woman
may be disreputable, although she may move in the first
set of the four hundred. These two elementary truths
seem to have startled many people in Chicago when I
enunciated them, as if they were heresies, not to say
blasphemies, against the social order. Heresies and
blasphemies though they may be called, they are sacred
truths, and if Christ came to Chicago, and were still of
the same mind that he was when he walked in Judea,
He would probably have said the same things with much
greater emphasis.

It is very odd to see how there has risen up a kind of
descendant of the noxious weed of the right divine of
kings to do wrong in the shape of the social idea that a rich
man must necessarily be "respectable." As a matter of
fact rich men and women are often, owing to the temptations which beset them, the most disreputable members
of the community; and it is one of the heaviest indict-
ments against the millionaire class, when it is not
steadied by responsibility and alive to its obligations,
that it tends inevitably to produce a class of mortals
which any well-regulated community would be justified in
sinking in the nearest bog until the breath had left their
body. Such was the treatment to which the ancient Germans resorted when their tribe was disgraced by a
coward. Such is the treatment which might fairly be
resorted to when a community breeds such social abor-

tions as the idle and the vicious rich. They are the social cancers of modern civilization, and it is they, not their hard-working fathers who have built up their fortunes, who will bring the class of millionaires to destruction. In the previous chapter I have referred to the trinity of Chicagoan millionaires, who represent the merits of their class. Unfortunately, as the sunlight is accompanied by a shadow, so over against the Chicago trinity there must be placed a companion picture, the diabolical counterpart of the benevolent and the public-spirited rich. Field, Armour and Pullman and their class, millionaires who regard themselves more or less as "God Almighty's money bags," who accept the stewardship of the money which has been intrusted to them, and who honestly desire to make the best use of their millions, constitute a class which, notwithstanding their shortcomings from the civic point of view, is worthy of considerable admiration. But side by side with those men, are others who use their inherited wealth for the worst purposes. These constitute what may be called the diabolism of Chicago. They can be conveniently divided into two classes, the predatory and the idle rich.

Concerning the predatory poor, all are agreed. It does not matter what temptation the man has been under or how severe the physical pressure under which he is put, if a man is a thief in the ordinary acceptation of the term that is the end of it. No conditions of extenuating circumstances are allowed to stand in the way of instant and ruthless condemnation of society. "He who takes what isn't his'n, when he's kotched is sent to prison," is the rule acted upon almost automatically by all civilized society in the Old World and the New. But the theft must be from an individual, otherwise the moral sense which is so prompt to vindicate the rights of private property does not assert itself. The old rhyme in England which contrasts the severity of the punishment of those who stole a goose from the common while nothing whatever was done to those who stole the common from the goose is as applicable as ever in the new conditions of the Western World.

This is partially due to a deficiency of the imagination, and also to the well-known fact, that what is everybody's business is nobody's business. A man who robs me of a dollar inflicts a wrong upon a definite individual, which leads me to actively resent the theft, and if possible to secure the speedy punishment of the thief. But fi the theft is committed, not on a definite John Smith or William Jones, but on a million such, and if the loss falls not upon a private purse, but the collective purse of a whole community, the indignation is so diffused as to be unappreciable as a force. There is no public prosecutor for thefts committed upon public property. The common weal is left to take its chances and as a result it fares very badly. Hence, the predatory classes in the community are naturally attracted to property which can be filched with impunity. This is equally true of all thieves, whether they be rich or poor. As a rule, however, property that is held in community is not of a kind that can be easily appropriated by the poor thief. To rob the city demands capital. And when brigandage is to be organized on a great scale the enterprise is usually above the means of the ordinary pickpocket or burglar.. But the man does not cease to be a thief because his robbery is conducted on a great scale, and still less deserves to be freed from the opprobrium attaching to dishonor because his robberies are conducted by means of a conspiracy and a corporation. Indeed, the more closely the matter is looked into, the more clearly will it be perceived that, while the garrotter and the foot-pad are poor enough specimens of humanity, they are, for the most part, infinitely less to be condemned than the wealthier scoundrels who wear broadcloth, pay pew rent and show an unfaltering front as respectable men. It would be unfair to hold the individual personally responsible for every crime against society of which they are themselves to a certain extent a product. There are wide tracts of territory even in Europe where brigandage is regarded as an honorable profession. In some parts of Italy and Sicily it used not to be uncommon for the brigand to regularly attend the confession to be shriven once a month or once a quarter, as the case might be, when he found time to spare from his more exciting avocations. It was not so very long ago when piracy was regarded as a laudable profession for an English gentleman, and in still more recent times, pious, humane and God-fearing merchants saw nothing contrary to the moral law in equipping vessels for the slave trade. So it would be uncharitable and unjust to confound the traffickers in public franchises, the trespassers on public property and the rest of the horde of wealthy brigands who are at this moment wallowing in the enjoyment of immense fortunes which they have plundered from the people, as if they were consciously as guilty as their poorer brethren, who, from time to time, are entertained at the expense of the city in the Bridewell or the penitentiary. But their offense is infinitely greater. When the slave trade was defined as the sum of all villianies, many estimable church members were sorely scandalized by the definition, which implied that they were the supreme villians of their time. Their own descendants to-day would not object to the statement. So in fifty years the grandchildren of many public robbers will admit that their fortunes were founded on acts of spoliation morally as indefensible as any of those that are treated as penitentiary offenses.

Regarded from the standpoint of an erring fellowman, there is a great deal to be said in extenuation of the offenses of many of the predatory poor which cannot be alleged in defense of the predatory rich. Take for instance the case of an ordinary crook who is at present serving his time in Joliet.

He may be, and very often is, the son of a ne'er-do-well, perhaps born of a nameless father on the highway;

hunted from his infancy by society, regarding the "copper" as his natural enemy. He grows up half educated or not educated at all. If he reads anything, it is probably detective stories, which form so large a part of the current literature of the English-speaking world on both sides of the sea. He robs for his living —gets sometimes one dollar, sometimes a hundred. Every now and then he is run into the police station and sent to the Bridewell or perhaps to the penitentiary. When he comes out he is still more of an outlaw. He is a jail bird and there is no place for him in the ranks of order and industry. So some day, down on Michigan Avenue or one of your other fine avenues, he crouches in the shade and holds up one of the citizens of Chicago and relieves him of his pocketbook. He is bad enough and ought to be laid by the heels in jail. There is, however, one good thing about him: he knows that he deserves to be so dealt with and so does everybody else in the community. There is no cant about your thief. He does not talk learnedly about the blessed law of competition or of political economy. He does not lay as salve to his conscience texts more or less misapplied, he simply takes his gun and holds a man up.

Take another class of men. These are not so bold; they are what we call in England area thieves. They are sneak thieves who wait until they can get hold of some man servant, or servant girl, and by promises of sharing the plunder, induce them to help them to the silver plate. He also knows that he is a thief and that if he is caught he will be sent to prison, and it will serve him right.

It is bad to rob your fellowmen on the street, but it is worse to rob your fellowmen of a whole street. It is bad to get hold of a servant girl and either by promises of plunder or by threats to induce her to guide you to the place where the silver spoons lie; but that dwindles into a comparative insignificance compared with what is done continually in Chicago by wealthy men, who bribe aldermen to give them franchises which belong to the citizens.

Of the predatory rich in Chicago there are plenty and to spare, but there is one man who stands out conspicuous among all the rest. He may not be a greater sinner than the rest of his neighbors, but he has succeeded in doing with supreme success what a great number of his fellow citizens have done or tried to do and failed. I refer to Mr. Charles T. Yerkes. Mr. Yerkes is a notable product of the present system. Of course, though Mr. Yerkes at an early stage in his career, before he was launched upon Chicago as a financier and street railway magnate, had served in a Pennsylvania penitentiary, I would not for a moment suggest that in his operations in Chicago he has brought himself within the clutches of the law. He who is once bit is twice shy, and the period of seclusion which he passed in the state establishment in the Eastern seaboard probably sufficed to convince him of the necessity for keeping strictly within the law of the land. But as a matter of fact Mr. Yerkes himself would be the last to complain of being classed among those who have become wealthy by the adroit appropriation of public property. Mr. Yerkes practically owns two systems of Chicago's street railways, the West and the North. Both the franchises, which make each of those lines worth more than most of the gold mines now worked in the States, were acquired by him without the payment of any adequate consideration to the city. No doubt the ordinances by which the franchises were originally granted were strictly legal and duly conveyed to Mr. Yerkes the privileges which are worth to him and his corporation millions of dollars per annum. But without questioning for a moment the legality of his title, even the most charitable of his friends shrug their shoulders when asked how it was the City Council showered such lavish generosity upon this immigrant from a Philadelphia penitentiary. It could hardly be for love of his beautiful eyes, nor can we suppose that Mr. Yerkes exercised any hypnotic power or fascination over the city fathers in the City Council. All that we know is that franchise after franchise was conferred upon Mr. Yerkes without any adequate consideration being paid for them. Two tunnels which the city had constructed under the river at an expenditure of millions of the city's money were handed over to him for equivalents which did not amount to more than twenty-five cents on the dollar. It is not too much to say that the City Council has given Mr. Yerkes and Mr. Yerkes' companies from time to time franchises, tunnels and monopoly rights which, if put upon the market to-day, could not be worth less than $25,000,000. Mr. Yerkes would certainly not be disposed to sell for less than that sum. But we may search the records of the city treasury from end to end without finding that the citizens received from him in return five per cent on the whole of this gigantic sum. What everyone in Chicago asserts is that the city fathers were bribed at so much a head to grant the franchises. No one can say that Mr. Yerkes bribed them; of that there is no legal proof—as little as there is that they were bribed. But if the mistress of a stately mansion in Prairie Avenue were to find her most valuable diamond ring on the finger of an Italian organ grinder who had been observed on terms of suspicious intimacy with her lady's maid, she would not hesitate to suspect that lady's maid very strongly, neither would she admit for a moment that the impecunious organ grinder had obtained possession of her diamond by any legal means. Just so in this case of Mr. Yerkes. The franchises are in his possession at this moment; of that there can be no doubt. Equally indubitable is the fact that the citizens with whose property these franchises make free have received no adequate consideration therefor. They were obtained by the votes of aldermen notoriously corrupt and from those three indubitable facts it cannot be said to be an uncharitable or far-fetched conclusion to assume that Mr. Yerkes has no reason to complain of being awarded a very conspicuous place in the ranks of the predatory rich. As the man said when asked if the fox had stolen the goose, " I would not like to say what I cannot prove, but I saw a good many feathers around his nose as he left the yard." Mr. Yerkes' nose is well feathered, indeed.

Rightly or wrongly, the citizens have an incurable suspicion of Mr. Yerkes, and whenever a franchise is going for a railway, surface or elevated, the immediate suggestion is that Mr. Yerkes is behind it. " I want to know if Mr. Yerkes owns Chicago," asked an indignant speaker at a meeting recently. Mr. Yerkes does not own Chicago. He only owns the greater part of it that is worth—well, not stealing, but conveying, the wise call it. Hence, when you ask a citizen if Mr. Yerkes is to be trusted to deal honestly with the city on matters of franchises the reply is almost invariably couched in similar terms to those with which the negro witness baffled the too searching inquiry of a judge as to whether the accused was or was not a notorious chicken thief. "Well, Massa," said Sambo " I don't know about that, but if I were a chicken and saw that darky loafing around, I would take care to roost very high."

Mr. Yerkes, having acquired so many millions from the city of Chicago, graciously deigns, now and then, of his munificence to throw a sop or two to the public. It was he who put up the electric fountain in Lincoln Park, which, however, might be regarded as a very shrewd business speculation, for the greater the attraction in Lincoln Park the more dense was the packing in Mr. Yerkes' cars. He, also, in his benevolence offered prizes for competition to the pupils in the public schools — prizes which, on the principle of not looking a gift horse in the mouth, were graciously accepted by the Board of Education. This form of benevolence was, however, discontinued after some of the school children had ventured to petition the autocrat for a slight improvement in the provision made by the street railway for conveying them to school.   By way of diverting the attention of inquisitive eyes which would keep squinting into his franchises he gave $250,000 for the construction of the largest telescope in the world, of which the University of Chicago is to be the proud possessor when finished.   It is much better for people like Mr. Yerkes that the scrutinizing gaze of the public should be turned to the heavens than to the scandalous manner in which he neglects his obligations to the people.   It is probable, however, that Mr. Yerkes, grown insolent by the impunity with which he has ridden roughshod over the people of Chicago, has overreached himself.   Had his railways been up to the standard of street car conveniences, had he used the power which he so mysteriously obtained in order to meet the necessities of the traveling community, he might have continued in unmolested possession of his monopolies.   Freebooters in olden times were able to acquire a certain degree of popularity even among those whom they plundered, by the genial free-handedness with which they would scatter largess among the crowd.   Mr. Yerkes may repent too late of his indifference to the welfare and convenience of the public.

Mr. Yerkes is a significant sample of the class to which I refer.   He lives in style, and apparently does not find it difficult to obtain the assistance of the gentlemen of Chicago in the managing of his companies.   There are too many like him on a smaller scale.   You can not drive a mile in any direction in Chicago without coming on instances of public plunder, only less heinous than those that are associated with the name of Mr. Yerkes. It is notorious that the franchises which have enabled the railway companies to lay no less than 1,900 miles of track through the heart of the city have been in many, if not most, cases due to corruption.   Rich corporations have used their wealth, as a brigand uses his carbine, in order to possess themselves of their neighbors' goods. And this system of public plunder will continue unchecked until the principle that the receiver is as bad as the thief is applied to all holders of franchises for which no adequate equivalent has been paid to the community, as well as to the fraudulent pawnbroker who acts as the banker of the light-fingered gentry who convey the watches of the citizens to the keeping of their "uncle."

The second division of the disreputables, and who are even more disreputable and a greater danger to the community than the predatory rich, are the idle, frivolous and vicious rich. Chicago has hitherto been spared the presence of many of these social cancers. This is due to the fact that the city is so new that it has not yet had time to breed an idle crowd. Again and again Chicago has been swept by national and public calamities, and most of her citizens have been constantly employed from the foundation of the city until now. The war, the great fire, the financial panic of 1873, have in turn swept away much of the realized wealth of the community and compelled successive generations to give their whole attention to the garnering of the golden grain. But a new generation is springing up of men and women born in the lap of luxury, shielded from childhood from all the rude blasts of adverse fortune, and endowed neither by precept or example with any idea as to their duties to the community in which they live.

The young noble in Europe enters upon a public career almost as soon as he is out of college. His course at the university finished, he steps at once into public service of one kind or another. He stands for Parliament, or the County Council, and he takes a seat on the bench. He is initiated into the administration of his estates. In a thousand ways he is reminded, not so much by precept as by the way in which the social machine works, that he has to take his place and do his duty in the exalted sphere in

which it nas pleased Providence to place him. The
plutocrat's child is shut out from this beneficent ministry of service. If, as usually happens, the son con-
ceives a postive distaste for the ant-like hoarding up of
money, he is left without an object in life. Here and
there, perhaps, a few studious young men devote themselves to science or literature, but they are few and far
between. For the most part they scout a public career.
It is bad form for a well-to-do citizen and member of the
Chicago four hundred to enter his son for the position
of alderman. To be an elected representative of the
city of Chicago in the municipal council is counted a
disgrace and it is even worse to sit in the State legislature. A story is told of a pupil in the public schools
who resented as an insult the imputation that his father
was an alderman. A youth without an object, without
an ideal beyond that of mere social success, and with
wealth beyond the dreams of avarice at his disposal, is
in a position perilous indeed.

Long ago in Switzerland I was much impressed by
the remarks made to me by Herr Boss, the veteran Alpine climber, who managed the great hotel of the Bear
at Grindelwald. Sitting on the stoop one evening looking out over the great expanse of the Bernese Oberland
and talking of the workings of Democracy in Switzerland, Boss suddenly exclaimed, "Do you know what
is the secret of the success of the Swiss Democracy?
Do you know what it is that has enabled us to keep all
these years a free republic, independent and strong, in
the midst of monarchical Europe?" I suggested their
schools, their popular system of government, and other
things which naturally occurred to the mind. "No,"
said he, "it is none of these. The secret of the strength
of Switzerland lies in this: we have realized that any
citizen who is not employed in some responsible work
for the community is a bad citizen, and a source of
danger to the republic. For instance," he said, "in this
valley of Grindelwald you will not find a householder

who has not some duty to perform for which he is personally responsible. It may be a very small duty, but it is a duty, and its performance is exacted by local public sentiment finding expression in the Commune. When a young man is finishing his course at college or at the gymnasium, and is about to return to his village and build a house for himself, the elders of the Commune come together and discuss what he shall be given to do. It may be only the supervision of a village pump, or the looking after the water course that comes down the mountain side, or the custody of the fire engine. It does not matter what it is, but before that young man returns from college and begins life as a householder in the little village there is a distinct duty set apart for him which he is expected to discharge. It is essential," said Boss "An unemployed citizen who had no duty laid upon him would be an irresponsible critic and fault finder. He would not feel himself attached by any binding tie to the community, and in a very short time he would become a center for all that is bad. The prevention of that is the secret of the success of the Swiss Democracy."

Boss's words often recurred to my mind when I saw in Chicago how many young, rich, cultured men, dowered with endless opportunity for serving the city, did nothing and cared nothing for its welfare.

This is the plague spot in Chicago which eats far more deeply into the vitals of the community than fifty sporting houses or one thousand saloons. It is impossible not to be moved with compassion in contemplating the monotonous round of the social treadmill in the sacred circle of Chicago society. When you have got money and got plenty of it you have arrived, and you cannot get any higher except by getting more money. And if you have no taste for piling up a monstrous pedestal of dollars, there is singularly little to excite interest. The machinery of dissipation which has been organized for centuries in such capitals as Paris and Vienna is only in its rudimentary state on the shores of Lake Michigan.

There are social jealousies no doubt as keen between pork
butchers and hotel keepers as between dukes and princes
of the blood. It is sad to see the same snobbery and
"tuft hunting" which have been the laughing stock
of all sensible men in aristocratic Europe reproducing themselves in a new society, where the distinction between those who are in the first file and those
who are in the last is almost indistinguishable to the
uninstructed eye of the casual observer. But there is no
doubt of the power of the desire to obtain a foot-hold
and to climb a little higher up than the social stratum in
which you were born. Newspapers in Chicago have
been named whose proprietors are so swayed by the desire of their wives for social distinction that it is impossible to rely upon them for an unhesitating and unsparing attack upon municipal or social abuses which command the approval of the keepers of the keys of the
social paradise.

Many tales, more or less malicious, are told of some
of the wealthy men of Chicago. Disraeli long ago described the English aristocracy as barbarians, who never
read books and who live in the open air. The first part
of that remark may be applied to many of the wealthy
men who have the means to establish themselves in
palaces on the Chicagoan avenues. The story is told of
one such, that when he furnished his house he ordered
as part of the furnishings so many yards of books. It
was necessary, he heard, that books should form a part
of the upholstery of his palace. So he ordered them by
the yard and paid for them accordingly. Another of
the same kind, when showing his library to an English
visitor, asked whether the bindings suited the furniture,
"Because," he said, "I don't know anything about
books, but if you don't think the binding suits the
furniture, I will have them all rebound at once."
These stories do not apply, however, to the younger
men, who are for the most part supplied with the
best education that the colleges can furnish. Culture,

however, even when combined with wealth, does not supply the saving grace of the enthusiasm of humanity. Neither does it give its possessor a passport to that healthy and varied existence which can only be reached when one lives in the close and constant contact of service with his fellow men. Infinite boredom reigns in many a luxurious home, and millionaires, wearied and sated with the narrow range of their amusements, turn with languid interest to any one who will invent a new toy. It may be a yacht, a race horse, or a new form of gambling. Anything is welcomed as a means of escape from the intolerable monotony of a listless life.

In this connection it may not be amiss to refer briefly to a commotion, chiefly confined to the columns of the newspapers and the drawing-rooms of one or two ladies of Chicago, by a short speech which I made to the Chicago Woman's Club. This club had done excellent work all through the winter in relieving distress among women and children. Its president, Dr. Sarah Hackett Stevenson, is one of the salt of the earth; public-spirited, energetic and self-sacrificing, a capable leader, whether of men or women, in any good work to which she puts her hand. I was invited to attend the meeting summoned by the Woman's Club, which I afterwards learned was composed largely of the women of the various relief committees in the city. I arrived late. Almost immediately after entering the room I was called upon to address the women present. I refused, saying I preferred to wait, nor did I wish to speak unless there was some practical question upon which I could say a few words that might be a help. After two or three speeches had been made I was again called upon, and seeing before me a great expanse of fashionable ladies, I spoke as the spirit moved me: simply, honestly and without the slightest intention of producing any effect beyond that of arousing the minds of some of those who were present who had no adequate realization of the situation to a sense of the need for exerting themselves. As my remarks were ridiculously misrepresented I venture to reproduce them here.

I am glad to have an opportunity of addressing you and to meet those who have been doing such good and active and self-sacrificing work in relieving the distress of their fellow citizens. At the same time I feel as if it were quite unnecessary for me to say anything to you, for those who are among the poor, working among them from day to day, know far better than I what they need and what should be done. But I think it may be useful for me to speak, because there are probably some sitting side by side with the active workers before me, and certainly many who are not here, but whom my words may reach through the press, who are among the most disreputable people in Chicago. Nothing is more obvious to any one who pays attention to the teachings of our Lord than the fact that the conventional judgment about the reputable and disreputable is foreign to the Christian ideal. Who are the most disreputable women in Chicago? They are those who have been dowered by society and Providence with all the gifts and all the opportunities; who have wealth and who have leisure, who have all the talents, and who live entirely self-indulgent lives, caring only for themselves, thinking only of the welfare of their brothers and sisters in the midst of whom they live. Those women who have great opportunities only to neglect them, and who have great means only to squander them upon themselves, are more disreputable in the eyes of God and man than the worst harlot on Fourth Avenue.

Among the many sad aspects of the present distress, the saddest is the way in which it presses upon women. More than ever before at times like this do I feel able to join in the old Jewish prayer, in which, every Saturday, man thanks God that he was not born a woman. For man in the midst of his misery and destitution is not tormented by the temptation to regard his virtue as a realizable asset. That is the supreme misery of a woman. Therefore I am glad to think that you women are bestirring yourselves for women. If you go down into the depths and come face to face with the actual facts of human life you will find that at this moment in the city the economic difficulty confronts you at every turn. This very morning I received a letter from the widow of a soldier who fought in the wars, who is in debt and difficulties and in danger of being turned out into the streets, but who is offered a shameful alternative by her debtor. "What have I to do?" she asks. "If I cannot raise $60, I must either give in or lose my home." Only the previous day I met a poor girl who is willing and anxious to leave the life she was leading. Yet when it is proposed to remove her there at once was the difficulty of a debt of $64 which she owed. So it is all around the chapter If all of those present were to rouse themselves as many of them are doing, then this great trouble and affliction would be a blessing, a blessing by no means confined to those whom they would help, but a blessing which you stand in need of yourselves. For unless all the teaching of all the religions is false it is better for a man to lose his life and be miserable and poor and tormented than be comfortable and the posse∫ or of all things and lose his own soul. None are in such danger of losing their souls as those who are wrapped up in their own selfish comfort and who forget the necessities of the brothers and sisters of the Lord.

No reporters were present. I left the meeting to fulfill another appointment immediately after I spoke. I went up afterwards at the close of the meeting and talked to some of those present, among them Dr. Stevenson and Madame Henrotin and others, nor did I gather from any one with whom I spoke that they misunderstood what I said. Unfortunately, however, half a dozen ladies present felt hurt and one of them confided her indignation to a newspaper reporter. Instantly it was evident to the sensationalists who manufacture scare heads for the Chicago papers that there was an admirable opportunity for working up a commotion. When Dr. Stevenson arrived home that night she found her servants in a state of alarm and the house surrounded by a band of reporters who were waiting to interview her, while the domestics feared the house was about to be attacked by burglars. Everyone who was present was cross-examined as to what I said, and as to what I didn't say, and as a result it was telegraphed throughout the whole land and across the Atlantic that I had grossly insulted the ladies of Chicago by declaring that they were the most disreputable of their sex. Nothing could have been farther from my thought than insulting anyone. I simply stated a truism, and those who argue that I was mistaken in assuming that some mere fashionable society ladies were present at the philanthropic meeting must be singularly unaware of the habits of the creature in question. When slumming or philanthropy is the fashion she is always foremost in the swim. Anything for a new sensation. Anything for a fresh thrill to break the ennui of a blasé existence. And I cannot regret that for once they should have received a somewhat stronger shock than they expected. There was so much discussion of the subject, and the phrase " disreputable " was so much discussed that I received an invitation to speak at the People's Institute in order to set forth what I

meant so that even the most perverse might not misin-
terpret my meaning.   Here is an extract from my speech :

There are worse people in the world even than the predatory rich.
When a man is preying upon his fellow men he is at any rate doing
something.   It is better almost to be at work in sin than doing nothing at all.   " The idle rich ! "   I was reminded last night by a friend of
Ruskin's terrible phrase when he said: " Every man belongs to one of
two categories : he is either a laborer, that is a worker in some way,
or he is an assassin."   Laborer or assassin !   Carlyle said the same
thing, although not so strongly, when he said " whenever you find a
hand that is not busy working you will find a hand that is picking
and stealing."   The idle rich !   What has been the salvation of the
people of Chicago in spite of all the City Councils?   It is this—that
heretofore you have been extraordinarily fortunate in not having had the
opportunity of breeding idle rich   In consequence of war, conflagra-
tion and panic your rich people have had all to work and hence they
have not been such demoralized rascals as those who abound on our
side of the water.   But you are breeding them fast ; and it is because
they are still only in the germ, as it were, that there is hope, if you
will turn your attention to it promptly, you may be able to prevent
the multiplication of the species.   It is difficult indeed to find language
adequate to express the sense of shame, of disgust and humilia-
tion with which we look upon those whom a bountiful providence
and a kindly society has showered all the wealth of the world.   They
have all their hearts can desire and they use all these blessings merely
in order to gild their own styes and to increase the quality and improve the flavor of the swill upon which they fatten.   It is difficult to
speak calmly of such people or to express the degree of confusion and
sorrow and indignation which that class of self-indulgent women excite
in the mind of any intelligent person.   I have been denounced because I said that the frivolous, self-indulgent women of fashion and
woman of society was worse, infinitely worse, than many a harlot.
It was a true word well spoken, and I am glad to know that it has
reverberated throughout the world.

I will ask you to take two typical cases.   There is a poor girl come
up from the country to this great city, and who is alone and friendless.
She is good looking and gets a position as saleswoman or as a stenographer.   Her health gives way and she is laid up.   When she comes
back her place is filled and she is out of a berth.   She goes from
place to place seeking work, and you who have never had to do so
do not know how hard it is to seek for work day after day and find
none.   In the midst of her trouble, when she is nearly at her last
cent, someone comes along.   He likes her looks, and proposes to her
with more or less preamble that she should go and live with him.
That is the way they usually begin.   She has no friends, she has no
money, and the man at least seems kind and sympathetic, which is
more than most of them are.   She must live.   She sees starvation
before her.   Her poverty, not her will, consents.   She becomes his
mistress.   After a while he tells her to go and do as the others do.
She is now down Fourth Avenue, loathing the life she leads and
drowning her thoughts with drink and often wishing that when she lies

down to sleep she may never rise again. That is a common type. There is another type, a woman who is young and strong and healthy, pretty and lazy. She does not want to work if she can help it. She sees that if, in the bloom of youth, she makes a market of herself she can earn more money in a week than what she could earn in a month by hard work. She sells herself accordingly. She says, "I suppose my body belongs to myself, and I do not see why I cannot do what I like with my own." So she does what she likes and makes a living out of it. That is another type. Both types are confounded under the common cognomen of fallen women and prostitutes. There is all the difference between them that there is between the fixed stars. I have given you both in order that you may compare them to their counterparts among the idle rich. There is a woman, she is young, she belongs to the cream of the cream of your society, she has all the education which wealth can secure her, she has carriages to bear her to and fro so that she will never have to put her dainty foot to the pavement. She thinks of nothing except pleasing herself, and uses her wealth to minister to her vanity and her glory. She uses her carriages solely for her own gratification, and uses that priceless and peerless influence which a good and cultivated woman can exercise upon her acquaintances to increase the excitement and frivolity of society. She does what she likes with her own. She uses it all for herself, but, having some self-respect, she draws the line at her carcass which the other does not. Between the two what is the difference? Each one uses what she has received to minister to her own gratification, her own vanity and her own excitement. Upon one society showers all its condemnation. Press, pulpit and women all unite in hurling the severest anathemas upon her who is often more sinned against than sinning, while they have nothing but adulation and praise for the pet of society who has never spent a single thought excepting upon herself. That is bad. It is not our Lord's way of judging.

Unfortunately there is even worse than that. Some of your wealthy women do not even draw the line at their carcass. There is one thing which strikes us over in the old country with a certain amazement— how the women reared in this great republic, the daughters of your millionaires, who have been born with every blessing which American civilization can give them, instead of taking pride in their American citizenship are ready in their lust for vainglory and their mad desire to outstrip, if only by a hair-breadth, some rival, to sell themselves as much as any harlot on Fourth Avenue to the most miserable scion of European nobility.

I remember one of our dukes who bore an ancient name. He was divorced on the charge of cruelty and adultery. On one occasion when I was editing the *Pall Mall Gazette* he wrote a letter for publication in the paper, which discoursed upon the subject of bimetalism. I sent it back. I wrote him I did not wish to publish that letter or any other letters in that controversy now. But I told him I should not be frank if I did not tell him that the reason why I sent the letter back, however, was not because of its subject, but because of its author. "Rightly or wrongly," I wrote, "you have the reputation of ruining women for your own pleasure, and therefore, in my opinion, you are infinitely worse than if you cut throats for hire ; therefore I return you your manuscript." Shortly afterwards he went to the United States and married an American woman of wealth. What do you think of your women if they allow themselves to be disposed of in this fashion? In feudal times when an estate was made over to a purchaser the contract was not complete until at the same time the seller took a handful of dirt from the estate and gave it to the purchaser. Your American beauties and American heiresses are no more than that handful of dirt which marks and accompanies the transfer of their fortunes to our stone-broke nobles.

You ask how can you help it? Well, at least, when one of them makes merchandise of herself, instead of filling your papers with eulogistic comments about her and her good fortune, you might speak the truth and say what you think. The idle rich have no moral sentiment. Their one law is to please themselves, and they will not touch with their little finger this burden which weighs the masses down. But were the idle rich created for that? They have education, leisure and great opportunities for influence or usefulness. They have received much and therefore they should render much. If they are higher than their fellows, therefore they should make themselves lower in order to be their servants and to help them. Is that not true Christian teaching? Is that not what our Lord and Master would say to those people?

In conclusion I would venture to appeal to those unfortunate sons and daughters of millionaires who are being brought up as idle gentlemen and idle ladies. They had better have been brought up saloon keepers. They had better have been brought up police constables a thousand times. But it is their misfortune that they have wealth and leisure without need to work and without stimulus to service. I would say to them, here in Chicago is the scene for your energies, here in Chicago where your fathers made their money, honestly or otherwise. In Chicago there are whole districts of your fellow citizens who have no conveniences of civilization, who have no opportunities of friendship. Why should your young men and women waste their lives and the divine enthusiasm of youth simply in their own gratification, and why should they give all these to wine and to women and to all the methods of fashionable debauchery when there are men and women and children at your very door whom you can help, and for not helping whom you will have to answer at the Day of Judgment? I do not ask you to deliver tracts, or to pray at prayer-meetings, but I do ask you to love your brother man. Why, instead of wasting your time and your life in idleness, why not devote yourself to the service of some precinct in this city and go and live among them? Do not act as high-toned, silk-stockinged gentlemen, but as a simple brother who is willing to go and live among men to help them to live a more human life than they are living now. You will then have many opportunities of usefulness and will be in brotherly union and living intercourse with hundreds of your fellow men, and then you will find that when you thought you had given up your position by going and living in the slums you have really found your soul and found your Lord.

I said all this at the People's Institute. It was toler-

ably plain speaking, but so far from exciting anything of the hubbub occasioned by the much milder
address to the ladies, one editor went out of his way to
remark concerning the moderation I had displayed in
the second discourse! The commotion which the first
speech occasioned was interesting if only as illustrating
how much need there is for the gospel to be preached
where heathendom in high places is masked by conventional homage to Christianity.

The graver offenses which spring from idleness and
wealth have not been specially alluded to in this chapter.
They need not be dwelt upon. It is a painful subject,
and every one can supply details for himself. Human
nature is the same all the world over. Exempt man or
woman from the necessity of daily labor, let no religious
or humanitarian enthusiasm bind them over to the service of their fellows, and there can only be one result.
That result is making itself manifest more and more
in Chicago. There is work of every kind waiting to
be done; there are multitudes of more or less untaught,
unkempt, uncivilized human beings to be brought into
some kind of human relationship, to be guided, to be
instructed, to be comforted. There are all the interests,
sorrows and sufferings of the helpless poor lying unattended to while the idle rich are racking their
brains in devising fresh means of excitement or new va-
rieties of self-indulgence with which to pass away the
time. It is not asked of them as it was asked of the
young man in the gospel to sell all that they have and
give to the poor, but they might at least give tithes of
their time and of their substance to those who have received so little and who need so much.

CHAPTER VI.

It is impossible to describe Chicago as a whole. It is a congeries of different nationalities, a compost of men and women of all manner of languages. It is a city of millionaires and of paupers; a great camp of soldiers of industry, rallying round the standard of the merchant princes in the campaign against poverty. This vast and heterogeneous community, which has been collected together from all quarters of the known world, knows only one common bond. Its members came here to make money. They are staying here to make money. The quest of the almighty dollar is their Holy Grail. From afar the name and the fame of Chicago have gone abroad to the poor and the distressed and the adventurous of all nations, and they have flocked and are still flocking to the place where a few men make millions and where all men can get food.

A scientific study of the city as a whole would be the work of a life time, and when it was finished it would possess only a historical value. For, while the scientist was correcting his statistics and checking his analysis, the kaleidoscope would be changing, and by the time his exhaustive survey was ready for the press, a new generation would have risen up which would not recognize the scenes which he portrayed. I cannot for a moment pretend to put the whole city, or even a single ward under the microscope. But I thought it might perhaps help us to appreciate the nature of some of the tougher problems that confront the reformer in Chicago if we paid a little attention to a single precinct in one of the thirty-four wards into which the city is divided.

For the purpose of this survey I have selected the

nineteenth precinct of the First Ward, not because it is an average precinct, but because it presents in an aggravated form most of the evils which are palpably not in accord with the mind of Christ. If Christ came to Chicago, it is one of the last precincts into which we should care to take Him. And yet it is probably the first precinct into which He would find His way. There are a good many of "the least of these, My brethren," in the nineteenth precinct.

The nineteenth precinct of the First Ward consists of the blocks which lie between Harrison and Polk Streets. It includes both sides of Fourth Avenue, the west side of Dearborn and the east side of Clark. It is easy of access. The Dearborn Street horse car traverses it on one side, the Clark Street cable on the other, while Polk Street station empties its passengers into Fourth Avenue. It contains a fair share, but not more than a fair share, of foreign-born citizens. According to the analysis of the voting at the election of 1892-3, the number of American-born citizens was only just ahead of those who had taken their naturalization papers. The figures are interesting and bring into clear relief the cosmopolitan character of the population of Chicago. I print the figures for the city, for the First Ward and for the nineteenth precinct.

CITIZENS, 1893.

Origin.	Chicago.	First Ward.	Nineteenth Precinct.
New England	7,522	410	12
Southern States	9,667	1,079	74
New York	9,721	822	26
Illinois	42,582	682	27
Other States	41,570	1,798	64
American	131,335	4,791	203
Canadian	6,693	143	3
German	45,005	477	12
Irish	23,578	382	4
English	7,844	138	2
Scotch	2,555	61	1
Swedish	10,838	44	1
Norwegian	4,832	19	2
Danish	2,333	20	1

French	643	29	5
Bohemian	5,721	5	...
Polish	4,865	44	1
Austrian	3,280	35	4
Russian	2,903	80	11
Italian.............................	1,032	137	8
Dutch	1,600	20	...
Miscellaneous......................	1,933	206	5
	128,812	1,740	60

The advantage of this small precinct organization, which was necessitated by the adoption of the Australian ballot, is that it cuts the city up into manageable proportions. There are in the city of Chicago thirty-four wards which are cut up into 800 precincts. Each of these may be said to constitute a unit of organization with an independent political life of its own.

It will be seen that so far as the nineteenth precinct is concerned that it is not a distinctively foreign precinct. The American-born citizen who barely holds his own in the city as a whole outnumbers the naturalized in the nineteenth precinct by more than three to one. It would, however, be a mistake to regard the population as indigenous to Chicago. More than one-third of the American-born citizens hail from the Southern States; that is to say, are men of color. Only twenty-seven were born in the state of Illinois.

In politics the nineteenth precinct is very evenly divided. Chicago cast a majority of nearly 35,000 for Cleveland in 1892, but his majority in the nineteenth precinct was only ninety-eight votes against ninety-one cast for the Republican. In the election for Governor the Democrats held their own to a man, but three of the Republicans voted the Prohibition ticket and as they were reinforced by another stalwart Prohibitionist the Prohibition vote in the nineteenth precinct is four strong, which, as the total Prohibitionist vote cast in Chicago was only 3,116, was rather more than its fair proportion.

At the mayoral election last December, the precinct

voted 85 for Hopkins (D), and 94 for Swift (R), while three voted for Britzius, the socialist.

If woman suffrage were introduced we should be better able to form an idea as to the constituents of the population. The female contingent would be largely foreign and more remarkable for its variety than its morality.

During the last year a great change has come over the population. The negroes have diminished and the Italians have increased. The large number of lodgers have to be taken into account in every election. They are registered and they vote. Where they come from no one knows; they are a floating, migratory population, but they are voted as any other residents of the ward.

The amusements in the precinct are few. The Park Theatre, a most infamous place of resort, stands within a few blocks, but in the precinct itself, the chief amusement is a little gambling, varied now and then by the excitement of seeing the inmates of an immoral house raided by the police, sometimes accompanied by their male partners. There is no public hall, no concert room in the precinct, and, as everywhere in Chicago, the saloons are the great centers of social intercourse.

This precinct, lying so close to the great arterial thoroughfares of the south and west, offers a tempting field to those who wish to do good to their fellow men. Here in these three blocks are some two or three thousand human beings without any of the civilizing influences which are usually supposed to be indispensible. There are, it is true, two doctors; but there is no resident clergyman, no minister of religion, no city missionary, nobody, in short, who has any moral, spiritual and educational oversight of the people. There is one Jewish synagogue, which is in an upstairs room in Clark Street, fronting a larger synagogue of another Jewish sect on the other side of the street. The Catholics also have a large German church just outside the precinct on the other side of Clark Street. This church stands open all day and every day. When I was present there were three black-habited nuns engaged in their devotions. The contrast between the garish females on Fourth Avenue and the sober suited nuns in the church was very striking. Men were kneeling before the altar, candles were burning before the central figure and there were, in short, all the indications of devotion on the part of the scattered worshipers that one expects to find in a Catholic country in Europe. It is as an oasis set in the midst of all the vice and squalor and drunkenness of a district in which, despite all, are to be found miracles of human innocence, girls as pure as driven snow, young men leading holy and upright lives, uncontaminated by the vice and filth in the midst of which their lot is cast. That this is so is only another reason why there should be something more done by those who love their fellow men, to supply every such precinct with a center, a human center of helpful friendship.

Near the center of Clark Street, on the western boundary of Fourth Avenue, stands my old friend Hank North's saloon, St. Lawrence House it is called, where at any time of the day Hank may be found dispensing free lunches to all and sundry. How he keeps it up is a marvel, but the free lunch goes on, hot soup with bread, apparently dispensed with equal freedom to those who take a drink and those who do not. There are several other saloons to the right and left, some of them very tough, but all supplying places in which the male denizens at least find a shelter and which are very generally used in the evening as a kind of general drawing-room or front parlor for those who have neither drawing-rooms nor front parlors of their own. Some of the saloons are equipped with billiard tables and other appliances for recreation. During the extreme cold weather one or two of the saloon keepers in the precinct allowed the homeless out-of-work free shelter in the basements of their saloons. The place was warm and the men lay together in any place where they could be out of the cold. Along Clark Street most of the stores are de-

voted to the sale of old clothes and are in possession
of gentlemen of Jewish extraction. The pawnbroking
business also flourishes, the poor man's banker being
able to make a living where other tradesmen starve.
The rates of interest charged by pawnbrokers is said to
be as much as ten per cent a month or 120 per cent a
year. Usury is forbidden by the Illinois statutes, but it is
nevertheless levied upon the poor. Neither church nor
state in Chicago has as yet risen to the height of establishing a municipal pawnshop, where the poor can trans-
act their financial business at something like a fair rate of
interest. It is here, as everywhere, those who are the
weakest have to pay the most for the accommodations
which they need. Anyone who would found a pawnshop on improved principles in the heart of the nineteenth precinct would be a benefactor to his kind.

An improved pawnshop is only one of the appliances
of civilization with which the nineteenth precinct
needs to be supplied. A reading room in which could
be found books and papers is another institution which
is needed but which there seems to be no possibility of
procuring. The streets back and front, including Fourth
Avenue, with its painted women at the windows beckon-
ing to every passer-by, will continue in the future as
they have been in the past, the common playground of
the children and the haunts of youth. There is in the
whole precinct not one house in which a genial hospitality is shown to the neighbors, where rich and poor
can meet and talk over their common interests and their
common wrongs. The policeman perambulating the
beat back and forth on his rounds is the only human
nexus which binds the precinct together, always excepting the political organizations which at least remind men
that they are members one of another and are united by
common interests and in common concerns. The political life may be low, the motives may be mean, and the
antagonism which is excited between Republicans and
Democrats may be often irrational, but it is difficult at

present to see, with the melancholy absence of intelligently directed humanitarian enthusiasm on the part of the better-to-do people, how the desired end could be attained better than it is at present. The cultured resident with kindliness, sympathy and helpful service is not forthcoming. In his place we have the Democratic and Republican heeler, each of whom is anxious to curry favor with and secure converts among the citizens, not so much for the good of the city as to weaken the other side and to secure a claim upon office. That motive may be poor—it is often sordid, and it works out frequently in gross corruption; but after all it may be compared, like the Kingdom of Heaven, to leaven which goes on leavening the lump until the whole is leavened.

In the nineteenth precinct there are 46 saloons, 37 houses of ill-fame and 11 pawnbrokers. This is an underestimate of the places which are commonly regarded as the moral sore spots of the body politic. Several houses described as stores or offices are more or less haunted by immoral women. The map which is printed in the first part of this volume does not overestimate, but rather gives an unduly favorable impression as to the influences in the midst of which the inhabitants of the precinct grow up. With so many saloons it ought not to be impossible to establish one place of call where visitors should not be expected to drink intoxicants in order to pay their footing and maintain the establishment. But in the whole of the nineteenth precinct, as in all the other nineteenth precincts, you will look in vain for any such place. Neither is there any bath or washhouse where cleanliness, which is next to godliness, can be cultivated; neither is there any public lavatory or public convenience, excepting in connection with the saloons. There are one or two drug stores and one rather imposing hotel, but otherwise the neighborhood is given over to persons who are conducting an arduous struggle against poverty. The only place of amusement is a shooting gallery in which the marksman can have three shots for a nickel. The only attempt to supply the intellectual needs of the district is made by two booksellers, one of whom was prosecuted some time ago for selling obscene literature, and whose windows still contain a large and varied collection of pornographic literature, together with an assortment of photographs of sitters whose chief characteristic is their absence of clothes.

A large portion of the inhabitants consists of Jews. The Jones public school, which stands just outside the precinct on the east, is the school of the district. I spent a morning going over the establishment and was much interested and not a little saddened at many things which I saw there. The principal of the school told me that forty per cent of the scholars are Russian or Polish Jews; a very large number of the remainder are negroes. The genuine American was in an extremely small minority. The school is large and lofty and on the whole is a commodious building. But the playground is miserably inadequate. It was a sight to see the muster of the little ones in the dusty playground on a bitter January morning for a ten-minute recess. The younger boys huddled up in rows, standing close together as sheep in a flock, waiting motionless until they could return to the warm school-room. The larger boys played and romped as best they could. The little ones crowded together for fear of being knocked over by the larger ones, for there was not room enough for them all to play. In such a crowded district land is perhaps too valuable to be used for playgrounds, but it ought not to be impossible to improvise a playground in pure air out of the dust by simply strengthening the roof and placing a railing round the parapet. Anything would be better than the miserable apology for a playground which disgraces the school at the present moment. Something also might be done to utilize the schoolroom after school hours, as has been done in London and other English towns.

But it ought not surely to be regarded as sufficient discharge of the obligations which thewealthy, leisured, cultured citizens owe to their fellow men that this service should be left to the hard-worked teachers and the more or less interested exertions of the political heelers.

The nineteenth precinct of the First Ward is by no means the only or even an exceptional precinct. When these pages are passing through the press Mr. F. W. Parker, of the Baptist City Mission, described before the Baptist Social Union a district which presents in a large scale the same evil features. Here is an extract from his paper :

There is a section of the city from Stewart Avenue to the river and from Twenty-second to Thirty-ninth Streets with a population of 60,000 people. From Twentieth to Fortieth Streets, along the lake front, is an equal area, with about the same population, rich and prosperous. It has more than three miles of splendid boulevard palatial residences. The river region has no boulevards; it has no lake shore, but instead the stagnant Chicago River. Its death rate is two and one-fourth times higher, and deaths from zymotic diseases are fourteen times greater than in the lake region; it has ten deaths from diphtheria to one in the other districts, and the death rate of infants is six times greater.

In the lake region there are seven hospitals. It has five asylums who help the unfortunate, while there is none in the river region. In the lake section there are six night schools to one in the other; ten kindergarten schools to one in the other; three business colleges to none in the other. The lake region has five sectarian schools, with 700 scholars, while in the river region there are eleven great sectarian schools, with 6,000 scholars. The lake section has ten book stores to none in its neighboring section to the west; the public library has three stations there to none in the other.

At the last city municipal election the lake region gave Mr. Swift 6,600 votes, Mr. Hopkins 3,700. The river region gave Mr. Swift 2,900 votes and Mr. Hopkins 6,900 votes. This illustrates a great difference between the two sections and the lack of political sympathy.

There are three Catholic churches in the lake region and six in the other; twenty-two Protestant churches in the one section and but six struggling Protestant churches in the other. In the lake region is intelligence, wealth, comfort and all that makes life enjoyable; on the other hand is ignorance, want, misery and degradation.

If Christ came to Chicago what would He do with the nineteenth precinct of the First Ward? One thing is certain, He would not pass by on the other side like the

High Priest or Levite.   He would much rather regard
it as the good Samaritan regarded the man who had
fallen among thieves.   Here is not one man, but some
two thousand brothers and sisters of Christ, who are
forced to live their lives here in the levee.   Their life is
squalid.   Life is dreary in this precinct, yet life must be
lived, the temptations of life resisted and the joys of
life cultivated with such success as may be.   But for
these two thousand and odd human beings, even if we
exclude the unfortunate women who are dedicated to
what is called by bitter irony a life of pleasure, there are
sufficient to afford a life's work for anyone who endeavors to unite himself by helpful service to his fellow man.

If any man or woman in Chicago to whom Providence and society have given wealth and leisure,
without at the same time destroying their generous
aspirations after the improvement of the conditions of
their fellow creatures, the nineteenth precinct of the
First Ward and many another precinct in the city may
be commended to them as affording an admirable field
in which they can turn their benevolent desires to good
result.   The gulf between rich and poor which modern
society seems to widen can only be bridged in one way,
namely, by the personal sacrifice of individuals in personal service to man and woman.   The healthy consciousness of human brotherhood and of community of
interest and sympathy is in danger of being forgotten
when the well-to-do live in stately mansions on boulevards and avenues and the poor are crowded together
in more or less noisome districts such as this of the
nineteenth precinct.

If Christ came to Chicago, where would He be most
likely to take up His abode—in the boulevards or in the
slums, in the region of the lake or the region of the
river?   If so, where is it that those who love Him
must seek and find their fate?

> Believe it, 'tis the mass of men He loves ;
> And, where there is most sorrow and most want,

Where the high heart of man is trodden down
The most, 'tis not because He hides His face
From them in wrath, as purblind teachers prate:
Not so: the most is He, for there is He
Most needed.   Men who seek for Fate abroad
Are not so near His heart as they who dare
Frankly to face her when she faces them,
On their own threshold, where their souls are strong.

CHAPTER I.

I WAS AN HUNGRED AND YE GAVE ME MEAT.

If Christ came to Chicago, by what standard would He judge the city and the inhabitants thereof? That is a question which Lowell answers as we have seen. The measure which our Lord would apply would be the image which we have made of the least of these His brethren. That conception is in consonance with the general sentiment of the Christian Church in all ages. It is entirely in harmony with the humanitarian aspirations which may be regarded as the latest and most authentic outgrowth of Christian principle in our age and generation. At the same time it must not be forgotten that Christ has not left us entirely to the guide of reason or imagination as to the standard by which we are to be judged. When He had finished His teaching and had delivered to His friends and His disciples all that He had to say upon going up to Jerusalem to be delivered into the hands of His enemies and crucifixion, He summed up all that He had said, and brought His teaching to its natural and definite conclusion, in His description of the Day of the Last Judgment. This description is—after the Sermon on the Mount — the most famous and most solemn of all the teachings of our Lord.

There is no greater surprise in the Bible than that which is occasioned when we come upon the simple narrative telling us that we shall not be judged by anything which we profess to believe or by any ceremonial or ritual to which we have conformed, or, still less, by the fact of our membership or non-membership in any organized body, ecclesiastical or otherwise.   The final decision as to our disposition, the definite appraisement of our character, will be made on grounds which many professing Christians would refuse to regard as being in any way distinctively religious.   Christ's test as supplied in the description as represented in the 25th chapter of St. Matthew's Gospel is throughout humanitarian as opposed to theological, and unless there should be any mistake it is stated twice, once positively, the second time negatively, as if to preclude any possibility of mistake.

The metewand of Christ on the Day of Judgment consists of the inquiry as to how far we have discharged the great secular acts of mercy in dealing with our fellow men.   Those six acts are ranged in regular sequence; they correspond to the simple elementary needs of mortal men.   Christ at the last day will not ask what we have said or thought about Him, neither will He ask us whether or not we belong to His Church.   His test, and so far as can be ascertained from His teaching, the only test which He will apply, is whether or not we have ministered to the physical, social and moral necessities of our fellow men.   His words are so distinct and so precise that there is no getting away from them.   Yet they have been ignored so much that salvation, which according to Christ was to be found in feeding the hungry, giving drink to the thirsty, clothing the naked, showing hospitality to the stranger and visiting those who were sick or in prison, is now almost universally held to consist in the acceptance of a more or less abstract series of religio-philosophical propositions.   I quote, therefore, the words of our Lord as the final authority on this point, if he came to Chicago.

31. When the Son of man shall come in his glory, and all the holy angels with him, then shall he sit upon the throne of his glory:

32. And before him shall be gathered all nations; and he shall separate them one from another, as a shepherd divideth his sheep from the goats:

33. And he shall set the sheep on his right hand, but the goats on the left.

34. Then shall the King say unto them on his right hand, Come, ye blessed of my Father, inherit the kingdom prepared for you from the foundation of the world:

35. For I was an hungred, and ye gave me meat: I was thirsty and ye gave me drink: I was a stranger, and ye took me in:

36. Naked, and ye clothed me: I was sick, and ye visited me: I was in prison, and ye came unto me.

37. Then shall the righteous answer him, saying, Lord, when saw we thee an hungred, and fed thee? or thirsty and gave thee drink?

38. When saw we thee a stranger, and took thee in? or naked, and clothed thee?

39. Or when saw we thee sick, or in prison, and came unto thee?

40. And the King shall answer and say unto them, Verily, I say unto you, inasmuch as ye have done it unto one of the least of these my brethren, ye have done it unto me.

It is not unreasonable to believe that since our Lord declares that this is the standard which He will apply when He comes to judge the earth, that He would apply the same standard if He came to visit Chicago. It may not, therefore, be unprofitable to briefly cast a glance over the city in order to ascertain what has been done, what is being done, under each of the half dozen divisions into which the whole duty of man is mapped out.

The first, most imperative want of man is food. The lack of it is the motive force which underlies revolutions. The dread of the want of it is the impelling force in almost all human labor. Men work not because they love labor, but because they are hungered to it. Chicago may rightly claim to have done more than an ordinary share in ministering to the needs of mankind in this matter of food. Situated at the head of the great alluvial basin of the Middle States, she has contributed to cheapen the price of bread and meat in every capital of Europe. The half penny of the English laborer, the centime or copeck of the European, will purchase for him a larger piece of bread or a heavier portion of beef and pork than it would have done if Chicago and the immense agricultural region of which Chicago is the outlet had never existed. All this, of course, was done in the way of business. But it is not only the poor of other lands that Chicago has helped to feed.   She has been for the last thirty years a hospitable host of the overflow of the poor of the Old World.   We might well apply Lowell's couplet originally written about the United States:

> Whose latch string was never drawn in
> Against the poorest child of Adam's kin.

Within her borders this day and every day, a million and a half of human beings, at least one half of whom were born beyond the sea, contrive in some fashion or another to get three meals a day with varying degrees of punctuality.

Chicago has done all that in her devotion to what an American humorist describes as the chief end of man, namely ten per cent.   But when we come to the feeding of the hungry under circumstances which preclude the making of a dividend out of the necessities of nature, the showing of Chicago is not quite so good.   And the moral aspect of feeding the hungry, comes in only where the work is done for the sake of the least of these our brethren, and not from motives which would operate quite as strongly in securing a supply of fire-arms or fire-water.

One of the first observations which occurs to a stranger who looks at the city from this standpoint is that while Chicago provides food wholesale, that is to say, wheat by the bushel, pork by the barrel and cattle by the ton, cheaper than any other place in the world, the retail price of these commodities when they are served up in portions suitable to the necessities of the poor is considerably in excess of that for which the same commodities are to be had in the capitals of the Old World.

The feeding of the hungry in Chicago was fortunately not accompanied by any scarcity of grain.   Never in the history of the city were the elevators more crowded with food, and this winter has seen wheat sink to the lowest price that it has ever touched.   With wheat selling at two cents per pound, it was strange indeed to see the streets of the city lined with men who were unable to obtain food.

The suffering in the city was very great and would have been very much greater had it not been for the help given by the labor unions to their members and for an agency which, without pretending to be of much account from a charitable point of view, nevertheless fed more hungry people this winter in Chicago than all the other agencies, religious, charitable and municipal, put together. I refer to the Free Lunch of the saloons. This institution, which is quite unknown in the Old World, is one of the features of the feeding of the hungry in Chicago which most amazes a stranger. There are from six to seven thousand saloons in Chicago. In one half of these a free lunch is provided every day in the week. And in many cases the free lunch is really a free lunch. That is to say, in many saloons, notably in my friend Hank North's in Clark Street, scores of people were fed every day and are being fed at this moment without fee, or reward or any payment for drink with which to wash down the more solid viands. In Hank North's saloon throughout the winter he has given away on an average about thirty-six gallons of soup and seventy-two loaves of bread every day. In very many cases those who took advantage of this open-handed hospitality were too poor to pay a nickel for the glass of beer which in other cases passed as a matter of course. In this respect I think Hank North was better than his neighbors; but both Frenchmen and Englishmen who have had practical experience of the working of the system declare that even when the nickel for the beer is insisted upon they get better lunch and more food. That is to say, better than they get anywhere else in town with a nickel and without the beer.

A very interesting article appeared in the *Chicago Herald* by a writer who has taken some pains in investigating the extent to which the free lunch system prevails in Chicago, and he came to some very remarkable conclusions which seem to me must be in excess of the facts. Calculating that three thousand saloons run free lunches, and that on the average at least twenty persons avail themselves of the free lunch at each saloon, the *Herald* calculates that 60,000 persons in Chicago were fed free every day by the saloon keepers. Even if we estimate the cost of the lunch as low as five cents this would represent a contribution from the saloon keepers to the relief of the destitute in Chicago amounting to $18,000 a week.*

Of course the enemies of the saloon will declare that this is a miserably inadequate attempt to remedy some of the incalculable evil that is wrought in the community. Without gainsaying that in the least, it is only just to remark that in the Old World, where we have the evils of the saloon, there is not even an attempt made to make such a compensation as that of the free lunch.

After the labor unions and the saloon keepers the most important feeders of the hungry are the Cook County Commissioners, who are intrusted with the control of what in England we call the administration of the Poor Law. The Central Relief Association occupies the third place in the work of coping with the distress this inclement winter.

It is the misfortune of Chicago that, like many other

---

*An attempt was made to abolish the free lunch in Chicago. In January a meeting of the Saloon Keepers' Mutual Benefit and Protective Association of Illinois held a meeting at Aldine Hall, 75 Randolph Street, in order to secure the abolition of the free lunch on the ground that it was bad business and entailed a ruinous expense on the trade. The *Chicago Times* of January 20, in a somewhat jocose fashion, thus chronicles the rejection of the proposal.

"The free lunch has been saved from the destroying hand of reform. It is a matter of regret that the deliberations of the mutual liquor dealers have not been reduced to print. But it was in no sordid spirit of profit and loss that the free lunch was discussed by the mutual association of free lunch dispensers. The debate proceeded. It reached its climax in the following peroration, with which Mr. Johnson at length overthrew all opposition :

"'I warrant you that the saloon keepers of Chicago with their free lunch have taken care of and fed more of the unemployed than all the relief societies put together.' Well did Mr. Stead say that the saloons in one direction were doing more good than all the churches put together.'"

"The name of Mr. Stead seems to have had a magical effect, for thereafter there was no more talk of abolishing free lunch. Who shall say now that Mr. Stead came to Chicago in vain?"

towns, she had no board of associated charities, similar
to those which have been organized in Cincinnati and
other cities.   The leading position among the charitable
distributing societies was occupied by the Relief and
Aid Association, which for some reason, whether on account of its virtues or its failings, cannot be said to be in
danger of the woe pronounced upon those of whom all
men speak well.   The Relief and Aid Society, I am
afraid, bears a family resemblance to the Charity Organization Society of London.   Nothing can be more
admirable than the principles upon which they are both
founded, and few things can be less satisfactory than the
way in which a good cause has been rendered distasteful
by the pessimism of their secretaries.   In London the secretary of the Charity Organization Society, Mr. Loch, a
very able man, has an absolutely unequalled way of dis-
suading people from doing anything.   No matter what it is
that is proposed to cope with the evils which afflict humanity, Mr. Loch is certain to produce an elaborate reasoned
brief setting forth all the dangers and all the difficulties
with much lucidity, with the inevitable result that nothing is done.   Mr. Trusdale, of the Relief and Aid Society, does not occupy so conspicuous a position as Mr. Loch,
but he seems to resemble him in the lack of that sympathetic fiber which enables him to enlist the sympathies
of the public.   His society has done good service
with its wood yard, but its attempt to provide lodging for destitute wanderers was a miserable failure.
Whether it was that they washed their inmates too
much or used too much carbolic acid or generally enforced too many rules and regulations, I do not know ;
but as a matter of fact, the home which was maintained
at considerable expense was a dead failure until Mr.
Lamorris took it off their hands and ran it on a commercial basis, when it at once became a dividend-earning
property.   The temptation of the Relief and Aid Society, as of all other societies, is to apply a cut-and-dried
standard to all cases, and to conclude that if the circum-

stances of the applicant do not fit their requirements, he is unworthy of relief. Had there been a more sympathetic spirit at the headquarters of the Relief and Aid Society, less red tape and more readiness to devise expedients for securing employment, the problem of distress last winter might have been coped with without the agitation. It is well that charitable societies should be scientific, but they should not at the same time cease to be charitable. It is quite as important that they should have the confidence of the benevolent public as that their relief should be administered according to cast-iron principle and hide-bound political economy.

Whatever the cause may be, when the distress came upon Chicago thus it was necessary to provide relief through other channels. The newly-formed Civic Federation took the question into consideration at its first meeting even before it was duly constituted and summoned a conference of all the charities and public bodies in the city. Action was taken almost simultaneously by the Illinois Board of Charities and Correction and the City Council. Both, however, were abandoned in order to follow the lead of the Civic Federation. A Central Relief Association was founded in order to bring into line all the existing charitable agencies and to cope with the more pressing needs of the unemployed. An influential central committee was formed and branch committees were constituted dealing with all branches of charitable relief. An appeal was made to the public of Chicago and all wage workers were asked to give one day's wages to the relief fund.

Before long a street cleaning brigade some 3,000 strong was formed which provided a labor test and utilized the surplus labor of the community for the welfare of the city. For the relief of the women sewing rooms were opened where more than a thousand willing workers were provided with means for maintaining themselves and their families. The principle on which both divisions of the relief work were founded was the same: let no willing worker starve, but if a man will not work neither shall he eat.

The women's branch of relief was under the management of the Woman's Club, Dr. Stevenson being the chief director of its operations. Their organization was more flexible than the department which looked after the men. The prejudice which prevailed in the minds of the chairman and the most active workers of the Central Relief Association against giving relief in money led to the issue of an inconvertible paper currency in the shape of ten-cent tickets which were only exchangeable for food and lodging in certain specified stores. The Woman's Club discarded the tickets and paid for the work cash down in the currency of the Republic. Whatever may be said in favor of the improvised inconvertible ticket currency, there is no doubt that if the question had been left to the decision of the workers who received it their vote would have been almost unanimous to be paid in money. The only advantage of the ticket is that it provides some check against its being used to purchase drink, as the saloon keepers were loath to take a currency which could only be redeemed on the day of issue. The other advantage claimed for it, namely, that at the depots of the association a ten-cent ticket would secure its owner more than he could buy for 15 or 20 cents in the open market, might have been overcome by the establishment of cost price stores which would limit their custom to those who were in relief work.

In New York, for instance, the Industrial Christian Alliance raised $10,000 for the purpose of founding people's restaurants, where a square meal could be had for five cents. At this institution a bowl of good soup, a bowl of coffee and three large slices of bread were supposed to answer the definition of a square meal. Tickets were issued at $5 the hundred, for distribution among the charitable. The cost of fitting up a restaurant with cooking apparatus, etc., was $1,500. The five cents was estimated to pay the exact cost of the raw material.

This is mere criticism of detail. Whether by one branch or another, a very great deal of arduous and voluntary labor was performed by leading citizens. Dr. Stevenson occupies the first position among the women, while Mr. Harvey was the first among the men.

Mr. T. W. Harvey, the founder of the town of Harvey, near Chicago, and well known for the leading part which he has taken in connection with Mr. Moody's work in Chicago, is one of the best-known and most public-spirited citizens of Chicago. From the first he threw himself into the work of the Civic Federation with the same energy which he displays in the management of his own business. Through the winter he subordinated the work of his office to the attempt to find work for other people. He was energetically seconded by Mr. W. R. Stirling and by Mr. C. H. S. Mixer, who had both devoted much attention to the subject and had rendered considerable service in connection with the Relief and Aid Society. Mr. W. R. Stirling has taken entire charge of the work in the 7th, 8th and 19th wards.

The following notes of a conversation which I had with Mr. Harvey in the middle of February, give a fair survey of the work which was done under his direction.

I found Mr. Harvey was suffering from a disagreeable neuralgic trouble brought on by excessive work. He was in excellent spirits and full of delight at the results which had been achieved by the Central Relief Association. Early in the day, when those who knew, or professed they knew, a great deal about the condition of Chicago were declaring that there were 100,000 men out of work, Mr. Harvey had assured me that the evil, although great, was by no means beyond the power of the city to cope with it. He had the satisfaction of refering to his prediction and pointing to the results of the steps which had been taken to grapple with the pressing difficulty of the unemployed.

"Yes," said Mr. Harvey, "It has been a labor of love. Laborious

no doubt, but with a rich reward in the consciousness that the necessary
work has been well done — thanks to the hearty co-operation of every
one and to the fact that these people who needed help were very good
fellows and men whom it was a joy to help." It was Sunday at lunch
time. "I have just come in," said he, "from being down on Water Street
where we have a thousand of our boys keeping the place clean. We
do not believe in Sunday work, but this was a Sabbath day's labor.
Water Street is full all the week and it is impossible to get it cleaned
and the boys are only too glad to put in their time in doing this necessary work."

"Tell me all about it, Mr. Harvey, for although we have read about
it from time to time in the papers it is difficult to grasp the salient features of the scheme."

"The salient features," said Mr. Harvey, "are very soon told. The
Central Relief Association, which was formed, as you remember, as the
first work of the Civic Federation, has grappled with the question in a
business-like fashion. It has secured the confidence of the citizens
and is now looking forward to the cessation of its more onerous
duties with the consciousness that it has done what it was appointed
to do; and, what is more remarkable, has done it to the satisfaction of
those whose distress was the immediate cause of action. When the
Relief Association was formed there were from two thousand to three
thousand men sleeping in the police stations and the City Hall and the
Pacific Garden Mission. Our first duty was to find sleeping places for
all these men. This we did. Not by the wasteful and extravagant
method of building or buying buildings of our own, but by taking advantage of existing lodging house accommodation and entering into arrangements with the lodging house keepers for providing each of these
homeless men with a clean bed where he could lie down and be warm
aι night. It took some organization at first, but we had a great deal
of assistance from Mr. Lammoris — a remarkable man is Mr. Lammoris.
We succeeded in establishing arrangements with lodging house
keepers in various parts of the city. Every homeless man was
provided with a bed at the cost of ten cents, which he paid for
by labor on the streets. No man was given relief without working for it, unless, of course, the man was incapable, and then
he was handed over to the County Commissioners to be dealt with
along with other hopeless cases by the County authorities at Dunning
and elsewhere. The work of the Relief Association properly understood is not to deal with hopeless paupers or incorrigible vagrants.
It has to provide temporary employment to tide over a period of
hardship. That is what we have done. We have had 4,500 persons
upon our hands at work, which is a tolerably large family to look
after and to provide for by an improvised committee. Of these about
3,800 were employed on the streets; the remaining 700 were looked after
under the Women's Committee, under Dr. Sarah Hackett Stevenson,
which has done excellent work in looking after the women. We have
found reluctance to go to work among a very small proportion of
the out-of-works, even although the rate of payment was only ten
cents an hour. Our difficulty has not been to find men to work ; it has
rather been in limiting them to the number of hours which we deem
wise. The Relief Association never set itself to enter into compe.

tition with the labor market as an employer of labor. Its aim was to pay the minimum upon which an able-bodied man could live. We provided work on the public streets which would procure him that irreducible minium of subsistence. We calculated that if a man took a pick or a shovel or a broom and went out to clean streets for three hours he would earn thirty cents, which would be paid him not in money but in tickets. We divided the tickets into three portions; one he gave for his breakfast in the morning before he started work, the second for his supper and the third went for his bed. We arranged it so that both breakfast and supper were considerably better than he could get elsewhere for 15 cents although they did not cost us more than ten. By this means the tickets, although nominally they had the face value of 30 cents, were worth 40 cents, and indeed if you take into consideration the advantageous arrangements made with lodging house keepers it might fairly be said that our 30 cent ticket was worth between 45 and 50 cents. This advantage comes out much more clearly, however, in the arrangements which were made for the married men. We had only about ten per cent of married men among our street workers. They were put on the long gang. That is to say they were allowed to work double shifts and sometimes eight or nine hours. A man who had earned 90 cents by doing nine hours' work in the street was able to get provisions at our store which could not be bought in the market for twice that money or nearly twice. This we could not do as a general thing but it was done in the emergency."

"But can you explain to me how it worked?"

"It is very simple," said Mr. Harvey, "and it is the most interesting part of the whole organization. You see we received a great many gifts of flour and food. These we sent down to our depots. We were also able to buy wholesale in the cheapest market, and in many cases when we made known what we wanted the goods for we were supplied, notably with boots for the mere cost of leather and the labor requisite to make the boots. The result was that we eliminated the profit of the middle man. We bought everything wholesale, and so we were able to supply our out-of-works with a pair of boots for ninety cents, which they could not have bought elsewhere for $2.50. So it was with coal and flour and everything else which they needed. We were, as you may say, the head of a great family with four thousand children, and by acting in that capacity and caring for them we were able to make a small sum of money go twice as far as would otherwise have been the case."

"Speaking about money, Mr. Harvey, how much do you think will carry you through?"

"We have raised $90,000 up to the present moment. We shall require another $100,000 to carry us through the next two months. I think that $200,000 will enable us to cope with all the floating distress which the association can regard as properly belonging to its province."

"Do you think you will get this money?"

"Certainly, we have no doubt of it. We have been very much pleased with the alacrity with which the wage earners and the lower middle classes have responded to our appeal. Sixty-five per cent of the money at present in hand has come from that class. The response has been very general and most gratifying."

"That is very good for the poor people," I said, "but it does not speak so well for the rich."

"Oh," said Mr. Harvey, "we shall get the money from the rich now. We could have got it already if we had wanted it; that is to say, we could have gone round and asked a number of men who are perfectly willing to supply all the money we need, but it is better that the whole of this movement of relief should be popular and should be from the people to the people. The result so far has fully justified our plan of operations."

"How far have you found the people whom you relieved strangers?"

"Seventy-five per cent of the persons who have applied to us for relief, and who are now on our books, have lived five years and more in Chicago. Many of them were born here. The popular accusation that we have been feeding a host of tramps from the outside is a delusion. The average, I tell you is, seventy-five per cent of residents in Chicago for more than five years. It is exactly the other way. Instead of bringing people to Chicago from the outside, we have sent away a great many persons who were lingering in our midst. They were very glad to get home and get a chance of regaining their old neighborhood, and who could not go because they had not the means, or they had been so broken down and dirty and ragged that they could not very well face their home folks. I should say there were fourteen hundred at least of persons whom we have given employment to, and have washed them and got them clean clothing, and they have been sent to the places where they belonged. There are more going home. We are getting to know the people better and to know exactly what they can do and what kind of character they have got, and we shall be able to find them places as soon as the winter passes. It is astonishing what you can do with men when you get into personal relation with them and establish confidence in them. It has been a great pleasure to me to go down morning after morning and see them parade before they go out to work. They breakfast from six o'clock to eight o'clock, and I go down to see that everything is going straight. If the coffee is weak they are very quick to make complaint, and on one occasion at least that complaint was very well founded. The supplier of coffee had substituted a fifteen cent for a seventeen cent coffee, and the men detected it at once. Our breakfast is a substantial meal; it is big enough to leave something over for a man to put into his pocket and make his lunch of, so that he could keep going until supper time. I have not been so pleased with working men for a long time. They are hearty and friendly, and there are very few kickers among them. If a man growls or tries to do anything mean the rest of the fellows round set upon him and hiss him. And why? Because they know we have really their interest at heart. They know also that we have not got so very much money to come and go upon, and that we are doing the best we can with what we have. We are really endeavoring to carry out with our street brigade of three thousand men something like the socialists' ideal on a small scale—that is to say we are endeavoring to give each man according to his needs. For instance, we parade the men and notice their shoes. Those that are in a very dilapidated condition we form into what we call New Boots

Brigade. They get an extra shift of work so that they can earn their boots. That is to say, instead of working only three hours they are put on the long shift and they will work six or nine. The average last week of hours worked by our men was five hours. So it is with laundry and with clothes, in fact with everything that a man needs. Then we look out for their health. We have doctors at all our stations, and they look at a man's physical condition. If he seems to be very much run down they give him more work, or a chance of doing more work. For we are not slave-drivers in our gangs, and if he cannot work from temporary indisposition he is put under treatment. We have had as many as two hundred men in the bad weather who had colds and other ailments. We had them laid up and attended to, and in a short time they got better. We have been very fortunate about small pox. There have been some cases, which were sent to the hospital, but we have been very fortunate in having singularly few deaths."

"Do you think," I asked, "that it would have been as well to have made the tickets into five cents as well as ten cents? Ten-cent currency is rather inconvenient."

"Yes," said Mr. Harvey, "we are going to do so to-morrow. We are issuing five cents because the men have to use a ten-cent ticket for a shave or for a bath or for whatever they may need even although it only costs a nickel. Now we are issuing nickel tickets and these will be good for the bath or for the barber. As for tobacco, of which some people have talked, that is not necessary; we have plenty of tobacco at the store. We are beginning this next week a more close and rigorous system of classification, so that we may know exactly the trade and the record of the men whom we are employing. A very great number of them are farmers' boys. We expect when the weather opens to get a thousand of them back on the land and that will be a very good thing."

"How have you got on with the labor unions?"

"Very well. At first they declared they would fight and protested against the ten cents an hour for labor, but they soon came to see that it was the best that could be done. I had one or two deputations from disgruntled kickers who came to demand that we should pay twenty cents an hour and employ everybody who was out of work. I asked them how many there were who were out of work. They said they thought there were about 40,000 who would willingly work upon the streets or anywhere else at twenty cents an hour. A very little calculation enabled me to show them that if we -started on that scale we should be out of funds in a week. The labor unions, however, repudiated those gentlemen, and on the whole we have no reason whatever to complain of the way in which the unionists of Chicago have treated us. They have been looking after their own men very well. We have relieved some unionists; we never make any difference between unionists and non-unionists, but speaking broadly, the unionists have helped the city very much by carrying their own people who are out of work.

"What about the churches?"

"The Catholics, for instance, have looked after their own poor, through the societies of St. Vincent de Paul and the Visitation and

Aid Society. Father Cashman and Father McLaughlin have both been very active, and all their subordinates and assistants have been specially active during this emergency in looking after the interests and welfare of the Catholics.

Some of our agencies claim that in the St. Vincent de Paul Societies each parish takes care of its own, without giving help to other societies that may be less favored with means. I don't know how true this is; but I should suppose that the richer parishes would assist those that were less able to care for themselves. At any rate I have no criticism for the work done by the Catholic denominations, as they certainly give much time, thought and money to the care of their own poor. Of course they are not able to care for all their wants, but the Chicago Relief and Aid Society and County and the Central Relief Association at this time supplement their efforts."

"What about the Jews?"

"The Jews," said Mr. Harvey, "as a rule have supported their own poor without assistance from us, but their funds have run rather low and Rabbi Hirsch is getting out a special appeal for funds."

"What about the other churches?"

"The other churches have done very well, but we have not succeeded in creating the general system of house to house visitation such as was at one time talked of. There are districts in the city where certain churches in one neighborhood are combined together and have undertaken a very thorough, systematic visitation of the district and have communicated to us daily all that they do, so as to avoid overlapping. But these are the exceptions. There is one district which is very well worked, and that is what we call the Hull House district in the seventh, eighteenth and nineteenth wards. This is extremely important because it contains many who are most in need of help. Ninety per cent of the Jews being helped are in that district; seventy-five per cent of the Bohemians and fifty per cent of the Italians are also located there. It is a matter of very great importance that they should be carefully visited, as they have been. We hope to have a very interesting and useful report of the Hull House visiting, where Mr. Waldo has charge of the registration. Miss Addams, of course, while she was in town was the center of this work.* The district which was best organized, outside Hull House district, is that of which the Rev. Mr. Inglis is the center. He has sev-

*The following particulars concerning the Hull House district will be of interest : In the Wards, Seventh, Eighth and Nineteenth, there are 887 men at work who are receiving 10 cents per hour for three full days in the week. This money all goes to families who are entirely dependent upon this work for their support. Each family has been visited and revisited to ascertain as to their needs and condition. Here are some interesting figures.

Of these men 684 are supporting 647 women, 1,597 children ; total, 2,908 persons. Average time in Chicago, 7.9 years ; average number of months out of work, 5 1·5. Total debts, $17,226.10 ; total rent overdue, $5,546.30 ; pawn tickets in their possession, 205. Total number of cases of sickness, 104 ; number of individuals needing clothing and shoes, 526 ; number of families needing coal, 351.

A summary of 134 other cases in these same wards who have been especially long residents of Chicago and of whom only eighteen were disapproved as unworthy shows 134 men supporting 129 women and 382 children ; total persons, 645 ; average time in Chicago, twenty years ; average time out of work, 6.3 months; total debts, $4,126.25 : total amount of rent overdue, $1,496.50 ; pawn checks in their possession, 30 ; number of cases of individuals needing clothing and shoes, 130; families needing coal, 63.

eral ministers associated with him and they do very good work. Most of the churches have one visitor and some of them have two and these are visiting and doing what they can, although there is a lack of organization."

"How did you succeed in regard to the County Commissioners?"

"There again there is work which we foresee will be better done next winter. We have been in friendly relations with them but we have not been able to secure from them the lists of the people whom they relieve. They are politicians and amateurs at the work of relief. The way in which they distributed at first created a public scandal. We have had people crowding upon each other in the streets. We have succeeded in impressing upon them the duty of having a waiting room where the people can wait, but we have not yet succeeded in opening their eyes to the fact that it would be well to provide them with chairs. Psychologically the chair is indispensable. If you meet an applicant for relief who has been standing for an hour before he comes into your presence, you have a man who is nervous and irritable, and he takes much more of your time than he would if he had been sitting for two hours on a chair in the waiting room. They have dealt, I should say, with about 8,000 families. They have not confined themselves to paupers, which is their proper function. They have relieved people more or less indiscriminately. Next winter I hope we shall be able to establish a more intelligent system of division of labor. The Chicago Relief and Aid Society, the old Chicago society, has done good work. That is to say, they will have distributed some $90,000 before the winter is over. They make allowances to families. They have the whole town mapped out and they know very well where the need is greatest. I had a curious illustration of the ignorance which prevails in certain well-informed quarters, as to the operations of the Chicago Relief and Aid Society. I asked a minister who was doing good work in a district on the West Side, whether the Chicago Relief and Aid Society was relieving any people in that district. He said he did not think they were. I asked him if he would be willing to relieve the Chicago Relief and Aid Society of all responsibility for cases in that district. He thought he would. In one week I asked the Relief and Aid Society's agent to draw me up a list of all the persons who were receiving relief from that society in that district. When the list was prepared I found that it contained no less than 1500 names. When I handed that to the minister he was simply knocked out, and admitted that it was no use, he could not undertake to do the work which the Chicago Relief and Aid Society was doing so unostentatiously and so efficiently that the ministers in the district were not aware of its benefactions. Mr. Mixer, who is Vice-President of the Relief Association and a leading member of the Relief and Aid Society, has been a valuable lieutenant through the whole of this work. He was a retired business man and having leisure he devoted it, without reserve, to the service of the poor. He has come to our office every day, six days a week, and has stuck to his work as he formerly stuck to his business. There are others who have done good work. Dr. Stevenson I have already mentioned in connection with the Woman's Club. We could not get all to work in cast-iron methods at first, and Mr. Sterling, who during the first weeks of the winter did very energetic service, was disposed to lament our inability to make things move according to rule and routine. We soon got them into shape and the work has gone very harmoniously and satisfactorily and I am particularly pleased at the hearty good feeling which exists among those whom we have relieved. We have got these men to understand that we are doing the best for them that we can, and they are cheerful and I never had to do with a body of men who made so few complaints."

The Society of St. Vincent de Paul, to whose work Mr. Harvey pays a tribute of well-earned respect, draws its resources almost entirely from Catholic subscribers. The Catholics, who number 40 per cent of the population of Chicago, include in their number more than 50 per cent of the extremely poor, while more than half the wealth of the town is in the hands of non-Catholics. Under these circumstances charitable relief by voluntary subscription falls heavily on those least able to bear it. Father Cashman, a public-spirited and enterprising priest, started a trampery in the parish of St. Jarlath which was a great success. He provided accommodation for the hungry and homeless, and succeeded in finding places for many of them. The good work done by isolated ministers and priests has never been adequately appreciated in Chicago. Were I to attempt to set it forth here I would have to convert this chapter into a catalogue or directory. Even then it would exceed the space at my disposal.

The work which Dr. Stevenson and the Woman's Club undertook was extremely interesting, dealing as it did more with the domestic life of the people. For everything that touches the woman touches the home. Mrs. Abbott was placed in charge of a department of immediate relief, with instructions to act in emergencies such as the prevention of evictions, the salvation of furniture from foreclosure and mortgage and all the other contingencies which suddenly threaten the destruction of the home. Various methods of relief were adopted; first of all was the employment bureau, where every attempt was made to obtain work, whether in the city or in the country, for those who were willing or anxious to work. Then rooms were opened for needle-work, for plain sewing, knitting and lace-making. The women as a rule worked seven or eight hours a day and received warm lunch at Hull House. They were paid fifty cents a day. In every way the club sought to tide over the distress of the winter. There was, of course, a certain proportion of reckless incompetents who gravitate to the bottom naturally, not having it in them to hold their own in the struggle for existence, but there was no skulking and very little fraud. Many were married women with families, but there was a good proportion of young women, several from the factories and some from offices.

Another women's organization which did good work was the Catholic Women's National League, which established soup kitchens in various centers and distributed coal and bread to those in the immediate neighborhood.

Among the many institutions which have been started during the past three months for the relief of the unemployed, that of the Brotherhood of St. Andrew is perhaps doing the most practical work. The office of this society is at 37 Michigan Street and is in charge of D. P. Welsh, who for a number of years has been connected with missions and charitable institutions. Mr. Welsh accepts all able-bodied men who come to him for work, and if they have no employment to which he can immediately be sent, they are taken in and cared for until something can be found for them to do. The bureau has the capacity of taking care of 140 men, all of whom are given three meals a day and a bed on which to sleep, in return for which they are expected to do a certain amount of work such as splitting wood, addressing envelopes and various other jobs. The home, at 37 Michigan Street, is fitted up with sleeping accommodations, bathing facilities, and, in addition, Mr. Welsh has introduced a system by which all the clothing of the applicants who are cared for is thoroughly fumigated so as to prevent the chance of any infectious disease being spread. The bureau is entirely undenominational and is supported by voluntary contributions.

Looking at the work of relief as a whole, it may be said that there was a well-meant attempt to cover the whole ground, that a central association was formed on sound principles with active and energetic men at its head, and that in two or three instances sections of the town were taken thoroughly in hand. But although the work was well begun, it is only beginning. The whole of the summer might be spent in elaborating a system of co-ordination and co-operation, which is indispensable to any effort to put the community in a state of siege against exceptional distress. Returns have been made from some of the churches, but they have been fragmentary, and the most sanguine would be the first to declare that the effort to systematically district the whole of the city under the direction of the Central Office, directed by the chief of staff of the army of relief, has by no means been realized. A good deal will have been done if by next winter the Central Relief Committee is in a position to issue a map of Chicago, showing the 190 square miles of the city mapped out into districts for visitation and relief. These districts should so far as possible be co-extensive with the wards into which the city is divided for electoral purposes. Within each ward the churches should be associated as far as possible in the work of visitation. If this were done, and an efficient visiting committee established in each ward, then should any fresh wave of distress overtake Chicago, the citizens would feel that they were adequately equipped to cope with any misfortune which may overtake the community.

A good deal however will have to be done in the way of active propagandism before the trustees of some of the wealthier churches realize that they owe a duty to the poor in their immediate neighborhood, which is not compounded for even by the erection of gorgeous ecclesiastical edifices or by the faultless performance of snatches of sacred opera by trained choirs on Sundays.

CHAPTER II.

Next to the relief of the hungry, by supplying of a certain modicum of solid food in order to maintain life, the second great want of our nature is something to drink. " I was thirsty and ye gave me not drink " is the second indictment which Christ says will be brought against us at the Last Judgment. Under the burning Asian sun the giving of a cup of cold water is a charity the nature of which is better appreciated than in the colder latitude of Chicago. In primitive semi-tropical lands the digging of a well has ever been regarded as one of the most meritorious of human acts; and in modern cities there is a wide field left for similar acts of beneficence, although, of course, their forms are varied.

The supply of water to the inhabitants of Chicago is one of the few monopolies of service which are in the hands of the municipality. The bounty of nature places an illimitable supply of pure water within two or three miles of the lake shore and the supply of that necessity of life is no longer left to the tender mercies of the individual citizen. But as man does not live by bread alone neither does he quench his thirst simply by pure water. When they drink water in Chicago it is usually iced and many people quench their thirst by beverages in which water is only one of the many ingredients. In America as in England the sanctified genius of temperance zeal has not been able to devise any drink that compares in popularity with beer. Therefore the saloon, after the municipality, holds the first place in the supply of drink to the thirsty.

According to the law of the State of Illinois the sale of drink is absolutely prohibited one day in seven. This is qualified by a municipal ordinance in Chicago which permits the saloons to be open on Sunday provided they keep their blinds down and admit people by the back door.   This ordinance is largely disregarded and almost all the saloons in Chicago are run wide open all Sunday.

In the question of prohibition after twelve o'clock, there is no municipal ordinance to break the force of the law of Illinois.   On the contrary, the municipal ordinances strengthen the law.   Merely for the purpose of testing how far prohibition prohibits, I employed an agent to make a personal investigation one evening in a district in the First Ward.   The following extract from an affidavit sworn before Mr. Justice Lyon, on December 14, 1893, gives the result of this investigation:

My field of examination was a territory bounded east and west by State Street and the Chicago, Rock Island and Pacific tracks, and north and south by Van Buren and Twelfth Streets.   The tour of investigation was made on Wednesday, Dec. 13, 1893, between the hours of 12.30 and 5 a. m., during which time I visited fifty-six saloons. These were chosen indiscriminately, as it was impossible to go to everyone in the district I have specified.   Out of the total number of saloons visited I found only four of them closed.   In the case of the other fifty-two, entrance was gained in thirty-seven places by the front door, and in thirteen cases by the side door.   At the remaining two saloons both the front and side doors were fastened, but they were immediately opened on my knocking.   In all but seven of the places visited I found men drinking, while in a number of them women were also to be seen.   In none of the saloons visited by me were the slightest attempts being made to keep secret the fact that the sale of liquor was going on, while in two cases I saw police officers drinking in the saloon.   The only difference to show that it was after the midnight hour being the fact that in most cases the window blinds were drawn down.   The gas in each place, however, was brightly burning.

The more zealous teetotalers of Chicago by way of compounding for their own inactivity in this direction turn to damning the saloon keeper.   He gives drink to the thirsty, as a matter of business of course, but as they disapprove of the quality of his beverage, they curse him up hill and down dale, through all the moods and tenses, but they do not raise a finger to minister themselves to the thirst of the community. Let me make here one exception.

The Woman's Christian Temperance Union has supplied the corridor of the City Hall with drinking fountains, which are so much used they occasionally run dry. That is good and deserves to be recorded to their credit, but like "a good deed in a naughty world," it stands out all the more conspicuously because it is unique. I shall discuss elsewhere the question of the saloon; but there is no doubt that, so far as ministering to the needs of the human mechanism for the wherewithal to quench its thirst, the saloon has done a great deal more than the churches. Even in the distribution of non-intoxicating beverages the saloon keeper does more than the churches or any institutions run by the churches. At the same time, if the saloon keepers are wise in their day and generation, they will follow the example of the English publican and supply soft drinks more widely than they do at present. Bovril or beef extract, coffee, tea, cocoa, as well as lighter beverages which are at present chiefly supplied by the drug store, are not supplied in the saloons to the same extent that they are elsewhere; and failing any effort on the part of the religious and temperance people to minister to the thirst of the community by non-intoxicants, the saloon keeper might well be appealed to for help.

"I was a stranger and ye took Me not in," the third head in the condemnation, recalls a virtue which has almost gone out of fashion in the civilized countries of the West. You need to go to Russia or still farther east to find what a high place hospitality holds among the distinctively Christian virtues. There are at the present moment millions of men and women who are wandering about the Russian Empire homeless, and in one sense of the word destitute, and yet they are at home wherever they can find a peasant with a roof over his head. These are the pilgrims to the sacred shrines, and the poorest peasant in all Russia would feel that he had denied his Lord if he did not extend to the pilgrim whatever accommodation his humble home possessed.

In Germany, by co-operation between private charity and the public authorities, labor farms have been established at intervals along the high-roads where a man can earn his board and lodging and go forth on his journey to whatever place he may be bound. In England the organization is not so complete, but casual wards in every Poor Law district are established, where in return for the stipulated stint of labor the tramp, or the working man on tramp in search of work, finds accommodation.

In America not even these municipal makeshifts for primitive hospitality have been provided. The result is that the tramp nuisance is becoming one of the most formidable of the lesser evils which afflict the Republic. The papers all this winter have been full of reports all pointing to the gradual evolution of the laborer in search of work into the mendicant tramp, and the still further evolution of the mendicant tramp into a species of banditti. In certain counties in Ohio, for instance, last winter, the tramps were little better than highway robbers traveling from place to place on freight trains. They alighted whenever they were hungry and made a foray into the neighboring villages or isolated farm houses, compelling the farmers to give them meals and then turn over whatever money might be in the house.

In another town, in Indiana, the Mayor provided every night watchman with a stout black snake whip and instructed them to use it with vigor upon all tramps. Every now and then the papers published telegrams describing how freight trains were boarded and their food and coal supply confiscated by the wandering wastrels of civilization.

In Iowa the tramps, forming into bands of six or twenty, made a practice of breaking into the most comfortable school house in the district and converting it into an improvised lodging house. There was usually coal enough in the coal house to keep the stove going until the morning, when they resumed their march. As it was in Iowa, Ohio and Indiana, so it was to an even more alarming extent in Texas and California. In Texas they were reported to have formed camps at stated points, where they rendezvoused and divided the spoils which they had either begged or stolen. The most formidable development was that which was reported from California in the month of December, for it marks a stage in the evolution of the tramp into semimilitary bands. The reporter telegraphed:

The army of unemployed is moving eastward from the Pacific in regular military fashion. Three hundred and fifty such men arrived in Colton, Cal., a week ago, en route to New Orleans, camped outside the city limits, ran up an American flag on a pole, and sent a delegation into town to ask for rations. The men were of good appearance, clean and orderly, and evidently were not tramps. The parties of unemployed are organized into companies, with captains and regular roll call. The officers serve two meals a day, all sharing alike when there is anything to share. The citizens of Colton gave this particular party 100 pounds of bacon, piles of bread, and several sacks of potatoes, beans and other provisions. The men wanted food to last them across the deserts of Arizona and New Mexico.

While the tramp was developing in this direction the most notable utterance on the other side came from Governor Lewelling, of Kansas, who had himself been a tramp in Chicago nearly thirty years ago. His letter to the police boards of Kansas created no small sensation throughout the Western States by he pointing out the fact that the right to go freely from one place to another in search of work was part of the personal liberty guaranteed by the Constitution of the United States to every human being. Even voluntary idleness was not a luxury forbidden to American citizens. The habit of fining tramps for being vagrants and compelling them to work out those fines as municipal slaves on rock piles was a flagrant violation of the Constitution. This institution he declared was a relic of the slave auction-block era. He declared that to be homeless and poor should no longer be considered a crime in the cities of Kansas. The method of entertaining strangers by converting them temporarily into slaves conflicted equally with his reading of the American Constitution and of the New Testament. When he was questioned as to why he issued the circular he made the following remarkable reply :

I know what it is myself to tramp the streets of a city seeking work and attempting in some way to earn an honest living. In 1865 I tramped up and down the streets of Chicago trying to get work. I was hungry, penniless, and was subject to arrest, but I was not a criminal and ought I to have been placed upon the rock pile simply because I was unable to get work when I was willing and anxious to do anything that would enable me to earn an honest living? I don't call these people without employment tramps, and no one should use such a name in connection with them. There is a large number of people out of employment. John J. Ingalls says there are 3,000,000, and Kansas has its share of them. The economic conditions of the present are the trouble, and men are compelled to wander around in search of work, not from choice, but from necessity.

The question as to what ought to be done with the tramp is a burning one in many American cities, but it is still as far from solution as ever. A circular issued to thirty-five Chiefs of Police showed that the opinion of the police authorities is almost equally divided as to whether or not public provision should be made for their accommodation. Sixteen thought it would be advantageous, while eighteen were of the opposite opinion. Twenty at present furnish lodgings without any conditions as to cleanliness or work.

The professional tramp proper, in the United States, is estimated at under 50,000, but this year this regular army has been swollen by a great influx of willing workers who are more or less undergoing a process of degeneration which urgently calls for the attention of the social reformer.

I have already described what is done for the stranger in Chicago without a penny, but the duty of showing hospitality by no means depends upon the impecuniosity of the stranger. As a municipality Chicago has not yet deemed it wise or necessary to intrust its Mayor with the discharge of civic hospitality, which is undertaken as a matter of course by the Burgomeister or the Mayor in the Old World. Such hospitality is only provided by a special vote of the City Council or is left to the sporadic action of individual citizens.

This, however, is a matter of comparatively small importance. What is much more serious is the absence in Chicago of any arrangement for providing clean, decent, habitable lodgings for the poor man. According to the best authorities, the floating population is about 30,000 single men, who are living at this present moment in lodging houses which are too often foul, verminous and full of every element which should not be included in the hospitality extended to the stranger. This army of 30,000 pays nightly for its lodgings, but owing to the scandalous inadequacy of the municipal regulalation of the city and the absence of the philanthropic enterprise, they are too often lodged like pigs and treated worse than cattle. The ten-cent doss house is by no means an ideal lodging house.

A description of one of these places will give an idea of what the poor and homeless men of this city have to endure. Within a stone's throw of one of Chicago's best private hotels can be found one of these lodging houses. It is a small, one-storied frame structure. Its sleeping accommodation consists of one hundred and fifty beds (?) which occupy the ground floor and the basement. Upon entering the front door one is almost overcome by the odor, which more resembles that of a long disused tomb than that of a human dwelling place. Pushing open the door the "office and parlor" is entered. Here in a room twenty-five by thirty feet were to be seen, a short time ago, crowded round a stove, twenty-seven men, whose clothing was more conspicuous by its variety and filthiness than by its adequateness. In one corner of the room was a desk at which sat a good specimen of the "genus tuff." This individual hailed the investigator as he hesitated at the door, with the question: "Say, dere, you, does you want a bed? if you don't, git! We want no loafers here." Stepping to the desk the visitor asked the price of a night's lodging, and after being told deposited a dime. Saying that he would like to retire, a doorway at the farther end of the room was pointed out, and he was told in a far from civil tone to take his choice of any of the beds. Following the direction pointed out, the investigator entered the sleeping room. For a few moments it was impossible to see anything in the place, the only light coming from a dirty lamp at the farther end of the room, which was about fifty by twenty-five feet in dimensions; while the darkness was made more apparent by the smoke from a dozen pipes of the men who were lying in the beds and smoking. The arrangement of the room was certainly unique in character. The beds consisted of a piece of canvas, which was fastened to the wall on one side, while on the other they were supported by upright wooden poles, which ran from the floor to the ceiling. They were arranged in tiers, four deep, and the covering on each bed consisted simply in one thin blanket, which in several cases was reeking with vermin. In the center of the room was a large stove filled with blazing wood which only served to dispel any breath of air which might by inadvertence have entered the apartment. In this place one hundred and fifty men sleep, no precaution being taken whatever to prevent the spread of any disease which may be brought in by any of the lodgers.

Nothing has been attempted in Chicago corresponding to the municipal lodging houses of London or the similar institutions which have long been successfully worked at Glasgow. It has been left to a private individual Mr. Lammoris, to do what can be done to provide clean and comfortable lodging accommodations for lodgers. Mr. Lammoris knows the lodging houses of Europe, and he has managed several large establishments in the city with great success. He is now preparing to put up a huge place, a veritable poor man's hotel, twelve stories high, with 1,200 rooms, and each room provided with an outside window. When that building is completed, Mr. Lammoris' hotel will form a precinct in itself in the ward organization of Chicago. Mr. Lammoris makes it pay and pay well. But even although there are dollars in it, yet this expert, who of all men in Chicago is best qualified to speak on the subject, has publicly declared the need which there is for the licensing, regulating and inspection of lodging houses. But as there is no boodle in it for the Aldermen, they will do nothing. Mr. Lammoris, speaking at a dinner which he gave on Thanksgiving Day to 750 guests, said:

I have tried for three years to get the City Council to take action for the inspection and regulation of hotels of this class. We have in the east end of the Eighteenth Ward twenty-seven lodging houses. We have from twenty-seven to 700 lodgers in each one, or an average of 250 in each one, or a total of 6,950 men. We have in this whole city only eight hotels that are run on the same or nearly the same principle as mine, yet we have on the South Side and on the West Side sixty-seven hotels that are run in every condition of disease and crime. I have known of men to reach the city with $3 or $4 in their pockets and through inability to find wholesome places within their means have gone to these filthy and dirty lodging houses to stay. After remaining a week or even less than a week they become filthy and dirty and get in with men that have no self-respect, and in less than a month they become criminals.

These are Mr. Lammoris' words, not mine. Judged on the evidence of this witness, the city of Chicago will cut but a poor figure if the third of the divine tests is to be literally applied. Her hospitality to the stranger is to convert him by rapid stages through dirt to crime.

One special feature of the housing of the penniless stranger, was the action taken by a certain number of churches, which, scandalized by the lodging of the homeless in the police stations and the City Hall, threw open their buildings as temporary lodging houses until better arrangements could be made for providing for them.*

This work was started by the Central North Chicago Ministerial Association, and was one of the outcomes of revival services held by the evangelist, Mr. Mills. Father Cashman also was not behind in this work of

---

*Those who took the lead in the matter were the following: Belden Avenue Baptist, Belden Avenue Presbyterian, Lake View Congregational, Grace English Lutheran, Wesley Methodist, Church of the Covenant, Fullerton Avenue Presbyterian, Christ Chapel and Union Park Congregational.

charity, and slung hammocks in the auditorium and lecture room of the old St. Jarlath's church, and supplied his guests with soup and sacred music.

The fourth article of condemnation, "naked and ye clothed Me not" is a text which does not fall very heavily on Chicago. Whether it is the severity of the climate that kills out those who have not sufficient to wear, or some other cause, I do not know; but the people you meet in the streets seem usually to be warmly clad. Even the little urchins who, at much too tender years, are allowed to vend newspapers in the streets, are comfortably rigged up. Of organized agencies for the clothing of the destitute there are not many apart from the charitable societies and the churches. The proprietors of a business establishment, however, gave away $200 worth of clothing for the Salvation Army last winter, and several other instances of like kind are reported.

The most systematic attempt to clothe the naked has been made by the admirable School Children's Aid Society, which has distributed about $10,000 worth of clothes to children who otherwise would have had to remain away from school owing to the lack of apparel. About 800 children a month were clothed .by this society, the funds for which were largely provided for by a Thanksgiving appeal. Most of the contributions were supplied by the children who were better off. For every dollar that the parents have given, the children have given five. A distributing room where both new and second-hand clothing was received was opened at 159 W. Monroe Street. The only criticism to offer upon the School Children's Aid Society is that, much as has been done, as the distributors know only too well, the work was very inadequately performed. While some were clothed, many more went without; there were many of these little ones who could not be warmly clad, because there were not enough clothes to go round.

Another point that may be noted in connection with

this "naked and ye clothed Me not," although it is not absolutely in accord with the scriptural interpretation of the words: clothing is a protection against cold, and there is great need in Chicago for something like those public warming places which have been established in Paris, where those who have no active work to keep them busy and who have to hang about the streets until night time can find shelter within reasonable range of a stove or radiator from the very cold wind which blows on the shores of Lake Michigan. Such institutions have been vehemently demanded for some time past in London, where the question seems likely to be solved by the unemployed taking possession of the reading rooms of the free libraries. They form part of the public, they can read or pretend to do so, and it is difficult for the custodian to discriminate between men who use the library simply for a warming place and those who are there for study. There are not many free institutions in America which could be utilized in that way. The fact that the evil has not obtained unmanageable proportions, is due to the much abused saloon. The saloon keeper is practically the only man who supplies free warmth to the chilled and shivering wanderers on the street. In this as in other things, it is one of the gravest questions which confront Chicago how long the saloon keeper is to be allowed a practical monopoly of ministering to the wants of mankind.

The care of the sick in a large city involves much more than at first sight appears. There is, for instance, the organization of first help to the injured, in which Chicago lags far behind other cities. Miss Ada C. Sweet, to whose energy and intellectual enthusiasm the city owes so much, has spent much time and trouble in endeavoring to bring about an improvement in this direction, with but partial success. In reply to my request for information as to how the matter stands now, Miss Sweet writes:

An Ambulance Association is contemplated, but at present there is nothing of the kind in Chicago. The Police Department has laid upon it the picking up of persons who fall sick in public places, or who are maimed, injured and dying. It has no trained men for this service, nor surgeons, nor nurses to go with its heavy patrol wagons on their missions of mercy, or even on its four ambulances. The entire city owns not more than six ambulances, two being used almost entirely for contagious diseases and cases by the Health Department.

Hundreds of men die annually in Chicago of injuries, when intelligent, timely aid might easily have saved them. The hospitals have no arrangements for responding to emergency calls; the whole matter of picking up and transporting to the hospitals persons injured or the victims of accident, is left entirely to the untrained, ignorant policemen on the patrol wagons and the three or four ambulances stationed about the city. Patients have to be carried miles over the rough pavements, generally in heavy, stiff-springed wagons; their lives are often jolted out or they bleed to death on the way to the County Hospital, where most accident cases are taken.

It is no uncommon occurrence for an injured man to die unattended in a police station. This happened to a man who had been struck by a train of cars in Chicago while these pages were going through the press.

The fifth head, "sick and ye visited Me not," recalls attention to the fact that here also the specialization and concentration necessitated by the condition of life in a great city have deprived many Christians of one of the means of grace which the Christian Church in all ages has urged with great stress. Instead of having the sick at their own doors, where Lady Vere de Vere or her Chicago prototype can visit her humble neighbors and cheer the dying couch by the grace of her presence, the sick poor lie many blocks and sometimes many miles away. They are cooped up in huge hospitals or carried off miles into the country and housed far away from all possibility of constant civilizing contact with the healthy members of the community. The accommodation of the sick is supplied on a more or less inadequate scale by various hospitals, the largest of which is supported by the county, while the others are of a more or less denominational character. A mere cursory survey, however, of the provision of the sick in Chicago, reveals an astonishing lack in the shape of convalescent homes. There are no institutions provided in which convalescents can recover or in which the incurable can be placed to die. Homes for the dying should be regarded as an indispensable necessity in every great city. Even supposing that here and there efforts have been made to provide for convalescents, it is broadly true that the accommodation for patients who have recovered sufficiently to leave the hospital is lamentably inadequate.

To visit the sick is no longer regarded as part of the indispensable duty of the Christian man or woman. It is considered sufficient to pay taxes or to subscribe to hospitals and to maintain district visitors or to support religious orders devoted to the task as part of the professional duty. The Nurses' Visiting Association and many other associations do noble work, but they would be much better if they were supplemented by more voluntary efforts, not merely for the sake of the sick so much as for the sake of the healthy who need to be brought into closer intercourse with their suffering neighbors. If each of us were to be asked when last we voluntarily visited a sick person we should most of us make a very poor showing. No one who has ever been an inmate in a hospital or poor-house and has lain silent, watching the long hours pass, can doubt that of all the charities which cost little in cash and are worth much in love and in service there are few which rank so high as that of the visitation of the sick. Yet what steps have been taken, or are being taken, by any of the churches in Chicago to secure a plan, let us say, whereby each church should take its proper share of responsibility for providing sympathetic visitors of the non-professional order who would take charge of their due proportion of inmates in the County Hospital or of the old and infirm in the poor-house at Dunning? In a village or country town where these sick persons would be lying within a stone's throw of their neighbors' doors such visitation would be regarded as a natural and necessary duty only to be avoided by those who had no longer the love of Christ in their heart. How is it that the obligation should diminish as the need for its discharge grows greater? That is a question which will have to be answered before our lives can hope to escape condemnation by the metewand of Christ.

The last division into which the duty of man is divided, that of going unto those who are in prison, is a duty which in the nature of things cannot be discharged by every individual in the whole community, especially if by prisoner is meant the ordinary convict prisoner. But even there much might be done by the contact of the civilizing influence of non-criminal kind upon caged-up convicts who are expiating their offenses in the Bridewell or at Joliet.

The condition of things in the Bridewell, for instance, where for years past juvenile offenders were crowded together in cells, the comparatively innocent with the incipient tough of the slums of Chicago, without any industrial training, was an infamy which ought to have roused the churches to action. But it did not, and it was not until Mr. Pomeroy publicly denounced the condition of things upon the platform of the Central Music Hall that help was given to Mr. Superintendent Crawford to enable him to carry out an object for which he had pleaded in vain for so long. All state institutions breed abuses as carcasses breed maggots, and the only way to remedy this and to minimize the evil is to perpetually keep every detail of the working of such institutions under the searchlight of the loving eye of Christ. But where is there among the churches of Chicago any recognition of their responsibility to the criminals in Joliet or the offenders in the Bridewell?

But it would be a mistake to limit the phrase, "I was imprisoned and ye came unto Me," to the convict prisoner. In the time of Christ the prison included a great many others than those who at present find themselves in the Bridewell and the penitentiary. All men under restraint may be said to be in prison: the inmates of lunatic asylums, those who are detained by the compulsion of circumstances in the poor-house, all prisoners of extreme poverty, who are reduced to a position of virtual slavery, and all those who are deprived of the right of leisure which distinguish the free man from the slave. In all these denizens of the prison houses of modern society we have to recognize the suffering Christ of our time. They are the least of these His brethren, and as we do it unto them, so we do it unto Him. There is a phrase that He used in relation to those who are in prison which has a curious significance. "I was in prison and ye came unto Me." To come to a person is to draw near to him, to be close to him, to be neighbor to him. Then there can be no great gulf fixed between him and us. But have we come unto Him? May it not be if we came unto Him, especially those of us who are weary and heavy laden with sins and troubles of our own; if we came unto Him as He lies scourged and manacled in the prison houses of our time, we should find the promise true: "Come unto Me, all ye that labor and are heavy laden, and I will give you rest. Take my yoke upon you and learn of Me; for I am meek and lowly of heart, and ye shall find rest unto your souls."

CHAPTER I.

THE BOODLERS AND THE BOODLED.

There is a story told of one of the early Caliphs which may well be recalled in this connection. When he succeeded to the dominion of the Mussulman world, he was asked by one of his friends, "Give me some money out of the public treasury." The Caliph looked at his friend in amazement and said, "What do you mean? You want some money out of the public treasury?" "Yes," replied his friend. "I have been your friend and would like some reward." The Caliph answered, "Come to me at sundown and I will help you to some money." His friend went away feeling that he had done well and that the Caliph had not forgotten that "to the victors belong the spoils." He came around that night punctually and found the Caliph in disguise awaiting him. He was provided with a pick-axe, a dark lantern and a spade. His friend was surprised and said, "I thought you were going to give me some money." "I said I would help you to get it," said the Caliph, "but you must also help me." So they crept through the by-streets until they came to the house of one of the wealthiest men in the city. "Now," said the Caliph, "Stop! I know where this man keeps his treasure chest. It is just on the other side of this wall, and if we only work steadily we shall be able to make a hole through the wall and you will be able to help yourself to the money." The man looked at the Caliph aghast and said: "Do you take me for a thief?" "Why," he replied, "I thought you said you wanted some money." "But," said his friend, "it was public money I wanted." "Then," said the Caliph, "when you and I stand before the judgment seat of Allah, whether do you think it will be easier, for us to listen to the reproaches of one man whom we have robbed or to those of all the millions of the Faithful, whose money you propose to take?"

This saying of the Moslem Caliph, with his archaic ideas of the responsibility of man to his Maker, not merely for his dealings with the individual, but still more for his dealings with the community, was far in advance of the morality of the City Hall of Chicago. It is perhaps too much to say that Chicago is and has been governed upon a system of corruption, but whoever did make that statement would not have much difficulty in making out a very strong *prima facie* case in support of his assertion. The sovereign people may govern Chicago in theory: as a matter of fact King Boodle is monarch of all he surveys. His domination is practically undisputed, and the recognition of its existence is the basis of the limitations which are placed upon the taxing powers of the City Council. It being expected as a fundamental principle that the Aldermen will steal, the longer-headed, well-to-do citizens, acting under the guidance of Mr. Medill, the editor and proprietor of *The Tribune*, then Mayor of Chicago, limited the taxing powers of the city of Chicago to two per cent of the assessed value of realty and personalty of the city. In order to limit still further the amount of money liable to be stolen by the representatives of the people, they elaborated the most extraordinary system of assessment that ever bewildered a financier or shocked a moralist. All this was not done to any desire on the part of the reputable citizens to place their city in leading-strings, but simply because they knew by experience that the rule of King Boodle would be supreme, and the members of the Council, whether Republican or Democrat, could equally be relied upon to act as his venal courtiers.

As a result of these expedients, which so severely limited the financial resources of the city, the Aldermen were driven to forage for plunder in other fields. Unfortunately they were only too numerous and the pastures to be obtained lay in tempting profusion on every side. The powers of the city, although strictly limited in the levying of taxes, are almost unlimited in relation to the common property of the city. The streets, for instance, have furnished an estate of incalculable value, which could be sold wholesale or retail to the highest bidder. This estate was much greater than might appear at first sight. For, as it is said of freehold property, the owner possesses not only the surface of the ground, but all that lies between it and the stars on on the one hand, and the molten core of the earth on the other. No one who proposes to cross the street in the air, either by an elevated railway or with telegraph or telephone wires or electric light wires, or any one who proposes to construct a balcony or bay-window overshadowing the roadway, is trespassing on the city's property. The surface of the streets of course affords an almost inexhaustible field for revenue. There is the right to lay down the street railways, and to permit railway corporations to cross the street or to run down a street, together with the right to make side tracks and connections with wharves and warehouses communicating with the streets,* to say nothing of the right to cumber the sidewalk with merchandise or advertising matter. All of these things of course belong to the city by right of its ownership in the streets. Below the surface it is the same thing. No conduit can be made for electric light wires, for gas or water pipes, for pneumatic tubes, to say nothing of tunnels for underground railways or subways, without infringing the right of the city in its streets.

---

* The permit for a switch track or the vacation of a strip of alley sometimes means more than a year's salary. There is said to be a recognized schedule of prices.

Switch track to a coal-yard..$1,000
Switch track to a brewery...$2,500

In the year 1892 the number of miles of streets was reported at over 2,000 miles. These streets are a portion of the civic domain, but only a portion. There are besides great portions of the city which belong to the Board of Education. These are what are called the school section, which are set apart for educational purposes. In the whole of Chicago, the area of which is 180 square miles, there were originally eleven square miles held in trust for the purpose of defraying the cost of education of the people.

These two reserves, the streets and the school sections, constitute a civic estate of almost incalculable value. No multi-millionaire would hesitate a moment to abandon his possessions if he could exchange them for the real estate originally devoted to education or the right of ownership in the streets. Unfortunately this immense estate, was left to the uncovenanted mercies of the city fathers, in the case of the streets, and to the Education Board in the case of the school sections.

The greatest part of the educational estate in the city has long been frittered away. Instead of allowing the space as a sacred trust to be retained or let out on lease until such time as their real value could be utilized, the thriftless and corrupt authorities jobbed away section after section until only a beggarly remnant remained, which last year only yielded a rental of about a quarter of a million dollars. The *Tribune* building stands upon one lot which has escaped the general scramble. McVicker's Theater is another prominent building which occupies a school section, and here and there throughout the city there are still parcels of property which are still held for their original purpose. One of these, lying on the outskirts, was saved from sharing the general fate by the action of a public-spirited young school teacher. Any proposal to to sell the school land must be approved by a plebiscite of the citizens, but as a rule the public was befooled and the trustees did just as they liked. On this occasion, however, the job was frustrated by the teacher, who, hearing of the corrupt deal, quietly whipped up a contingent of citizens and when the matter came to the poll the scheme was voted down. The result is that the tract of land which would have been sold for a few hundred dollars is now worth as many thousands. Unfortunately there was not a young teacher to stand in the gap in other cases and now there is but a miserable remainder of what was formerly a magnificent estate left in the hands of the Board of Education.

Even this is by no means made the most of. On the day when the people of Chicago wake up and decide to look after their own property they will find that they will be able to realize a much greater revenue than they do at present from the school sections. One section was made over almost bodily to the railways for use as railway tracks at a mere nominal figure. A searching inquisition into the present status of the school sections, with full particulars as to the terms on which they are held by the present occupants, would suggest many lines of inquiry that might be profitably pressed home.

It is not, however, with the school sections that I propose to deal, but rather with that other great urban estate, the streets of Chicago. The streets cannot be sold in small pieces so that the purchaser can take them away in his pocket. All that the city can part with is the right of way ; but this right of way, whether over, on or under the streets, is a property the net value of which cannot be valued at less than $5,000,000 a year, while it might very easily amount to twice or three times that sum. This estate yields $5,000,000 a year in hard cash, not one penny of which would be earned except for the permission to use the streets. As this revenue, moreover, represents surplus profits, after paying all working expenses and the capital involved in the construction and maintenance of the plant, this represents the sum available for the purposes of boodling. Boodling is a euphemism signifying the corrupt disposal of public property by the representatives of the people in return for price paid not to the public but to their dishonest representatives. It would have been cheaper for the city of Chicago to have paid every one of her Aldermen $10,000 a year, if by such payment the city could have secured honest servants, than to have turned a pack of hungry Aldermen loose on the city estate with a miserable allowance of $156 a year but with practically unrestricted liberty to fill their pockets by bartering away the property of the city. Sixty-eight Aldermen at $10,-000 a year would only cost $680,000 per annum. That would have been money well spent if it could have saved for the city $5,000,000 a year, which they have been flinging away in exchange for bribes which in no way correspond to the value of the property for which they were given. The Aldermen knew that they were dealing in stolen goods; they were fraudulent trustees who, in order to fill their own pockets, conveyed away the property of the city. Now it is an invariable rule that the thief is at the mercy of the "fence" or receiver of stolen goods. He cannot fix his own price. A $100 watch will often fetch not more than $10 when it finds its way to the "fence." It is just the same in relation to the purchasers of city franchises. The predatory rich, the unscrupulous corporations who are forever endeavoring to snap up bargains, never dream of paying to the Aldermen the full value for the franchise which they purchase. There is no exact proportion whatever between the value of the franchise and the bribes which are necessary to secure its passage through the Council.* The

---

*In the Chicago *Record* of February 19, 1894, I find the following information on the subject :

How much does it cost to pass a franchise ordinance through the Council?

There is no set price, because one franchise may be worth more than another. The highest price ever paid for aldermanic votes was a few years ago when a measure giving valuable privileges to a railway corporation was passed in the face of public condemnation. There were four members of the Council who received $25 000 each, and the others who voted for the ordinance received $8,000 each. An official who was instrumental in securing the passage of the measure received the largest amount ever given in Chicago for a service of the kind. He received $100,-000 in cash and two pieces of property. The property was afterward sold for $111,-000 In one of the latest "boodle" attempts the Aldermen voting for a certain franchise were supposed to receive $5,000 each. One of them, however, had been de-

Aldermen, like all thieves, are bad men of business and are compelled to take what is offered to them. Occasionally they make a struggle to raise the price of their votes from $750 to $1,500, but they never venture to value their support at the value of the privilege which their votes confer. Hence the city receives nothing, while the Aldermen get very much less than what ought to have been the fair market price of the boodler if the market had been open and the transaction had not had to be carried on in secret.

The method of boodling as prevailing in the City Council of Chicago for many years is very simple. Some man or some corporation wants something from the city. It may be some right of way or it may be a franchise for tearing up the streets in order to lay gas pipes, or it may be an ordinance sanctioning the laying of a railway down a street or to make a grade crossing across one of the innumerable thoroughfares of the city. He can only obtain permission by obtaining it from the City Council. Now the majority of the City Council consider that they are not in the Council "for their health." As each of them went into it " for the sake of the stuff" and for whatever there was " in it " for themselves ;" they think these favors should not be granted without the receipt of a corresponding *quid pro quo*. Hence it is necessary, if you wish to get anything through the Council, to "square" the Aldermen. The "squaring" is done discreetly and with due regard to the fundamental principle which sums up the whole law of the boodler, namely : thou shalt not be found out. If it is a small thing, such as an ordinance sanctioning a projection over the street, it is not necessary to square more than

ceived and was to get only $3,500. When he learned that he had been "frisked" of $1,500 he wept in anger and went over to the opposition, assisting in the final overthrow of the steal.

The " $5,000 per vote " is the high-water mark in the Council for the last four years. During 1891 and 1892 there were a dozen ordinances which brought their "bits," yet in one case the price went down to $300. In spite of what has been said of the good old times these two years were among the most profitable ever known in criminal circles.

When it becomes necessary to pass an ordinance over the Mayor's veto the cost is 25 per cent more than usual.

one Alderman.   This can be done directly or through an intermediary.   In all cases, however, the Alderman must be "seen."   Remittances through the post are discouraged; bank checks are at a discount; the transaction takes place in the presence of no third party, but face to face.   If it is a very small matter a trifle will suffice, for your Alderman is not above small pickings by the way. It is a very different matter, however, when the question is one involving a railway franchise or a new gas ordinance.   Then much more elaborate machinery is employed.   The Council is sometimes divided and redivided into various rings.   In the present Council one Alderman, who usually can be found in the neighborhood of Powers & O'Brien's saloon, can control forty others. The head of the big ring is the boss.   There is also a smaller ring of ten, subsidiary to the greater ring and working together with it.   The support of both rings is necessary when an ordinance is to be passed over the Mayor's veto.   The smaller ring, as the larger, has its own chief.

When a franchise is applied for, or in other words something is proposed to be stolen from the city, it is necessary to ascertain on what terms the Aldermen will consent to hand the stolen goods out of the windows of the City Hall.   For carrying on such negotiations, the first desideratum is a safe man, one who can be relied upon to keep his own counsel and who can be depended upon not to take more than a certain proportion of the swag.   This gentleman is usually outside the Council, but he commands the confidence of both parties to the transaction.   He is the go-between, and all transactions are conducted by him by word of mouth.   He seeks the head of the ring to acertain whether the boys are hungry and with how little they can be induced to stand "pat."   Into the conferences between the go-between and the boys the world is not admitted.   The secrets of a papal conclave are not more sacredly preserved than the details of the conferences between the chiefs of the corrupt ring in the City Hall and the corporations who are in for the deal. As both parties mean business they arrive at an understanding, and the money, whether it be $500, $750, $1,000 or $1,500, is agreed upon. The money is then put into the hands of the go-between and deposited in his own name in the strong room of a national bank. There it remains, the purchase price of the fraudulent trustees of the people's property. When the boys are assured that the money is banked in the name of say " Mike," " Pat " or " Billy," as the case may be, the safe man whom they have trusted many times in the past and who has never gone back on his word, they proceed to fulfill their part of the bargain. An ordinance, usually drawn up by the corporation which proposes the steal, is intrusted to one of the gang, who introduces it with such garnishings as he deems desirable. If the franchise is not very objectionable on the face of it, it usually goes through. Aldermen are bound to oblige each other and as the city property has been chucked away every month without any protest, it is quite possible for the ordinance to pass without serious debate. If, on the other hand, there are any of the Aldermen who do not consider that they have been properly treated or who have been left out in the cold in the promised distribution of the boodle, there may be a debate with heated discussion. Sometimes, of course, this opposition may be perfectly genuine and due to the natural indignation of honest men against a bare-faced swindle. But even when this is the case, the opposition is generally aided by one or more of the boodling Aldermen who oppose the ordinance with a view of putting up their price.

This maneuver is very familiar in the City Council. It is discounted by the manager of the ring, who knows the price of his boys as well as the farmer knows the price of his hogs. Sometimes, however, the recalcitrants are formidable enough to endanger the passage of the ordinance, especially if the Mayor vetoes it and the requisite two-thirds majority is required to pass it over his veto. Then it is necessary that the boss "should be seen," with the usual result. Aldermen will reverse their votes with the most extraordinary facility, and this occurence is so familiar as hardly to call for a passing comment. A story is told of a very well known boodler in the town, who was at that time a member of the City Council, and is now an aspirant for a federal office. A railroad corporation was endeavoring to secure a franchise to give it the right of way into the heart of the city. The Alderman in question had not been offered, so the story runs, so much for his vote as he deemed it worth. He made an eloquent and impassioned speech against the tyranny of the railroad corporation, dwelt upon the devastation which it would make coming into the city, and he voted against the ordinance. The ordinance was passed, however, and vetoed by the Mayor. It was therefore necessary to secure the necessary two-thirds majority. The gentleman in question was to all appearances unshaken in his opposition. He had previously intimated to the ring that they would have to pay him his price or he would vote to sustain the Mayor's veto. As they made no sign before the debate opened, he took part in it and began a denunciation of the railroad company and expressed his strong determination to defend the rights of the people. While he was speaking the chief of the ring laid an envelope before him, on the corner of which was written "$1,000." Hastily thrusting it into his breast pocket he continued his speech, when suddenly, to the great amusement of those who were in the secret, he wound up with the declaration that, notwithstanding his detestation of railroad tyranny, and his reluctance to see the streets interfered with, still, under the present circumstances, seeing the great advantages which would accrue from having another depot in the center of the city, he would vote for the ordinance which he had previously opposed. The ordinance was passed and the Alderman was warmly congratulated by his new allies upon his conversion. When the Council broke up they crowded him so that he did not have a chance of examining his $1,000. When he returned home that night he said complacently to his wife, as he produced the envelope from his pocket, "See, dear, I have made $1,000 this day," and handed her the envelope. She opened it and found a $100 bill! The Alderman was sold. His vote was recorded and the ordinance was passed and the boodler was boodled. But as a rule, unless an Alderman plays very fast and loose, he is dealt with on the square.

Of course every boodler swears that he has never touched boodle and as a matter of fact boodle is seldom distributed until after the campaign is over. It would never do for any Alderman to so far compromise his conscience as to give a corrupt vote in the Council. In most instances the Aldermen have never fingered a red cent on account of the ordinance for which they have voted. It is only after the ordinance has been passed and the stolen goods duly placed in the hands of the receivers that the division of the boodle takes place. The degree of secrecy which is observed in distributing their respective shares depends upon the degree of caution on the part of the boys or the amount of fuss there has been in the papers.* As a rule the distribution is managed with discretion. The stipulated sum is sometimes placed in blank envelopes addressed to the Aldermen in an unknown handwriting, who find them in some mysterious way in the pockets of their overcoats. In some instances, notably one in which a late mayor was said to have been involved, the money was said to have been placed under the pillow, for the virtuous man refused even to touch it—at least until his visitors had left the room. By this means the needs of the Aldermen are satisfied, their consciences escape any pangs of remorse and there is no legal evidence of money having passed.

---

*In the distribution, the men are graded on a ratio of "one," "one and a half" and "two." The man who handles the funds and the bright gentlemen who indulge in the "con" talk would get $2,000 each. Another half-dozen or so would get $1,500 each and the price of a plain, untrimmed vote would be $1,000.

The fact that money does pass is not disputed even by the Aldermen themselves. There are some members of the Council who are professional Aldermen, that is to say, they have no other profession except that of being an Alderman. They certainly do not live on the three dollars a sitting which is paid them for their loss of time. Aldermen of the city of Chicago have some special privileges which are denied to meaner mortals. On the production of their aldermanic star they are allowed to ride as dead heads on the street railways and enjoy all the conveniences of locomotion which have been secured by the corporations by the votes of themselves or their predecessors. They have also free entrance to all places of amusement, a privilege which they share with police-men and other servants of the public, but none of these recognized and legitimate privileges can explain the sustenance of a full bodied Alderman and his mainten-ance in style befitting a city father on three dollars a week. Where the money comes from is not known. It is not well to ask too many impertinent questions, but that it comes from somewhere and somebody may be taken for granted. " In a fruitful year," says the *Rec-ord*, " the average crooked Alderman has made $15,000 to $20,000."

The precise number of boodlers in the City Council is a question upon which there is often much discussion. A lawyer of a railway corporation, speaking on the sub-ject the other day, said, " There are sixty-eight Aldermen in the City Council and sixty-six of them can be bought. This I know because I have bought them myself." This was probably a little exaggerated bluff on his part. No other authorities put the percentage of non-boodling Al-dermen so low as this. I have gone through the list of the Aldermen repeatedly, with leading citizens, both in-side the Council and outside, journalists, ministers and men of business. The highest estimate of non-boodlers that I have heard was eighteen out of sixty-eight. Be-tween the minimum of two and the maximum of eighteen it will probably be safe to strike an average. We shall probably not err on the side of charity if we admit that there are ten Aldermen on the Council who have not sold their votes or received any corrupt consideration for voting away the patrimony of the people.

Ten righteous men would have saved Sodom ; but ten righteous Aldermen out of sixty-eight are not sufficient to save the City Hall from the reproach of being under the dominion of King Boodle. This is the abomination which maketh desolate set up in the Holy of Holies, for the City Council is the machinery through which the Kingdom of God should be established in Chicago. It is the agency by which, if at all, progress will be made towards a happier and juster social state. The City Council is the direct heir and executor of the Christian church, and holds in trust many of the great Christian duties which in the earlier ages were exclusively performed by the Church. Yet here in this innermost Temple of the Lord we have this supreme infamy — swindlers and scoundrels sitting in the center of the whole machine and treating their duties and their trust as means by which they can fill their own pockets. Since Antiochus Epiphanes slaughtered a sow on the Mercy Seat in the Holy of Holies there has seldom been a more authentic fulfillment of the prophecy which speaks of the abomination which maketh desolate being set up where it ought not to be.

These boodling Alderman are indeed the swine of our civilization, but unfortunately there is no Antiochus to offer them up as a sacrifice to the offended gods.* It is a constant amazement to me that secrets which are in the possession of at least fifty mortals, most of whom

*The *Chicago Herald* is the leading Democratic paper in Chicago. This is hcw it describes the Democratic Aldermen of the existing Council:
" The average Democratic representative in the City Council is a tramp, if not worse. He represents or claims to represent a political party having respectable principles and leaders of known good character and ability. He comes from twenty-five or thirty different wards, some of them widely separated, and when he reaches the City Hall, whether from the west, the south or the north division, he is in nine cases out of ten a bummer and a disreputable who can be bought and sold as hogs are bought and sold at the stockyards. Do these vicious vagabonds stand for the decency and intelligence of the Democratic party in Chicago ? "

are married and many of whom are given to their cups, should continue to be secrets, or that such a system of organized plunder can go on, without any authentic legal proof being attainable.   To unearth such scandals, to bring them to light, to clear out the Augean stable of the City Hall seems to be an enterprise peculiarly inviting to the indomitable genius of an American newspaper.   Unfortunately, whether it be, as I am frequently assured, because there are so many in it whom the newspapers dare not offend, or because of simple lethargy of conscience and indifference to the welfare of the town, which seems hardly less credible, or to some other cause, there is no doubt as to the fact. Every newspaper man in Chicago will tell you first that the system of government by boodle is going on all the time and in the same breath he will tell you that no newspaper has ever been able, excepting on one occasion, to secure legal evidence as to the actual passage of money.

For the purpose of uncovering frauds which cost the city millions, it ought not to be impossible to purchase the confession of a boodler.   Boodlers, according to the dealers in boodle, are divided into two categories, the honest and the dishonest boodlers.   The honest boodler is the Alderman who, when bought, "stays bought," and does not sell out to the other side ; the dishonest boodler is perfectly willing to take money from both sides and dispose of his vote, not according to the first bid, but the last.   Among these dishonest boodlers who are for sale all the time, it ought not to be impossible to make a deal for a squeal, although the price might run high.   Then again public-spirited citizens at the coming elections might find a much worse use for their money than to spend it in securing the election of an experienced detective to the aldermanic chair, with a mandate to take care to be in everything that was going, with a view to a timely exposure of the secrets of the gang. If such a competent representative did his work well, he would probably not have much difficulty in landing forty or fifty of his fellow members in the penitentiary at the end of the first twelve months.

Discussing this question with a leading editor in Chicago, after he had put forward the usual futile pleas as to the difficulties of getting evidence, I suggested to him that nothing was easier than to obtain evidence as to the identity of the boodlers. All that it was necessary for him to do was to apply to the Council for a franchise, and he would soon be approached by the guilty parties. At present it might be somewhat difficult, owing to the fuss which has been made on the subject, but last year there would have been no difficulty whatever; for the boodling was carried on with such comparative recklessness that there would have been little or no difficulty in landing the boodlers.

A gentleman who had applied to the Council for a franchise a short time ago and who had met with no success because he would not part with the needful, told me that he had been approached by an Alderman who intimated to him that he was the center of a group of ten who acted together in the Council, and he was able to communicate with another Alderman, whom he named, who was the head of a ring of forty and who could be got at, with the whole of his men, on the same terms that the Alderman and his ten were willing to dispose of their votes. The price, which he stated with business-like directness, was $1,000 each, with probably an extra $1,000 for the Alderman who arranged the business. My informant said that he had taken no steps to carry the matter further, inasmuch as he was determined not to bribe.

"But," said I, "why don't you carry it a step further, and obtain legal evidence as to the identity of the Aldermen? Get two or three persons if need be behind a screen or in a closet, who will be able to hear the whole of the conversation and who can confirm your testimony."

"All very fine," said he, "and what would become of any hope of my getting a franchise hereafter? I might, no doubt, as you say, convict one boodler, possibly two. Even if I had the whole of the witnesses' statements taken down and sworn before a justice of the peace, even if they had furnished me with the lists of the forty and ten for whom I had to provide $1,000 each, that would not be legal evidence against anyone but the two persons with whom I had business. I might get two men sent to Joliet, but forty-eight men would remain in the Council, every one of whom would regard it as a personal question to refuse me my franchise if I wanted it. Even if half of them were rejected at the coming elections, the rest would still regard me with implacable hatred. A boodler never forgives a man who has shown up a brother.boodler. You cannot expect me to do anything in the matter unless I am prepared to give up all hope of getting a franchise, or unless you reformers, on your part, would undertake to clear out the whole boodling gang from the City Hall. As for me I shall lie low and say nothing."

That conversation brings out very clearly the difficulty of obtaining evidence from the people who are approached. It is equally obvious that those who are receiving bribes are not likely to give evidence against themselves. Therefore, if anything has to be done, a detective Alderman should be elected, or a dishonest one should be bought up, or someone should promote a franchise for the express purpose of being approached. One of these methods would suffice to let daylight in upon this particularly discreditable section of Satan's invisible world displayed. If one or other of these methods are not adopted, boodling is likely to remain the chief motive power of the City Council of Chicago.

CHAPTER II.

The first impression which a stranger receives on arriving in Chicago is that of the dirt, the danger and the inconvenience of the streets. Those accustomed to the care that is taken in civilized cities to keep the roadway level and safe for teams and carriages stand simply aghast at the way in which the thoroughfares are corduroyed by ill-laid, old-fashioned street car lines, the flange of which projects so much above the body of the rail on which the traffic runs as to be perpetually wrenching wheels off the axle. The civilized man marvels and keeps on his way. But from marvel he passes rapidly to disgust and indignation when he comes to the steam railroad tracks. Here indeed is the climax of reckless incompetence in city management, the supreme example of the sacrifice of public safety, public property and public convenience to the interests of great corporations. The Pope has always clung to the title of Pontifex Maximus, but Chicago seems rather to aspire to be known as Pontifex Minimus. For instead of bridging her railroads or making them bridge her streets she has avoided bridge making wherever possible and allowed the railroads to run along and across the public thoroughfares of a crowded city at the street level.

If a stranger's first impression of Chicago is that of the barbarous gridironed streets, his second is that of the multitude of mutilated people whom he meets on crutches. Excepting immediately after a great war, I have never seen so many mutilated fragments of humanity as one finds in Chicago. Dealers in artificial limbs and crutches ought to be able to do a better

business in Chicago than in any other city I have ever
visited. On inquiry I found that the second salient
feature of Chicago was the direct result of the first.
The railroads which cross the city at the level in
every direction, although limited by statute and ordinance as to speed, constantly mow down unoffending
citizens at the crossings, and those legless, armless men
and women whom you meet on the streets are merely
the mangled remnant of the massacre that is constantly
going on year in and year out.

"Can nothing be done?" you ask in amazement, and
you are told that the Mayor is trying to do something
but that it is very doubtful if he can succeed, the railroad corporations are so powerful. "But what about
these infamous street car tracks with their murderous
flanges? Can nothing be done to substitute more civilized tracks?" Another shake of the head, a shrug of
the shoulders. "Ask Baron Yerkes! He owns Chicago." So you go from one to another and always meet
the same despondent, hopeless reply. Everywhere it is
the same story. The corporations have grabbed or
stolen everything. The citizens have not even a miserable revenue from the franchises which gave the corporations their power. They have barely a right-of-way
in their own streets. It did not begin all at once, this
usurpation, but now it is complete.

It is the old story of the Arab and the Camel. That
camel was the ancient prototype of the modern American corporation. The citizens are crowded to the wall
by the corporations which they permitted to occupy their
streets. If the citizens don't like it they can quit.

The novelty, the wonder of all this is bewildering to
an Englishman. His old ideas about the sovereignty of
the American citizen, the free and independent way in
which the denizens of the great Western Republic
were believed to vindicate their rights, the traditions of
liberty associated with the American people, all combine
to obscure the truth. He cannot believe that things

are as bad as every one he meets tells him they are.
Even after many disillusions he clings to the fond
delusion that he is sojourning among a free and self-
governed people where the rule, "of the people, for
the people and by the people," is universally recognized.
It is only after a long time that he begins dimly to discover that upon the ruins of popular liberty and republican theories there has been established a plutocratic
despotism as sordid, as tyrannical and as lawless as ever
was permitted to scourge a people for its sins.

I have watched the rapid evolution of Social Democracy
in England. I have studied Autocracy in Russia, and Theocracy in Rome, and I must say that nowhere, not even
in Russia, in the first years of the reaction occasioned by
the murder of the late Tzar, have I struck more abject
submission to a more soulless despotism than that which
prevails among the masses of the so-called free American
citizens, when they are face to face with the omnipotent
power of the corporations. "Wealth," said a workman
bitterly to me the other day, "has subjugated everything.
It has gagged the press, it has bought up the Legislature,
it has corrupted the judges. Even on the universities it is
laying its golden finger. The churches are in its grasp.
Go where you will, up and down this country, you will
find our citizens paralyzed by a sense of their own
impotence. They know the injustice, they know
better than any the wrongs which they suffer, they mutter
curses, but they are too cowed to do anything. They
have tried so often and have been beaten so badly they
have not the heart to try again."

What this man said, I have been hearing on every side,
in all classes of society. There is the most helpless hope-
lessness, utterly strange to me. The Russian peasant,
suffering under a corrupt tchinovnik, who bows his head
with the fatalism of his race, does not submit more ab-
jectly to illegal exactions than the American citizen
to the endless tyrannies of his plutocratic task-masters.
The Russian peasant at least has faith in God and in the

Tzar, and though, as he says, "Heaven is high and the Tzar is far off, still who knows but that some day the wicked tchinovnik may meet his deserts?" But the American, if he is religious, does not think the affairs of this world interests the Divine Being who is chiefly concerned with chants and prayers and sermons; and if he is irreligious, he does not think of God at all. As for the Tzar, there is no Tzar; the only substitute on this side of the Atlantic for such a deliverer is the far-off, semi-mythical conception of arousing of public opinion. "If public opinion were aroused," say some more sanguine citizens, "something might be done." "When or how?" sneer the pessimists. " You forget that the country is not governed by the opinion of its citizens, lawfully expressed at the ballot box. It is controlled by the Dead Hand. Read our Constitution and the Constitution of our State, and see how cunningly the money power is intrenched behind constitutional battlements. Think you that in a country where it is unconstitutional even to pass a truck act to save workmen from being plundered by their employers, you can do anything? If you carry your reformers at next elections, the corporations will buy them up. If by some miracle they proved incorruptible, their legislation could be declared unconstitutional by the courts. And if you want to amend the Constitution, you have a very long row to hoe."

The root of the whole trouble is lack of faith in God. If there be no God, or if He does not heed such trivialities as mundane affairs, if there be no law, invisible but eternal, which is the silent but secret ally of every forlorn fighter for justice and for liberty, then it is not surprising that·men's hearts fail them for fear and they refuse to rouse them for the fray.

The citizens have acted each man of them upon the principle of "each for himself and the devil take the hindmost." They have made their fortunes if lucky, or they have failed if they were unlucky, but the devil has taken among other hindmost things the government of the city. Instead of seeing to it that the authorities were just men, upright, fearing God and hating covetousness, they left the worst elements in the community to convert the city government into a joint stock corporation for the spoliation of the people and the promotion of perjury, corruption and all unrighteousness. And now, having accepted Cain's gospel and lived up to it, they are reaping the consequences.

The more I look into the operations of the laws which have reduced the city of Chicago to this present unendurable position face to face with the spoiler in the streets, the more I am reminded of the old familiar story of the fate of the Children of Israel after they had established themselves and had waxed fat and comfortable in the Land of Promise. As it was then, when the hosts of Moab and of Midian and of the Mesopotamians fell upon the chosen people and smote them and spoiled them, so it is to-day in the city of Chicago.

Just before the French Revolution, Gibbon, on concluding his history of the Decline and Fall of the Roman Empire, complacently congratulated civilization upon the fact that there were no longer any hordes of barbarians on its frontiers who might repeat the havoc of Attila the Hun, or Alaric the Goth. But a few years passed and the Reign of Terror proved that civilization could breed her own savages within her own frontiers, and that in the slums of her capitals were hordes as capable of devastating the land as any of the hosts that followed Attila to the sack of Rome. The American Republic, in like manner, although too strong to be in any danger from without, is now learning that democracies can breed tyrants and that the conquerors of old who overran empires for the sake of plunder, and impoverished whole nations to fill their treasuries, have their legitimate heirs and successors in the coalesced plutocracy of the United States.

Chicago is as much under the rule of the Assyrian as were the Jews in olden time. Only our Assyrians seem to come not from the Euphrates Valley, but from Philadelphia. It is a great mistake to imagine that the Assyrian or any other Eastern conqueror established the minute despotism of the modern state. What these ancients wanted was not so much to interfere with the liberties of their subjects as to plunder them and to deal with them as they pleased. They killed a few, not more than they wished to, the rest they spared to earn the tribute money. Their interests were solely selfish. They left like the Turk of this day the local tribal or national organization, almost uninjured. All that they wanted was plunder, and in collecting that plunder they were as indifferent to the comfort and life and convenience of their luckless subjects as any street railway company or railroad corporation or gas trust in the whole United States.

As the Assyrian crushed Israel as the direct result of the misgovernment of the country and the indifference of its rulers to the welfare of the poor among the people, so the present plight of the citizens of Chicago is the direct result of their past indifference to honesty and justice in their elected representatives Hence it is that Isaiah's words apply almost without an alteration to the present situation:

1. Wo unto them that decree unrighteous decrees, and that write grievousness which they have prescribed ;

2. To turn aside the needy from judgment, and to take away the right from the poor of my people, that widows may be their prey, and that they may rob the fatherless!

3. And what will ye do in the day of visitation, and in the desolation which shall come from far? to whom will ye flee for help? and where will ye leave your glory?

4. Without me they shall bow down under the prisoners, and they shall fall under the slain. For all this his anger is not turned away, but his hand is stretched out still.

5. O Assyrian, the rod of mine anger, and the staff in their hand is mine indignation.

6. I will send him against a hypocritical nation, and against the people of my wrath will I give him a charge, to take the spoil, and to take the prey, and to tread them down like the mire of the streets.

That, at least, it must be admitted, is exactly what our Assyrian has done and is doing. He takes the spoil, he takes the prey and he treads us down like the mire of the streets.

To those who have never visited Chicago, and to many who have grown up and become accustomed to the condition of things as they exist, the comparison between the great corporations and the Assyrian who oppressed the children of Israel may seem rhetorical or far-fetched. But anyone who will take the trouble to look into the facts will see that the comparison is strictly just, and after due allowance is made for the fervor and vivid imagery of the Jewish seer, no language can more exactly express what the corporationss are doing in Chicago than the verses in which he addresses the Assyrian.

Chicago has not yet a patron saint. Considering the intense feverish restlessness which characterizes the city, an unkind wag suggested that St. Vitus, of St. Vitus' dance, would be the most appropriate selection. Those, however, who take a bird's-eye view of the city, looking down on it, say, for instance, from the Auditorium tower, would have no hesitation in deciding that Chicago is the living prototype of St. Lawrence, who was stretched upon a gridiron and whose torture is one of the familiar horrors of Catholic picture galleries. This great city with a million and a half of population is stretched over a gridiron of rails which cross and recross the city and form a complex network of tracks, every mesh of which is stained with human blood. It is not for nothing that the dismal bell of the locomotive rings incessantly as it tears its way into the heart of Chicago through the streets. In England the locomotives use the whistle, not the bell, and this solemn weird tolling of the bell is very impressing to the imagination of the visitor who hears it for the first time sounding every hour, year in, year out, summer and winter. As regularly as the sun rises these great engines slay their man in and upon the streets of Chicago. No other great city in the world has allowed its streets to be taken possession of to a similar extent, and the massacre resulting there-

from is greater than that of many battles.   We in England have always one or more little wars upon our hands on
our frontiers where they impinge upon the lawless tribes
in Africa and Asia, but I do not think that it is too much
to say that in the last five years we have had fewer soldiers
killed in our wars all round the world than have been
slaughtered in the streets of Chicago at the grade crossing.   The figures are: in 1889, 257; 1890, 294; 1891, 323;
1892, 394; 1893, 431.   As might be expected, the number of these railroad murders steadily increases with the
growth of the population.   In the city of Chicago there
are under 2,500 miles of roadway, but there are 1,375
miles of railroad track within the same area.   The railroads traverse the streets at grade in 2,000 places.   Under Mayor Washburne a commission was appointed to
investigate the matter, and an effort was made to ascertain the obstruction to traffic caused by this system.   Mr.
E. S. Dreyer, speaking at the Sunset Club, where the subject was discussed on February 1, said :

> Our terminal commission caused to be taken, by careful enumera-
> tors, a count at thirty-six of our most dangerous crossings on a certain
> business day, from the hour of six in the morning to seven in the even-
> ing, and their report showed that there passed during that time over the
> thirty-six crossings 68,375 vehicles, 9,145 street cars, 221,942 street car
> passengers and 119,181 pedestrians.   The gates at these crossings were
> lowered 3,031 times, and the total time the gates were closed on the
> thirty-six crossings was over twelve hours, delaying 15,000 vehicles,
> 2,320 street cars with 51,367 passengers and 18,212 pedestrians.

These figures, be it noted, have only regard to thirty-
six of the 3,000 crossings in the city   For years past
the city has protested, but protested in vain.   The railroads ride roughshod over the convenience, the rights and
the lives of the citizens.   Sisera with his 900 chariots
of iron never tyrannized more ruthlessly over the
Hebrews than the railroads with their fire chariots of
steel have lorded it over the city of Chicago.

Every week in Chicago you read of grade crossing acci-
dents, and it is very seldom that you hear of anything
being done to saddle anyone with the responsibility for
the loss of life.   The evidence before the jury is usually to

the following effect; the gates were not lowered, the watchman was not in attendance, no whistle was sounded, no bell was rung. The deceased was crossing the track all unwitting of any danger, when a train dashed up with the inevitable result. In many cases the bodies are mutilated out of all human semblance. The nightmare imagination of those gruesome artists who exult in describing the torture and mutilation of helpless victims could depict nothing more terrible than the human sacrifices which are offered up daily on the altar of the Railway Moloch by the city of Chicago. Very rarely is anyone saddled with responsibility. On February 2 a jury returned a verdict against one of the division superintendents of the Chicago, Rock Island and Pacific Railroad, but nothing seems to have come of it. The only redress is to prosecute the railroad company for damages. This often involves a law suit with the casualty companies with whom the railways have contracted for all liabilities for injury to life and limb. The railraods have taken the precaution of protecting themselves by law. By an infamous act, boodled through the Illinois Legislature by railroad influence, no jury is allowed to award more than $5,000 damages against the railroads for causing the death of any citizen.

The usurpation of the streets of the city is none the less a usurpation because it was achieved by gold and not by steel. In many cases railroads have laid their tracks through the streets without even going through the formality of asking for a franchise. They have treated Chicago as a conquered territory. The strolling Tartar, who in the Middle Ages wandered absolute lord over Russia, was the prototype of the railroad corporations in the capital of the West. For the use of the streets the railroads have not paid a cent into the City Treasury. Whatever payment they made was made corruptly and went into the pockets of the Aldermen, and sometimes of the Mayor. If they paid $100 a mile for way-leave that would bring in the city a revenue of nearly $200,000. So far from doing any such thing, the railroads have imposed upon the city an expenditure which is estimated at $30,000 in the salaries of twenty-five policemen and other employes, paid by the city for the purpose of raising and lowering the gates and of warning citizens to escape slaughter. Further, they have put the city to the expense of millions in the building of viaducts over their tracks where the expenditure of life became too great even for Chicago to tolerate. In 1892 the cost of maintaining these viaducts was no less than $146,000. For the privilege therefore of keeping the annual total of human sacrifices down to a victim a day the city pays blood money amounting to $176,000 a year.

But, it may be urged, the city has in its own hands the power of taxation and it can recoup itself from the enormously valuable property within its limits. Here again we are confronted with another specimen of the way in which the citizen goes to the wall. Mr. Washburne, when Mayor of Chicago, stated publicly that the value of railway property in the city was not less than $350,000,000. It is to-day assessed at less than $19,000,000.

The steam railroads are the worst oppressors from the point of view of human life, but from the point of view of plunder and of injury to health and happiness the street railways leave them far behind. In a city like Chicago, where the distances are so great as constantly to occasion the regret that the building of the city had not been postponed until the race had developed wings, street railways are as indispensable as the streets, and they should no more be handed over to speculative corporations than the highroads. From the practical point of view it is pretty much the same thing, for the owner of the street railway has not only the railway but has also the street. He breaks up the driveway and treats the road as though it belonged to him. The arguments against municipal ownership of street railways would have more force if the speculative corporations who are in possession of the monopoly of streets

could be kept up to mark by competition. In the necessity of things this cannot be.   The street railway is a
monopoly, and a monopoly of service for the whole
people should be in the hands of the representatives
of the whole people.   The usual result has followed in
Chicago.   There is nothing about which there is more
clamor than about the infamies of street railways.

The overcrowding of the cars is little less than a public
scandal.   The city railway companies have plenty of cars,
and plenty of power, for the cables run just the same
whether there are few cars on the line or many, but in
order to save conductors' salaries they cynically compel
one-half of the traveling public of Chicago to travel
without seats.   A Chicago car at the rush time, in the
middle of the day or early in the morning or late at night,
is a sight which once seen is not easily forgotten.   Every
seat is filled and all the space between the seats is choked
with a crowded mass of humanity.   The unlucky individuals are holding on by a strap from the roof.   At the
platform at each end of the car a crowd is hanging on by
its eyelids as thick as bees when they are swarming.
The first time I saw it, it reminded me of one of Doré's
pictures of a scene in Dante's hell.   When appealed to
to give better accommodation those companies which are
paying from 9 to 24 per cent reply that their dividends
come from the people who hang on by the straps, and that
things are to remain as they are.   The cable service, especially on the North Side, is perpetually breaking down,
the horse cars are miserably slow, badly horsed and most
inadequate.   It was quite recently that the tyrants of the
car scouted the idea of heating them in winter time and
compelled their luckless travelers to shiver for an hour
at a time in unwarmed vehicles.   The rails are laid in
such a fashion that they provoke the incredulous comments of a stranger, and some of the busiest roadways of
the town are crossed and recrossed by a corduroy of steel
inconceivable to anyone who has ever lived in a civilized
country.   When the snow comes the companies simply

sweep it to either side of the track ; and notwithstand
ing the city ordinances compelling them to remove the
snow, they leave it lying on the streets with the result
that this winter the indignant citizens retaliated by piling the snow over the tracks and stopping traffic. Scrim-
ages ensued which threatened on more than one occasion to end in serious riots.   Even if they could not run
more cars, the South Side cable could follow the universal
custom of the Old World and carry passengers on the
roof, where in five days out of six it is much pleasanter
than the inside.   Mr. Pullman has devised an admirable
double-deck car, but as its adoption would require the
changing of the rolling stock that is not to be thought of ;
for nothing is bad enough for those who use the street
cars in Chicago so long as it does not fall to pieces on
the line of track.   And this right to compel the citizens
to endure all these costs and exactions was obtained by
bribery of the most barefaced kind.

It is not only the surfaces of the streets which were
handed over to the street railway companies by boodling
Aldermen.   They are in possession at the present moment
of two tunnels under the river, both of which have been
handed over to them without any adequate return.   The
Washington tunnel, which it would have cost the companies thousands to build, was given them on condition
that they moved the Madison street bridge to Washington.   This cost them a bagatelle.   A similar preposter-
ous agreement handed over the La Salle tunnel to Mr.
Yerkes' company on the North Side.   Two bridges were
put up, at Clark Street and Wells Street, which cost the
company about one-tenth one-fifth of what the tunnel cost
the city, and much less than what it would have cost the
company to construct the tunnel at the time they took
it over. The city was plundered in the matter of the tunnels to the extent of at least one million dollars and it
would have cost the railway corporations twice as much
again to have built the tunnels themselves.*

The financial result of these privileges would make the

mouth of a Turkish Pasha water. The following are the figures :

	Capital.	Dividend.	Net earnings after pay- ing interest on bonds. 1894.	Paid to the City.
North Chicago....	$ 8,000,000	11½	$1,600,000	22,687
West Chicago.....	10,000,000	9	2,340,000	20,874
City of Chicago...	....	24	8,500,000	11,811

Five or six years ago the street railway companies secured by the usual means an extension of their franchises for another fifteen years ; the net result of which is that they will continue to enjoy the undisputed monopoly which brings them in these enormous dividends until 1904. If the franchises, instead of being renewed six years ago, had been allowed to lapse, as they would have done about the present time, it would have been possible for the city to have possessed itself of the car lines upon terms which would have been equitable to the company and would have yielded the city a net annual income of at least four million dollars. That is to say that the city has been robbed by its corrupt Aldermen of nearly twice as much as the total sum raised every year by the pew rents, collections and by all the machinery of church finance. Or to put it another way, the tax upon real and personal property in the city of Chicago does not amount to more than $4,800,000 a year. Almost the whole of this sum might have been raised by the city railway corporations in the hands of an honest City Council. †

*See an admirable article in the *Chicago Tribune*, April 4, 1892, on this subject. It is reprinted in a most useful pamphlet by Barton A. Alrich, entitled, "How Should Chicago be Governed?"

†On this point I may quote the published statement of Mr. W. J. Onahan, who for two years was Comptroller of the City Treasury. Mr. Onahan says:

"If the city, since it became a city, had received proper annual compensation for all the franchises that have been ignorantly and corruptly disposed of for nothing, Chicago would today have income enough to run its affairs without levying a dollar taxation on real estate or personal property. I can prove it if called upon. Consider the privileges that have been given the steam railways from the Illinois Central to the last to come in. In connection with these steam railways look at the countless private switches and tracks—all given away. Then the street railways, the gas companies, the electric lighting companies, the telephone companies, the water privileges, dock privileges, and I don't know what all. Why, every one of these favored interests, which secured their privileges by bribing Aldermen and corrupting officials, ought to be millions in annual tribute to the city. I repeat that if our rights in this regard had been looked after in the beginning and been carefully guarded ever since, there would be no need now to talk about taxes or their injustices and inequalities."

Instead of this sum the city railway companies pay over to the city a license tax amounting last year to $50,000. Even here there is a swindle into which Mayor Hopkins is making diligent inquiries. The companies pay a tax of $50 a year upon the cars in service. But no car is held to be in service by the companies unless it makes thirteen round trips every day. As half the cars do not make thirteen round trips a day, they do not pay the license, and the city loses $50,000 a year in consequence.

The total capital of the street railway companies, as shown by latest published account, is only $26,500,000. If all the working expenses were unchanged and the company received five per cent upon its stock, this would still leave a balance available to the city of $4,000,000, the sum which the Assyrians levy upon the citizens of Chicago.*

The third of the oppressors under whose tyranny Chicago is groaning is the Gas Trust. To begin with, there ought not to be any gas trust in Chicago. By the law of the State of Illinois, trusts are illegal, and have no legal rights. The seven companies, however, who form the Trust, keep their accounts separate, and swear that they are no trust—for subterfuge and trickery are among the weapons of the oppressor in every age. Among the other limitations of the prerogatives of the city of Chicago it is not allowed to own or operate its own gas plant. It has therefore tried to get cheap gas by encouraging competition. Franchises were granted to various corporations, but they always amalgamated and combined in order to plunder the

---

*The fact is that in a city like Chicago a street railway franchise is worth more than most gold mines, and if a good bargain is made the cars will not only carry the citizens, they could also carry the cost of governing the city. Take for instance the case of Philadelphia. Ten Street Car Companies in ten years, ending 1891, on a paid up capital of $5,840,000, drew out in dividends $15,000,000, an average of 26 per cent. The market price of their stock in February, 1893, was $38,500,000. If the city of Philadelphia had invested the original capital on behalf of the citizens had charged 5 per cent interest and had applied the balance to the city treasury, it would have made an annual profit of $1,200,000 plus an actual investment in the value of the property amounting to $3,250,000 a year. Philadelphia therefore lost nearly $4,500,000 a year because the city did not run the street cars.

public for the benefit of the share-holders. Instead of being a check on each other, they are now all united in maintaining their monopoly. They stayed prosecution by virtue of an illegal agreement executed under the Washburne administration, by which they were able to purchase the acquiescence of the city in their illegal position, in consideration of a reduction which has brought the price of gas down to $1.15 per thousand, and secured to the city three and a half per cent of its gross income which amounted in 1891 to $150,000. Before the companies amalgamated Chicago paid $1.00 per thousand feet. After the amalgamation the price was raised immediately to $1.25, from which it is to be reduced each year at the rate of five cents until it reaches the old level of a dollar. As the cost of manufacture is not more than 33 cents per thousand feet, and the cost of distribution, leakage, etc., does not exceed 33 cents, which is a very liberal allowance, that leaves at present prices fifty cents available for profits and dividends. Before the Gas Trust the Gas Light and Coke Company, using the old processes, could not manufacture the gas at less than 65 cents per thousand feet, but it was nevertheless able to sell it at a dollar a thousand feet, and pay a dividend of seven per cent on its capital stock, besides putting an additional two per cent into an expansion fund. By the introduction of water gas and new and improved processes of manufacture, the cost of production was cut in half, the figures for the last year on the North Side being 30.13 cents, and on the South Side 29.16 cents. Thus the immediate result of the illegal monopoly formed by the combination of the seven gas companies has been to raise the price of gas to the consumer at the very time when the cost of its production was reduced fifty per cent to the producer. In order to profit by this the Gas Trust has watered its stock to an extent almost inconceivable. According to the best authorities in the gas making business, there ought not to be a greater capital expenditure for every thousand feet of gas supplied than $3.00 but three years ago the capital of the Gas Trust was $10.65 per thousand feet. The process of inflating, or watering, or whatever the term is which implies the creation of fictitious capital value, has gone on apace since then, and it probably reaches now near $12 per thousand. The watered stock and outlying bonds mount up to between fifty and sixty million dollars. Now the whole of the city of Chicago could be supplied with gas, and a brand-new plant, at an expenditure, taking the present consumption of gas at four thousand million feet, at a capital expenditure of $12,000,000, interest upon which at five per cent would only be $600,000 a year. If you add $400,000 for a sinking fund, you would have a net charge of a million dollars a year as sufficient to pay interest upon capital, and extinguish the whole debt in twenty years; whereas the Gas Trust is at present distributing from two millions to two millions and a half in interests and dividends every year. A sum, therefore, between one million and one million and a half represents the enforced tribute extorted from the oppressed citizens by this illegal monopoly, under virtue of an illegal agreement made two years ago, in order to evade a law suit.

If the Gas Trust had supplied ideally pure gas, and if in every respect it ministered to the convenience of the consumer, the hatred with which it is regarded would be considerably modified, and it is probable that the citizens would not object to pay a dollar for their gas rather than face the inconvenience of tearing up their streets. But the consumers complain bitterly of the quality of the gas and of the rule by which the trust compels every consumer to deposit $10 before a meter is placed on the premises, only $7 of which is ever returned. By this means the trust obtains possession of a capital of at least a million dollars, and, what is much more serious, it practically shuts gas out from all the smaller householders, who might be willing to pay even $1.15 for their gas, but who are not able to put up $10 in advance. Besides this the Gas Trust is as arbitrary as any Persian Satrap in its dealings with the citizens. No matter how much the gas may be called for in various regions to which it has not yet laid its mains, it turns a deaf ear to all appeals. It has got a very good thing as it is and it does not see why it should trouble itself merely to please consumers, who, after all, are as the mire under its feet.

There is only one way out and that is for the city to own and operate its own gas plant. When that comes to pass the Gas Trust will be confronted with the alternative of handing over its mains and its meters at a fair valuation, which ought not in any case to exceed the sum for which the plant could be duplicated, or if it refused these terms, then the city would be obliged to bring it to terms by introducing municipal gas. This could be supplied at 75 cents per 1,000 feet. It would be a great nuisance tearing up the streets, a nuisance which should not be incurred excepting when the work was done by the municipality for the municipality. It might, however, be worth while doing it in order to rid the town of the garrote of the Gas Trust.

Compared with those great oppressors other minor monopolies hardly deserve notice, but it is worth while illustrating the tyranny of the Gas Trust by the interdict which it succeeded in placing upon the development of municipal lighting. At the present moment the municipality owns and operates its own electric light plant. This was permitted by the Legislature on the strict condition that no private consumers should be supplied by the municipality. The result is that the municipal plant is idle half its time. Even as it is the introduction of municipal electricity into the town enabled the city to reduce the cost of each arc lamp from $175 to $100 a year, and if the plant could be still further utilized that would be reduced still further by $25 per annum. That is the fine imposed upon the city by the

Gas Trust and other monopolies to check the legitimate development of municipal enterprise. For private illuminating purposes electricity is far too dear and the price would be cut at once if the municipality were allowed to use its engines, which are standing idle. So little does the Gas Trust care for the interests of the citizens that, instead of lighting the streets for nothing, as it might well be expected to do, it actually charges the city 25 per cent more for what is consumed in the street lamps than it charges the private consumer. The charge for street lamps is $25 a year, and this amounts to a charge of at least $1.42 per thousand feet as against $1.15 charged to the private consumer! Twenty-six cents a thousand feet is the extra charge levied upon the city for all the gas which it consumes. That is the gratitude of the Gas Trust for its franchise. It is a kind of Gessler's cap, the last crowning insult which exulting tyranny inflicts upon its victims.

Another monopoly which owes its existence to a franchise recklessly disposed of is the telephone company. This is in possession of the field. Its prices are fixed at an excessive rate, and in return for this privilege to plunder, it pays the municipality a peppercorn rent upon its net receipts. But as it publishes no accounts and gives no information, the municipality is obliged to take whatever the Company pleases to pay. This, however, will be looked into.

When once an honest Council is established at the City Hall it will be found a matter of comparative ease to check the tyranny of the Assyrian. That at least is my belief. At the same time I must admit that the opinion of the majority of those who have spoken to me on the subject is that it is hopeless. I have talked until I have been tired to one citizen after another and have received from them the most despondent and discouraging replies. "It is no use," they say, "do what you please, they will best you in the long run; there are too many in it to hope for any success," and so forth and so forth.   It is as if they were Christian Rayahs in a Turkish province and I was a Pan-Slavonic emissary endeavoring to rouse them to a struggle against the oppressor.

There is always the despairing shrug of the shoulder and the remark that it is no good putting a man up to be slaughtered.   The others are too strong.   Fortunately Mayor Hopkins does not seem to think so and behind Mayor Hopkins are the awakened intelligence and the aroused moral consciousness of the city.

It is no use pretending that these tyrants are so strong that they cannot be grappled with.   They have franchises, no doubt, and many legal privileges, and they are in possession; but a resolute Mayor backed up by an honest City Council could very soon bring them to their reason.   It is the old story of the Normans and the Jews.   The nobles after the Crusades were practically helpless in their hands.   Their estates were mortgaged and the astute money lender of those days had taken as much pains to complete the ruin of his victim as Mr. Yerkes, the corporations and the trusts have taken to secure their hold upon the vitals of Chicago.   At last the tyranny became intolerable.   The noble, being a practical man was indisposed, after fighting the infidel in the Holy Land, to submit calmly to the exactions of the Jew at home.   He replied to the protests of his creditor, who pointed to his bonds and his papers, by saying, " It is true, you have my bond, but I have got your person, your property and all that is yours." When the Jew did not at first appreciate the significance of this argument, the noble clapped him into his dungeon and used strong and piercing arguments in the shape of the extraction first of one eye-tooth and then of another until such time as he consented to be reasonable and make fair terms with his jailers.   Herein lies a hint for every city administration which lies prone beneath the heel of the oppressor.   The corporation may have franchises, but the right of enforcing new conditions lies in the hands of the City Council.   And, moreover, they can soon bring the corporations to reason if they insist that no further concessions under any conditions shall be granted to any existing railroad, street railroad or gas company until it has delivered the citizens from the present tyranny. No railroad ought, for instance, to be allowed to lay another rail within the limits of Chicago until it has undertaken to elevate the tracks. By imposing new conditions, or by the refusing of new franchises, the city has the game in its own hands. But besides this there are great resources dormant in the hands of the authorities in the shape of a searching inquiry into the provisions of the existing franchises, and an inquiry into the extent to which the corporations have already forfeited their rights by non-use or mis-use of the privileges intrusted to them. It will be found in almost every case that the corporations have trespassed without warrant upon the public domain. They have laid down two tracks where they had only received permission to lay one, they have laid down rails in streets for which they had obtained no permission at all, and they have failed to take any adequate precautions to make the streets safe for the people who have a right to use them.

The leading case which may be quoted in this connection is not to be found in the law books but it applies admirably nevertheless. It is to be found in the Merchant of Venice, where Shylock insists upon having his pound of flesh. " 'Tis so written in the bond ;" to the bond he has appealed, to the bond he must go. It would seem that already in Chicago a Daniel had come to judgment in the person of the Mayor.

CHAPTER III.

DIVES THE TAX DODGER.

If Christ came to Chicago and took any practical interest in the establishment of His Kingdom in the city, the assessment system would be radically reformed. This is not a question of politics or of administration or of finance. It is a question of elementary morality. For the assessment system is based on a lie. It is worked by perjury, and it has as its natural and necessary results injustice, corruption, and the plunder of the poor. Its continuance for another year would be a practical recognition of the devil's dominance and ascendancy in Chicago, which it is idle to attempt to counterbalance by such lip worship and devout genuflections as we blasphemously dignify by the name of Divine service in our churches.

A great deal has been written about assessment, but many good people in Chicago are still utterly unaware of what it means or how it is worked. Otherwise, it is impossible that in a city nominally Christian, which is studded with churches and littered with Bibles, such a supreme embodiment of fraud, falsehood and injustice could have been allowed to exist for a single hour. Therefore it may be that the best service I can render is to print in plain English the simple truth about the system and how it works.

The first remarkable feature about the assessment system of Chicago is that it puts a higher premium upon perjury than upon any other vice or virtue under heaven. The culture of perjury is not usually regarded as one of the legitimate objects of a civilized, to say nothing of a Christian, government. But in Chicago perjury may almost be regarded as a protected industry. Cer-

tainly there is a fuller reward offered to professional perjurers than to any other officials in the employ of the
city. It may perhaps be argued that the virtue of the
Chicago citizen is so austere that it is necessary to offer
abnormally high inducements to induce them to damn
their souls by perjury; but judging from the eager competition there is for the post of professional perjurer,
there would seem but little basis for this argument.
Whatever may be the cause, there is a heavier sum in
solid dollars pocketed every year by the official perjurers
in Chicago, than is paid to any other officials in the service of the city.

Perjury ought not to be so rewarded. When the Lord
cometh, it is written on the last page of the Old Testament Scripture He would " come near in judgment as a
swift witness against false swearers." "For I am the
Lord, I change not," was the message given through
the Hebrew prophet, and if He has not changed there
will be a very poor lookout for the Town Assessors of
the City of Chicago when they stand before Him to render
account. For each and all of the whole eleven of them are
false swearers. They perjure themselves habitually and
necessarily as a part of the system. As the calling of a
pirate is based upon the negation of the moral law concerning theft and murder, so the calling of an Assessor
presupposes the annulling of the condemnation which
the moral law pronounces upon the false oath. This is
a strong saying, but it is literally and exactly true and
is proved on the authority of the latest official document
issued by the Comptroller of the City of Chicago. Mr.
Ackerman, the Comptroller in question, in his report on
the system of assessments says:

There are now eleven Assessors, whose duty it is to assess values
in the South, West and North Divisions of the city and in the towns
of Lake View, Jefferson, Hyde Park, Calumet, Norwood Park, South
Chicago, Town of Lake, and Rogers Park. When they return their
books to the County Clerk they make oath that the book contains
a correct and full list of the real property subject to taxation in their
town, so far as they have been àble to ascertain the same, and that the
assessed value set down in the proper columns opposite the several

kinds and descriptions of property is in each case the fair cash value of such property to the best of their knowledge and belief (except as corrected by the Town Board).

The Assessors must, therefore, as a condition of their office, swear that the returns which they make in their official capacity are correct and full and that in each case they have set down the fair cash value of the property to the best of their knowledge and belief. Lest they should be liable to make any mistake as to what constitutes "the fair cash value" of the property they assess, it is expressly laid down by the Statutes of Illinois how that fair cash value is to be ascertained.

The Revenue Law of the State, Revised Statutes, Chap. 120, Sec. 4, page 1,266, in the rules for valuing real estate, provides:

1. That each tract of land or real property shall be valued at its fair cash value, estimated at the price it would bring at a fair voluntary sale.
2. Taxable leasehold estates shall be valued at such a price as they would bring at a fair voluntary sale for cash.
3. When a building or structure is located on the right of way of any canal, railroad or other company, leased or granted for a term of years to another, the same shall be valued at such a price as such building or structure and lease or grant would sell at a fair voluntary sale for cash.

There can be no possible loophole of escape for the Assessor. He must swear that he has made a full and correct return, that each item of property is assessed at its fair cash value and that he has estimated it at the price it would bring at a fair voluntary sale.

Now there is not one of the whole eleven Assessors, if they were put in a row and asked the question at the Day of Judgment, or even before a Grand Jury, who would deny that they each and all habitually make false oaths. They know they never make either full or correct returns, they never assess any item of property at its fair cash value, and they never estimate their assessments at the price the article assessed would bring at a fair voluntary sale. That this is so is obvious the moment the matter is looked into, whether we take the

totals of the realty and of personalty or whether we ex-
amine the details of particular assessments.

We will begin with the totals. The fact that Chicago
has grown enormously in population, in area and in
wealth in the last quarter of a century is one of the
most conspicuous and indisputable facts of contemporary
history. Its increase is one of the phenomena which
have attracted the attention of the whole world. Without going back farther than 1867, the following figures
will suffice to illustrate the way in which Chicago has
advanced by leaps and bounds to the proud position of
being on the eve of securing recognition as the Capital
of the New World.

	Area Square Miles.	Population.
1867	24	252,054
1873	36	367,396
1883	36	629,985
1893	180	1,438,010

No other city in the world has such a showing. But
when we turn to the returns of the assessments, duly
sworn by eleven different Assessors as a full and correct
statement of the price which the real and personal property owned by the citizens of this marvelously increasing
city, we are staggered by the discovery that Chicago
would, according to the oaths of these eleven responsible
officials, sell for less to-day than she would have brought
at a fair voluntary sale twenty years ago! Here are the
figures :

	Area Sq. Miles.	Population.	ASSESSED VALUE.		
			Realty.	Personalty.	Total.
1867	24	252,054	$141,445,920	$53,580,924	$195,026,844
1873	36	367,396	262,969,820	49,103,175	312,072,995
1883	36	629,985	101,596,787	31,633,717	133,230,504
1893	180	1,438,010	189,299,120	56,491,231	245,790,351

Therefore if we are to believe the Assessors, Chicago,
with close up on a million and a half inhabitants and
with 180 square miles of territory, would bring 66 millions dollars less if put up to auction and sold than
what the Chicago of 1873, with only 367,000 population

and 36 square miles of land, would have brought at a fair voluntary sale.   Such an astonishing shrinkage in value is even more amazing than the amazing growth of the population.

Let us look at it another way.   If we average it up we have the following remarkable results :

AVERAGE ASSESSED VALUE.

	Square Mile. (Million Dollars.)	Per Head. (Dollars.)
1867	8.1	774
1873	8.5	850
1883	3.6	211
1893	1.3	170

At this rate, in another twenty years Chicago would be stone broke, and couldn't be sold for a red cent.   Yet these figures are all official, and not one of them was inscribed on the returns except over the solemn oath of the Assessor.   In reality the value of property in Chicago would be underestimated at 2,000 million dollars.

The extraordinary thing about the unaccountable drop in the value of Chicago real estate is that all the data available for estimating the value of the property in the city points in exactly the opposite direction.   According to the statements of the Department of Public Works, there were 71,545 buildings erected in the city between 1883 and 1892, the estimated value of which was $316,-857,000.   But when we turn to the Assessors' statements, the addition of these 71,000 houses to the real estate of Chicago did not raise the total value of the assessment more than 88 millions of dollars, even if we exclude from consideration all other descriptions of realty.   Two and two do not seem to make four in the Assessors' office at Chicago ; for if you add 316 millions to 101 millions the result is 189 millions.   The comparison with other cities only brings out the same astonishing contrast all the more clearly.   For Chicago, while its assessed value has been shrinking, has not been increasing its debt.   It has a less assessed value than any great city except New Orleans, and it has a smaller debt per head than any city, barring none.

Statement showing the assessed value of real and personal estate for the last year and the population and debt of the leading cities of this country:

City.	Assessed Value.	Popula-tion.	Debt.	Valuation per Head.	Debt per Head.
New York...	$1,933,518,529	1,923,031	$100,762,407	$1000	$0.52
Brooklyn....	506,054,676	1,000,000	47,334,214	500	.21
Boston	924,134,300	500,000	33,720,111	1800	.67
*Philadelphia	769,930,542	1,046,964	29,065,845	750	.29
St. Louis	280,991,420	574,569	21,376,021	500	.37
Chicago	245,970,351	1,500,000	18,431,450	160	.12
New Orleans.	137,000,000	265,000	15,335,037	500	.60

So much for a comparison of the totals. Now let us look at the full and correct returns of property assessed on oath at actual and the fair selling price to the best of the knowledge and belief of the Assessor. Take as our first instance the personalty of Mr. C. T. Yerkes, erstwhile of a Pennsylvania penitentiary, now the street railway despot of Chicago, a millionaire and a resident in a handsomely furnished mansion at 3201 Michigan Avenue. Mr. Yerkes, according to the oath of the South Side Assessor, has got $1,000 worth of personal property in his residence, excluding the piano. In his stables he has two horses, which the Assessor values at $150 each, and a carriage which is assessed as high as $1,000. It is singular that Mr. Yerkes, who rides in a thousand dollar carriage, can furnish his whole house for $1,000. The carpets on the floor, the pictures on the walls, the plate on the table to ordinary eyes would seem each to be dirt cheap at $1,000. But the Assessor swears that to the best of his knowledge and belief the whole of the personal property of Mr. Yerkes, excluding the piano, would not fetch more than $1,000 at a fair voluntary sale! In strange contrast to the beggarly value of the Yerkes' household furnishings is the costly piano. It is assessed

---

*Real estate only.

at $1,700, or nearly as much again as all the rest of his furniture.

Mr. Yerkes, however, is peculiar in possessing so valuable a piano. I have made bold to acquire what the value, the assessed value, of millionaires' pianos may be in Chicago. I find that, according to the sworn valuation of the Assessors, they average little more than $150 apiece. That is the fair selling price according to the oaths of the Assessors of the instruments which are to be found in the drawing-rooms of Mr. Marshall Field, Mr. George Pullman and Mr. J. W. Doane.

Mr. Yerkes' horses are also much more valuable than those of the millionaires of Prairie Avenue. Chicago is one of the greatest horse markets in the world and South Town Assessors may be supposed to have some kind of an eye for horse-flesh. Hence it must surprise the public to learn that to the best of the knowledge and belief of the South Town Assessor, the carriage and riding horses of the millionaires would not fetch more than $20 apiece! Judging from their appearance in harness these steeds must be the cheapest in Christendom. But the Assessor may know that despite their fine appearance they are broken-winded and spavined, for he assesses them on his oath at only $20 a head. Their carriages, also, in notable contrast to Mr. Yerkes' thousand dollar chariots, could be bought, always on the sworn opinion of the Assessor, at $30 each. Here are a few extracts from the returns :

Millionaire.	Horses.	Each Valued at	Carriages.	Each Valued at	Piano.
J. W. Doane	5	$20	5	$30	$150
Marshall Field	6	20	6	30	150
Marshall Field, Jr.	2	20	2	30	...
G. M. Pullman	10	20	6	30	150

The total valuation of the personalty of the millionaires is equally astonishing. Including horses, carriages, pianos, and everything, the following are the returns of the Assessors, under oath, of the personalty of some leading citizens :

Marshall Field $20,000	J. W. Doane $10,000
Marshall Field, Jr 2,000	H. H. Kohlsaat 1,500
P. D. Armour 5,000	C. T. Yerkes............ 4,000
George M. Pullman 12,000	Potter Palmer........... 15,000

None of these gentlemen make out their own returns. They prefer the unerring judgment and trained experience of the Assessor. He stands between them and their conscience, and why should they complain if he, the elected representative of the citizens, should decide that it would be unfair to tax Mr. Marshall Field, for instance, upon a higher valuation than could be realized by the sale of the Corots and Millets and Teniers which are the gems of his picture gallery?

This is no jesting matter. It is, in plain English, a colossal lie, bolstered up by habitual perjury, and operating to produce roguery of every kind. If it does not speedily go by the board, there will be very little value in the apparent revival of the spirit of righteousness in Chicago.

It is not difficult to see how the system came into existence. Like Topsy, it growed. No lunatic in Kankakee is quite mad enough to have invented such a labyrinth of fraud and make-believe all of a piece. The evil is of comparatively recent growth. As the Comptroller says :

In 1867, under an act of that year, there was a Commissioner of Taxes appointed by the Mayor. He was a man selected for his knowledge of real estate values. His books were open to the inspection of the public, and affidavits were required of tax-payers as to the value of their real and personal property. By act of 1st of July, 1877, an unfortunate change took place. The city of Chicago was required to assess and collect its taxes in the manner provided for in the general revenue law. This is set forth in Art. 8 of the Revised Statutes, and is the system in use at present.

The net effect of this system is that while the value of the property in Chicago, if it were correctly assessed, is nearly 2,000 millions, the officially assessed value of the whole state of Illinois, including Chicago, is only 700 millions. Hempstead Washburne, when Mayor of Chicago, said that the Supreme Court of Illinois had decided that all property should be assessed at 33⅓ per cent of its actual value, but even this liberal standard of 66⅔ per cent reduction would hardly bring Chicago up to the sum at which the whole state, including Chicago, is now assessed. When you begin to inquire you find that the city throws the blame upon the state and the state upon the city. If the Assessors of the city were not to perjure themselves, these worthy officials remark, we should simply be enabling the state of Illinois to run tax free. All the taxes would be paid by Chicago. If you can get all the Assessors throughout the state to assess full value or any regular proportion of the value, we might fall into line and keep our assessments up to the agreed standard. But at present what can we do? We must do as the others do, or hand over the city to be knifed by the state.

The state, however, would co-operate if Chicago were in earnest. The Revenue Commission, appointed by the joint resolution of the two Houses of the Legislature in 1885, reported as strongly against the present system as any one could desire. The Commissioners' report that the Assessors, although sworn to assess all property at its fair cash value, "are far from doing so. Real estate is generally put down at one-third of its value, frequently much less, and personal property at a much smaller fraction. If there was uniformity in the reduction perhaps but little harm would be done ; but there is not. The Assessor, having forsaken the standards of the laws without guide or restraint except his own varying judgment, and subject to the pressure of importunate tax-payers, falls heavily downward. The practice is widely different from the theory. The realty of one man is assessed at one-third, one-half, two-thirds, or even the full measure of the actual value, while that of his neighbor is assessed at one-sixth, one-tenth, one-twentieth, or, as was shown in one instance of considerable magnitude, one-twenty-fifth of its actual value. The owner of the one pays as his annual tax five or six per cent of the whole capital invested, while the owner of the other pays one-fourth or one-fifth of one per cent. Such distinctions are too invidious to be meekly borne." *

In order to understand the true significance of this system of tax dodging from the point of view of financial pressure, it is well to remember that while the city of Chicago can only levy two per cent, the other taxes which are collected on the same assessment mount up to over $7.00. Broadly speaking, Chicagoans in the South, West and North Towns pay from $6.79 in the South to $7.98 in the North Town. The difference is due to the rate of taxation for parks and boulevards, which falls heaviest on the west and north. The total is made up of the following items which are uniform all over the city :

```
State ................ 0.310
County .............. 0.778
City................. 4.608
Library ............. 0 199
Sanitary ............ 0.500
```

The other items vary. They are highest in the West and North. The figures for the other taxes for the West are as follows :

```
Town................ 0.500
Park ............... 0.450
Park Bond........... 0.050
Boulevard........... 0.050
New Park Survey..... 0.150
```

Roughly speaking, the citizen of Chicago pays from $7 to $8 local rates and taxes for every $100 of his assessed value. It is therefore his constant object to cut down his assessment. He can not materially alter the rate of taxation, but he can and does reduce the assessment.

If Chicago were assessed at its selling value it would not need to be taxed more than one dollar per hundred for all purposes. One dollar per hundred would yield almost exactly as much as $8 does to-day, for the net result of manipulating assessment is to reduce the real

---

* Report of the Revenue Commission, Springfield, 1886.

value from 2,000 millions to an assessed value of 245 millions. But in that case all would pay according to the value of their property, and not, as at present, upon the fantastic value at which they can induce the Assessor to perjure himself.

In England we have no tax upon personal property; local rates are based upon what is called ratable value. This is ascertained by a calculation based upon the letting rental. If a house lets at $1,000 per annum it is rated at about $750 or $800 ; the 20 or 25 per cent being thrown off as an allowance for repairs, etc. When I occupied my house on a repairing lease, that is to say, when I as tenant undertook to keep the house in repair, I was rated on my net rental. The system is not perfect, but as the rental can be ascertained from both landlord and tenant and the valuation is subject to independent revision it does not work badly on the whole.

The result of the Chicago system is too ludicrous for belief if it were not so cruel and unjust as to stifle laughter. It is of course absurd to blame the rich citizens who have been born under the system and have never realized their personal responsibility for what the tax-farmer does in their name. Neither do they realize, the most of them, what hardship their maneuvers inflict upon the poor. But if they will study the comparative tables which I publish in the appendix, they will see how the system works.

Speaking broadly, the average assessment is one-eighth the value of the selling value of the property. There is no rich man assessed at more than one-eighth. There are many assessed at much less. There are few poor men assessed at all whose assessments do not run above the average of 12½ per cent—of course except the poor Aldermen, who, with half a dozen exceptions appear to have no personal property at all. They have probably spent it all in trying to live upon their official salary of $3 a week.

The curiosities of the assessments collected in the appendix speak for themselves.

First and foremost be it noted how careful the Assessors have been to assess lightly all those who have a pull, political or otherwise.   Mr. Melville Stone told me that some years ago when he was editing the *Daily News* he was assessed at about the same as his stenographer.   He protested and got his assessment raised, but he attributed his low assessment entirely to the fact that the Assessor hoped thereby to secure the support of the paper which he edited.   Newspapers in Chicago have certainly, from this or from some other cause, a very low "fair selling value," in the opinion of the Assessors.   He would be a smart man who could equip a first-class newspaper office with plant, type, machinery, and so forth, for the total sum of the combined assessments of the Chicago press. The average assessment of the morning paper is about $15,000, about the price of a single printing machine. The personalty of the *Dispatch* is as low as $300, a very modest sum on which to run an evening paper.   Newspaper real estate is equally cheap, in the opinion of the Assessor.   It is rather odd to find that the *Inter Ocean* is assessed at more than double the assessment of the *Tribune.*   The total value of the realty and personalty of the *Record* and *Daily News* is about a month's profits, if common report be correct.   Mr. Lawson does not seem to have inherited his late partner's objection to low assessment.

After the newspapers, the Aldermen are most influential in Chicago.   They are hopelessly impecunious—according to the Assessor.   Mr. Madden, Chairman of the Finance Committee, is not assessed at one red cent.   Mr. Mann, Chairman of the Judiciary Committee, has only $100 of personalty.   It is an extraordinary illustration of the way in which Chicago is governed, that the control of the city revenues, which amount to almost exactly the total value of all the gold mined in the United States in a twelvemonth, should be vested in the hands of sixty-eight Aldermen, of whom fifty-five have no personal property at all and the remainder only own, in the opinion of the Assessor, sufficient personal property to fetch $1,550 if they were sold at auction.

The millionaires—but stop, there are no millionaires in Chicago, according to the Assessors. No one pays taxes on a million. The personal property and the real estate combined do not in any single instance amount to that sum. There is no tax roll compiled by the Assessor so as to show at a glance what each tax-payer is assessed at. The real estate of a millionaire is scattered around to such an extent that it is difficult to ascertain how much he is really assessed at. But if we take their personalty and the cost of their residences it is astounding how cheaply they are housed and how economically they furnish their palaces. The Chicago millionaire drives blooded horses which the Assessor does not think would sell for more than $20 cash, if he lives on the South Side, but on the North Side they average $50. Their carriages also vary in cost from $30 to $100 according to the district in which they are assessed. Their pianos also come cheap—from $50 to $180; and one of them, Mr. McCormick, has actually got three watches, worth, on an average, $33⅓ each.

The list abounds in strange contrasts. Who, for instance, could have imagined that Carrie Watson down Clark Street had four times as much personalty as Mr. John R. Walsh, President of the Chicago National Bank, chief proprietor of the *Herald*, and head of the Western News Co.? Such, however, is the fact, according to the sworn information of the Assessor. Carrie Watson's personalty is $4,000; Mr. John R. Walsh's only $1,000. Whatever Carrie Watson's failings may be in other respects, she seems to do her duty as a tax-payer better than many other people who would not touch her polluted fingers. I had heard that she lived in style and had amassed considerable wealth, but I did not expect to find that with the exception of Mr. Yerkes she owned

the finest horses in the city.   She has four assessed at
$125 each.   Mr. Yerkes has only two, but they average
$150 apiece.   If Mr. Yerkes beats her in horse-flesh,
she leaves Mr. Marshall Field far behind in carriages.
The multi-millionaire modestly rides to town in a $30
chariot, whereas nothing less than two $350 coaches will
suffice for Madame.   Mr. Medill, poor man, can only indulge one piano valued at $100, whereas Carrie Watson
has two, each of which is assessed at $150.

Speaking generally, the total personalty of millionaires is assessed at about the sum necessary to furnish a
single room in their palaces, and that by no means the
best.   The jewelry worn by some ladies at an evening
party far exceeds the total value of the whole assessment
of their personalty.   Mrs. William Astor is said occasionally to dazzle New York society by appearing
plastered with diamonds valued at a million dollars,
There are fortunately no such peripatetic jewelers' show
cases in Chicago, but more than one lady in Chicago,
could sell her jewels for more than the entire assessed
personalty of the Prairie Avenue fraternity.

The contrasts between the assessments of the immense
business buildings and those of humble stores, upon
which the *Chicago Times* lays such stress, is notable
enough to need no comment.   Much of this may be explained by the fact that, as a wealthy man remarked the
other day, " I buy my taxes cheap as I buy everything
else."   When we find the Auditorium assessed at just
about the sum which it cost to fit it with radiators, it is
not marvelous that people shrug their shoulders.   What
can we think also of the assessing of the Plaza, a seven-
story building at the southeast corner of Clark Street
and North Avenue, at $10,000 in 1892, when the pur-
chase money of the ground on which it stands was
$95,000?   The premises as they stand are estimated as
being worth well-nigh a million.   But even now they
are only assessed at $30,000, an increase of $20,000 since

the previous year. The assessment lists are full of similar scandals, but few are quite so gross as this.

If the evil were confined to rich people it would be bad enough. But there is just as much discrimination or indiscrimination between the poor and the poor as betweed the rich and the poor. The canker of corruption has eaten through and through the whole social system.

The Assessor, who having forsaken the standards of the law, says the report is without guide or restraint, except his own judgment and the pressure of the importunate taxpayers. This is a euphemism for saying that the Assessor is without any guide excepting his own interests as they are influenced by Dives the Tax Dodger. The place of Assessor is not worth very much if it is estimated by the value of the legal salary, but every one knows that in Chicago an assessorship is the shortest cut to fortune. As Roman Emperors were wont to give their favorites consulships in a fat province, in order that they might replenish fortunes wasted in gambling and debauch, so the political system in Chicago distributes assessorships as plums to politicians who have deserved well of their party. Assessors are not bribed in the same way in which Aldermen are corrupted, but although the method varies, the end in the long run is arrived at all the same. The representative of the people uses his position of trust in order to cheat the people and feather his own nest. That is all there is of it, take it as you please. Sometimes the Assessor is bribed by liberal subscriptions to his election fund, the balance of which goes into the Assessor's pocket. At other times the matter is arranged in hard cash, either between the tax-farmer and the Assessor, and sometimes between the individual citizen and the man who can fine him to three or four times as much taxes as are being paid by his neighbor or who can cut down his estimate to next to nothing. An anecdote was told me of an Assessor who, calling upon a cobbler in one of the towns of Chicago for the purpose of fixing his assessment, asked significantly, how much a first-class pair of boots would cost for him. The cobbler's honesty wilted under the temptation, and he replied, as any luckless Christian would do whose goods a pasha or kaimakan had taken a fancy to in Macedonia or Armenia, that to him the boots would cost very little. As a matter of fact the boots were given, and if the assessment was not reduced it certainly was not raised.

An Assessor, no doubt, when he leaves office marvels at his own moderation. He has practically carte blanche to steal where he pleases, nor is there any possibility of any check upon his corruption provided he acts with ordinary caution. Here, for instance, is a case in point. Mr. Washington Hesing, present Postmaster of Chicago, mentioned the following instance of the kind of plunder that goes on. Speaking of Assessors suddenly becoming rich, Mr. Hesing said:

There is Chase, who was Assessor on the North Side. A few years ago a friend of mine came to me, and with him was Chase. My friend said: "Mr. Hesing, this man is Mr. Chase. He is poor and has nothing to do. He wants to be Assessor in the North Town. The salary is only $1,500 a year, but that will keep Chase and his family from starving. Will you help him get the office?"

Chase got the position all right, held it either four or five years, and went out of the office rich.

I make no comment on this at all. I don't need to do so. I just simply state these facts: Chase went into the office penniless. He held it either four or five years, drawing a salary of $1,500 a year, and came out of it wealthy. He built himself a handsome and costly house on Vernon Avenue. Where did he get his money?

So well recognized is it in the town that assessments are fraudulent, and it is considered perfectly legitimate to resort to any expedient to avoid taxation. Of course in this kind of a game, the rich, and especially the corporations which have no souls to be damned or bodies to be kicked, play a leading part. The law is the poor man's friend. Civilization consists, as I am constantly saying, in the substitution of the law for the arbitrary caprice of an individual. Civilization means the protection of the weak against the rapine of the strong. The strong and the rich can always hold their own under anarchy. Under a system in which might is right, there is no law save only the will of him that is strong; the poor and weak go to the wall. That is just what happens in Chicago where civilization has still to penetrate many of the departments of the city administration. The very poor in Chicago do not pay taxes at all. They are excused on account of their poverty. The very rich, at the other end of the social scale, do their best to approximate to the condition of the very poor by reducing their assessments to a minimum. The burden of taxes, therefore, falls on the middle classes. The middle class man is not wealthy enough or powerful enough to employ tax-farmers to reduce his assessment.

I shrink from using language which would be adequate to describe the injustice of this proceeding. Fortunately there is no need for me to say what I think, seeing that my sentiments and those of every person who looks on this subject from the outside have been expressed with sufficient emphasis by Postmaster Washington Hesing in an interview published by the *Chicago Times.* Mr. Hesing's official position and his familiarity with the facts of which he speaks give great authority to the following scathing indictment of the tax system of Chicago:

There is not a large corporation in the city of Chicago that is paying taxes on over one-tenth of the real value of its property. It is the greatest outrage on a municipality ever perpetrated. The poor men of Chicago pay the bulk of the taxes and it grinds them and galls them to do it. Some of them get to thinking about it and once in a while you'll hear of a man declaring himself an Anarchist. No wonder. Can any one blame him?

The lowness of Chicago's tax list is the result of the most villainous bribery and perjury. It is enough to make honest, decent people boil with indignation to hear the naked facts. The property of a big corporation is never assessed for more than one-tenth of its real value. Here, for example, is a syndicate owning a big building. The property is worth a couple of millions. At a forced sale it would bring in the neighborhood of $1,200,000. That is the figure it should be assessed at. But it never is. It goes on the Assessor's book at about $125,000. The Assessor and his go-between pocket their bribes and go out on Blue Island Avenue or Clybourn Avenue and find a poor man—a small shop keeper—owning a little place worth $2,000. He pays taxes on $1,500. There is a great merchant in this town. I will not mention his name; everybody knows who I mean. His place was burned out once and he produced fire insurance policies for between $950,000 and $1,000,000. He got the money, I presume. At least the companies never made any public objection to paying. That insurance was on his stock—that is to say, chattels—which is taxable. When I heard about it I sent a man over to the Assessor's office, and I declare to you that a member of the firm had sworn that the stock was worth $72,000, and that was what they were paying taxes on.

The rank dishonesty of the Assessor amazes me. I don't see how a man can accept bribes, flagrantly disobey the law, and escape unscathed. The Assessor, however, always tries to cover up his tracks and works behind another man. To show how these persons operate let me tell of a case that was brought to my attention. There is a business man in this town whose taxes amounted to $1,500. He was going to pay that sum without a kick. One day a man went to him and said: "Your taxes are $1,500. I can get them cut to $750. What will you give me if I do this?" After some talk the business man agreed to give $400. His taxes were reduced and he saved $350. The city was cheated out of $750. That is only one case. There are scores of others. Of the $400 bribe the Assessor got $200 and his agent $200.

There are men in the city of Chicago whose business it is to swear to lies, to perjure themselves. A merchant does not like the idea of going on record as a perjurer. So he says to one of these professionals: "Here, I am going out of town. You fix up my taxes. Make the amount so much," naming the small sum on which he wants to be assessed. The perjurer does this and gets his price.

Whatever is done, the present infamous system should go. It forces men of little means to bear the burden; it takes but a trifle from the rich; it results in bribery; it causes perjury; it is outrageous. Let it be wiped out, and that without delay.

Mr. Hesing went on to describe how his efforts to secure an adequate assessment of his own property utterly failed. He protested against a building in which he was interested being assessed as being worth a little more than its annual rental, but it was in vain. Mr. Hesing's house, for which he would not take $40,000, was assessed for $3,637. He owns land in Ravenswood that is worth $80 a foot, and is assessed for a mere bagatelle which would hardly pay for putting up a fence around it. It is very seldom, however, that the tax-payer manifests an eager desire to be assessed at his full value. They take the goods the gods provide them and they do not care to look a gift horse too close in the mouth. They secure themselves on the ground that these things form part of a wrong system and that they ought not to make martyrs of themselves in changing it. What they forget is that they might at least make voters of themselves in order to improve it, but that is what they heretofore do not seem to have taken into consideration. So the rotten system goes on. How it works out may be seen from these fragmentary examples given in this chapter. Those who care for further information will find in the appendix a list of many of the wealthiest people in Chicago together with some samples of the way in which the property of the smaller tradesmen and the lower and middle class is assessed.

The reform of the assessment system can only be effected by action at Springfield through the State Legislature, and this brings us to another difficulty. A leading citizen and universally respected ex-official of the city administration said frankly that he despaired of doing anything because " there are too many in it," to use his own words, for any measure of reform to be carried through the Legislature at Springfield. He said: "Our Aldermen are bad enough, and cannot be said to be ideal representatives of the city; but they are gentlemen compared with the creatures whom we send to represent us in the Legislature of the State of Illinois. Hence, even if you were to reform the City Council of Chicago and get them unanimously to indorse a bill reforming the assessment system, it would have no chance at Springfield. The rich, who at the present moment escape their fair share of the burdens of the city, would simply go down to Springfield and buy up the Legislature. Congressmen are not only a more disreputable lot than the Aldermen, but their price is much lower. You can buy up the Legislature of Illinois at much less per head than you can the City Council of Chicago. It is ludicrous, if it were not a matter for indignation, to see the kind of men who are considered fit and proper persons to represent this great city in the Legislature of the State. I remember some time ago I had a young man who was a pretty fair clerk in my office, a man of no special capacity, who was earning fair wages but who was totally destitute of any training that would qualify him as a legislator. One fine day I was told that he was listening to the proposals which were being made to him for standing for Congress as a representative of one of the wards of the city. I sent for him and begged him to dismiss such nonsense from his head. 'You cannot make an honest living at Springfield,' I said, 'neither can you continue to earn a salary as a clerk in my office if you are attending to your legislative duties in another place. Besides you know you are quite unfit for the post. You cannot write the introduction to any bill which might be introduced, to save your life. Drop all that and stick to your business.' He hung his head and looked ashamed, but then picking up courage he said that he would try, because if he did not get it some other d— fool would. He did get elected and went to Congress. He became as corrupt as any of the boodlers there and as corrupt personally as he was politically. His moral character went, he took to drinking and now he lies in a drunkard's grave. He is one among many who have gone down to destruction because our Legislature, even more than our City Council, is a sink of iniquity. What are you going to do against such a state of things as this?"

"Well," I replied, "there is more work to be done than I at first realized, but it will be done all the same."

I can only say that for my own part I marvel with exceeding great wonderment that a system so rotten and so unjust could be allowed to continue for a quarter of a century in the midst of a nominally Christian community. In England we have been accustomed to consider that Americans as a race are fond of liberty, with a keen sense of justice and an inveterate impatience with injustice when it takes the form of taxes. I am afraid I shall return to my own land with a very different conception of American citizens. The men who threw the tea into the bay at Boston and severed the tie which linked the American colonies to the mother country have left few descendants among the citizens of Chicago. The amount of taxes in dispute which lost us this continent was only $400,000 a year. Many times that sum is every year unjustly shifted by the wealthy tax-dodgers of Chicago from their own shoulders to those of their poorer neighbors, and no one seems to care. Yet the number of tax-dodgers is comparatively few. They could be snowed under at any election by majorities of at least ten to one, but this meek and patient majority has gone on year after year, suffering without protest a system of taxation compared with which that of George III was ideally just. There has been no tea thrown into the harbor in Chicago; there has hardly been an articulate protest against a system of spoliation which admittedly robs the poor to enrich the wealthy.

I read in the *Chicago Times* the statement that "the Chicago system of taxation is systematized crime against the poor; that for twenty years the burden of taxation has rested upon the poor and that it is the history of tax-dodging, discrimination, bribing and perjury, written upon every page of the tax books of Cook County. The trusts, the corporations, the millionaires of Chicago pay taxes on less than one-tenth of the value of their enormous accumulations of wealth, while the small property owners are being taxed on from one-half to one-third of the value of their humble possessions. The millions belonging to the rich are sheltered by bribery and perjury from paying tribute, while the humble homes of the poor have no protection." Yet, although these facts are undenied and have been in the possession of the public for years and are no worse to-day than they have been any time since 1880, there is no agitation, no protest, no revolt. Here and there in a few obscure corners a few Socialists are organizing, and in still more obscure corners the Anarchists are muttering threats and perhaps dreaming of dynamite, but for any trace of an out-

burst of healthy indignation which such facts should
elicit in any self-respecting community, I have looked
in vain. The Chicago tax-payer may have the meek-
ness of the sheep and the patience of the ass, but he
can hardly be said to have the independence and self-
respect of a human being or the public spirit of an
American citizen.

But human nature being human nature all the world
over, even in Chicago, and the stock of patience and for-
bearance under spoliation and plunder being a limited
quantity, the time of its exhaustion must be drawing
near.   I have had some little experience of agitation in
the Old World and I must say that I never have seen a
condition of things in an English-speaking land where
the signs point unmistakably to change, and it may be to
violent change.   Evils often exist which are keenly felt
but whose origin and source is so obscure that it is
almost impossible for the sufferers to place their finger
on the cause of their trouble, nor do they know how to
redress it. In Chicago for the first time I have found a system of taxation admittedly unjust, undeniably and palpably based upon corruption, maintained for the benefit of
a handful of persons, none of whom dare defend in the
light of day what they are doing in secret; and we
have the facts officially certified by the chief authorities
in the city.   Successive Mayors and Comptrollers have
placed on record so that no street sweeper could mistake
their meaning, their deliberate judgment that Dives is a
tax-dodger and that he is now and has been for years
thrusting the burden which he should have carried upon
the shoulders of Lazarus.   Here, for instance, is a passage from the last report of Comptroller Ackerman:

There appears to be a general disposition to escape this form of taxation, and evasion and misrepresentation appear to be almost the rule.
It is notorious that many instances occur every year in which em-
inently reputable citizens have made returns equal to about one-fiftieth
and in some cases one-hundredth part of the value of their personal
estate.   The whole system is demoralizing in its effects from beginning to end and should be remedied by such legislative action as will

enable the officers of the city to have complete and entire control of its resources.

Changes indeed! But what sign is there of its being changed at the present moment? Even a worm will turn, but the poorer tax-payers of Chicago seem not even to have the spirit of a worm; they are rather like caterpillars, bruised and mangled beneath the gardener's spade, without even strength to crawl or resolution to bestir themselves to remedy their miserable condition. Even the loss of the beloved dollar fails to nerve them to action. Possibly the tax-dodger knows his neighbor and assumes upon his apathy and indifference; but he will do well to remember that this assumption is the infallible mistake of all tyrants and oppressors in all lands. They think that the injustice by which they profit will last their time and after that may come the deluge. But sometimes the deluge does not wait until they quit the scene. George the Third made that mistake, among others, with the result that the English-speaking race was reft in twain, and Britain lost her empire in the New World, owing to a dispute about a less sum than that annually plundered from the poor by the tax-dodgers of Chicago. There is a grim saying in the Old Book which may be commended to the gentlemen who are skulking, ashamed but resolute, in their trenches of the assessment system: "Rob not the poor because he is poor, neither oppress the afflicted in the gate, for the Lord will plead their cause and spoil the soul of those that spoil them." And there is another like unto it: "their feet shall slide in due time."

CHAPTER IV.

GAMBLING AND PARTY FINANCE.

Every city in Europe, with one exception, Monte Carlo, which is not a city, has put down public gaming hells. They flourished in other places until 1870, but when reunited Germany smote down the French Empire and unified the Fatherland, the clink of roulette was heard no more in Homburg and the other German watering places, for the croupier went out as the Kaiser came in.

There is plenty of gambling in England, but the European conscience has decided apparently once for all that gaming hells are not institutions for civilization to tolerate. This would also seem to be the opinion of the Legislature of the State of Illinois, and the same doctrine has received the approval of the City Council of Chicago. Nevertheless, so far from this having brought Chicago up to the moral level of the most immoral European city, the contrary is the case. The gaming hell open and nn-ashamed is one of the indigenous institutions of Chicago.

The love of gambling is almost as deep-seated in the human nature as the animal appetite on which the race depends for its preservation and multiplication. The craving for excitement ; the longing to be suddenly rich without exertion or expenditure, are too deeply seated to be expunged by municipal ordinances or statutes of the Legislature.

Gambling seems to come to most men as naturally as lying, and therefore it is claimed by some it is best to place no obstacle in the way of this strong, inherited and natural propensity. Common sense would seem to point in exactly the opposite direction. One does not need to be a moralist to admit that the gaming table is not an institution which makes for righteousness in a community. That would not be maintained by anyone, least of all by its habitues, of which in this city, it is said, there are about 5,000. If, therefore, it be regarded as an object of sound policy to minimize any evil which cannot be annihilated, the object of the administration must be to compel those who gamble to do it as much out of sight as possible, in order that the temptation and fascination of the pursuit may be kept out of the minds of others. Because it conduces to unrighteousness, the public gaming hell has been suppressed everywhere in the Old World, and it is not likely that any new arguments can be discovered in Chicago to justify a contrary policy from a moral point of view. The defense, if defense there be, must be based on other than moral considerations. At the same time, while regretting that Chicago should deliberately adopt a lower moral standard in relation to gaming hells than any European city, there is no ground for Phariaism on the part of European critics.

The great gaming hell of England is the race course, and I have never been able to understand the nicety of the distinction which damned the gaming table and upholds the race course. Everything is strongly in favor of roulette and unloaded dice as against the gambling machines used not on the green table, but on the green turf of the race track. Monte Carlo is a fair play itself compared with the betting ring. Nothing can be more odious than the way in which some English newspapers which derive much of their circulation and profit from pandering to the race course, hold up their hands in holy horror against the Prince of Monaco for drawing a handsome revenue from the gaming tables of Monte Carlo. At the same time while we recognize that the race track is worse than the gambling hell we need not sanction both evils because one is less than the other, and refuse to do one good thing because we cannot do two. This is an absurd policy which should be left strictly to the party of temperance, falsely so-called.

The peculiarity about the Chicago plan of dealing with the gambling hells is not that the houses are allowed to run; anybody could allow houses to run, if they were prepared to take the moral responsibility of allowing pitfalls or temptations to be opened up before the feet of citizens. That which is peculiar about Chicago is the way in which gaming is utilized as an engine of party finance. Chicago taught the world how to make the dice box and the wheel of fortune and the pack of cards a resource of partisan finance. It is ingenious and immoral. It is simply the adoption by the Mayor of the city of the methods and morals of the policeman who levies blackmail on the street walkers on his beat. Between the blackmailing Mayor and the blackmailing policeman there is not a pin to choose, except the man in the high position is much more to be condemned than his poorer and humbler fellow citizen. The principle in both cases is exactly the same. The gaming house has no more right to exist in Chicago than the woman has to solicit vice in the public streets. The law against gaming houses is much more precise and more emphatic than that which forbids solicitation. It is inconvenient for the policeman to be perpetually arresting street walkers, and it is much more agreeable for him to make a deal with her in consideration of which he lines his pocket and she is left uninterrupted to pursue her vocation. The same argument precisely led the late Carter Harrison to conclude the famous deal with the gamblers' syndicate, which brought in so golden a harvest. Of course, if anybody asks for proof that any particular policeman took blackmail, the proof is not forthcoming. There was the same universal conviction as to the nature of the bargain which was struck between Carter Harrison, as Mayor of Chicago, and the gambling fraternity, but the evidence which should be produced in a court of law is not forthcoming.

A Mayor can on an occasion be as discreet as a boodling Alderman, and they usually console their consciences by reflecting that, after all, the money is not used by them for their own private needs; it is a contribution to the expense of getting elected and a safe financial expedient for recuperating the party war chest for the lavish outlay of dollars which a contested election will cost.

The way in which it was done, according to the story circulated everywhere in Chicago, is as follows:

Before Carter Harrison's last election, a certain number of the gamblers, as is the custom in this city, made up a purse and subscribed several thousands of dollars (authorities differ as to the precise amount) to Mr. Harrison's election fund. When he was elected he took steps to recoup those patriots who had supplied him with the sinews of war. A small syndicate was formed for the purpose of securing a certain liberal percentage of the profits on gaming, and in return practical immunity from prosecution was secured to the gaming houses by the arrangement with the Mayor. How large that percentage was has never been definitely settled, but reports put it as much as 65 per cent. A certain well-known citizen who was trusted by the Mayor was at the head of the syndicate, and in that capacity he became the favored shepherd of all the gamblers in town. In dealing with the gaming houses he had practically a free hand. Whom he would he slew; whom he would not, he kept alive. That is the theory ; but in practice it was found that the houses that were shut were those which had not agreed to pay the stipulated percentage while those who punctually paid up their dues to the gambling shepherd were allowed to run free. This sum, which amounted during the World's Fair, in some districts, to a colossal fortune, was divided. Many people had a finger in the pie before the residue reached Mr. Harrison. But however many there were who fingered the profit en-route, there was enough left to make it well worth the

Mayor's while to allow the houses to run. This arrangement was in full force when Carter Harrison was shot, and the houses continued running all the interregnum. Everyone in Chicago knew perfectly well that they were running; there was no attempt at concealment. They were all in existence and prospered under the protection of the administration. One of the most famous hells was running immediately over the saloon of Alderman Powers.

A Grand Jury last autumn suddenly struck evidence as to the existence of gaming houses. They asked the police why they were not suppressing them, the patrolmen declared under oath that gambling was running wide open in the city by the consent and under the protection of the authorities, with an occasional exception where the parties were not in sufficiently good standing to obtain a permit. They were reminded that each one of them was commanded by law to close up each gaming house and seize and prosecute the gamblers. They replied that their hands were tied by their superior officers, and that no houses were closed without special and direct orders from these superior officers. The Grand Jury summoned the Chief of Police. Of course he knew nothing about it; the duty of closing the gaming houses was left, he said, to the patrolmen. The Grand Jury thereby reported that the conflict of evidence led its members to the conclusion that there was collusion between the police force of the city and the gamblers so general and wide that its devil-fish tentacles reached over a large portion of the police force. Of course everyone who read this laughed at the innocence of the Grand Jury, and wondered how long after the deluge begun these worthy souls would discover that it looked like rain, and prepare to unfurl their umbrellas. The Grand Jury, however, at least established the fact beyond all doubt or gainsay that gambling was running wide open by the consent and under the protection of the authorities in direct contravention both of municipal ordinances and the laws of the state of Illinois. Although this fact was thus officially brought before the Chief of the force and acting Mayor, nothing was done. The gaming houses were crowded every night, and at the dinner hour by the dinner-pail brigade, just as they always had been; and the gambling syndicate collected their share of the gaming receipts, and, it is hoped, handed over the due proportion to their heirs and representatives of those who had arranged the deal. So matters remained until the election of Mr. Hopkins.

Nothing was said on the subject either by the Republicans or Democrats in the mayoral campaign. The Republicans were too busy discussing the city's financial situation and the infamy of the Queen of the Sandwich Islands. The Democrats laid low and said nothing for reasons of their own. Gamblers, acting in accordance with their usual sagacity, put up large sums of money (the exact amount is again uncertain) for campaign purposes. A leading Democrat on the West Side told me that Mr. Hopkins, who was receiver of the Chemical National Bank, noticed, with some curiosity, a heavy check paid into the Republican campaign fund by some leading gamblers of the South Side. He immediately ordered all checks from the same source to be sent to him for examination, and as a result of this scrutiny he came to the conclusion that the gamblers were putting more money upon Mr. Swift than they were on Mr. Hopkins. Therefore the Mayor, who is quick to resent an injury and slow to forgive a slight, is said to have marked down those gamblers for condign punishment. He said nothing, however, and when the election was over he still kept his silence, until one fine day, early in January, the Rev. O. P. Gifford and a gambler, by name Ficklen, waited upon the Mayor and asked him what he proposed to do about the gaming houses. Mr. Gifford had previously made a radical speech at Willard Hall, in which he declared he and other ministers were determined to put the law into motion against gambling hells or perish on the threshold. His first move was to take counsel with the Mayor. He reported when he came out that he was more than satisfied with his visit. He (the Mayor) told Mr. Gifford he considered gambling an evil which could not be suppressed in a city of this size, though he thought it could be regulated, and he assured Mr. Gifford of his hearty sympathy in every effort he might make to exterminate open gambling in Chicago. This was on the fifth of January. The same day he summoned Chief Brennan and as a result orders were issued the next day ordering all the police to close the gambling houses in the city. The next Saturday night every gaming hell was closed up tight. On the next Monday, the following interview appeared in the Chicago papers:

The Mayor expressed some surprise when questioned concerning the order.

"Who told you the gambling houses had been closed?"

His honor was informed that the information had come direct from Chief Brennan's office.

"Well," remarked the Mayor, "I don't know anything about any order on the subject. But I do not issue instructions to my department chiefs. I presume Chief Brennan can tell you all that is to be told about closing the gambling houses. I think it not improbable," the Mayor continued, looking very grave meanwhile, "that the closing is entirely voluntary on the part of the gamblers. I understand they have been complaining about the hard times. Then within the past few weeks two of these gambling houses have been robbed. I am informed that Chief Brennan is talking of reducing the police force. In view of these things, it is possible that the gamblers fear they will not have adequate police protection hereafter, and have concluded to go out of business. This is only a suggestion, however, which I offer for what it is worth."

Chief Brennan was appealed to.

"Does the order include all gambling houses?"

"All gambling houses."

"For good?"

"For good."

"All forms of gambling?"

"All forms of gambling—gambling houses, crap games, pool rooms."

"They will not be allowed to reopen under certain promises, then?"

"They will not. The pool rooms of the city were closed on my orders after I had conferred with the Mayor on the matter. They will remain closed if it takes the entire police force to do it."

From this it will be seen that the Mayor in addition
to his other gifts possesses a broad sense of humor.   It
also shows that the actors in the little comedy had not
arranged their parts with sufficient care; otherwise the
Mayor would hardly have expressed surprise at the action of the Chief of Police and disclaimed all responsibility for what he was doing, at the very moment when
the Chief in question was declaring that the gaming
houses were closed after he had conferred with the Mayor
on the matter.

Another reporter declared that the Mayor had said if
anyone could find an order of his closing the houses he
would give them a new suit of clothes.   The *Inter Ocean*
in announcing the closing of the houses embodied the
general conviction of the gamblers themselves in the
following " Scare heads : "

Not on the square ! Gambling houses are ordered to suspend
operations ! It is only a blind ! Done for the purpose of concen-
trating the privilege to rob ! Houses will open again as soon as those
under the ban are driven out !

"We shall all be open again in a week," was the
opinion of most of the professionals; but they began to
look rather blue when a week passed and no permission
was received.   They began to fear that the Mayor, after
all, might really be in earnest.   After a time they decided
to give him a hint.   To remind him of his dependence
upon the gamblers they made it hot for him by an election petition.   The petition called attention to the
various irregularities which had taken place in the contest which had resulted in the return of Mr. Hopkins
and compelled him thereby to defend his seat.   This led
to Mr. Hopkins' second declaration on the subject of gambling, from which it may be seen plainly enough that he
regarded the whole question from the point of view of the
politician and not from that of the moralist.   When asked
about the current rumor about the petition he said : " You
can say this: no gambler who spends his money in fighting me in this contest will open his place while I am

Mayor. I may not be able to stop gambling entirely, but I will be able to stop these men from running open houses." This was on the 23d, the houses having been closed for more than a fortnight. The papers, which at first had been very dubious about the Mayor's will or power to close the gaming houses, now declared that gambling could be suppressed, and had been suppressed, and must continue to be suppressed. Judging from the utterances of the Chicago newspapers there was nobody in the town who wished gambling to continue. Meanwhile some of the gamblers who had been through similar experiences smiled audibly.*

Then one or two of the papers announced that the Mayor was going to weaken on the policy of restriction. The 25th of January a gaming house proprietor stated that the Mayor had owned himself beaten: that the gaming houses would all be running full blast as soon as they could get their rooms in order. " He (Mayor Hopkins) has been driven to toleration by stress of circumstances. He has thrown up both hands and confessed his failure. I am willing to give him credit for a conscientious attempt to suppress the gaming tables, but, like everybody else who ever tried it, he has found his efforts futile. He has been successful in exterminating the downtown gambling houses for the time being, and what is the result? Simply that the fever has broken out all over the body corporate. There are small games all over the city and invariably will be as long as the legitimate outlet for the disease is closed.

---

*The gambling houses should not be permitted to reopen under the pretense that they are to be "regulated." There can be no "regulation" of that which is plainly illegal and which is overwhelmingly condemned by the best public sentiment. Let the gambling houses remain closed throughout Mayor Hopkins' term.—*Herald.*

Mayor Hopkins' first step toward the "regulation" of gambling is to close up their places. The next logical step is to cause the arrest and prompt conviction of the gamblers as common vagrants. "The laws will be enforced." That seems to cover the case.—*Times.*

The recent onslaught of Chief Brennan has afforded ample proof that gambling can be suppressed if the authorities wish to suppress it.—*Record.*

If the police mean business, they will swear out warrants, they will raid the gambling houses, will smash the implements, and prosecute all the offenders they catch. If that policy is pursued the establishments which where warned Saturday can be kept closed permanently. There will not be the least difficulty about it. —*Tribune.*

From various and sundry quarters complaints have been lodged with the police that residents were annoyed in their homes by the proximity of gambling houses."

The same paper which published this statement reported that the Mayor declared that he had stopped open gambling and he proposed to keep it stopped if he could. Meanwhile the gaming house keepers went on furnishing and preparing their establishments for the reopening, which they confidently predicted would speedily come.

At the beginning of February the rumor as to the reopening of the houses began to gain, and it was not until the eve of Valentine's Day that the interdict was removed, no one knew why or how. The last statement which appeared from Mr. Hopkins was that while gambling could not be suppressed he was determined to prevent houses from running open, and that as long as he was Mayor there should be no open houses in Chicago, whatever might be done secretly. His declaration was so emphatic that it is difficult to account for what followed.

On the 12th of February several houses opened and were closed at once by the police. Chief Brennan said : " In closing the gambling houses that were opened last night the police acted only on my standing instructions. I guess if any houses open up the police will know their duty ; there has been no change in orders." That utterance was reported on the morning of the 14th of February. On that day every gaming house in Chicago started playing in full blast, nor was there even a pretense of secrecy. Notwithstanding this, two days after the houses were running open Mr. Hopkins declared that he was doing all he could to stop gambling.

"Day before yesterday," said the Mayor, "I was going to lunch with a friend, when we passed under the shelter shed on La Salle Street, in front of the Stock Exchange Building. This shed is placed there to protect the people passing from falling bricks and timbers from the hands of workmen laboring high up on the uncompleted structure. When we reached the center of the shed we encountered a big crowd. Peeping over the heads of the men on the outskirts of the crowd I saw a man with a chuckaluck cloth spread out and a dozen or more men placing their money on the turn of the dice. I did not wish to create a disturbance of so quiet a game, and concluded to go to the corner of La Salle and Madison Streets and send a policeman back to arrest the fellow. Afterwards I wished I had used my authority as head of the police force to make the arrest myself, for on reaching the corner no policeman could be found. I went back myself, but before I got there the fellow had flown.''

"After dinner I called Chief Brennan to my office and told him what I had seen. He informed me that this was a common occurrence; that the gambler always had a confederate to watch for the arrival of a policeman and when one loomed up on the horizon the gambler, being warned, stuffed his cloth and dice into his pocket and walked off in the crowd.''

"This simply shows," continued the Mayor, "that we cannot stop gambling. I am trying to the best of my ability. Chief Brennan had his orders soon after I entered upon the duties of my office and he has had no modification of the orders since. There is bound to be gambling and it is surprising how many reputable business men want it to continue. I have had representatives of prominent wholesale houses tell me that they have great difficulty in entertaining their country customers because they cannot take them around to gambling houses. It is a fact, too, strange as it may seem, that 75 per cent of the brewers want gambling houses open.''

Chief Brennan's orders were still unchanged and yet the public was asked to believe that the Mayor and Chief of Police were totally ignorant that everything was going on just as before.

Mr. Harrison at least was bluff, cynical but straightforward in the matter; he openly avowed that he was permitting gambling to go on for reasons which he set forth ; he did not pretend to be doing one thing while in reality he was doing the other. He did not, of course, admit that he was subsidized by the gamblers ; that would be expecting altogether too much from human nature. But he did not say he was doing all he could to suppress it, while a dozen houses were running full blast under his nose ; nor did he declare he was opposed to gambling and that no house should run open while he was Mayor, and then permit the gaming houses to be run as openly as they are in Monte Carlo. Mr. Hopkins may have reasons for the course he has taken ; that the future will show. But at present he has unfortunately given the enemy so much reason to blaspheme that it will require very energetic action hereafter to remove the impression that Mr. Hopkins is no better in this respect than his predecessors.

CHAPTER V.

THE SCARLET WOMAN.

" Servant, awake, arise, for the people have slept o'er long!" is the opening line in the soul stirring summons which Mr. Grant Allen in his newly published volume of poems, hears reluctant " In the Night Watches."

Sing of the maiden, thy sister, whom men thy brothers have sold,
Cast on the merciless world, on the tide of the ravening years,
Bought with a price in the market and paid with dishonor and gold,
Courted and loved and betrayed and deserted to desolate tears.
* * * * * * * *
Sing of a pitiless race and the blast of a terrible wrong,
Poisonous, fiery, venomous.
                "Master, I hear and obey."

There is as much need for such a clarion cry to the servants of God in the New World as in the Old. The terrible wrong "ancient as infinite ages and young as the morn of today" is as poisonous, fiery and venomous in Chicago as in modern Babylon on the Thames.

I regret to have to number among the illusions dissipated by this visit to the western hemisphere the belief that the Americans were leading the world in the sincerity of their respect for womanhood. The woman with money in her purse has more homage—at least from the lips outward—than in England, but the poor woman is cheaper in Chicago than in London.

A leading member of the Knights of Labor said the other day that the Americans as a nation no longer believed in God. They worshipped, he said, three things, first gold, secondly women, thirdly children. I wish I could have found more proofs of their devotion to women and to children in their laws. The statutes made and provided for the protection of young girls are in many states a very grim and ghastly commentary upon the traditional respect of the Americans for their women.

In some states it is true the law has been amended—largely under the influence of the same cyclone of moral indignation which raised the age of consent in England in 1885 from 13 to 16, but in many others the law is still in a condition to be a disgrace to heathendom. The legislatures of Delaware, of Wisconsin, and other states in the following list would seem to be composed of Yahoos rather than of Christian citizens of a Republic founded by the descendants of the Puritans. The age of consent—the technical term used to denote the number of years that a girl must have lived before she is regarded by the law as competent to consent to her own seduction —varies all over the Union. I quote here the black list of dishonor from a table compiled by the *Philanthropist* from official returns:

AGE OF CONSENT.

Delaware	7 years.	Kentucky	12 years
Texas	10 "	Indiana	12 "
Idaho	10 "	Wisconsin	12 "
South Dakota	10 "	Virginia	12 "
Carolina, North,	10 "	West Virginia	12 "
" South	10 "	Louisiana	12 "
Georgia	10 "	Iowa	13 "
Alabama	10 "	New Hampshire	13 "
Minnesota	10 "	Tennessee	13 "
Colorado	10 "		

These are the worst states in the Union from this point of view. There are others nearly as bad. Seventeen states fix the age of consent at 14 and two at 15. Six follow the English rule and place the age of consent at 16. Florida the most southern of all the states raises it to 17, while Kansas and Wyoming place it at 18.

The time is coming when such laws as those which practically hand over innocent and unsuspecting girl children of 7 and 10 to 12 to be the lawful prey of brutes in human shape if they can but get their consent—forsooth! to something of which they know nothing until it is too late will be regarded with as much shame and indignation as the Fugitive Slave Law. Certainly as long as these

States persist in leaving defenceless maidenhood without the protection of law, the vaunts about American chivalry and high regard for women and children sound as hollow as did the Declaration of Independence in the old Slave States.

The increase in the number of young women in America who make their living as clerks, shop girls, teachers and other callings which take them away from home, has not been accompanied by increased safeguards for their protection. Young children are employed as cash girls in Chicago at a much earlier age than would be permitted in Europe, and in more than one of the great stores ugly stories are current of wages being fixed at a rate which assumed that they would be supplemented by the allowance of a "friend." The recurrence of this worst feature of Parisian shops in the far west is a much more painful phenomenon than the appearance of the familiar figure of the street walker. In one of the largest of the dry goods stores in Chicago the head of the dress making department, now happily discontinued, was the manager of a house of ill-fame down the levee. She is said to have found the combination very convenient as she recruited in one establishment by day for assistants in the other at night. These things are only too well known to the unfortunate victims, but as public exposure would add the last drop to their bitter cup, they suffer in silence. The Missions and Refuges which receive the shattered wrecks of lost womanhood, know only too well how deadly is the system by which the daughters reared in American homes are lured to their doom. Another lost illusion is the belief that American girls are trusted with knowledge instead of being kept in that cruel ignorance which is confounded with innocence. It is not the case. If legal protection peremptorily denied the American girl by the men who monopolize the legislative function, neither are they delivered from the dangers of ignorance by their mothers. No disability of sex stands in the way of the timely performance of the

most necessary duty which maternity ever imposed upon
woman.   But even that is denied the American girl.
Anna B. Gray, M. D., writing in the February number
of *New Occasions*, a monthly magazine edited by Mr.
B. F. Underwood, and published at Chicago, on "Ignorance at the Price of Depravity" bears testimony on this
point that is worth noting.   She writes:

> I have given years of attention to the subject, and have arrived at
> this much of knowledge.   In nine out of every ten cases of seduction,
> the woman in America has erred through affection, not passion; that
> instinct of common humanity, most highly developed in women, to
> please the beloved, but chiefly through *ignorance*.   They feel no
> passion; they are totally ignorant of its signs in others, even if they
> feel, they are in equal ignorance of what it means.   While that
> much lauded ignorance prevents any thought of evil, the result is
> that before they know they have arrived within sight of it they have
> crossed the threshold of sin.
> I have not arrived at my conclusions hastily nor do I state them lightly.
> I have talked with all sorts and kinds of women from the common
> prostitute to the purest matron, from the girl who committed suicide
> when told of the consequences that would follow her error, to those
> whose sins never became known, and this is my sure conviction:—The
> commonest, and largest factor in the seduction of unmarried women
> is unadulterated ignorance.   Ignorance of any love less innocent than
> that which teaches her to clasp a baby in her arms, caress its tender
> limbs, smother it with kisses, and half crush its life out in a passion
> of tenderness.   If she wonders at the fervor of the caresses bestowed
> upon her, they mean no more to her, than those she so freely bestowed
> upon her baby brother or sister.

If any good is to be done in dealing with this saddest
of all social maladies it must be done betimes.   Prevention is a thousand times better than cure and many
thousand times easier.   The chief difficulty that stands
in the way of frank sensible speech on such subjects
between parent and child is the absurd prudery which
in the old days led American matrons to put frills round
their piano legs and which quite recently led an Amer-
can girl to call legacy limbacy, in order to avoid the
improper first syllable.   A prudish silence with ignorance
as the necessary results lands many an innocent girl in
Fourth Avenue.   This is a subject npon which an ounce
of fact is worth a pound of theory.   The facts are indisputable.   The keepers of houses of ill-fame who reap the

harvest of these blighted lives are authorities on this point. Take for instance the evidence of Mrs. Vina Fields, who next to Carrie Watson is the best known Madame in Chicago. Vina Fields is a colored woman who has one of the largest houses in the city. During the Fair she had over 60 girls in the house, all colored, but all for white men. Now she has not more than 30 or 40. She has kept a house for many years and strange though it may appear has acquired the respect of nearly all who know her. The police have nothing to say against her. An old experienced police matron emphatically declared that "Vina is a good woman" and I think it will be admitted by all who know her, that she is probably as good as any woman can be who conducts so bad a business. I had a talk with her about it one afternoon and some days after she wrote me a long letter, upon this subject. She says:

> The present state of affairs results from the want of proper knowledge regarding self. When cultivation of self is made universal, a better condition is possible, and not until then. The cause for prostitution will continue until it is made honorable for the sexes to seek knowledge of self and their duties toward each other. The most important things of human life ought to never make an honest educated man or woman blush. It is ignorance that causes shame and all this distress. Let the causes of life and common things be more understood and the greater things will take care of themselves, in private matters between man and woman the same as in other things.

Therein Vina spoke wisely and well. The result of not teaching young people the truths of physiology at home is that they usually acquire them abroad when it is too late.

Vina Fields is a very interesting woman. She is now past middle age. She has made a moderate competence by her devotion to her calling and she prides herself not a little upon the character of her establishment. The rules and regulations of the Fields house, which are printed and posted in every room, enforce decorum and decency with pains and penalties which could hardly be more strict if they were drawn up for the regulation of a Sunday school. In it the ladies are severely informed that even if they have no respect for themselves, they should have for the house. She is bringing up her daughter who knows nothing of the life of her mother in the virginal seclusion of a convent school, and she contributes of her bounty to maintain her unfortunate sisters whose husbands down south are among the hosts of the unemployed. Nor is her bounty confined to her own family. Every day this whole winter through she has fed a hungry, ragged regiment of the out-of-works. The day before I called, 201 men had had free dinners of her providing. She had always given the broken victuals away, she said, but this year the distress had been so great she had bought meat every day to feed the poor fellows who were hunting jobs and finding none.

"What brings your girls here?" I asked. "Passion, poverty, or what?"

"Misery," she answered quietly. "Always misery. I don't know one who came that was not driven here by misery. Unhappy homes, cruel parents, bad husbands. Misery, always misery. I don't know one exception."

On this subject Vina wrote me afterwards at some length. And I cannot do better than quote this homily on home, the duty of making home happy—although few, perhaps, would be prepared to listen to such a discourse from the colored keeper of a house of ill-fame.

It is not necessary to go to houses of prostitution to find the cause that places girls there. All you have to do is to investigate the homes of the people. These women called prostitutes come from these homes from every grade of life, from the upper classes as well as the others; and I am sorry to say that they give a good percentage to this class, as the daughters are educated to an idle, frivolous life. As a rule the marriage policy does not work very charmingly, and only a few succeed in obtaining comfortable homes, the balance have to find shelter wherever they can, and as houses of ill-fame are open to this class of woman—they prefer it to dying and starving on the street; many of them find it more pleasing and preferable to their married lives. These women are no more lustful than their sisters in other positions in life. They simply have not been successful in marrying a home, and as many, very many do not know how to do any kind of work, they come here.

The only remedy for prostitution will be to educate woman in the value of home life.

It is natural only for man to provide. He cannot make a home alone. It is absolutely necessary that there be the mother and wife, and as girls enter into the most important condition of life without any previous culture or consideration of the new life that they enter, as a rule, there will be failure, and more is to pity than to blame for the results. The men from necessity are forced to houses of prostitution. Why? Because the women are uneducated in the business of becoming wife and mother, and they, as a rule, know nothing about the formation of a new home; that is left to chance. Is it any wonder that there is trouble and ruin all around us? Do you think that there is even a single instance where a young girl leaves her mother to-day to form a new home, that she is taught by that mother to believe that the grandest and best work of women is to be able to produce a grand, noble woman or man; and that to do this her home must be a heaven, and that it rests with her, more than all things else, whether her home is a heaven or hell? The great cry of today is the advancement of woman—that means for all to make a grand rush for outside employment, other than home work. While the husbands and sons are walking the streets idle the mother and sisters are earning the living, and by so doing, the homes from necessity are dirty and the younger children uncared for or left with ignorant nurses, and this state of affairs makes the women tired and fretful, the husbands, when they have money, naturally seek the house of ill-fame, as wives are too tired from work or devoting their time to society, to give husbands even a pleasant word. Yes, I say, the only way out of this trouble is to teach girls the value of home, and when women in a mass elevate their homes and make them all that the word implies, that is, clean, home-like and cheerful; their kitchen the cleanest and most cheerful room in the house, and their parlor for use of the family instead of strangers; the houses of ill-fame will have to shut up shop. They will have to close for want of patronage.

When this is made the highest ambition of girl's life, to be a possessor of a model home by her own virtues; and the boys, by mother, are taught to value a good woman; they will then think it an honor to keep those homes clean and wear a bright smile for husband and little ones, and will then know the value of a clean calico dress, a gingham apron for work and a white apron for eyes of father and dear children. There is not a man living that would not prefer a dear little home to "a wandering, no-account, hap-hazard life."

An other typical scarlet woman of Chicago is Carrie Watson, whose brown stone house in Clark Street has long been one of the scandals of Chicago. She was there before the fire and is there still. She does not have quite as many girls as Vina Fields but they are white and not colored and as she is at the head of her shameful profession prices run higher. Business is carried on openly enough with carriages standing at the door at all hours of the night waiting for the "gentlemen" inside. Carrie Watson and Lame Jimmy her violin player are a typical Chicagoan pair. Lame Jimmy acquired an unenviable notoriety this year for at his annual benefit-ball one of the best known police officers in Chicago was shot dead in the midst of the orgy. Lame Jimmy's benefit is one of the saturnalian nights of the Levee when all the professional forces of debauchery are let loose to disport themselves in a Music Hall with the assistance of the police as the above incident shows. Carrie Watson herself has made a fortune out of her trade in the bodies of her poorer sisters. She is the exploiteur, the capitalist of her class, for the same conditions reproduce themselves everywhere. In the brothel as in the factory the person at the top carries off most of the booty. Carrie Watson is a smart woman, said to be liberal in her gifts to the only churches in her neighborhood, one a Catholic just across the way and the other a Jewish synagogue which local rumor asserts is run rent free owing to Carrie's pious munificence. This is probably a slander but its circulation is significant as proving that Carrie Watson can be all things to all men. She is emphatically a smart woman, and cynical as might be expected. Prostitution is to her the natural result of poverty on the part of the woman and of passion on the part of the man. She regards the question from the economic standpoint. Morals no more enter into her business than they do into the business of bulls and bears on the Stock Exchange. Girl clerks and stenographers she says are often unable to earn salaries to keep them in clothes to say nothing of the numberless relations who are often dependent upon their labor for a livelihood. If they have youth, health and good looks they can realize these assets at a higher price down Clark Street, or on Fourth Avenue than at any other place in the city. Women who are desperate go to Carrie Watson and her class, as men go to the gaming

hell in the hope of recouping their fortunes. The misfortune of it is, that women can almost always secure
their stakes at first, whereas the gambler quite as often
as not is deterred by an initial failure. Few people
realize that a young and pretty woman can make more
money for a short time by what may be called a discriminate sale of her person than the ablest woman in
America can make at the same age in any profession.
But as life's enchanted cup but sparkles near the brim so
the profits of that life are of very short duration. When
the bloom is off the rose, a very rapid process of
degradation sets in which ends in the lock hospital, the
jail or the drunkard's grave.

Carrie Watson agrees with Vina Fields in believing
that girls do not take to the life from love of vice, neither
do they remain in it from any taste of debauchery. It
is an easy lazy way of making a living, and once they are
started either by force, fraud or ill-luck there is no way
of getting back. They have to go through with it to
the bitter end. They bury the memories of the past by
drinking the waters of that temporary Lethe, which
men call strong drink, and quiet their conscience by the
thought that after all they are not worse than the highly
respectable men who visit them and that they are able
by suffering these things to help relations who would
otherwise often be in very great straits. Carrie Watson
for instance says that almost every girl in her house
has three to four persons depending on her who share
with her the wages of sin.

Dora Claflin, who was interviewed at length by a
representative of the *Mail*, which published a series of
articles suggested by some remarks which I made at the
Central Music Hall last November, spoke with great
good sense on many phases of this difficult and appall-
ing problem. Like everyone also who has thought
much upon the subject, either from the inside or from
the outside she was of the opinion that prevention is a
far more hopeful field of work than that of rescue.

"Prostitution is an effect," said she, "not a careless, voluntary choice on the part of the fallen. Girls do not elect to cast themselves away. They are driven to the haunts of vice. The more distinctively womanly a girl is—and I mean by that the more she has beauty, delicacy, love of dress and adornment, feminine weakness—the easier a mark is she for the designing. And the designers are not wanting.

"Girls, and I say this empathically, are not seducers. They have innate delicacy and refinement. I say honestly that I do not believe that one woman in 10,000 would cast herself at the feet of lust except under duress or under the force of circumstances.

"The recruiting grounds of the bagnio are the stores, where girls work long hours for small pay; the homes that have few comforts and practically no pleasure; the streets, where girls are often cast, still unknown to sin, but in want and without shelter; in a word, places outside the levee, where distress and temptation stand ever present as a menace to purity and rectitude, behind every effect there is a cause. In the case of prostitution the real cause lies not in the girls who fall, but in the social conditions that make the fall easy and the men who tempt to the step and furnish the money to support degradation after the step has been taken. Before reform in the levee is possible there must be reform in the home, on the mart. The people to enlist in the work of reform are the fathers, the husbands, the sons, especially the fathers and husbands."

I excited much animadversion by saying that if you wished to do any good by reforming any section of society it was a good plan to take counsel of those who were the least disreputable of their class in order to know where we are to begin. These three women whom I have quoted are probably better qualified than anyone else in Chicago to speak as to the profession which they have successfully pursued. They all lay their finger upon ignorance, poverty and misery, as the three great causes of prostitution.

The question of assignation houses of which the police say there are between 400 and 500, is far more difficult to deal with nor is it possible to deal with it by the favorite specific of some people by placing them under a system of license. Such a remedy would be worse than the disease. The utmost that can be done is to keep an eye upon notorious houses and when the concourse of couples becomes so large as to become a public scandal and to leave no doubt as to the character of the house it should be proceeded against as a public nuisance. But a fresh ordinance would probably be required if not an amendment of the statute law of Illinois.

The only licensed houses of ill-fame in Chicago are the massage parlors, fully 90 per cent of which places are nothing more nor less than houses of prostitution. The City Council on May 9th, 1893, passed an ordinance licensing these places with a hope that it could thereby control them.

One condition of the license is:

That it shall be unlawful for any proprietor, manager or employe of any room, establishment or place wherein any of the kinds of business, treatment or operations mentioned in the first section of this ordinance are carried on to furnish, provide, permit or suffer female attendants to bathe, treat, manipulate, operate upon or attend male patrons.

It shall be unlawful for any female attendant, employe or inmate of any rooms, establishment or place wherein any of the kinds of business, treatment or operations mentioned in section one of this ordinance are carried on to bathe, treat, manipulate, operate upon or attend any male patrons thereof.

At the first glance this ordinance will appear to be a measure for the suppression of the immoral massage parlor. It has had the exact opposite effect. The criminal code of the State of Illinois says that no person can be convicted of a crime where the witness to the crime have been guilty of participating in the offense in order to procure the necessary evidence to convict. This fact was prominently brought out at the trial of three of the proprietors of massage parlors in this city two months after the passage of the ordinance mentioned above. The case, in question, was put on trial in the Criminal Court of Cook County for three days during which nearly a dozen police officers testified to the fact that they had gone into the houses in question and had taken the baths and massage (?) treatment in order to procure the evidence on which to arrest the three defendants. On this admission being made a verdict of not guilty was returned by the jury on the defendant's attorney quoting the law which prohibited the obtaining of evidence in such a manner. By the passage of the ordinance the power of putting down these places has been virtually stopped. Previous to the action of the City Council the massage parlors were frequently raided and so kept under some kind of subjection. At the present time, however, the mayor of the city has no power to refuse a license to any persons providing their characters are good and although he may be morally certain in his own mind that such places are going to be run in direct violation to the law he has no facts on which he would be justified in refusing to grant the license asked for.

As might be expected the employers of girls are very sure that if any of their employes go wrong it is not because of insufficient salaries. Indeed it would seem from their statements that the standard of female morals is higher in a Chicago store than it has ever been anywhere since the expulsion of Adam and Eve from the garden of Eden. I sent a representative to question some of the leading men in the city on the subject. Here are their answers in brief.

E. Hillman, the manager of the Boston Store said "As far as I can remember I never have had a girl who has gone wrong who was employed in this store and we employ about 1,900 girls. We take every precaution for their being of strict moral character. It is a strict rule with us that no young man is allowed to come in and talk with the employes or wait for them when they are through work so as to escort them home. If this rule is broken and we learn of it we immediately discharge the offender."

H. G. Selfridge, of Marshall Field & Co., has only known of three girls who have gone to the bad in the last five years. In his opinion it was not want of food but a craving for jewelry and finery that led girls into prostitution.

Arthur Keim, the Superintendent of Siegel, Cooper & Co's. store said in talking on such a subject there is always a feeling of delicacy. "Generally I cannot say much upon the matter but I know that girls in this store are paid good living wages. I think that wages makes but little difference as only those girls go wrong who have a tendency that way."

Another gentleman who was principally engaged in employing girls and young women at the Fair said: "From my own experience I have found that the question of wages caused but little difference with these girls who go wrong. It is the training which they have received. Girls in this store all receive $5 or $6 a week and on that money a girl can live easily in Chicago."

Not food but clothes, not plain clothes but finery,

that is no doubt the want that drives many to a life of shame. The fact that I venture to remind the Woman's Club of is that the peculiar temptation of a woman is that her virtue is a realizable asset. It costs a man money to indulge in vice, but for a woman it is money into pocket. This temptation has naturally greatest force when work is scarce, and when sickness is in the house. Even if they have a living wage in ordinary homes, these periods of stress and strain break them down.

"I lived at home," said a girl in a house of ill fame, "and had a mother and a sister to support on $5 a week. One time, however, my mother got ill and I could not get the necessary medicine for her. Then some young man whom I knew in the street and who came quite frequently to my counter to buy goods, offered me a good deal of money if I would go with him to an assignation house. I wanted the money for my mother and so I went. Having gone once I went again until I gradually drifted into a house of prostitution."

So it is with many. But there are many employers who are not so careful as Mr. Selfridge, who says: "It is and has been my custom to ask all girls whether they live at home or with friends before engaging them and I always make it a practice if they have to pay for board and lodging to pay them a larger salary. When a girl is inexperienced I refuse to employ her rather than pay her a salary on which she cannot live morally."

A keeper of one of the best houses on Fourth Avenue spoke to me very thoroughly on the subject. She said that one of the large dry goods managers had been complacently assuring her—he was a customer of hers—that he never employed any girls for $2.50 a week unless they could live at home. Pin money girls as they call them who are maintained in part by their relations, keep the rate of wages down below living point. If blood relations fail, other relations are too often established. As Mr. Hillman, of the Boston store says: "A girl who boards out cannot support herself on a low wage. We have to enforce the rule as to living with the family or with friends to insure the moral character of our employes.''

The procuress plies her trade in Chicago as in other large cities, preying upon youth and inexperience. They haunt the railway depots, they are quick to discover the pretty girl who is out of work, and they are quite often in attendance at the County Hospital. Excellent societies of good women have done much to warn inexperienced girls of their danger and to provide them with a place of shelter. But their efforts are inadequate and there are many girls in houses of ill fame who have been taken there by plausible ladies who ''knew of such nice lodgings, you know, with a teacher of music who takes such an interest in young girls.'' They did not know anything until it was too late. These girls are as innocent of any wish to go wrong as the deer is innocent of any wise to be shot or snared.

The keepers of houses always deny indignantly the accusation that they recruit their establishments with unwilling volunteers. They profess to detest ''green horns.'' They prefer experienced women well broken to the work, etc., etc. All the same there are many who are only too glad to obtain young simpletons whom they can fleece even if they cannot, as is sometimes the case, realize heavily upon them for rum. One well known procuress, Mrs. Davis, was arrested twelve months ago for one of these offenses, but she escaped. Criminals ''who have a pull'' can usually escape in Chicago. And procuresses, of necessity, ''stand in'' with the police whom they subsidize for permission to live.

Cabmen in Chicago are frequently the active agents of the houses of ill fame. If they find a pretty girl who has not enough money to pay her fare they can usually raise the money by delivering her at a sporting house. That this is done may seem incredible but it was not merely admitted but even complained of by keepers of houses, who being overstocked objected to the practice of an imposition. One madame on Fourth Avenue told me that on three occasions last year she had received consignments in this fashion. She did not want the girls so she handed them over to the Annex to Harrison Street police station. If only any one will take the time and trouble to watch some of the depots and houses of prostitution on Plymouth and Custom House places in the "levee" district, and those on Dearborn street and Armour avenue, in the vicinity of 22nd street they will realize the sad state of affairs.

An ex-police reporter in this city said recently: "I have to my knowledge had four distinct cases of cabmen tak ing young girls, who had just arrived in the city and engaged him to drive them to a hotel, to a house of ill fame. In each of these cases the girls were only saved by police interference, and yet no effort was made to punish the guilty driver of the vehicle in which the girls had been driven to the houses where they were found."

The best proof that the practice exists is the fact that the City Council has passed an ordinance expressly directed against it. It runs as follows:

It shall be unlawful for any licensed owner or driver of any coach, cab, public cart or other vehicle to convey any person without his request to any place or house of ill-fame, or deceive any person in relation to any railroad or other ticket or voucher for conveyance which is worthless, or make any false representation or statement in regard to any voucher or ticket for conveyance that may be shown to him, under the penalty of not less than ten dollars for each and every offence.—*Municipal Code, p. 291, Sec. 1202.*

When once a young girl is ensnared there is very lit tle chance of her escaping. The police report that 20 per cent of the girls between 14 and 18 reported miss ing are never heard of. Those zealous A. P. A. emis saries who work themselves up into a fever heat of indignation and of passion because of more or less imaginary narratives of the way in which convents are used to imprison unwilling maidens, would find a more profitable field for their emotions in contemplating the underground railway by which keepers of houses of ill-fame move girls out of the way. After a girl has been ruined in one town, especially if there is any trouble, she is exchanged for a safer girl in another city. A case of this kind, which can be vouched for, occurred about a year ago. L. M., a girl of 18, came to Chicago from a well-known city in the western part of New York. While here she was seduced under a promise of marriage and taken to a house of ill-fame on South Clark street. Meanwhile she had ceased writing to her parents, and they, fearful that she had met with an accident, communicated with the police here. She was located soon afterwards, but before the authorities could arrest her she was sent to Council Bluffs, Ia. A few weeks later another girl arrived at the South Clark street resort to take the place of L. M. Strange to say, she *had come from the same house in* Council Bluffs to which her fallen sister had been sent. Her story was also on the same line with that of the deported girl.

Many other girls are taken from the County Hospital, where the authorities could interfere with effect in enforcing some standard of civilized decency.

In places of amusement, the Park Theatre is an outrage as it has been and is being conducted. The whole theatre is an exhibition which would be more in place in Sodom and Gomorrah than in Chicago. The proprietors, it is said, make friends of the powers which be by subscribing to the funds of both parties. Whether that is so or not I cannot say. As a matter of fact it is but the antechamber to a lupanar. The moral level of its stage is below that of a decently conducted sporting house. The Midway dance was one of its standing attractions long after it had been banished from Boston and New York. Although the manager lied to me like a Trojan on the only occasion when I visited the place, I had no difficulty in obtaining trustworthy information as to the orgies which have given an evil fame to the wine room.

In a book called "In Darkest Chicago" it was stated that dancing by naked women was one of the regular performances of this theater after the play concluded. That, however, I think, is no longer true, the only difference, however, being that when the women dance the cancan in the Park they pay such homage to decency as is implied in the wearing of a single garment which enhances rather than interferes with the obscene suggestiveness of the performance. An outward semblance of decency could be secured by cancelling their license whenever their decorations or entertainments violated the municipal standard of decency. There is no necessity for making that standard extreme or puritanical, but in a civilized city the goatlike gambols of Satus might be forbidden. It would be too much no doubt to expect certain classes, including some of the most respectable so-called citizens, to comport themselves like human beings, but they might certainly be compelled to preserve the natural decency of an ordinary brute beast. The unnatural and worse than bestial performances which are carried on in certain places in Chicago well known to the police ought to land a considerable number of persons in Joliet for the rest of their natural lives. Offences which in England a very short time ago sent men to the gallows and still entail penal servitude are among the sights of Chicago which are not interfered with by the police, because it is held by large wholesale houses, so the story runs, that it is necessary for them to have certain amusements for their country customers. Entertainers are attached to the large wholesale houses, and when the country customer comes in to make his purchases the entertainer personally conducts him round the sights of the town. As Mayor Hopkins remarked when discussing the gambling houses, it is surprising how many merchants in this city approve of their existence for the sake of their country customers. They say that the first night a country customer comes to town he is taken to the theater; next he is taken round to the questionable resorts, and on the third night he insists upon going to the gambling hells. The questionable resorts to which the Mayor referred as occupying the country cousin's second night may be said to be run, if not under the patronage of the police, at least with their cognizance. A friend of mine who made the round was personally escorted by a detective. When the police and the large wholesale houses and country cousins are in collusion to support unnatural crimes which the good people of Chicago fondly imagined existed only in the corruption of the later Roman Empire, it is obvious that the moral reformer has a very up-hill task before him.

CHAPTER I.

THE CHURCHES OF THE SECTS.

I shall never forget the almost overpowering sense of sympathy and sorrow which overwhelmed me on the morning of the conference in Central Music Hall. I had been discussing, until long past midnight on Saturday, with policemen, saloon keepers, gamblers and keepers of houses of ill fame what Christ would think of them and of us in this city of Chicago. I had heard their unconventional exclamations as they were suddenly confronted with this unwonted suggestion. I had seen the brutalization of men by drink and vice until the human, let alone the Divine image, had almost disappeared, and the still sadder sight of women who were somebody's daughters continuing a life of vice from the terrible conviction that there was no escape.

A feeling of sorrow for these people—a feeling of bitter heartache at the thought of my own inability to do them any good or give them any relief, was after a time completely swallowed up by a new emotion which took possession of me almost in spite of myself. I felt so sorry for Christ! I have never been able to indulge in these devout but sombre meditations on the actual facts of our Lord's passion with any sense of real anguish. It was hard no doubt—all that wandering down the dolorous way, and cruel, brutally cruel, the martyrdom of the Cross, but it happened a long time ago. The halo of supernatural glory which surrounds His tragic death cannot disguise the fact that so far as mere physical pain was concerned His suffering could not compare with

261

that of uncounted myriads of His brethren who had gone down to the invisible world amid protracted agonies of torture, compared with which the way of the Cross was a comparatively swift and easy relief. But when I had this fresh realizing sense of the greatness of the sorrow which he came to relieve and which still remains unstanched and of the maimed souls crushed and mangled out of all semblance of the Divine image, the sense of failure of it all, the thwarting of the great aspiration came home to me with a freshness almost inconceivable, considering how long I have been familiar with some of the saddest sorrows of the world. Was it for this He came to earth? Is the 19th precinct of the 1st ward with its poor girls in the Fourth Avenue houses, and its toughs and the crooks down the levee, the fruit which He might expect to find after nineteen hundred years? If I felt it so much, having but seen for a few moments one infinitesimal shred of the world's garment of mourning and heaviness, if I, all flawed and faulty as I am, yet feel the iron enter my soul, what must He have felt, who has heard the dropping of their tears in heaven these nineteen hundred years?

It is this which is the real passion of our Lord! The unabandoned sin, the unstanched tears, the abounding bitterness of the human heart, these are the real crown of thorns which the world has crushed upon His wounded brow.

Long ago, Darwin's Descent of Man, gave me a similar sense of the immanence of God. Until then, in a vague sort of way, I had had the feeling, common I suppose to most of us, that the world had been created long ago and that creation was as much a past event as the Norman Conquest, or the war of the American Independence. But Darwin made me see that the creative work is going on today as much as at any previous time in the history of the world, for we stand in the very work shop in which the Eternal is from day to day fashioning the world in which we live. So in the bitterness of that dreary night I felt that our Lord's passion and crucifixion was no longer a bygone instance in the history of the human race. The Passion and the Cross are for us day by day and hour by hour, moment by moment. Nor will He cease from dwelling amongst us—the living word made manifest in flesh—as long as men and women live, and love, and sin, and suffer, and go down forlorn into the pit.

There was sadness and anguish in the thought, but there was also a great consolation, and a wonderful stay and solace in this new realization of the omnipresence of the Cross. And then there came the comforting thought in the midst of it all, that He who saw it all from the beginning never lost heart, never struck sail to a fear, never doubted even when the sky was blackest and hope seemed dim, that God was love, and that in the end we shall see as He saw that even those things will work out for those who suffer and those who bleed a far more exceeding weight of glory.

At present we must work by faith and not by sight, and if Christ came to earth His first instinct would surely be to seek out those who are called by His name, if only to ascertain how it was that these things were so after all these years, and what they were doing to banish evils which banish love from the lives of so many of his brethren.

Of all the churches in Chicago the first place to which He would turn his steps, would be the Catholic Church, over which Archbishop Feehan presides as the representative of that Vicar of Christ, whose seat is in the Eternal city. Archbishop Feehan is a good and saintly man, ascetic in habits of life, devoted to his offices and the punctilious discharge of all the duties of his high office. Behind him there is all the spiritual authority derived from the traditions of the Roman Church and their vital connection with a hierarchy which encompasses the world.

Under him as spiritual chief and director general of

the forces of the Catholic Church, there are two hundred and fifty celibate priests. Some of them zealously enthusiastic, humble and devoted saints of God, working with a zeal that never tires, and with a self-sacrifice of which the world knows little or nothing in order to maintain Christian law and Christian discipline within the polyglot host which worships in the one hundred churches over which the Archbishop has supreme control. Every Sunday in these churches they gather together from as early as four in the morning twice as many citizens of Chicago as attend all the other churches of all the other denominations put together.

Five hundred thousand of the inhabitants of Chicago believe more or less implicitly that Archbishop Feehan is their divinely appointed commander-in-chief in the great campaign that is ever being waged against the forces of evil.

But while recognizing the perfection of discipline and drill which the Catholic host has attained by the daily or weekly maneuvers on the ecclesiastical parade ground, while doing glad homage to all that is high and noble and self-sacrificing in the great communion with its saintly sisterhoods, its enthusiastic orders and its consecrated priests, I must admit a sense of bewilderment that a power so great should be lodged in hands so feeble, and that the army maintained at so great an expense, both of money and labor, should have so little influence on the civic life of Chicago.

Much is said, and foolishly said, by persons who hate Rome much more than they love anything in heaven or earth, against the intrusion of the church in politics. But if the church be the divinely appointed instrument for the reconstruction of society in accordance with the law of God, if in short the church be the chosen organization, as, presumably, Archbishop Feehan believes, by which the mandate of God is to be established here on earth among men, it cannot keep out of politics excepting by delivering them over to the devil. That is what seems to have been done in Chicago, nor has the Evil One shown any lack of alacrity in accepting the charge.

But if Christ came what would He say concerning the organization called by His name offering Him constantly sacrifice of prayer and praise, and the sacrament of the mass, but which refuses to lift a finger or stir a hand in the great struggle for honesty, justice and righteousness in the government of Chicago?

The A. P. A's., or the modern Know-nothings, who call themselves the American Protective Association, probably because most of their members are not Americans but Canadians or Britons, whose reason for protecting American citizenship is not quite apparent, assert that the Catholic Church is only too active in politics in Chicago, and in proof thereof they parade the following tabulated statement of the offices which are held in Cook County by Catholics.

The Catholics of Chicago have:

> The Mayor.
> The Chief of Police.
> The Chief of the Fire Department.
> The Postmaster.
> The City Attorney.
> Clerk of the Circuit Court.
> Clerk of the Probate Court.
> Clerk of the Superior Court.
> A number of the Judges.
> Forty-five of the sixty-eight Aldermen.

Ninety per cent of the police force, eighty per cent of the members of the fire department, and sixty-seven per cent of the school teachers are Catholics, while eighty per cent of the pupils are Protestants—as half the Catholic pupils go to priests' schools.

Mr. Hopkins is the first Catholic Mayor the city has ever had, and had it not been for Protestant support he would have been ignominiously defeated. His majority was made up of 75,000 Catholics and 38,000 Protestants. Both the Chief of Police and the Chief of the Fire Department were in office before his election, and by general consent are the fittest for the post whatever their religious belief. The fact that the Catholics predominate in the police and the fire departments is more due to the fact that they are Irish than because they are Catholics. The alleged preponderance of the school teachers has nothing whatever to do with politics. Every teacher is appointed after an open examination, conducted by Protestants, and if sixty or seventy per cent. are Catholics it would seem to indicate the intellectual superiority of the Catholics who go in for teaching. This is surprising, but it is in no way due to the political influence of the Catholic Church.

Still these figures are sufficient to show what an enormous interest the church has in the administration of the city. And the fact that the Catholics preponderate so largely in the City Council ought to rouse the church to spare no effort to rid the City Hall of the reproach under which it at present labors.*

But to use the influence of the Church merely to get jobs for Catholics is a conception that reeks of the Ring. For the church to go into politics for the spoils would be a church that had gone into politics not for the kingdom of God, but for the boodle, and would be morally on the same level with Alderman Powers and other distinguished but unhonored members of the City Council.

The evils which afflict the city as the result of our forgetting God fall with heaviest weight upon the poorest citizens. The majority of these belong to Archbishop Feehan's flock. Yet so far as they are concerned, he

*Archbishop Hennessey of Dubuque, who preached in Chicago in December, spoke words which ought not to have fallen on deaf ears. He said: "There is a tradition, brethren, that 900 years before the birth of Columbus this country was colonized by a band of Irish people. It was called the Great Ireland of the West. I can see in a vision the future of America and the Catholic Church wherein it will be again called the Great Ireland of the West. What are you doing? There are half a million communicants in the church in this city. Chicago is the most Catholic city of America in proportion to its population All nations of the earth are here represented, and there is a multitude of societies. Take my suggestion and work for the future of the church of Christ. Build up your schools, make them commodious and ample. make them free. schools, so that the children of the poor may enjoy their benefits. Elevate the standard of education to the plane of the government of God's divine church. Marshal your forces, and you shall become the center of the Catholic Church in America."

might as well be the Archbishop of Timbuctoo as Archbishop of Chicago. *

No one would dream that the Catholic Church in Chicago should sully the purity of its sacerdotal garments by arraying itself on the side of corrupt republicans or corrupter democrats. Partisanship of that kind is alien to the spirit and contrary to the whole conception of the church. But not less hostile to the whole traditions of the church are the lethargy and callous indifference with which the Archbishop and his advisors have seen this half Catholic city plunged into the mire of corruption without one word from the Archbishop to warn the faithful as to the sin which they were bringing upon their city and the danger which would follow to their own souls and to those of their children after them.

It was said of old time in one of the early writings of the Christian Church, "If the neighbor of an elect man sinneth, the elect man has sinned himself." How much more then must the sin of the Catholic boodlers in the council and the corruption of the Catholic wards in the city lie at the door of the Catholic Archbishop in Chicago! He sees things going from bad to worse under the very shadow of the spires of his churches but has he ever said a word or done a deed to rally the forces under his com-

---

* Some people complain of the Pope's interference in American affairs. It is much to be regretted that he cannot intervene much more than he does in Chicago. Leo XIII would have very little patience with such inertia in face of the present social crisis as prevails in this Diocese. That is to say if we may assume that he meant what he said in his recent Encyclical. The Pope is not a mere preacher or letter-writer. He is a general or commander of a great black-coated army of ecclesiastics all over the world. He reigns over the Empire of the Confessional, as England reigns over the Empire of the Sea. When he says that the Church ought to concern itself with the solution of the Social Question, he practically asserts that every Catholic priest everywhere should do his uttermost to bring to bear the teachings of the Encyclical upon the community in which he lives. For political questions tend to become more and more social questions, and in all social questions the Pope tells us the influence of the Church is essential to their right solution. If, therefore, the Church stands apart from their consideration, she makes their right solution impossible.

The Encyclical deprives Archbishop Feehan forever of the excuse of Cain. At present, when a strike or an agrarian revolt breaks out, there are many members of Christian Churches who shrug their shoulders, saying, "It's no affair of ours. Am I my brother's keeper?" "Yes," replies the Pope, "you are your brother's keeper, and his blood will I require at your hands." Henceforth, whenever any social question disturbs the community, the Catholic priests will feel that they have failed in their duty if they have not in some way or other made their influence and their teaching helpful to the solution of the problem.

mand in support of the cause of honesty, justice and fair dealing with the poor?

When Gregory the Great was told one day that a solitary unknown beggar had been found dead from starvation in the streets of Rome, he excommunicated himself for having allowed such a thing to happen in a city under his rule. For days he abstained from communion, shutting himself up in his silent cell, to make atonement by tears and penance for his sin of omission towards that poor starveling.

If the Archbishop of Chicago had but something of the heart and soul that was in St. Gregory, the sufferings and privations of this last winter would not have left him unmoved.

If Christ came to Chicago would he find a greater disappointment anywhere than the spectacle the greatest of all His churches doing ecclesiastical goose step in the parade ground, but refusing to go forth to battle against the powers of wickedness in high places, and against all the tyrannies which oppress the poor, because, forsooth! —it might endanger the church and create difficulties even with some of its own members. As armies exist in order to fight so churches are founded in order to encounter dangers and to face difficulties. Nor would there have been an Archbishop in Chicago to-day had earlier archbishops been as timid and incapable of rising to the height of great opportunity as Archbishop Feehan.

Turning from the Catholic Church to the non-Catholic churches in the community which number in the whole city about 200,000 members, and having an attendance every Sunday which is probably not more than 100,000 and sometimes considerably less, we have spiritual forces which at least are free from the paralysis of a commander in chief whose ideal of strategy is to keep his army out of the field. In the non-Catholic sections of the church of Chicago there exists great diversity with no unity. The spirit, however, of co-operation exists and at the conference held this winter representa-

tives of the various parties expressed a great desire to
co-operate so as to take more effective action in the
campaign against the evils which afflict the city.

The various churches are wealthy, comfortable,
served by able and zealous ministers and sung to by
choirs of ecclesiastical nightingales. Very few are as
fruitful in good works in the shape of institutional side-
shows as we are accustomed to in England but here and
there you will find a church that reaches out on all
sides to minister to the wants of the community.

The Salvation Army lives among the poorest people,
works with them, gathers them together every night
and contributes a valuable element to the building up
of saner and sounder citizenship than that which yet
prevails in many precincts of Chicago.

But the Protestant churches for the most part, judg-
:ng by the complaints which are heard from inside
the church rather than from the outsiders, has succumbed largely to the temptation of "being at ease in
Zion." The Methodist ministers were told somewhat
rudely by a speaker recently that men were needed who
would do more than make faces at the devil from behind
the pulpit.

And the most enterprising of their number are at
present considering whether they could not establish
some mission resembling that of Mr. Price Hughes in
the west of London in some of the spiritually destitute
districts of Chicago.

The growth of Epworth Leagues and Christian
Endeavor Societies is a sign of progress in the right
direction, but I do not know of any church in Chicago
which utilizes the whole of its ecclesiatical plant as vigorously as do some of the leading churches of England.
Two services a day on Sunday and a prayer meeting,
possibly once or twice a week, can hardly be said to
be making the best use of an investment in real estate
which is estimated to amount at least to $13,000,000.
All money sunk in church buildings is God's trust

money. If it belonged to anyone else and were invested by trustees so as to yield interest only one day out of seven the trustees would either be sent to the penitentiary or the lunatic asylum. They would certainly not be held to have used the trust to the best advantage.

As it is with the church buildings so it is with the membership. Instead of regarding the church members as saved souls come together for the purpose of saving others, the tendency is too much to regard them as the members of a select club, meeting together for their spiritual edification, and for harmless æsthetic indulgence.

Some ministers have roundly asserted that many of the richer churches in the city are nothing more nor less than social clubs, which are quite out of touch with the masses of the people. They represent not so much sacred dynamos for the generation of spiritual force capable of lighting the whole district, but huge fly-wheels driven at great expenditure of coal without any driving belt. It is too much in the fashion to lay the blame for all this on the ministers. Some ministers are to blame, no doubt, but the responsibility lies at least as much at the door of the congregation and especially at that of the trustees.

In America the Erastian theory of a church under the influence or domination of the state is scouted and rightly scouted, but Erastianism is very much like Mother Nature. Even if they expel it with brute force it will find its way back again after a little delay.

Each of the churches is free. It represents in theory a spiritual power entirely free from the control of the world, but as many a minister knows full well he is very effectually tethered by the secular power in the shape of a trustee or a liberal contributor to the collections. It has been said to me repeatedly that the devil has a mortgage upon many of the pulpits in Chicago, and he will promptly foreclose if ministers are to presume too much upon the liberty of prophesying.

On the last occasion on which I addressed an audience in Central Music Hall I made some observations on this point which I venture to reprint here:

I have talked a great deal to ministers of religion of all denominations, since I came here. Some of them shrug their shoulders and say "Well, it is all very well talking, but if I were to denounce a man whom I knew to be a scoundrel who was standing for alderman I would offend some very influential members of my congregation and that would not do for the interests of religion." But if the Church of God exists for anything in this world is it not in order to raise men and women who are prepared to take a little risk for God and his Christ, and if the ministers of religion think it is sufficient answer to any appeal made to them to enter into a campaign for righteousness that it might offend some members of their congregations, then there is a great need for a revival of religion among ministers of religion.

I have spoken, also, to other ministers. They say "We are with you heart and soul and to the best of our ability we have preached in this sense. We have laid righteousness to the line, and justice to the plummet, and we have endeavored to stir up our congregations but they do not like it." Said one eminent minister in the city recently, "When I preach a sermon like that to my people they are not pleased. They do not come to the church to hear that, they want to hear a sermon which would make them feel good. They want to be told concerning the good people of old times and have Christian doctrine expounded, and they wish to have a blissful future portrayed to them of the place where they will go when they die. I am of a very sympathetic nature and I have never felt unsympathetic to anyone who wishes to feel good—feel comfortable, I mean. I have a great deal of sympathy with those good men and women who have been toiling and moiling through the week and who wish to get into a place where the world and all its cares would be shut out, and where they could sit down and sing their souls away to everlasting bliss." It is very natural but it does not follow that it is right because it is natural.

I will take you to another scene which is also very natural and which appeals even more strongly to many men and women than the seductive influence of a fashionable church and congregation. Go with me down the Levee. Go along until you come to a down stairs dive. You go down the steps and knock on the door in a peculiar kind of a way. A long pigtailed heathen comes to the door. You then find yourself in an opium joint of which there are a good many in that quarter fulfilling many useful offices among others tending to enable our hard worked police to increase their perquisites. The atmosphere is not incense ladened, but through the dim light you see reclining on tressel beds or bunks persons, each of whom has a pipe and is carefully engaged in putting a little pill of opium into it in order that they may smoke it. You sit down a while and talk to that Chinee and after a time you begin to find out that there is a most wonderful spiritual resemblance between the opium joint and the fashionable church. Because the poor wretch who is lying there wishes to get away from the world and its cares and the turmoil and troubles of this evil life and he likes to smoke himself away for a brief season into everlasting bliss into a realm which is not a real realm and which has no bearing upon real life. That man feels good and I sympathize with him. H feels that for half an hour or so he gets away from all his troubles and cares into another region, a more exalted region it seems to him, and there is just about as much religion in it as there is in the other one. Perhaps there is a little bit more, for the man with the pigtail does not sing hymns protesting all the time he is pleasing Jesus Christ who resents faithful preaching urging present duty because they prefer to be lulled into pleasant imagining of a blissful future or a miraculous past. Those people are just like the habitues of the opium joint. It is not religion. It takes them away from the duties of religion and leaves them in a region which is neither heaven nor earth but is betwixt and between, and which from the point of view of citizenship is precious little good.

I hope it is not necessary for me to protest that I have no wish to underestimate the amount of sincere religion that exists in every church. It is not because I disbelieve in the church that I appeal so strongly and protest so vehemently against the misuse of the immense power which the churches could wield if they were to but concentrate their forces with ordinary common sense, upon the redemption of the city. But if we endeavor to place ourselves in the position of our Lord, were He to visit Chicago, to see what progress had been made towards the establishment of His kingdom in this city, is it not obvious that His heart would be saddened by the present condition of the churches called by his name?

Instead of finding each of these congregations, which gather together for worship every Sunday, in His name, working hard to get His law fulfilled and His brethren saved from the wicked injustices to which they are now subjected under the existing city government, they are comfortably assembling once or twice a week, for the purpose of hearing a good talk about Him and of having their senses thrilled by choirs who offer the service of praise in the hearing of the congregation.

Is it uncharitable to say that of all the disappointments caused by the comparison between the real and the ideal the greatest disappointment which Christ would find in Chicago would be in his own church?

The sectarian churches, whether they be of Rome or against Rome, are not in touch with the whole community. They have no close direct bearing relations with every householder. There is no system in the ecclesiastical organization corresponding to the ward and precinct organization which enables the municipal government to cover the whole town. Although the churches may fraternize and their members be on visiting terms with each other, ecclesiastically as well as socially, there is no attempt to create a central executive empowered to wield the united force of all the churches against the common enemies of all. It is something gained that they should be civil to each other Some of them are not even that. Yet there is in the more advanced churches a genuine desire to enter into closer relations with each other. Of this the recent formation of a Ministerial Federation is a hopeful sign.*

Once more let me conclude with an extract from the Gospel according to Russell Lowell, for the great American puts the truth more forcibly in verse than we can express it in prose. In no poem has he uttered thoughts as to the non-ecclesiastical church more thrillingly than in "The Search." In this poem Lowell tells us how he went to seek for Christ, "for Christ, I said, is King." He searched for him in the solitude of nature, and found him not; and then, "'mid power and wealth I sought, but found no trace of him." The churches had become the mere sepulchre of their risen Lord, and divine service a mere formal mustering, as for roll-call, of men in the empty tomb:—

> And all the costly offerings I had brought
>   With sudden rust and mould grew dim:
> I found His tomb, indeed, where, by their laws,
>   All must on stated days themselves imprison,
> Mocking with bread a dead creed's grinning jaws,
>   Witless how long the life had thence arisen;
> Due sacrifice to this they set apart,
> Prizing it more than Christ's own living heart.

---

* See Appendix. The Federation of Ministers of Religion.

The poet-seeker then turned to the heedless city, where he came, led by fresh-trodden prints of bare and bleeding feet, and found his quest:—

> I followed where they led,
>   And in a hovel rude,
> With nought to fence the weather from His head,
>   The King I sought for meekly stood;
> A naked hungry child
>   Clung round His gracious knee,
> And a poor hunted slave looked up and smiled,
>   To bless the smile that set him free;
> New miracles I saw His presence do—
>   No more I knew the hovel bare and poor—
> The gathered chips into a woodpile grew,
>   The broken morsel swelled to goodly store.
> I knelt and wept; my Christ no more I seek,
> His throne is with the outcast and the weak.

CHAPTER II.

If Christ came to Chicago and sought to discover His church He would not be likely to mistake any of the existing ecclesiastical sectarian institutions for the society which he founded for the purpose of carrying on the work of the redemption of the world.

Where then would He find it? To answer that question it is necessary for us to ask ourselves what Christ meant by the church and what as a matter of fact the church was and did in the early days of the Christian era. If we further consider the evils which exist in Chicago, which must be exorcised if the city is to be won for Christ it is obvious that the church militant must be the organization which can combat those evils. The church in every age has been an association of those who endeavor to do Christ's work and make Christ's will supreme among men. "Thy will be done in earth as it is in Heaven." If we keep those two ideas steadily before us we shall not be far wrong in coming to the conclusion that if Christ came to Chicago, the City and County administration would seem to Him to be more like the church which He founded nineteen hundred years ago than any other organization lay or ecclesiastical which exists in Chicago at this moment.

Considering the iniquities that are permitted under the rule of the City Hall it is a somewhat startling paradox to assert that Christ would regard that as the cathedral of his church in Chicago. But the temple in Jerusalem was none the less the temple of Jehovah because false incense was sometimes burned on its altars to false gods. So although the council chamber is packed with boodlers nevertheless it is the Council and the County Commissioners which are doing most of the work that the Christian church in the early ages regarded as its distinctive function. The City Hall is more faithful than any of churches to certain of the great ideals of Christ, and it is only through the City Council and the Town Commissioners that Satan's invisible kingdom can be effectively attacked.*

If we look at things as they are, resolutely refusing to allow ourselves to be blinded by their labels, we shall not be long in discovering that the City government, both in theory and in practice, much more closely resembles the ideal Christian Church than any of the existing ecclesiastical churches. To begin with in the Apostolic times there was one church for one city. There was the Church of Thyatira, the Church of Philadelphia and so forth. In Chicago there are 500 churches but there is only one city government.

Secondly the fundamental principle of the Christian Church was that of a brotherhood so broad as to include men of all ranks, of all conditions, of all nationalities. The City government more than any of the churches is based on just such a recognition of human brotherhood. In the citizenship of Chicago as in the old Christian Church, there is neither Greek, nor Jew, bond nor free, Barbarian or Scythian, all are one before the ballot box. Only in one respect does it fail to come up to that Christian ideal. Chicago is not yet sufficiently civilized to recognize the citizenship of women so that part of the

---

*It cannot be too often insisted upon that however great may be the shortcomings of the city government the churches cannot dissever themselves from a large share of responsibility in the matter. What is the use of lamenting the absence of a strong sense of civic religion if the official ministers of religion seldom or never preach or teach the religious aspect of municipal or social duties? What is the use of deploring the indisposition of competent and leisured men to undertake the irksome and uncongenial work of municipal administration when those whose special duty it is to rouse the conscience of the community never preach the dedication of the citizen to municipal work as one of the most important and most sacred means of helping to bring in the kingdom of Christ on earth? What conception of civic religion is possible to the ordinary man if on the eve of municipal elections the church takes not the slightest pains either to urge the best men into the field, or even to impress upon her congregations the importance of electing the best men from the candidates before them? If the churches are the divinely appointed instrument for carrying out the divine will in the affairs of this world in Chicago, it would seem as if either God had forsaken His church or His church had forsaken Him.

text which says "in Christ neither male nor female," does not apply here.

Thirdly, the City government recognizes as does no other organization in Chicago, the great truth that the community is one body of which we are all members and that if one member suffers, all the other members suffer likewise. This sense of interdependence results from the fact that the evolution of the social organism is much further advanced on the municipal side than on any other. The conception, however Christian, has made more advance under the ægis of the municipality than under the dome of any Christian temple in Chicago. Those who doubt this should compare for the moment the different way in which a material evil is handled by the municipality and a moral evil by the various churches. Nothing is more inspiring than to see the way in which the conception of the unity of the social organism operates under the city government. It is tested by the outbreak of a fire. A drunken tramp drops a match in the outhouse of some miserable shanty in the outskirts of Chicago. The straw alights and the fire blazes up. The nearest patrolman who sees it hastens to his patrol box and sends in a fire alarm. Instantly in every police station, and newspaper office throughout the 190 square miles within the city limits that alarm is reproduced and almost before the patrolman has quitted the patrol box the fire engines are clattering along the streets from the nearest stations to extinguish the fire. Should the wind be high and the flames baffle the efforts of the local force, fresh alarms are sent in and instantly more fire-engines and firemen are dispatched, until in case of need the whole resources of the city in apparatus and in men will be concentrated upon the point of danger. There is no question as to rich and poor, no discussing in police stations or at the fire department as to whether or not the locality was a long way off or what might be its ratable value or anything else. There is fire and there is need and that is enough.   The whole machine splendidly equipped in perfect discipline, acts almost automatically on any appeal from any section of the community.

Contrast this, where we have the social organism functioning at its best under municipal guidance and direction, with the way in which the ecclesiastical churches act, when some moral pestilence which it is no exaggeration to compare to an outbreak of hell-fire, takes place in any quarter of the town.   To begin with there is no special patrolman to give the alarm, and if there were, there is no arrangement by which the cry could be heard, let alone be heard instantaneously throughout the churches of Chicago.   But supposing that by some telepathic miracle, the spiritual watchman could sound his warning note in the ears of all the churches, how many of them would respond?   Some would shrug their shoulders and say it was outside their parish, others would remark that it was among the Catholics and not for their people, others again that there were no Catholics in the region, but they were all Jews and that they ought to look after themselves.   As a result of this refusal, born not of selfishness or of cruelty, but due simply to the fact that the evolution of the Christian ideal of the unity of the social organism has not yet attained so high a point in the churches as it has done in the municipality.

Fourthly, the City government is organized upon the simple democratic basis which was natural to the company of fishermen whom the carpenter of Nazareth selected as the nucleus of His church.   Whatever may be the faults of the City government, it is simple and it is close to the people.   No social and ecclesiastical hierarchy stands between the common people and their elected representatives any more than there was between the early believers who gathered together after the day of Pentecost and those whom they appointed to dispense charity and to serve tables.   The poor man, the laborer rude and uncultured feels more at home in the City Hall than he would in most of the wealthy churches in the city of Chicago.

This it may be said is only theory. But the fact is, that the City government is much more like that early Christian Church than the existing Christian churches which claim to be its direct descendants. This is largely due to the success with which the early Christian Church and its medieval successors Christianized the whole conception of secular government.

The moment you begin to study the state from a historical point of view, and trace the origin of the institutions which we now possess, you are brought sharply face to face with the fact that the modern state, especially the modern municipality, is very largely the heir and acting legatee of the mediæval church. That is to say, many of the functions which the City Council has to perform were in old times the exclusive work of the church. Not many centuries ago it would have been blank heresy in the eyes of churchmen, and absurdity in the eyes of statesmen, to assert that much of the work discharged by the City Council could possibly be entrusted to any body excepting the religious orders, the monasteries, and other ecclesiastical authorities. That is to say, according to the old conception of the functions of church and state, the City Council, and the County Commissioners, from the work which they perform, are quite as much Church as State, for they perform duties and accept responsibilities which for centuries were regarded as the exclusive prerogative of the Church.

Take, for instance, the care of the poor. This was in early times regarded as the province of the church. Pure religion and undefiled was defined by the apostle as consisting in the first place in providing for the fatherless and the widow. This function, however, is no longer entrusted to the ecclesiastical organizations. The fatherless and the destitute today, are sent to Dunning, or to some other institution, which, whether it is governed by the City Council or the County Commissioner, is a secular institution doing distinctively Christian work.

Take another instance. The hospitals were founded by the church, and for hundreds of years were exclusively maintained by the church. Today there are still hospitals in connection with various churches, but the greatest hospital of all is a County institution, and its management is in the hands of the elected representatives of the people. The same is true concerning prisoners whether it is in the Bridewell, the Penitentiary or in other places wherein these wards of the state who have forfeited their liberty are kept in temporary servitude. The work of redeeming and reclaiming those wandering ones is left to the state, it is no longer the prerogative of the Church.

Education is another great department which in early times used to be regarded as much the right and duty of the Church, as the conducting of divine worship is today. That also has passed into the hands of a secular board appointed by the Mayor, who is elected by the citizens of Chicago. Another institution— the Public Library—which mankind has come to regard as indispensable, formerly had no existence save in the monasteries. Now it is domiciled in the City Hall, and cared for by the civic authorities.

Cleanliness which is next to godliness, has entirely passed under the control of the City which supplies the water, superintends the drainage, and is responsible for the removal of those physical causes which contribute so much to the moral degeneration of the people. In fact, the more closely it is examined, the more clearly will the facts stand out that if any of the great saints, who, a thousand years ago Christianized and civilized Europe, were to come to Chicago, they would, after surveying the whole scene, decide that three-fourths at least of the work which they did was in the hands either of the City Council, the Mayor or the County Commissioners, and that not more than one-fourth remained in the hands of the clergy and their so-called church. The state, or rather the city, has become the executor of the church for three-fourths of the work which the church was instituted to accomplish. This is right enough, for it is the duty of the church ever to press forward, and when it has Christianized the community sufficiently to entrust any of its own duties to the elected representatives of the people, there is always more work to be done further afield. But the responsibility for the due discharge of all these functions of which it has relieved itself remains with it intact yet.

But unfortunately no sooner does the church rid itself of the onerous responsibility with which it was formerly saddled, than it seems to abandon all care or interest in what used to be its own special work, and what was heretofore regarded as distinctly Christian work, is often handed over to men who have not the slightest trace of Christian principle. In this respect the church behaves not unlike the unfortunate mother of an illegitimate child, who, finding it irksome any longer to maintain her offspring, hands it over to a baby farmer, and thanks God she is well quit of her brat. Everyone knows what results follow when the baby farmer is substituted for the mother as the custodian of the infant. Much the same results follow in the secular sphere when the moral influence of the Christian Church is withdrawn from the bodies to which it has been handed over the duties formerly discharged by the church.

Yet it is not only the theory of its constitution and the actual work with which it is entrusted that the City government would lead the steps of our Lord to the City Hall. He came to earth to seek and to save those who are lost, to deliver the oppressed and redeem mankind from the evils which afflict them. In His progress through this city many sad and grievous sights must have afflicted Him whose eyes are too pure to look upon iniquity; but when He had made his sad pilgrimage through our streets, and considered how best to deliver the least of these His brethren from the afflictions with which they are encompassed, He would find no agency in the whole city which was capable of coping with the evils in question, excepting the City government. The ecclesiastical churches, even if they were filled with His love and inspired by His spirit, could no more remove those evils than a sunbeam can drive a locomotive. What are these evils? There is the injustice by which the rich, who are strong, and are able to bear the burden of taxation, transfer hundreds of thousands of dollars to the shoulders of those who are poor, and not able to support so heavy a tax. That can only be dealt with through the legislature, and by the elected representatives of the people. There is the evil of corruption established as monarch in the center of the civic administration, while aldermen like servile courtiers fawn around his throne for sops which are purchased by stealing the heritage of the poor. That evil also can only be attacked at the primaries and the ballot boxes. Whether we are dealing with the tramp or with the willing but workless worker it is by politics, through politics and in politics that the work of redemption must be wrought. Gamblers, open their trap doors to perdition in our streets; it is the duty of the police to close them. The insanitary precinct, where the children of the poor are reared under conditions which defraud them of their natural inheritance of health, and the prospect of happiness belongs also to the municipality. The predatory rich can only be kept in order by the same agency. In fact the way of deliverance from most of the evils which afflict the community, must be sought through the City Hall, rather than through the direct agency of any of the churches of the town.

Hence I think that from whatever point we approach the question we shall arrive at the same conclusion, if Christ came to Chicago, the center from which He would work to establish His kingdom here and now in the city of Chicago, would be the City Hall.

CHAPTER III.

MAYOR HOPKINS.

Few things impress a visitor from England more than the dearth of leaders. Next to the distrust which people have of each other, this phenomenon impresses the stranger most unfavorably. The lack of leadership is, perhaps, the natural Nemesis of a people which has forgotten how to trust. But the conditions of society are rapidly compelling even the most indifferent of these Anarchists of Comfort to see that society will not get on much longer without leadership. Hero worship is innate in the human mind. Not even the feverish temperature of the Board of Trade can banish that original instinct from the heart of man, although the ambition to lead is singularly absent among the natural leaders of the Democratic society.

Nevertheless, here as elsewhere, in the wise leadership of the preoccupied many by the capable few lies the hope for the future. The majority of men or women, whether in democracies or aristocracies, do not think for themselves. They have not the mind in the first place and would not take the trouble if they had the mind. The wise, the thoughtful and the men of character and initiative are always in a very small minority, but it is that minority which rules, and must rule if the state is not to drivel down to a heap of ruins. The supreme merit of Democracy is not that of permitting every Tom, Dick and Harry to steer the ship according to the untrained unwisdom of the forecastle, but because it gives the one capable man, whether he be in the forecastle or in the forecabin, a chance of proving his capacity and obtaining possession of the helm.

Conspicuous among those who have arisen to do battle

in the popular cause against the tyranny of the corporations and the scandalous corruption which honeycombs
civic life in America, is a sturdy New Englander, who is
now serving for the third time as Mayor of Detroit. Hazen
S. Pingree, like most of the men who have contributed
largely to the building up of the middle and western
states, is from the east coast. He did not come over with
the Mayflower, for the historic vessel had made her epoch-
making trip fourteen years before Moses Pingree settled
in Massachusetts. England was at that time just foam-
fretted from end to end with the beginnings of a civil war
which was not to end until Charles Stuart's head fell beneath the headsman's axe, and Moses Pingree brought
over with him the Puritan hatred of tyranny and all
unrighteousness. Hazen Pingree, the present Mayor
of Detroit, was born on a farm in Maine in 1842.
When fourteen he left the farmstead and began to
serve his time in a shoe factory in Massachusetts.
When the war broke out he was twenty years old
and was the first volunteer from the village in
which he was working. They talked of buying him
off, but he laughed the proposal to scorn. "Who
would not give a farm to be a soldier?" he said, a saying
which, being repeated, passed from mouth to mouth and
acted as one of those potent suggestions kept up the
morale and re-enforced the ranks of the Army of Emancipation. Pingree, who possessed a strong constitution,
fought through the whole war from Bull's Run to the
collapse of the Confederacy with the exception of
six months which he spent as a prisoner of war in
Andersonville.

After the war was over he came to Detroit and resumed work in a shoe factory. After a time he saw
an opportunity of beginning business on his own account in a small way, and from that moment he never
looked behind him. Keen business instincts, united
with a sterling honesty which was universally recognized
by his customers, and the rapid growth of the north-

western states, combined to make him the owner of the largest shoe factory west of New York. He settled down, married, and became a comfortable citizen, full of restless energy. He built up a considerable fortune and furnished a mansion, every room of which bears testimony to the culture and refinement of the Detroit cobbler. Notwithstanding his business he made time for travel, visiting Alaska on the one hand and all the picture galleries and museums of Europe on the other. His drawing-room contains some of the gems of European art, trophies of his continental expedition, while the library is full of choice and well-thumbed books.

There was great dissatisfaction in Detroit in 1889 owing to the corruption and mismanagement which prevailed in the municipality. An influential deputation of citizens waited upon Mr. Pingree and begged him to accept a nomination to the mayoralty. Up to this time he had been engrossed in business and had given but cursory attention to the management of the municipal affairs. He hesitated, then refused, but finally was induced to stand. He threw the whole of his irresistible energy into the campaign and was elected by a majority of 2,318. He is a Republican, but he speedily made it known that in the City Hall, partisan politics were to be severely subordinated to the public good. As soon as he entered office he saw that it would be impossible to do anything in the perfunctory fashion which had previously prevailed. The Mayor of Detroit in those days did not come down to the City Hall till half past eleven, where he spent half an hour in signing documents and then for the rest of the day went about his private business. Mayor Pingree changed all that. He went down immediately after breakfast and stayed there till six at night. He ran the city in the same businesslike fashion in which he had previously managed his shoe factory.

As soon as he grasped the situation he found that he was confronted by a corrupt Council, whose members re-

garded their position as chiefly valuable for the opportunity which it afforded for selling public franchises.
He found the streets practically handed over to the domination of the street railway companies, while the murderous grade crossings of the steam railways were increasing and multiplying to the peril of the citizens and
the continual interruption of public traffic.   The
tax-dodger flourished and by so doing laid the greater
proportion of the burden of taxation on the poorer classes.
The town was being spiderwebbed with wires, notwithstanding an ordinance which had been passed, but never
enforced, compelling the electric lighting, telegraph and
telephone companies to place their wires under ground.
The gas company was in full possession of the municipality, it charged the consumers $1.50 per thousand
feet and acted in the usual high-handed fashion of gas
companies in similar positions.   Valuable franchises
were given away without compensation.   The electric
light company rendered shamefully inadequate service;
and in short, Mayor Pingree found Detroit suffering from
all the evils which afflict Chicago and most American
cities. The city, instead of being governed in the interests
of the citizens, was practically farmed out to corporations
who were about as honest as the farmer generals in
France before the French revolution, and who had as
much regard for the welfare of the people as distinguished
a hungry Roman proconsul just appointed to fatten upon
the wealth of a conquered province in Asia.   Seeing
which Mayor Pingree took off his coat, turned up his
sleeves and set to work.

It is not necessary to describe here the details of that
great fight which began in 1890 and is still going on.
It is a campaign in which all the glory and most of the
triumph has been on the side of the Mayor.   He is a
silent man of as much pertinacity as the taciturn general
who led the armies of the Union in triumph to the rebel
capital.   In his first message he announced that the
time had come for the city to assume control of the public

lighting and own and operate its own plant, in order that it might escape the caprices of tyrannous corporations. After a prolonged struggle with the city railway companies he brought them to their knees, and only this year he has achieved a brilliant, although not decisive victory in the law courts to which he had appealed against their franchise. The net value to the city of the judicial decision, if confirmed by the Supreme Court, is not less than $5,000,000. This, although the latest, was by no means the first of his encounters with street railway companies. He had given them a taste of his quality by refusing to call out the militia to shoot down their employes in a strike which took place soon after his election. Instead of calling out the militia he wrote a strong letter to the company counseling a resort to arbitration. His advice was followed under duress and the strike ceased. The principle of arbitration then established has been in operation ever since, and when I was in Detroit this year arrangements were being made for the reassembling of the Arbitration Board for the settlement of a question which had arisen as to a proposed reduction in wages.

He fought the gas companies and compelled them to reduce their rates from $1.50 to $1, with a prospect of a still further reduction to 80 cents. The quality of the gas was improved, meters were protected against fast running, and no extra charge was to be made for their use. The gas company was not allowed to destroy the pavement in laying its pipes, as all gas pipes had to be laid in alleys whenever possible, and gas mains were to be extended on the petition of one consumer for every 100 feet. Detroit, like Chicago, is debarred by its charter from owning its gas plant and the gas companies were not brought to their knees without a severe fight, in which the police, acting under orders of the Mayor, arrested the gas men who were tearing up the streets in defiance of the city authorities.

The most sensational incident which attended his fight needs to be told at a little greater length. From his first entering office the Mayor had set his heart upon municipal electric lighting. After infinite trouble in getting permission from the Legislature for the municipality to operate and own its own electric light plant, he was disgusted to find that the corrupt members of the City Council, disregarding the permission given them by the State, had passed an ordinance handing over the electric lighting of the city to a private corporation in almost as cynical a fashion as the majority in the Chicago Council passed the Watson Gas Ordinance. The Mayor promptly vetoed it with as much emphasis as Mayor Hopkins. The boodlers of Detroit had either more nerve or were in greater need of money than those of Chicago, for a two-thirds majority was prepared to pass the ordinance over the Mayor's veto. Mayor Pingree was in despair. But light arose in the midst of darkness. An hour or two before he had to go down to the City Council to assist as an impotent spectator at the triumph of the boodle, an Alderman presented himself at the Mayor's house. He stated that an agent of the electric light company had just been to see him. They were rather anxious about their majority and they wanted another vote. The Alderman replied he was not going to vote for the ordinance. The agent assured him that they would make it worth his while to pass the ordinance over the Mayor's veto. On asking what he meant he was told that if he voted for the ordinance he would receive $800, in proof of which he handed him there and then $200 on account in hundred-dollar bills. The Alderman, wisely dissembling, accepted the money, thanked the gentleman and hurried down to the Mayor, in whose hands he placed the $200.

With a light heart, notwithstanding the fire which burned within, and with victory in his eyes, Mayor Pingree drove down to the City Hall. The Council was assembled. The ordinance was about to be passed over his veto. Just before the roll was called the Mayor rose. Amid the dogged and mutinous silence of the boodlers the Mayor, as his habit is, plunged into the middle of his subject. " Before you vote for the ordinance I wish to inform you that I am well aware that illicit means have been employed to secure your votes. In fact I hold in my possession two hundred dollar bills which were this very day handed over to an Alderman whose vote the electric light company wished to purchase in support of this ordinance. This $200 was a twenty-five per cent instalment of the total sum to be paid for that vote." A murmur of alarm ran through the Council and one or two of the bolder members ventured to cry, " Name ! Name ! " " Yes," said the Mayor, " I can name him : he is Alderman so and so," naming his informant. " He will testify that it is true. Here are the $200 which he has handed me. It is impossible to believe that he is the only Alderman who has been approached. Now gentlemen, let us call the roll." Consternation is a mild word to express the dismay which was depicted on the faces of the boodlers. The blow struck by the Mayor hit the Aldermen between the eyes and when the roll was called they simply bolted. The Mayor's veto was sustained, and as a result Detroit expects to be the best and most economically lighted city in the whole of the United States. Success was gained in this case by the opportune discovery of legal provable facts as to the boodling that was practiced in the Council. From that time forth the Mayor has gone on conquering and to conquer.

He is bent at the present moment upon giving the inhabitants of Detroit free water, founding a citizens' street railway company which is to construct and operate street railways in certain streets in Detroit under conditions the most onerous which the wit of man can devise. The franchise is to be forfeited whenever any of these conditions are ignored. Girder-grooved rails have to be used. The roadway between the tracks is to be repaved. No overcrowding is to be permitted in the cars, which have to be of the most approved design for service and for comfort. The fare is

to be twenty-five cents for eight tickets, carrying right
of transfer within the city limits. The street railway company is to pay from $1,500 to $6,000 a mile on
tracks paved and railed by the city, and the corporation
is to deposit $10,000 in cash as a security for the com-
pletion of the trolley system. The City Council is to have
the right to purchase it at valuation to be fixed by arbi-
tration at the expiration of fifteen years, or to take over
the whole plant, exclusive of rolling stock, free gratis
and for nothing, at the end of twenty-five years.

I went over to Detroit in order to see this champion of
the rights of the common people against corporate tyranny. I found Mayor Pingree a solid, stalwart, resolute man, who has established a reputation of being as
immovable as the Rocky Mountains in all cases where
public interests conflicted with the claims of private
speculators. No one can move him when once he sees his
objective and he goes for it with an irresistible dash and
keeps up the momentum of the charge until his enemies
are scattered like chaff before the wind. He is a terror,
is Mayor Pingree, a terror to evil-doers and hated accordingly by all that class. Notwithstanding the opposition
of all the monopolists and all the corporations he has
twice been re-elected, and each time by a larger majority.
If ever there was a man who sits firm in the saddle and
rides his steed with a steady hand Mayor Pingree is that
man. Senator Palmer, whose family has been so long
connected with the city, said that there was no doubt
that Mayor Pingree was absolutely incorruptible and that
he was consumed with an unquenchable zeal for the public service. "There is no doubt," said Senator Palmer,
"that he has succeeded in making a stand which has
given him a position very few men hold in the Union;
and I am not afraid to say that if the Republicans are
likely to have a hard fight for the next presidential election Mayor Pingree might be the strongest candidate
whom they could put into the field. He is a strong man
who stands for a principle which is likely to come to

the front more and more and I am not by any means sure that his nomination would not be good party policy."

Into such lofty regions I do not venture to intrude. All that I know is that Mayor Pingree is an honest man, fighting a heroic battle against immense odds, and encompassed by a host of enemies who have spared no effort in order to ruin him both financially and politically. The extent to which this is carried may be inferred from the fact that last year an Alderman in the City Council, who had supported the Mayor's reforming policy, was waited upon by an influential deputation, including, I am sorry to say, some leading members of St. John's Episcopal Church in Detroit, who gave him to understand, without ceremony, that he must either quit supporting the Mayor, or abandon his seat in the Council or make up his mind to be ruined. The Alderman was a plumber with one of the best businesses in Detroit. As a high-class plumber his business connection lay chiefly with the rich people, and on looking into the matter he saw that the members of the deputation were perfectly able to make good their threat in case he did not oppose the· Mayor or abandon his seat in the Council. The Alderman came down to Mayor Pingree with tears in his eyes and told the story. "What can I do?" he said. "I am over 60 years of age, my business is worth $25,000. I shall lose it all if I remain in the Council and support you, as I must if I sit there. The only thing that I can do is to resign." And resign he did. It is a curious instance of the modern tyranny of the predatory rich that not one paper in Detroit would publish the truth about this Alderman's resignation for the information of the citizens.

Mayor Pingree is a Republican, who has no bitterer enemies than some of the Republicans in Detroit. Mayor Hopkins, who was elected last December as the successor of Mr. Carter Harrison in the mayoralty of Chicago, is a Democrat, and unless all appearances are misleading, is likely to find his worst enemies among men of his own party. That, however, is all in the day's work and must be expected. But just as Mayor Pingree has made reputation for the Republican party in the Union at large, so Mayor Hopkins may become one of the elements which contribute to the national strength of the Democratic party. Mayor Hopkins has the advantage of Mayor Pingree in being a younger man. He is the youngest Mayor that Chicago has had, with one exception, and he was elected by the heaviest vote which Chicago ever cast for a chief magistrate. There is much in his career to fascinate the imagination, and if he should continue to progress as rapidly as he has done up to the present, the story of his early life and his rapid rise is likely to figure in the school books of the English-speaking race side by side with the story of how Abraham Lincoln from a rail splitter became President. To an Englishman the possibility of so sudden a promotion from the ranks to one of the foremost positions in the Republic is one of the few elements of romance and of charm in American politics. The fact that the man who, the other day, was working as a lumber shover or a day laborer, should now be autocrat of the capital of the New World, is a distinct contribution to the romance of contemporary history. The Arabian Nights element is always the most interesting in history of nations and individuals and there is a great deal of the Arabian Nights element in the rapid rise of Mayor Hopkins.

John Patrick Hopkins was born in Buffalo. He was educated in the common school, and was the third son of a family of twelve. His father and his brothers are dead, and when quite a boy his sisters had to take to dress making in order to keep the family in bread and butter. As soon as he left school, which he did at a comparatively early age, he set to work to earn his living. His first place he found for himself. He started in life by heating rivets in an iron foundry.

From there he went to work in the Evans elevators and by the time he was twenty had established a good enough reputation for regularity and industry to be appointed weighmaster of the place. When he was twenty-one he came to Chicago, the city which fourteen years later was to elect him to the highest office in its gift. For four months he looked around. He fixed up his sisters in dressmaking business, and then started out to look for work for himself. He was not quite twenty-two when he went down to Pullman and asked the superintendent of works for a job. In reply to the question of what he could do, he replied that he would do anything. Being asked if he meant what he said he was taken at his word. The superintendent was rather pleased at his determination to try his hand at whatever turned up, and sent him to shove lumber down in the yards. There he worked as an ordinary laborer for some months, until he had satisfied the management that he had good stuff in him which could be better employed elsewhere. Whatever may be said concerning the autocracy which Mr. Pullman has established in the city which bears his name, no one can deny that the autocrat and his agents have a keen eye for capacity, at least up to a certain point. Mr. Hopkins' career illustrates this. In August, 1880, he was called into the storekeeping department. The April next year he was appointed timekeeper in the store ; in the following August he became general timekeeper. Two years later he was made paymaster by Mr. Pullman.

But notwithstanding his rapid promotion and the responsible position which he occupied as paymaster of the great industrial army which recognizes Mr. Pullman as its captain general, Mr. Hopkins was singularly independent. It used to be said of him in those days that he was the only man in Pullman who dared to call his soul his own. He was a Democrat, although Mr. Pullman was a Republican. He was young, a comparative stranger, without capital or resources of his own, but

not content with his position of salaried employe, he
went into business on his own account in the Arcade.
A friend of his who knew him at Pullman, and to whom
I applied for some information of those early days and
of the struggles by which Hopkins established his reputation, wrote me as follows :

This Arcade is one of the original and peculiar institutions of the
little manufacturing city of Pullman, which is now, much against Mr.
Pullman's will, part of the great metropolis of Chicago. It is a
big, red structure with passage-ways running north and south
and east and west throughout and on either side booths and shops.
In the upper stories there is a small theater, a public library, offices
and flats. In one corner of the main floor is the Pullman Savings
Bank, through which the pay-roll runs and which is ready to care for
the deposits of the workingmen. There is no other place in the settlement where shops other than groceries and markets can be kept,
and those are for the most part centered in one great market building,
modeled after the same plan. It is possible for the company to dic-
tate in these matters, as it controls every inch of the ground, and not
even the streets have been dedicated as public highways. It has its
own hotel, which has always lost money for the company, but which
is sustained for the convenience and gratification of the officials and
especially Mr. Pullman. Even the church is the property of the company. The Catholics were indeed after a long time permitted to build
on consecrated ground, but before they were given a deed it is said
that a priest who had espoused the laboring men's side in a great
strike had been compelled to resign. However that may be, it is sure
that the reverend father without any apparent reason did fold his tent
and desert his flock against their protests and despite their tears, leaving another to finish the church which he had begun.

This was before I came to Pullman, and I speak therefore only by
hearsay. But John Hopkins had been the companion of the reverend
father in guilt and his resignation had been demanded as a punishment for the crime of openly sympathizing with the workingmen. It
was forthcoming without a murmur, and after a little time spent in
silence and without either suing for restoration or complaining, the
young man was invited to return and his demand for a largely increased salary was granted. It was Pullman's first surrender. But
the fact was that it was not easy for any one to fill young Hopkins'
place ; he knew Ole Olson in the brick-yard and Ole Olson in the
foundry, and he never forgot either or mistook one for the other. So
much of his work was in this way personal that the conveniences for
a merely mechanical system of paying were not at hand and his successor made a sad botch of it. Besides, the absence of swagger or
bitterness on the young man's part was a strong recommendation for
a new trial; but, state it as you will, it was a great victory for the
mayor-to-be, then little more than twenty-five years old. A similar
victory was afterwards scored by a young man named Harper, who
served as chief accountant, and was discharged for insubordination

and requested to return after a time to straighten out a set of books which some of the best experts in Chicago had failed to decipher. He was really a wonderful accountant, whose equal I have never known ; and what because of this and what because of a fellow-feeling for him, Mayor Hopkins has chosen him to unravel the muddle at the City Hall, a task which he seems to be performing with perspicuous ability and great dispatch. But though Mr. Pullman restored both of these gentlemen to their positions without requiring an apology and with increased salaries, he did not fail to place persons with them to learn the work so as to supplant them, and each found a short shift for himself as soon as the powers felt able to dispense with his services. Perhaps this may have been apparent to John Hopkins all along, and may have had much to do with his indifference.

Politics was the cause of war. If there was anything which Mr. Pullman could not endure, it was stiff-necked rebellion politically. Like so many American manufacturers, he had come to think protection a necessity to his business, support of it loyalty to his interest and that of his employes, and voting the wrong way in some manner a treachery unpardonable. But the imperturbable paymaster merely smiled in his usual confident and provoking way, and proceeded to do his best to carry Pullman for the Democratic ticket.

It was not an easy thing to do. The people were accustomed to subserviency, and yet more so since the unsuccessful strike referred to in the foregoing. But Hopkins was indefatigable, and he knew Ole Olson in the brick-yards and Ole Olson at the foundry—in short, he knew them all. To be sure, they worked for the Pullman Company. Doubtless largely because of their admiration for the brave fellow who had stood unabashed and victorious before the company, they did give a considerable Democratic majority in spite of the ever-increasing rumors of official vengeance. Really, by his words, his magnetic presence and, yet more, by his example, Hopkins brought manhood and courage to the surface in men who never gave any signs of either before and have since lapsed into the old, lack-luster, subservient mode of life.

This was too much, and the brilliant young paymaster had to get out without ceremony: and (whether as a fearful warning or not I cannot say) fourteen hundred others, to a man Democratic voters, were sent out too. The reason assigned was lack of work. As a Republican victory had been scored in the nation, this could hardly be ascribed to their future votes. But to an outsider it seemed as if the company, by one fell blow, thought to make such things impossible for the future. Not only was the leader but the flock as well this time driven out of the gates. As before there was not a word of complaint from the imperturbed young paymaster, who only entered a formal protest when the rent was suddenly and greatly increased on the store-rooms occupied by himself and partner in the Arcade. Amid the sneers of the company and its satellites, he prepared to remove his business to Kensington, and for that purpose pushed, with true Chicago enterprise, the construction of a new store building.

He established himself in " Bumtown," on the outskirts of Pullman, which had been abandoned to saloon keepers

and disreputable houses. His advent changed everything.
His store was a wonderful success.   His wagons delivered
goods in Pullman, for the autocracy of the company
could not be stretched so far as to prevent its late paymaster from using the public thoroughfare.   Mr. Hopkins is
still in litigation with the company to recover the exor-
bitant rent exacted from him.   He has also had more
than one opportunity since becoming Mayor of making
it even with his adversaries.   Not that there is any
trace of bitterness in him ; no one could be more smiling,
affable or debonair.   But he has not lost a chance since
he arrived of reminding the public of the seamy side of
the Pullmam administration, whether in gas or in water
or of the district containing 100,000 population on the
boundaries of Pullman which has not yet been provided
with a common sewer, owing to the opposition of the
owners of real estate in the neighborhood.

Mr. Hopkins was always a politician but he was twenty-
seven years old before he was appointed to an office.
The position which he held was that of Treasurer to the
village of Hyde Park.   Two years later he endeavored to
obtain the nomination to the National Democratic·Con-
vention. As usual with young aspirants he had to fight his
way to recognition. He was defeated in 1888, but he made
so plucky a fight against Mr. Green that his standing in
the party was recognized without further hesitancy.   He
was placed on the committee and in the presidential campaign Pullman was delivered over to his hands by the
Democrats.   It was Mr. Hopkins who first startled the
Republican close borough by a torch light parade
through the streets and by this and other electoral sensa-
tions he achieved a victory which startled everyone. The
next year he followed it up by a municipal success quite
as notable, for as Chairman of the Annexation Committee
he played a leading part in adding 225,000 population to
Chicago.   Among the towns annexed, Hyde Park was
one of the most important, and the Pullman Company
had the chagrin to see their estates annexed to the city

of Chicago against their opposition. After this he became President of the Cook County Democracy. He took the boys down first to Springfield and then to Washington. His name was first coupled with the mayoralty in February, 1890, when with a thousand members of County Democracy Marching Club he went down to Des Moines to attend Governor Boies' inauguration. Hopkins, who has an extraordinary memory for names, resembling therein the Queen and Mr. Gladstone, who are said never to forget a name they have once heard, presented each member of his thousand marching Democrats, and it is said that he never made a mistake in the name of a single individual. Mr. Hopkins having complimented Governor Boies on his gray hair, the Governor replied, " By the time you have hair like mine I trust you will be Mayor of Chicago." Not a single streak was visible on the Mayor's glossy raven locks when Governor Boies' prediction was fulfilled. Mr. Hopkins went everywhere with the marching club. " He would always wear a plug and carry a cotton umbrella like the rest of us," said one of the members, " he never made an enemy in this club." He was never absent from one of the fifteen funerals which occurred during his membership and he was just as punctual in attending inaugurations, ratifications and celebrations of all kinds ; indeed, the County Democracy Marching Club may be said to have been the creation of Mr. Hopkins. It is remarkable that he should have held his own as its chief and trusted captain, for he never drinks, and many of the marching Democrats need to be well primed before the parade. He was always pleasant and genial to everyone, never forgot anyone's name and was always in his place when expected. All this time he was building up a big business. He entered upon other work, dealing with street cleaning and street work, and he had become a very substantial citizen. All his mind was concentrated on business and politics. He took no part in society, although he belonged to several clubs. He spent most of his time in

his store or at home with his mother and sisters. He
dressed well and kept in well with the influential people,
including President Cleveland, who last year appointed
him receiver of the Chemical Bank, the duties of which
responsible post he discharged with the vigor and dispatch which characterize all his actions.

When Carter Harrison was shot and the election was
ordered to be held for the appointment of his successor,
there was no intention on the part of the official gang in
the County Democracy to run Hopkins. They would
willingly have nominated one of themselves, but Mr. Hopkins came in and said he wished the nomination, and all
opposition went down before him. He does not owe
anything to the party managers unless it may be a few
grudges, which he will probably pay off in due time.
He refused absolutely to make any pledges or to bind
himself to any course, but insisted on having his hands
free in case he were elected. With many a wry face his
rivals bowed to the inevitable and Mr. Hopkins entered
for the campaign against Acting-Mayor Swift. It was
hot and furious while it lasted, but so far as Mr. Hopkins was concerned the contest was not characterized by
any asperity, nor did he commit himself recklessly in his
election pledges. The policy of the party was defined
in a manifesto which compared very favorably with the
singularly barren and jejune production which emanated
from the Republican Committee. His portrait was in
every saloon and in a great many other places besides ;
for Mr. Hopkins is a presentable looking young man,
whose countenance is good to look upon. In the end he
was elected by a majority of over 1,200.

No sooner was the Mayor in the saddle than he began
a campaign which bore the strongest resemblance to
that of Mayor Pingree in Detroit. He addressed himself
to the elevation of the grade crossings, ordered a list of
the killed and wounded to be made up and read to the
Council at their meetings. He prepared himself for a
battle royal with the boodle element in the Council,

which he saw would endeavor to use the attempt to elevate the tracks as a means of levying blackmail on the railways in order to embarass him in his enterprise. Finding the city hopelessly behind in its finances he cut his own salary ten per cent and insisted on a general reduction all round. He surrounded himself with competent and public-spirited advisers and began a systematic inquiry into all the abuses which have disgraced the city. Comptroller Ackerman drew up a report upon the scandalous system of assessments, which is the disgrace of Chicago, and the report was published to the dismay of all the tax dodgers of the community. He took energetic measures against the street railways to compel them to fulfill their obligations in repairing the tracks, in paying the license duty and in discharging the other obligations which they owed to the city.

His first battle with the Council took place over the Northwestern Elevated Railway Ordinance, which the Aldermen had passed, it is said, in return for $1,000 a vote, for making an elevated railway to the northwest. The Mayor vetoed the ordinance because it did not secure any return to the city in the shape of a percentage upon the gross receipts. His veto was sustained. The ordinance as amended provides that the city shall share in the gross profits of the railway. A committee was appointed to inquire into the unauthorized encroachments on the public domain by steam railways, with results which are not a little surprising to the public and disagreeable to the railroads. He stopped the disgraceful system of levying fees for inspection. He waged war against the system of collecting and retaining the taxes by which collectors were able to pocket scores of thousands of dollars which ought to belong to the public, and generally set on foot an investigation of the shady places of the city administration. By a ukase he peremptorily suppressed the raids for revenue upon houses of ill fame, which have been the scandal and the disgrace of Chicago for many years, and ruined at least for a time the business of the professional bailer and the justice of the peace. In dealing with the police his avowed policy has been to remove the police from politics, but the temptation to avenge himself on his adversaries was too strong to enable him to carry out that programme in its entirety. Captain Shippy disappeared, Captain Mahoney was reduced and Inspector Ross compelled to resign. There was no attempt to justify these acts, other than upon political grounds.

Mr. Hopkins' great fight, however, was waged with the boodle gas ordinance. For a whole week the victory was in dispute, nor did anyone know to which side it would incline. At the Council meeting Mayor Hopkins launched one of the strongest messages which has ever been addressed to such a body. His veto was sustained, although forty-two members of the Council voted in its favor while only twenty-two voted against it. He was saved from defeat by the defection of a certain number of Republican Aldermen. The Democratic boodlers stood firm, with the result that the Mayor's next task is the ridding of the City Council of the presence of the corrupt members of his own party.

Personally Mr. Hopkins impressed me very favorably, partly, I must admit, at first on account of his resemblance to Cecil Rhodes, the Prime Minister of South Africa. Cecil Rhodes is the ablest man in the British Empire from the administrative point of view, and if Mayor Hopkins is anything like Cecil Rhodes he will not stop far short of the presidential chair. He is, however, younger than Mr. Rhodes and of a more nervous temperament. When he presides over a Council meeting his fingers are continually playing with his mallet, and at times even this method of disposing of his surplus energies fails and he gets up and walks backwards and forwards like a caged lion on the raised dais on which the mayoral chair is placed. He may get over this when he grows older, otherwise it will wear him down, for the Aldermen are a tough crowd and he has a very long row to hoe before he gets to the end of his job in Chicago. He is a demon for work, and his constitution, which has not been impaired by any excess either in drink or tobacco or other forms of dissipation, will stand a much greater strain than would ruin the strength of most of his opponents. There is a joyous elan about him which will stand him in good stead. He has not been elected three months, but he has established a reputation in Chicago which no other man possesses, and it is admitted reluctantly, even by those who are opposed to him, that if he were to stand on an independent ticket he would be elected Mayor at present by a majority of three to one. " He has a spine like a telegraph pole," exclaimed a banker, admiringly, after reading the message on the boodle ordinance. It would be difficult to describe more picturesquely the kind of backbone which is needed by a man in Mayor Hopkins' position.

Mr. Hopkins is not an orator, but if he were to take a little more trouble he would be able to excel as much on the platform as he does in administration. There is a bonhomie about him which is attractive to the masses, and he is quite Bismarckian in the reckless candor with which he expresses his opinions. He is not a scholar nor a student of books. He reads the newspaper, and he lives in the midst of his fellow men. His vernacular is expressive and at times vigorous. When it was told him that Andrew Foy, a City Hall employe, was refusing to support his wife, who, had borne witness against him and Coughlin in the Cronin trial, he told him he would have to quit if he did not support his wife. "I will be d—— if I will have a man in the employ of the city who will not support his family." Mr. Hopkins is perhaps a trifle vindictive, but in the campaign on which he has entered if he will but qualify his vindictiveness by a large magnanimity he may find that part of his nature an element of strength. He has got an Augean stable to clear out and many of the other labors of Hercules to put through. He will need all his youth, all his strength and all his good temper and all the support of the honest citizens. His experience at Pullman shows that he is capable of fighting a winning fight against apparently hopeless odds. He will have against him every scoundrel who is fattening on the plunder of the poor. He will also have to face the determined opposition of the so-called respectable citizens who have profited and are now profiting by the success with which they have avoided the proper share of their civic obligations. But as Mayor Pingree said to me, " I could never have succeeded if I had not thrown myself upon the people, and at every crisis in the struggle appealed to the people to support me in the campaign, and they have never failed in Detroit." Neither will they in Chicago if Mayor Hopkins but sticks to his guns and trusts the people to help him to carry their cause to victory.

CHAPTER IV.

BISHOP BRENNAN AND HIS SECULAR CLERGY.

"Give me control of the police force," said Commissioner of Police Sheehan of New York, "and I do not care a tinker's damn who has the majority of votes." I was told much the same thing in Chicago. "Do not make any mistake," said one of the leading business men in the town, "Mr. Hopkins may be mayor but the people who run the town are the police. They are on deck when the captain is in the cabin and it depends upon them far more than upon him what kind of government we have got." Government by police is hardly an ideal system of administration, but it would not be so bad if it were not permeated through and through by the influence of politics. The policeman is a good servant but a bad master, and he has all the faults of the tyrant and all the vices of the slave when he at the same time lords and tyrannizes over the people and is compelled to cringe before the pull of the political boss.

One of the planks of the Democratic party which carried the mayoral election for Mayor Hopkins was that the police should be taken out of politics. It can be done no doubt, but the process is very much like taking a man out of his skin, and so far there does not seem to be very much evidence that the operation has begun. The first act of Mayor Hopkins was to dismiss Inspector Ross, who was supposed to have been Mr. Swift's candidate for the chieftainship of the police. His second was to reduce Captain Mahoney because, as the aggrieved officer put it in his letter to Mr. Hopkins, "At the special election for mayor I exercised my right as an American citizen, entitled to the suffrage in voting for the choice of my party, and in my humble opinion, for the best man for the position." Captain Mahoney said he failed to see how Mayor Hopkins was fulfilling his pledge to take the police out of politics by reducing him in position. That is because Captain Mahoney is somewhat dull of perception and fails to appreciate the humor of a position which is really very humorous although it was somewhat tragic for him.

I asked Farmer Jones what he thought of the way in which Mayor Hopkins was fulfilling his election pledges in this matter of the police. "He is all right," said Farmer Jones, "there is nothing the matter with him." "But," I said, "he is only firing out Republicans, and is that not a rather peculiar way of divorcing the police from politics?" Farmer Jones looked at me curiously and then said with somewhat of his old smile lingering in the corner of his eye: "It is all right. This is one of the first steps which must be taken towards that end. You see that the Democrats believe that the police can be divorced from politics, the Republicans do not, therefore the Republicans will do all they can to make the experiment of a non-political police a failure. To give it a fair chance therefore it is absolutely necessary to clear all the Republicans out of the force in order that the police divorced from politics may be worked by those who believe that there ought to be no politics in the police force, that is to say by Democrats. Otherwise this reform would have no chance at all." Farmer Jones, it will be seen, has in him the making of a famous casuist, but the Mayor, fortunately, has shown no sign of going to the lengths which Farmer Jones' apology would justify.

The ideal before Mayor Hopkins, as indeed before everyone else in Chicago, is the Fire Brigade. Fire Marshal Swenie has remained in command of the firemen for many years and the administration of the department has been conducted on business principles, with results in efficiency which are a standing reproof to every other department in the city. As the necessity of rescuing at least one department of the administration from the all pervading pestilence of party politics was burned into the mind of Chicago by the great fire it almost seems as if it would require a similar cautery to brand upon Chicago a similar conviction in relation to other departments. Even with the memory of the fire fresh in the minds of the citizens Mayor Cregier was so unmindful of it that immediately after his election he proposed to replace Fire Marshal Swenie by a creature of his own. The way in which he was restrained from doing so was told me by Mayor Hopkins. As soon as it was known in the city that the Mayor was going to apply the spoils system to the fire department, a deputation of fire insurance men waited upon Mayor Cregier. Their communication was brief and to the point. They said, "Your Honor, we are only citizens engaged in the fire insurance business, we have nothing whatever to do with the distribution of the mayor's patronage, and if you dismiss the Fire Marshal that is your business with which we cannot interfere. Our business is to make rates at which we are willing to take risks on the insurance of property against fire. The moment the Fire Marshal goes the rates upon all descriptions of fire risks will go up 25 per cent." The deputation then withdrew but the Fire Marshal retained his position.

Chicago appreciates an argument which can be stated in percentages payable in dollars. Chicago is not yet sufficiently alive to arguments which relate to the administration of justice, to the prevention of crime and to the repression of vice. These things are important, no doubt, but negligence in their enforcement does not entail an immediate money fine upon the respectable citizens. Were it not so they would make their police as non-political as their firemen.

The Chief of Police in any city corresponds more nearly to the early ideal of a Christian bishop than any modern prelate. If his manifold functions are looked into it will be found that there are few people who deserve to be regarded as the true episcopus or overseer than does Chief Brennan. His jurisdiction is limited to the prevention of sin in the comparative and superlative degree; when sin becomes vice or develóps into crime then it demands the attention of the Police Bishop of the city. Day by day in the New World as in the Old the tendency is more and more to saddle the police with ever increasing duties, responsibilities and obligations, thereby increasing the resemblance which the police bears to the medieval bishop. Indeed the moment the idea is suggested to anyone analogies crop up in all directions. Chief Brennan does not wear a mitre or grasp a crozier. He does not even wear a helmet and his uniform is the reverse of conspicuous, but in his inner sanctum he reigns like a prince-bishop of the olden times over the whole of his diocese of Chicago. His inspectors are his suffragans, his captains are his deans, his lieutenants his canons, while the patrolmen who every day and night keep ceaseless watch and ward over the city constitute his secular clergy, sturdy and stalwart specimens of the church militant containing as is wont with all human institutions a fair share of recruits from the Devil's Brigade.

It is a thousand pities that a force which should be allowed to perform its arduous and responsible functions with a single eye to the enforcement of the law and the maintainance of order should be perpetually interfered with by the politicians. It is quite incredible—the extent to which this system is carried. Over and over again I have had to ask myself whether I was really in an American city or whether I had been spirited away and dropped down in some Turkish pashalik so entirely has the very conception of impartial justice died out in the police courts of Chicago. That is a strong statement to those who do not know Chicago but those who know the city will only wonder and be surprised that I should regard it as a subject interesting enough to be talked about. I might as well discuss the rising or the setting of the sun or the order of the equinoxes. These things happen they say, but as no amount of talking will stay the equinoxes, or delay the rising and the setting of the sun so no amount of discussion or denunciation can cause justice to be administered in Chicago without fear or favor. The mayor, the aldermen, the saloon keeper, the heeler, everybody in fact who is anybody or anything in Chicago has got a "pull" when justice is to be administered excepting that abstract entity justice herself. Justice has no "pull."

There is no secret about this in the force. The men talk quite freely about it on their beats and as it is with the patrolman so it is with those much higher in station. There is no secure reward for ability and the most faithful service counts for nothing compared with the ascendancy of the spoils system. As Major McClaughry the late Chief of Police in Chicago said bitterly to the chiefs of police assembled at Bloomington:

If the policman resists all the temptations which beset him he has in most cases, under our admirable system of city government, the prize set before him of being abused and hounded and misrepresented, and of being turned out to graze the moment there is a change of administration, either in the ward in which he resides or in the city government, of which he forms a part.

But it is not worth while dwelling here upon the way in which the spoils system spoils the men who administer it. That is an old story. What is not so familiar is the extent to which politics interfere not only with patronage but with the actual administration of justice from day to day. One night as I was returning from Harrison Street police station to my hotel I ran across an elderly policeman who belonged to the first precinct. The conversation which took place left a deep impression upon my mind. I had said something about the infamous system by which the professional bailer and the justice of the peace drew fat revenues by levying legal blackmail on the unfortunates in the streets. The policeman said, "There are no greater robbers in Chicago than you will find at the police stations."

He said they were all robbers at the police station, the justices, the bailsmen and everyone else. But he added, "That is not the worst of it, politics are in everything and they poison everything. The police department and the administration of justice ought to be taken clean out of politics altogether. It just tires us out seeing how everything we do is brought to naught by politics."

I asked "How?"

"Well," he said, "every justice is a political man and he is under the thumb of the alderman and the politician. The bigger the thief the greater the politician and the more influence he has in Chicago. A tough who is always prominent at ward meetings and fights for the candidates of his party gets the protection of his party. Hence we may arrest him red-handed and take him to the police station; in a very short time he will march out having the laugh on us."

"How is it done?" I asked.

"Oh, the charge will be reduced from larceny to disorderly conduct by discretion of the judge who will then fine him $50 or $100 but before our backs are turned he will suspend the fine, that is to say he will remit it. The whole system of suspending or as you would say remitting fines is bad. It is simply that a fine which is imposed according to law is taken off according to politics. Politics rule everything and no one in the force dare go against an alderman. If I saw a man commit a robbery now and I arrested him and if that man were in politics I would be a fool not to let him go, because he would at once appeal to an alderman who would see that he got off. Some men are so dull-headed they cannot take a hint. I thought once that it was my duty to arrest a thief even if an alderman were his friend but I always found that I got the worst of it in the long run. It is that which spoils us. When you have a clear good case against a man and work hard to get him to the police station you are horribly discouraged when you find that all your labor is thrown away because your prisoner is in politics. It is politics everywhere and justice takes a back seat to politics. For instance if an alderman came along here and struck me across my face with his fist I would be a fool to arrest him unless I wanted to be fired out of the force."

Repeating this conversation in another police station on the other side of the river an officer who was present said he thought the patrolman had exaggerated somewhat, for his part he remembered that an alderman was once arrested in Chicago.

"When?" I exclaimed.

"Well," said he, "it was a very long time ago," so long indeed that he was not able to settle a date. I asked the policeman from the first precinct whether he would give me specific instances. "Instances!" exclaimed he, "oh, every Tom, Dick and the devil know about that. Go down any day and see it for yourself."

Without for a moment admitting that the whole administration of justice in the justice courts of Chicago is as hopelessly rotten, the chances of the conviction of a political offender in Chicago are slender enough indeed. The law, even when it is honestly administered without its being rendered unworkable by the interference by people with pulls is very faulty. The system of taking appeals is simply licensed larceny, for this the law is to blame not the police or the justice. For instance: Jacob Mendelsshon, late chief clerk in Justice Foster's court, said last winter:

"If the legislature would amend in some way the law relating to appeals in city cases it would do good. For instance, if a thief is fined $100, $11.50 will get him out of the trouble. He appeals from the decision of the justice, puts up $11.50, has a bond signed and then is on the streets again, and this is the last of the case. Only yesterday two women were fined $100 and costs each for nearly stabbing a man to death because he would not give them any money. They appealed the case, paid $11.50, and were at liberty again in ten minutes. The justices are not to blame for this state of affairs.

Under the circumstances it is a marvel that there is so

little serious crime in the city.   Over and over again
when I have reflected upon the way in which justice is
outraged in her very courts, and when I see how the administration has been poisoned with political prejudice
and twisted everywhere by the zeal of faction, I have
marvelled that society does not show a much greater de-
moralization.   Nearly everything happens that ought
not to happen, and yet things go on fairly well.   The
administration of justice is carried on in a hugger-mugger
fashion in a hurley-burley almost inconceivable to those
who are accustomed to the graver and more serious
methods of the Old World.   I sat on the bench at the
Harrison Street police station beside Mr. Justice Brad-
well for an hour one morning, and could not help smiling at the rudeness of the accommodation which was
provided for the magistrate and his assistants, and the
extraordinary way the accusers and accused were thrust
almost like a flock of sheep into a pen in front of the bar
of the court.

As might be expected perjury is regarded as a very
venial offense by many policemen in Chicago.   This is
the besetting sin of the police all the world round.
There is a tendency in every policeman to hold that the
end justifies the means, and when a police officer is
quite sure that he has got hold of a crook he feels that it
would be almost a mortal offence not to strengthen his
evidence by a little hard swearing if the occasion
demands it.   A prosecution of a policeman for perjury
would be almost inconceivable in Chicago.*   To such
an extent has this been carried that one judge in
Chicago, Goggin, by name, has on more than one
occasion astonished the court by dismissing all prisoners
against whom there was nothing but police evidence.

---

*Writing on this subject the Chicago *Herald* of December 29 makes the
following emphatic assertions: "The courts of Chicago have been defiled by repeated police outrages. Wherever members of the force have had a personal or
factional interest in causes undergoing judicial scrutiny it has been repeatedly
shown in evidence that officers tampered with witnesses, secreted or distorted or
manufactured testimony, conspired for or against a defendant, and did not hesitate
at rank perjury to accomplish an unjustifiable end."

On January 25, on releasing a man on habeas corpus, Judge Goggin said:

"The carelessness and irregularities in procedure observed by the Police Department are very great. Many of the officials are either entirely ignorant of the first element of law or else do not take the trouble to proceed in a legal manner. I am inclined to think that the members of the city prosecutor's staff who attend the police courts are not careful, or else I would not have continually to release prisoners."

The fact of the matter is, as Judge Goggin very well knows, the police are a law unto themselves, and have the very scantiest respect for any law which they can evade without getting themselves into trouble. One great cause of this is that the city ordinances are so far in advance of what is attempted to be done that a policeman naturally feels that he can pick and choose. The Municipal Code is very strict. Section 1790 runs as follows:

"Any member of the police force who should neglect or refuse to perform any duty required of him by the ordinance of the city or the rules and regulations of the department of police, or who shall in the discharge of his official duties, be guilty of any fraud, extortion, oppression, favoritism or willful wrong or injustice, shall forfeit and pay a penalty not exceeding one hundred dollars for each offence.

Under this ordinance every policeman might be fined $100 every day from the highest to the lowest for there are municipal ordinances by the dozen which are never enforced at all. Whether it is in relation to the saloon, or the gaming house or the house of ill-fame every member of the police neglects to perform the duties required of him by ordinance and therefore he has very little of the reverence which policemen in other countries imperceptibly absorb for a law which is inexorably enforced. Every policeman has more or less discretionary power to suspend the law in individual cases, just as a justice of the peace has to suspend a fine at his own caprice. The way in which this works is obvious, it works directly in the levying of black mail.

Hence the duty of the police in Chicago is twofold. He is a representative of the majesty of law and he does not bear the sword, or to translate it into the vernacular, his staff, in vain. He is also the representative of his own interests and of the *modus vivendi* which has been established between the disorderly classes and the authorities. In his first capacity he has his duty clearly marked out for him, he must be upright, incorruptible, just and vigilant in the enforcement of the law, but in his second capacity he is left to the resources of his own mother wit. The policeman divides his time in unequal proportions between keeping a sharp eye upon every evil doer whom he must arrest and in winking both eyes hard when he comes across those other evil doers who have either in money or in "pull" established their right to be invisible to the patrol. Such a position is enough to demoralize a saint and although the majority of the Chicago Police are recruited from the Isle of Saints, the family of Saints, as Mark Twain said of the descendants of Washington who could not tell a lie, "has dwindled much of late."

There are refinements in the black mailing trade which are not suspected by the public. Take for instance the following story told by Mr. Supt. Byrnes of New York as to the way in which certain policemen under his control are blackmailing the peddlers who sell fruit, fish and vegetables in the open market which is held in Hestor street at the east side of New York:

It seems each of the several policemen employed an agent, and the latter informed the peddlers that every Friday they would have to pay him 50 cents or $1 or more, according to the location of their push-carts. The policemen on post demanded these sums, the agent averred and if the peddlers desired to do business they would have to pay for the privilege. Then, when Friday came around, the agent would start to make his rounds. The policeman was sometimes a yard back of him, but as often alongside, walking with him. From one peddler to another they would go, the agent taking the cash and the policeman counting it. Sometimes a peddler would refuse to be blackmailed, and then his stand or cart would be kicked into the street, sometimes all its contents—the poor fellow's stock in trade—being overturned and destroyed by falling into the mud.

If that can be done to peddlers who are driving a legitimate trade, it can fairly be assumed that every immoral resort, whether it be a low drinking saloon, an opium joint or a house of ill-fame, yields a steady revenue to the policeman on the beat. Nor is it only the patrolman who levy irregular fines upon the outlaws of society, the captains at the police stations have a touch upon the houses and collect their money in large sums. They have had great trouble at the Harrison Street police station, I was assured at police headquarters by the way in which the superior officers had succumbed to the temptation of feathering their own nests in this fashion. A captain who had plundered the district very badly was removed and one who was supposed to be a reformer was placed at his desk. As often happens the little finger of the reformer was heavier than the loins of the unregenerate whose place he has taken. The new man levied blackmail so constantly and in such large quantities that human nature could stand it no longer and the Madames of Fourth Avenue rose up and protested against being bled so unmercifully. "D— you," said the officer, when he received their complaints, "what are you made for but to be plundered?" That is the police theory stated with cynical brutality and acted on more or less constantly day in and day out every 24 hours in the 365 days in this year of grace.

Another mode by which the police augment the slender income of $1,000 a year allowed them by the city, is by going shares with bondsmen. A young lawyer in the town told me an incident in his own experience which brings out the *modus operandi* very clearly. I do not give his name, but he is personally known to the mayor and may be found any day at the City Hall. My friend was one of a party making the round of the opium dens under the guidance of a couple of detectives in the district where they are thickest, that is to say between Michigan Avenue and Clark Street in the neighborhood of 12th Street. They had gone from one house to another, seeing a great number of American citizens in various stages of opium intoxication. As they were rounding up their tour their guides decided to take them to just one more joint before they went home. On entering it the detectives discovered to their surprise a well known crook whom they had been seeking for in vain and whom they had now found quite inadvertently. The doors were instantly guarded, the patrol wagon was called and the whole joint was raided. Every individual from the proprietor downwards was put in the wagon and carted off to the police station. There were more than would fill one wagon so they had to wait for it to return when they were all taken to the Harrison police station, including the two detectives and my friend. On their way the detectives stopped and roused up a professional bailer. The man got out of bed and came down. He was told he was wanted at the station as they had just raided a joint. "All right," he said, "I will come along directly," and leaving him to complete his toilet, the party arrived at the station where they promptly lodged their captives in the cells. Soon after in came the professional bailer and bailed out all those who could put up any money for their bail bond. As soon as the little ceremony was over and the justice had profited to the extent of a dollar a head on the issue of the bonds and the professional bailer had pocketed his money he went back to his saloon accompanied by the two detectives and my friend who wondered somewhat at what was to happen next. He did not have long to wait, for no sooner was the party ensconced in the saloon than a vehement discussion arose as to the extent to which the detectives were to share in the bail money. The controversy waxed hot and my friend had no difficulty in hearing the whole of the discussion. Ultimately a divide was agreed upon. Each of the detectives received $10 for his share in the raid while the bailer kept the rest. This kind of thing goes on constantly wherever there is discretion left in the hands of the police officer as to whether or not the law shall be enforced. Out of that discretion the policeman coins money.

The policeman has many privileges in Chicago, including many other things a discretionary right to kill. In the equipment of a Chicago policeman, one indispensable item of expense is $11 which he must pay for a first class service revolver, and this revolver is bought for use and not for show. It is his own property, and he has a right to do with his own what he likes, even to the extent of firing promiscuously at any citizen who does not choose to obey his summons to halt. Chief Brennan assured me that the shooting was greatly exaggerated, and that a great many more shots were fired at the police than what they returned. There is a good deal of shooting, however, anyway, as was brought pretty forcibly to mind the other day, when one of the best known officers in the force was shot by his comrade who was endeavoring to allay a drunken brawl in a disreputable dance house.

Chief among the great temptations which confront the policeman are the allurements held out to him by the saloon-keeper, the courtesan, the dishonest pawnbroker, the shrewd gambler and the cunning thief.

It is difficult if not impossible to devise any expedient whereby this vice can be eradicated. Indeed if the policemen of Chicago flourish upon black mail, it is not because he is driven to it by poverty. There is no salary paid in the whole force under $2.00 per day and as soon as the officer becomes valuable as a patrolman, he receives $1,000 per year; out of which, he pays 1 per cent to the Pension Relief Fund, and 2 per cent more to the Benevolent Association, which provides for him in case of sickness.*

---

*New York has 41¾ square miles of territory and 3,800 men. They are paid: Chief, $6,000; inspectors, $3,500; captains, $2,750; sergeants, $2,000; roundsmen, $1,300; patrolmen, first year, $1,000; second year, $1,100; third year and thereafter, $1,200.

In Boston 906 men police 58 square miles of territory. There the patrol men are paid $1,000 the first year, $1,100 the second year, $1,200 the third. Brooklyn has 26 square miles of territory and 1,225 men. Brooklyn patrol men are paid $900 the first year, $1,000 the second year, and $1,100 the third year and thereafter.

In San Francisco the police territory covers 41¾ square miles and is guarded by 457 men. The chief receives $4,000 a year; captains, $1.800; clerks, $1,800; detectives, $1,500; sergeants, $1,500; corporals, $1,404; first class patrol men, $1,224. From his salary $2 per month is deducted for the pension and relief fund.

The policemen in Philadelphia, St. Louis, Cincinnati and Denver, are paid as in Chicago, but in those cities the uniforms are furnished.

This compares disadvantageously with the salary of policemen in other great cities of America; more especially as the policeman in Chicago has to provide his own uniform. One outfit costs him close upon $100. The force is unprovided with police surgeon, and if he is sick he is docked of his pay. His hours are longer than those which are put in by the New York police, for the eight hours system has not yet been adopted by the Chicago police. At night he puts in nine hours; by day he puts in twelve; whether by night or day he always puts in seven days per week.

The City Authorities in Chicago in drawing up the regulations for the police have evidently arrived at the conclusion that Col. Ingersoll should revise and extend his lecture "On the Mistakes of Moses" in order to draw special attention to the great mistake made by the Hebrew Law-Giver in insisting upon one day's rest in seven. The Chicago authorities know better than that. Moses may have been right about the Jews of his time, but the patrolman, who is constantly on his beat in the "Windy City" stands in no need of Sunday rest!

Considering the immense expense of territory that is patroled by the police, and considering the nature of the population that is congregated into the heart of the city, it must be admitted that Bishop Brennan and his secular clergy have their diocese very well in hand. Mr. Brennan declares that there is less crime in Chicago than any other city in proportion to its population, and you may certainly wander unmolested through the league-long avenues and boulevards, and also through the more disreputable districts in the first ward without being conscious of the near proximity of some of the dives and crooks with whose exploits the police reporters keep the public so well informed.

If the police were divorced from politics, and if Chief Brennan were to show that he would prove as capable in his own department as Marshal Swenie was in the campaign against fire, the force might enter upon a new and happier era as a result of the election of Mayor Hopkins. But Mr. Brennan is an anxious, somewhat timid man who is mistrusted by many on account of his connection with the Clan-na-Gael, and it is yet to be proved that he is quite equal to the exigencies of the situation, which would try the resources of the ablest man, who ever wore a uniform. Still we can hope for the best, and Mr. Brennan, if he is allowed a free hand, will probably do a great deal better than even an angel from Heaven if the angel were liable to have his wings pulled every now and then by the Mayor on the one hand and the Aldermanic Hierarchy on the other in the interest of political partisans.

CHAPTER V.

"*Vox populi, vox Dei,*" is an old adage not much respected in great American cities, where Lincoln's noble prayer at Gettysburg for the success of the great experiment of government of the people, by the people and for the people, does not seem to elicit a loud "Amen." Leading citizens in Chicago have repeatedly assured me that there is no hope and no future for the city of Chicago under the system of popular government. To abolish the whole system of administration, stock, lock and barrel, and to place the city under a federal triumvirate, appointed from Washington, who would govern Chicago as Washington is governed, is one favorite specific. To make the Mayor a Democratic Cæsar is another proposal. Universal suffrage is roundly declared to be a failure, and the whole hope of improvement is said to be the abandonment of the Democratic principle and the adoption of some form or other of one man power.

All that is of the devil, and those who think to make a short cut to the millenium by using the scepter of the despot are on the broad road that leadeth to destruction. Democratic institutions are all right, and would work all right if the people who are talking about their future would only take ordinary trouble to see that they worked right. The people's instincts are sound, and their interests are those of the community. But in order to give them a fair chance, they should not be left to the uncovenanted mercies of the boss and the heeler. Those who have principle, education and wealth should go into politics and consult the oracle themselves, instead of leaving the divine voice to be misinterpreted by thievish

319

hierophants of that polling place, that modern cave of Delphos.

The custody of the Delphic cave is left to two sets of partisans, respectively known as Republicans and Democrats, who instead of really desiring to know what the sovereign people have to say, concentrate all their efforts upon the supreme duty of working the oracle so as to make each deliverance tell against their adversaries and in favor of themselves. That is all they care for the welfare of the city. The future of the millions it will contain are as dust in the balance compared with the great object of getting an advantage honestly or otherwise over the other side. Thus there has come into existence in the party organizations a new and hideous dual form of the old plague of legitimate right. No Bourbon was more sure of his right divine to govern wrong than an American party manager is of his right to subordinate every consideration, divine and human, to the interests of his faction.

The result works out very disastrously in the cities when the welfare of the greatest of modern communities is sacrificed remorselessly to the exigencies of a national policy absolutely foreign to the questions which are of life and death to the people of Chicago.

One of Tom Moore's familiar fables for the Holy Alliance describes how a Scythian Philosopher who strayed into the temple of Memphis—

> "Saw a brisk blue-bottle Fly on an altar,
>   Made much of and worshipped as something divine;
> While a large, handsome Bullock, led there in an halter,
>   Before it lay stabbed at the foot of the shrine."

Surprised at such doings, the Philosopher inquired why such a useful and powerful creature should be thus offered up to a blue-bottle fly. He was told—

> "That Fly on the shrine is Legitimate Right,
>   And that Bullock the people that's sacrificed to it."

If our Scythian could come to Chicago to-day he would see the same marvelous sight, but in this case there are two flies on the shrine, and they are the rivals Republicanism and Democracy. Opposed to each other in every point, they agree in demanding the sacrifice of all other interests before the shrine, where they keep up their eternal feud.

What is wanted for Chicago is the election of the best men regardless of party strife. Whenever votes are given to the worse candidate for the city because he belongs to the better party from the point of view of the nation, the bullock is offered to the blue-bottle fly. Chicago's good government, Chicago's welfare should not be subordinated to the interests of the party caucus.

Here in Chicago, for instance, the looseness of the registration laws, the reckless facility with which anybody and everybody is registered as a citizen, is a direct encouragement to those vulgar Catilines to aspire to pack not a primary or a ballot box, but the register of the electorate. To put matters simply, registration in Chicago is a farce. Any naturalized citizen can vote, and anybody and everybody can be naturalized as a citizen if they are males over twenty-one years of age. All the careful stipulations of the laws to insure a due term of residence and an acquaintance with the principles of the American Constitution * are brushed to one side as so many spider webs. I am unfortunately not able to remain in Chicago till the April election. Had I done so, I am assured by an ardent politician that he would guarantee to qualify me if I would be a safe vote for Bath House John. I do not see why every English-speaking man should not be recognized as being naturalized by virtue of his speech wherever he is on English-speaking land. But so long as the distinction is kept up between the subjects

---

* A story which Americans love to tell as illustrating the process of naturalization, is as follows: An Irish politician brought in a foreign voter to be naturalized. In reply to the question whether the applicant had read the American Constitution, his sponsor admitted that he had not. " Until he has read it," said the judge, " we can not make him a citizen." Pat retired with his candidate for citizenship, but in five minutes they were both back before the judge. " Well," said the ruler, " has he read the Constitution?" "Indade, he has, your honor," said Pat, "and he thinks it a damned fine document." Naturalization followed as a matter of course, but in this case possibly Pat's assurance may be held to have deserved it.

of the Queen and the citizens of the Republic it would
be more seemly to make the process of naturalization
something more than a premium on perjury. The process of registration is almost as great a farce as the
process of naturalization. The list of voters registered
in a precinct in Chicago may have as little connection
with the ward in which they are registered as Boss Mc-
Kane's gang of rowdies had with Coney Island.

The most amusing tales are told concerning the frauds
practiced by politicians in registering electors. Tramps
and nondescripts of every description, raked together from
anywhere and everywhere, can be registered under any
name and with any address, so as to swamp the resident
electorate. In Chicago in one ward on one occasion,
the registration agents falling short of names and lacking the imagination of a novelist, registered as citizens
of that ward every man whose name was printed on
the familiar print representing the prize fight between
Sayers and Heenan. None of these worthies had ever
been in the ward, few of them had ever been in the
country, many of them were dead ; that was immaterial.
The politician had registered them all as citizens, and
when polling day came he had his obedient drove ready,
who voted punctually as Tom Sayers and J. C. Heenan
or any other of the ornaments of the British prize ring
of thirty years ago.

The only chance of exerting any influence for good
on a primary is by what may be described briefly as incipient mugwumpery. That is to say, if before the primaries, the better elements of each party meet together,
mustering as strongly as possible, and were to let it be
distinctly understood at the headquarters of the respective parties, that this section would bolt the ticket unless
good candidates are selected, this would in most cases
result in preventing the nominations which at present
are a disgrace to the city. In default of such organizations honest men are practically disfranchised.

As long as party leaders know that if they nominate

the devil himself, the sworn Democrat or Republican will vote the party ticket rather than turn to the archangel Gabriel if he were nominated by the other side, they will simply consult their own convenience, which in nine cases out of ten consists in taking the line of least resistance by pandering to the ugliest and most aggressive members of their own party. But once let it be known that each party has its sworn contingency of honest men who will put up honesty before party, and who would rather defeat their own side than be accessory to the election of a thief or a boodler, and we shall see a great change for the better. Even the toughest and most unmanageable of the heelers of the ward politicians would bow to the inevitable, and recognize that it was no use trying it on with any man who was not up to what might be regarded as the mugwump standard.

However natural it may be to an Englishman to compare American election methods with those with which he is familiar in the old country, it is almost impossible for an American to conceive of elections conducted under the strict rules of the English Corrupt Practices Act. Whenever I described to citizens of Chicago the penalties exacted under that Draconian law, they declared with one consent that if it were put in force in America there is not a single candidate who could not be unseated on petition for the acts of his agents. Yet any one who has any regard for the purity of elections, and for the checking of this Saturnalia of corruption and debauchery which prevails in contested elections in America, as it formerly prevailed in Great Britain, can hardly refrain from sighing for the Corrupt Practices Act in the United States.

That measure is the most unique illustration of a law which cuts up by the roots one of the most deeply rooted cancers in the electoral system at a single stroke. Its provisions are simple but searching. Every candidate, on the eve of election, is compelled by law to nominate an agent through whom alone all expenses incurred by the candidate must be paid. These expenses must not exceed a certain statutory maximum, and at the close of the election a full account of all moneys expended must be returned within a certain limited period. If during the course of the election the candidate, his agent or any of his subordinate agents were to pay any elector any sum of money, no matter how small, or even to defray the cost of his railway fare or recoup him for the loss of time on voting day, that act in itself is sufficient when proven before an election judge to vitiate the election. That is to say, if a candidate gave an elector a dollar to pay him for his loss of time and railway fare in order that he might register his vote, that act would be sufficient to vitiate the election even if the candidate had a plurality of thousands of votes. Nor would he be allowed to stand again when unseated, for that constituency during the existing legislature. The law is equally strict, although the penalty is not so severe, as regards the disqualification of a candidate, in case of treating or intimidation.

Citizens of both political parties have assured me repeatedly that were such provisions enforced in the United States, there is not a representative of the people, from the President down to the Constable, who would not be unseated when the conduct of his election was made matter of inquiry before an impartial judicial tribunal, taking evidence on oath on the spot.

The practice of treating is carried to what seems to our English ideas an absolutely ruinous extent, and candidates of both parties might well welcome legislation which would reduce such irregular claims upon their purses.

Chicago is in the throes of what for the want of a better name may be called a Civic Revival. The good men and women of all parties have begun to realize how disgraceful to the city is the condition of its municipal administration. The Mayor has placed himself at the head of a movement directed against the worst vices of the system of organized boodle, which has so long had everything its own way in the City Council. The financial exigencies of the city treasury, the extreme suffering occasioned by the lack of employment throughout the winter and many other things have combined to prick the conscience and arouse the moral sense of the community. Flagrant instances of corruption have occurred in the City Council on the very eve of the elections, and we are justified in turning to the April polls with the hope that they will show that Chicago has at last wearied of being represented and governed by the vilest of her citizens. It is fortunate that no national issue has arisen to complicate the question which will be submitted to the people. The April election is simply to select new Aldermen, Town Assessors and Collectors. It is likely to be fought out from first to last on municipal grounds. This is as it should be.

Even if the pending fight should result in a brilliant victory for the forces of reform, the campaign will not be over. The enemy never sleeps. The forces of corruption exercise an influence as permanent as the law of gravitation, whereas the reformers act by fits and starts. There is an inevitable tendency on the part of all well-to-do citizens to go to sleep politically the day after they have recorded their votes. The system of checks and counter checks, which the Americans have borrowed from the English Constitution as it was when George the Third was King, tends directly to encourage this sluggard tendency on the part of the citizens. An English city like Chicago would have no limitations upon its powers of taxation, nor would the Mayor have any veto upon the decisions of the City Council. With us the Mayor is simply the Chairman elected by the City Council. He is nominally the chief magistrate, but his vote counts for no more than that of any other Alderman in the Council. In Chicago the Mayor counts for more than two-thirds of the Aldermen minus one, and his veto is relied upon as the sole effective check against excessive corruption, to which the Aldermen, as their votes prove, would otherwise be prone.

If the citizens of Chicago felt that there was no limit to the taxation which the Aldermen could impose, and that there was no check upon the City Council in the shape of the Mayor's veto, they would, perforce, be compelled to see to it that their representatives in the Council were honorable citizens. As it is, what with limitations here and vetoes there, the citizens for the most part lull themselves to sleep with the feeling that the Alderman cannot do very much harm after all, and that they can afford to allow them to play tricks within the limited area allotted to them. But no city can afford to allow their representatives to ignore honesty and good faith.

CHAPTER VI.

THE WATCHMEN OF THE CITY.

"Son of Man," came the word of the Lord to the Hebrew prophet, "I have made you a watchman unto the House of Israel." The same word might well be applied to the editors of the press of Chicago. They are the watchmen of the house of our local Israel. They stand on the battlements keeping watch and ward while the citizens sleep, and upon them, first and foremost of all men, lies the responsibility and warning and rousing of the community as to the perils which encompass it. Chicago, prolific in all things, has been exceptionally so in the production of journals. It gives you the headache merely to read the list of the periodical publications in the directory. Of the great majority of these, however, it may be said as it was said bitterly of one of the ancient churches, "they have a name to live but indeed they are dead." There is no place in the city where all of them can be purchased, and as it would take a long day's march to make a pilgrimage to all their publishing houses they remain unknown to the majority of the citizens. Its periodicals are as polyglot as its inhabitants, and even its newspapers are printed in seven different languages. For practical purposes, however, the newspapers which do watchmen's service for the whole of the city are printed in English with the exception of Mr. Hesing's *Staats Zeitung* the only non-English paper which is on evidence at the bookstalls. There are several other daily papers in Chicago which no one outside the office where they are published seems to see. Omitting all these we may compare for practical purposes the watchmen of Chicago to the staff of the ten English papers, five of which appear in the morning and five in the evening.

The *Record*, which is published at one cent, has the largest circulation of the morning papers, while the *Tribune*, the *Herald* and the *Inter-Ocean* in the order named circulate over or under .100,000 copies a day. The *Times*, the remaining paper, belonged to the late mayor, Mr. Carter Harrison, by whom it was valued more for its influence than for its dividends which were usually represented by a minus quantity. Of the evenings, the *Daily News*, which when Mr. Melville Stone was connected with it, attained the phenomenal circulation of 200,000 per day in a city of less than a million inhabitants, still has the largest circulation of all the evening papers and by far the greatest advertising revenue. The *Evening Post*, the afternoon satellite of the *Herald* is as much in advance of all its evening contemporaries in ability and influence and general quality of make up and appearance as the *Daily News* is ahead of them in circulation and advertisements. The *Journal* is an old established paper with fine crusted prejudices of the olden time concerning Catholics and "sich" which its editor expresses with refreshing vigor. The *Mail*, judging from its appearance, has more ability, than capital, and more assurance than either. The *Dispatch*, the drunken helot of journalism, is the only remaining paper. Its character can best be judged from its advertising columns which are stuffed with advertisements of houses of prostitution and of assignation. Like attracts like.

With the exception of the *Dispatch* and perhaps of the *Mail*, the other Chicago dailies are conducted as respectably as any newspapers in the world. They are all owned and controlled by men who have sunk thousands of dollars in their journalistic investment, and who do not mean to get left if they possibly can help it. The internicine war which exists between the newspapers in some towns does not exist in Chicago where all the respectable journals have combined for regulating their business on common lines. Neither with the exception of the *Inter-Ocean* and the *Evening Journal* can they be said to be fanatically partisan. The *Tribune* is Republican, but it is national Republicanism with its protective adjuncts which excite its devotion; it is reasonable and impartial in relation to city affairs. The papers as a whole and the men who write them are good average press men without any very great enthusiasm for their profession, doing the best they can from day to day. They turn out readable copy and manufacture scare heads to the best of their ability which is not inconsiderable and which appears all the more conspicuous when the material to be operated upon is as dull as ditch water. Chicago journalists are good business men. Since Mr. Melville Stone left the *Daily News* there are not many editors who take their position seriously. They seem to feel that it is more important to build up a great property than to exert a great power. Mr. Medill, of the *Tribune*, on one famous occasion laid down the doctrine that a journalist was not a teacher, he was not a leader, he was simply a huckster whose duty it was to supply whatever articles his customers required without allowing his own convictions to interfere with the conduct of his journalistic shop. Fortunately, Mr. Medill's practice is much better than his precept, otherwise he would have deserved the retort which was made at the time that if he were right, Dana, Greely and Bryant and all the greatest men in American journalism had mistaken their vocation. The *Tribune* has often shown that it was more than a shop where hucksters sold news or traded opinions according to the demands of their purchasers, but all the newspapers are more or less under the influence of the commercial theory of journalism. To lead public opinion may be glorious but it is not always profitable. The true policy, according to the counting house theory is to be just a little behind public opinion rather than ahead of it and for the most part the newspapers live down to that conception of their duties.

That is an abdication of the position of power which in a free democracy they ought naturally to occupy. In a democracy the newspaper is or ought to be chief scepter of power and to degrade an instrument of government to the mere level of a corner store—and sometimes to the level of a corner saloon—is not worthy our high calling and not calculated to help either journalism or Chicago. The ambition to lead, to direct, to educate and to act as the uncrowned kings of the American democracy does not seem to exist among a majority of newspapers, which really often seem to have no other ambition than to heap up an immense fortune and fatten on their gains. I wish sometimes that newspaper proprietors of the present day had as much of the fear of God before their eyes as the old medieval robber-baron. It is not, perhaps, a very lofty idea, but it is not one which is lived up to by the newspaper proprietors. In the old days when a man, who was stouter, or shrewder, or more cunning than his neighbors, raised himself above the level of the common fighting herd and succeeded after a time in carving out for himself a domain, in the center of which he built his castle, from being a mere filibuster, a militant adventurer, fighting for his own profit or for such of his neighbors' goods as he could seize, he often developed under the pressure of the spiritual power wielded by the old church into something like a civilized ruler. Having "made his pile," he used it in order to govern and civilize and educate the people in the midst of whom he had established his castle. But there is no such recognition of responsibility on the part of many newspaper proprietors nowadays. Instead of regarding the wealth which they have acquired by the success of their journals as merely giving them a starting point from which they might be able to civilize and educate and humanize the conditions of life in the midst of the people whose support has given them their wealth they live self-indulgent, self-centered lives. This system can be changed only by bringing back into existence the real live church. The old medieval baron would probably have been no better than the modern newspaper proprietor if it had not been for the spiritual power which, by a judicious use of hell-fire, succeeded in scaring him into something like humanity and decency. We want to substitute nowadays something for the old church, and I do not at present exactly see where it is to be found, except in the gradual growth of a healthier public opinion on the part of the newspaper men themselves and an unsparing and unflinching use of the newspaper as a social pillory.

Unfortunately the effectiveness of the newspaper from this point of view has been impaired by the continual straining after exaggeration and emphasis which is equivalent to an incessant bawl kept up in private conversation. If you always howl through a speaking trumpet you find it difficult to attract attention when you have something really important to say. This straining after effect and the unsparing use of the superlative all tends to weaken the influence of the pointed word which, like everthing else in the world needs to be used with reserve if it is to be used with power. When newspapers denounce every political opponent as if he were the incarnation of every crime, people learn to take every invective as merely a journalistic method of indicating their dissent from the opinions which he holds. Sometimes, however, the need arises when the journalist should speak with emphasis and some great evil is to be prevented, they find it difficult to arouse the attention of the public which is so accustomed to being scare headed that it can hardly be roused to more than a languid interest even if the capitals in the scare head were printed six inches long.

The papers are all in line this spring. But they have all been united before when they all fought Carter Harrison, with the exception of the *Times*. But he was returned at the head of the poll by an overwhelming majority. Carter Harrison was an astute man, who knew how to minimize the influence of the newspapers. He represented himself as being the victim of a newspaper trust, as the other papers had never forgiven him on account of his ownership of the *Times*. As the allied papers were weighted with a very undesirable candidate, Mr. Harrison's victory was complete. The result has made the Chicago papers think twice or even thrice before they commit themselves to a similar enterprise. They had gone forth to battle and were beaten, and felt very sore about it. They are once more in battle array, and they certainly do not lack enemies against whom to direct their shot.

Newspapers can do more good by bringing facts to light than by the most Ciceronian invective. It was this which led me to address the following appeal to the press at my last meeting in the Central Music Hall:

I have been for twenty years a pressman, and I am proud of my profession. It has always seemed to me that the newspaper editor was the descendant of the spiritual power which in the medieval times exercised so great and salutary an effect over the barbarians who overran Europe. I regard the modern editor as in the direct spiritual succession to all the prophets and all the spiritual teachers who have ever lived, and, therefore, in dealing with those who need to be revived, if the community is to be revived, I begin with the representatives of the spiritual power, the press first, and then the pulpit.

Think of it! Every day, and in Chicago, I am sorry to say, seven days a week, the newspaper editor has to speak out what he thinks to be true, and what he thinks is necessary for the welfare of his readers to know. He has that opportunity, which no other man has, of impressing such truth as there may be in him upon his fellow men. Yet somehow or other our newspaper editors do not seem to feel ashamed and disgraced by the existence of such a state of things as there is to be found at present in the City Hall.

Has it ever occurred to your confreres, editors of Chicago newspapers, that the shame and the disgrace of this state of things lies more at your door than at the door of any other class of citizens in the community? I know that some have done all they can, and I know that others would have done a great deal more if they had not been hindered by the influence that comes from the counting room and the advertising columns rather than from the editorial sanctum. But taking it broadly, without laying any blame on any individual, is it not a right and true thing to say to the editors in this city of Chicago, where you have some of the most prosperous and enterprising papers in the world, that it is a disgrace to the newspapers that they cannot clean out your City Hall? They advise the electors for whom to vote, they criticise the city fathers, and they proclaim the gospel day by day as they see it, and you see the result before you.

Over in the old country, pressmen and the general public believe two things firmly about American newspapers. It is a tradition with us that the American newspaper man is one of the smartest and sharpest and most indomitable of all men, and that Argus with his hundred eyes was not in it compared with an American newspaper reporter; that if there was anything in the whole world which was covered and hidden, that would be the one thing which an American reporter would unearth and publish to the world. That was one belief of mine which, I am sorry to say, has been rudely shattered since I came to Chicago. There was another idea, and that was, that after an American reporter had got the facts and verified them there was no power on this earth that could prevent an American editor from publishing it. This is also a delusion. I suppose we got that idea from several what you would call remarkable journalistic "beats" which were done by American press people, chief among which was the well-known instance when James Gordon Bennett sent Stanley to find Livingstone in the heart of Central Africa. You remember how Livingstone had disappeared, no one knew where he was, and then an American editor said to an American reporter: "There is the map of Africa; Livingstone has got lost somewhere in the middle of that continent. Go and find him." Mr. Stanley, nothing loath, packed up his things and went through the wilds of Central Africa, regarding all the perils through which he had to pass as all in the day's business, until the day on which he took off his hat and said: "Dr. Livingstone, I presume." That has given the American press a great prestige. But alas for the illusions of our childhood! When we come to this city of Chicago, we learn that there is a work which is as important, and more important to you than that which Stanley undertook. When he had to find Livingstone, the only direction given him was Central Africa, somewhere near the equatorial lakes. If James Gordon Bennett would send a Stanley to Chicago to discover the boodlers and name them, I think he would not have such a wide area to go over as Central Africa. He would say, "Go to the City Hall and you will find them somewhere in the neighborhood of Powers and O'Brien's saloon." I know that there are men on every Chicago newspaper who would be only too delighted to take the commission to find the boodlers and get legal evidence, but then they are held back.

There is a secret which has been diligently cloaked up so that nobody can get at it. You ask how many people know the secret? There must be at least thirty, forty or fifty who know the secret, and yet this secret, which is of so much importance to all of you in this city, is too much for the Chicago newspapers to find out. James Gordon Bennett can send Stanley to the heart of Central Africa, but the Chicago papers, either individually or collectively, cannot find out who it is that boodles in the City Hall.

It is one of the most wonderful things I ever heard of. Here are four or five of the brightest newspapers with millions behind them, and there is the City Hall just across the way. They all admit corruption. And yet, when I ask who it is that gets that money, and who it is that pays that money, no one can tell me, no, not even a Chicago newspaper.

The boodler has not yet been run to earth, but he obligingly came forth from his retreat and displayed his boodle-branded forehead unabashed before the community. There are 42 of them, of whom Mr. Powers of the 19th ward seems to be the chief. All the newspapers, always with the exception of the *Dispatch*, seem to be vigorously impressing this upon the attention of the public. While wishing them all God speed in this work, it seems to me that the Civic Revival would be powerfully helped if it had a distinctive organ of its own, and this without any disrespect to the daily papers, who indeed would find such an organ an invaluable auxiliary. In addition to newspapers which are properties and run for profits, there might exist one journal which might aspire to be a power and a prophet, even if it were run at a loss. It is somewhat odd that in the midst of all the periodical publications of Chicago there is no one weekly newspaper in the English sense; that is to say, there is no weekly two cent paper which the citizen can read who has neither the money nor the time to read the daily press. The consequence is that a great many people have all the daily papers on their tables and are constantly failing to read things they ought to see and want to see. They cannot see the wood because of the trees. There is such a mass of printed matter laid before them, without much perspective, that the weightier matters relating to the good government of the city get overlooked or are thrust into the background by the more sensational happenings of the hour. A newspaper which would survey the progress of the city from week to week, summarizing everything that was of permanent importance appearing in the press from day to day, and which would preach civic reform, would have a distinct mission in Chicago.

Were such a journal to be established and distributed

to every household in the city every week, either by the aid of the churches or the help of the post, it would be an organ of incalculable influence in the town. Everything of course would depend upon how it was edited and the nature of its contents. Bright enough writers, however, could be found to turn out a weekly journal whose advent would be looked for impatiently and whose non-delivery would be resented sharply. Such a distribution could be provided for either by endowment or by the sale of advertising space.

In order to give a little more substance to this suggestion I ventured to draw up a preliminary prospectus of such a newspaper. An appropriate title would be simply, " Chicago," with the motto, " I will Thy will." Here is the draft :

" CHICAGO."

On the first Saturday in —— —— there will be published the first number of a weekly paper entitled "Chicago," the aim and object of which is indicated by its motto. "I will Thy will.

The aspiration of its conductors is to familiarize every citizen of Chicago with the conception that this city should be made and can be made, the ideal city of the world.

To achieve this end every resource of journalism, poetry, romance, prophecy, art, prizes, etc., will be employed to quicken interest and to concentrate attention upon this civic ideal, and for the first year at least a copy of this paper, which will be published at two cents, will be delivered at the door of every family in Chicago.

Nothing short of this regular weekly distribution to every household, regardless of nationality, religion, color or station, can suffice in so cosmopolitan a community to bring the great ideal adequately before the whole body of the citizens.

The aspiration, born of the World's Fair and its congresses, to make Chicago worthy of its position as the first city in the United States has already brought about what may be described as a civic revival whose influence may be perceived in many directions.

The new weekly will chronicle the fruits of this civic revival, will encourage the citizens to fresh efforts by the record of successive advances made towards a better social state, or rouse them to more earnest action by emphasizing the lesson of occasional reverse and, in short, will endeavor to be the popular gazette of the campaign for the realization of the ideal Chicago. There is nothing Utopian or revolutionary about this programme of "Chicago." It is severely practical and persistently opportunist. While recognizing as the ultimate the fulfillment of the petition "Thy will be done in Chicago as it is Heaven," every step, however faltering, in the right direction will command our support. To refuse to do anything until you can do everything is to do nothing. Our policy will be to do what you can as soon as you can, wherever you can, with whatever instruments are within reach in order to make life happier, healthier and more human for every man, woman and child in Chicago.

To achieve this, no new patent nostrum of a social specific is required. All that is needed is the intelligent and resolute use of the existing civic organization as the natural and constitutional instrument for securing for the citizens of Chicago the best of everything which exists in the world.

If Chicago is to be the Capital of Civilization, it is indispensable that she should at the very least be able to show that every resident within her limits enjoyed every advantage which intelligent and public spirited administration has secured for the people elsewhere. Only in this way can Chicago vindicate her right to the position to which she aspires, and it will be the constant endeavor of the conductors of "Chicago" to call attention to the flaws in her social armor, to describe improvements which have been made in other communities and to indicate the ways and means by which such improvements can be most easily secured for the city.

"Chicago" will not be a party paper, neither will it be identified with any religion save that which finds expression in the Service of Man. Its constant aim will be to promote the union of all who love, for the service of all who suffer. Instead of seeking for points of difference as for hid treasure, it will endeavor to discover points of accord and, therefore, a basis of possible co-operation among parties and sects which are most opposed to each other. To see each other as we appear to those who love us at our best moments is more profitable than to dwell constantly upon the gloomy portrait painted by those who hate us when we are at our worst.

"Chicago" starts with the promise of hearty co-operation in distribution and in support from many organizations never before united in the promotion of a common enterprise. It will combat as the common enemy all that breeds distrust whether of nationality or of sect, and will constantly seek to promote the growth of a hearty brotherly comradeship among all the citizens of this great city. Its great ideal which will ever be presented before its readers will be such a transformation of the conditions of life that no one's child in the poorest district of Chicago will be doomed to miseries, temptations and wrongs which we should regard as intolerable for our own children.

To succeed in arousing a sense of the responsibilities and opportunities of citizenship it is necessary to present the issues involved in civic questions in such popular fashion as to enlist the sympathies of all—especially of the women and children. Hence, while "Chicago" will endeavor to give every week a summary and a survey of all that has been published during the week relating to the improvement of the city, it will have special features of its own in the shape of short tales, stories from real life in Chicago, ballads based on the events of the week, character sketches of leading citizens, and other articles which will enable the reader to understand the inner human and therefore the divine element that underlies the dry and uninviting discussions of public questions.

To stimulate public interest in all classes in the questions of the city prizes will be offered every week for contributions bearing upon the improvement of the conditions of life in Chicago, and every effort will be made to develop the growth of a civic literature in prose and poetry.

So far from being the rival of any existing periodical "Chicago" hopes to become the supplement or auxiliary of all, and will rejoice if it is able to co-operate with each of them in helping to realize the great aim of all in making Chicago the ideal city of the world.

Such a journal, once well established, would do more to give the cosmopolitan heterogeneous mass of the residents of Chicago a sense of the unity of their city and greatness of its destinies than any other scheme which could be devised. Some such paper seems to be much needed in every great city. The churches of the sects have their weekly organs, but for this city, in which there are a million and a half of human beings, there is no organ and no pulpit from which the whole of the citizens can be reached. What an audience would hear that prophet voice, and, as Russell Lowell said, with "never as much as a nodder even among them:"

And from what a Bible can he choose his text—a Bible which needs no translation, and which no priestcraft can shut and clasp from the laiety—the open volume of the world, upon which, with a pen of sunshine and destroying fire, the inspired present is even now writing the annals of God! Methinks the editor who should understand his calling, and be equal thereto, would truly deserve that title which Homer bestows upon princes. He would be the Moses of our nineteenth century; and whereas the old Sinai, silent now, is but a common mountain stared at by the elegant tourist, and crawled over by the hammering geologist, we must find his tables of the new law here among factories in this Wilderness of Sin (Numbers xxxiii. 12) called Progress of Civilization, and be the captain of our Exodus into the Canaan of a truer social order.

CHAPTER I.

THE CONSCIENCE OF CHICAGO.

If Christ came to Chicago He would do as He did in olden time and endeavor to band together those who loved Him and believed in Him in an organization which would work for the realization of His ideals, and for the removal of the evils which afflict the least of these His brethren. In other words, He would form a church in which all might be one, even as He was one with his Father. Such unity is impossible on any basis excepting that of the practical life of service and of sacrifice. But the one church, that is His Church Militant, can and will be founded upon the basis of His life and His love, for that is broad enough to include all existing churches and others beside, of whom He said: "Other sheep I have which are not of this fold." The only possible definition of theChurch Universal is the union of all who love for the service of all who suffer. And that church, from the very fervor of its love for its Divine Master, will not ensconce itself in pews stuffed with comfortable ecclesiastical cushions, enjoying as sweet morsels spiritual caramels dispensed from the pulpit, but will find the true service of the sanctuary in going down into the depths, even to the depths of ward politics and electoral agitation, in order to attempt, amid the dust and the din of the world-struggle to rebuild society on the foundation of the Kingdom of God.

The old idea of the union between church and state, has long since been recognized by the modern mind as an anachronism at the present time. It is a survival

from the past which must either be readjusted to meet
different conditions or cease to exist. Cavour's formula
"A free Church in a free State," is accepted by Americans in the plural number—free Churches in a free State,
But the problem of the relation between the spiritual
power which the conscience of the community and the
civic power which represents the will and the executive
mind of the nation is far from settled by the mere enun-
ciation of a formula. The Mayflower sailed across the
Atlantic not in order to found a free church in a free
state, in the sense of a state in which the church had
nothing to say, but rather to found a state in which the
church should be supreme. Our Puritan forefathers,
labored for a theocracy as all earnest men have always
labored whether they call themselves Mohammedans,
Catholics, Puritans or Latter Day Saints. No one
at this time of day would propose to endeavor to
realize the theocracy or the rule of right and the attainment of the ideal by the worn out machinery of church
meetings or ecclesiastical synods, but the essence of the
problem remains the same. The community which we
call a state stands more than ever in need of being
directed and controlled and dominated by the moral
sense of the community. In other words, the state must
have a conscience as well as a will and a mind. That
community will be best governed in which the moral sense
of its members has most authority. This indeed is only a
re-statement of the old proposition that the society
which always endeavors to do what it believes to be
right will be a better governed society than one whose
members subordinate right to considerations of selfish
interest and who act upon the unavowed but practical
belief that it is quite possible to cheat God. Mr.
Bigelow's caution that "you have got to get up early if
you want to take in God" has been forgotten by many
smart citizens who imagine that they can run a town
safely and well by entering into a practical copartner-
ship with the Devil.

The address to all English-speaking folk, written four years ago, will at least serve to show that whether in London as an editor or in Chicago as a visitor I have clung with tenacity to my one central conception of the Civic Church.

There exists at this moment no institution which even aspires to be to the English-speaking-world what the Catholic Church in its prime was to the intelligence of Christendom. To call attention to the need for such an institution, adjusted, of course, to the altered circumstances of the new era, to enlist the co-operation of all those who will work towards the creation of some such common centre for the inter-communication of ideas, and the universal diffusion of the ascertained results of human experience in a form accessible to all men, are the ultimate objects for which this review has been established.

This is done distinctly on a religious principle. The revelation of the Divine Will did not cease when St. John wrote the last page of the Apocalypse, or when Malachi finished his prophecy. "God is not dumb, that He should speak no more," and we have to seek for the gradual unfolding of his message to his creatures in the highest and ripest thought of our time. Reason may be a faulty instrument, but it is the medium through which the Divine thought enters the mind of man.

Among all the agencies for the shaping of the future of the human race, none seem so potent now and still more hereafter as the English-speaking man. Already he begins to dominate the world. The British Empire and the American Republic comprise within their limits almost all the territory that remains empty for the overflow of the world. Their citizens, with all their faults, are leading the van of civilization, and if any great improvements are to be made in the condition of mankind, they will necessarily be leading instruments in the work. Hence our first starting-point will be a deep and almost awe-struck regard for the destinies of the English-speaking man. To make him worthy of his immense vocation, and at the same time to help to hold together and strengthen the political ties which at present link all English-speaking communities save one in a union which banishes all dread of internecine war, to promote by every means a fraternal union between the British Empire and the American Republic. These will be our plainest duties.

It follows from this fundamental conception of the magnitude and importance of the work of the English-speaking race in the world, that a resolute endeavor should be made to equip the individual citizen more adequately for his share in that work. For the ordinary common English-speaking creature, country yokel, or child of the slums, is the seed of Empire. The red-haired hobbledehoy, smoking his short pipe at the corner of Seven Dials, may two years hence be the red-coated representative of the might and majesty of Britain in the midst of a myriad of Africans or Asiatics. That village girl, larking with the lads on her way to the well, will in a few years be the mother of citizens of new commonwealths; the founders of cities in the Far West whose future destiny may be as famous as that of ancient Rome. No one is too insignificant to be overlooked. We send abroad our best and our worst; all alike are seed-corn of the race. Hence the importance of resolute endeavor to improve the condition, moral and material, in which the ordinary English-speaking man is bred and reared. To do this is a work as worthy of national expenditure as the defence of our shores from hostile fleets. The amelioration of the conditions of life, the levelling up of social inequalities, the securing for each individual the possibility of a human life, and the development to the uttermost by religious, moral, and intellectual agencies of the better side of our countrymen, —these objects follow as necessary corollaries from the recognition of the providential sphere occupied by English-speaking men in the history of the world.

Another corollary is that we can no longer afford to exclude one section of the English-speaking race from all share in the education and moralizing influences which result from the direct exercise of responsible functions in the state. The enfranchisement of women will not revolutionize the world, but it will at least give those who rock our cradles a deeper sense of the reality of the sceptre which their babies' hands may grasp than would otherwise be possible. Our children in future will be born of two parents, each politically intelligent, instead of being the product of a union between a political being and a creature whose mind is politically blank. If at present we have to deplore so widespread a lack of civic virtue among our men, the cause may be found in the fact that the mothers from whom men acquired whatever virtue they possess have hitherto been studiously excluded from the only school where civic virtue can be learnt—that of the actual exercise of civic functions, the practical discharge of civic responsibilities.

We believe in God, and in Humanity! The English-speaking race in America and elsewhere, is one of the chief of God's chosen agents for executing coming improvements in the lot of mankind. If all those who see that, could be brought into hearty union to help all that tends to make that race more fit to fulfil its providential mission, and to combat all that hinders or impairs that work, such an association or secular order would constitute a nucleus or rallying point for all that is most vital in the English-speaking world, the ultimate influence of which it would be difficult to overrate.

Our supreme duty is the winnowing out by a process of natural selection, and enlisting for hearty service for the commonweal all those who possess within their hearts the sacred fire of patriotic devotion to their country. Whatever we may make of democratic institutions, government of majorities, and the like, the fact remains that the leadership of democracies and the guidance of democracies belong always to the few. The governing minds are never numerous.

Carlyle put this truth in the must offensive aspect, but truth it is, and it will be well or ill for us in proportion as we act upon it or the reverse. The wise are few. The whole problem is to discover the wise few, and to place the sceptre in their hands, and loyally to follow their leading. But how to find them out? That is the greatest of questions. Mr. Carlyle, in almost his last political will and testament to the English people, wrote: "There is still, we hope, the unclassed aristocracy by nature, not inconsiderable in numbers, and supreme in faculty, in wisdom, in human talent, nobleness, and courage, who derive their patent of nobility direct from Almighty God. If, indeed, these fail us, and are trodden out under the unanimous torrent of hobnails, of brutish hoofs and hobnails, then, indeed, it is all ended. National death lies ahead. . . . . Will there, in short, prove to be a recognizable small nucleus of Invincible Aristoi fighting for the Good Cause in their various wisest ways, and never ceasing or slackening till they die? This is the question of questions on which all turns." In the answer to this, could we give it clearly, as no man can, lies the oracle response, "Life for you: death for you."

Our supreme task is to help to discover these wise ones, to afford them opportunity of articulate utterance, to do what we can to make their authority potent among their contemporaries. Who is there among the people who has truth in him, who is no self-seeker, who is no coward, and who is capable of honest, painstaking effort to help his country? For such men we would search as for hidden treasures. They are the salt of the earth and the light of the world, and it is the duty and the privilege of the wise man to see that they are like cities set on the hill, which cannot be hid.

The great word which has now to be spoken in the ears of the world is that the time has come when men and women must work for the salvation of the state or of the city with as much zeal and self-sacrifice as they now work for the salvation of the individual. For the saving of the soul of Hodge Joskins, what energy, what devotion, is not possible to all of us! There is not a street in Chicago, nor a village in the country, which is not capable of producing, often at short notice and under slight pressure, a man or woman who will spend a couple of hours a week every week in the year, in more or less irksome voluntary exertions, in order to snatch the soul of Hodge Joskins from everlasting burning. But to save the country from the grasp of demons innumerable, to prevent this city or this Republic becoming an incarnate demon of lawless ambition and cruel love of gold, how many men or women are willing to spend even one hour a month or a year? For Hodge Joskins innumerable are the multitude of workers; for the city, or the state that embodiment of many millions of Hodges, how few are those who will exert themselves at all? At elections there is a little canvassing and excitement; but except-ing at those times the idea that the state needs saving, that the democracy need educating, and that the problems of government and of reform need careful and laborious study, is foreign to the ideas of our people. The religious side of politics has not yet entered the minds of men.

What is wanted is a revival of civic faith, a quickening of spiritual life in the political sphere, the inspiring of men and women with the conception of what may be done towards the salvation of the world, if they will but bring to bear upon public affairs the same spirit of self-sacrificing labor that so many thousands manifest in the ordinary drudgery of parochial and evangelistic work. It may no doubt seem an impossible dream.

Can those dry bones live? Those who ask that question little

If Christ Came to Chicago.

know the infinite possibilities latent in the heart of man. The faith of Loyola, what an unsuspected mine of enthusiasm did it not spring upon mankind? "The Old World," as Macauley remarks, " was not wide enough for that strange activity. In the depths of the Peruvian mines, in the hearts of the African slave caravans, on the shores of the Spice Islands, in the observatories of China, the Jesuits were to be found. They made converts in regions which neither avarice nor curiosity had tempted any of their countrymen to enter ; and preached and disputed in tongues of which no other native of the West understood a word."

How was this miracle effected? By the preaching of a man who energized the activity of the church by the ideals of chivalry and the strength of military discipline. What we have now to do is to energize and elevate the politics of our time by the enthusiasm and the system of the religious bodies. Those who say that it is impossible to raise up men and women ready to sacrifice all they possess, and, if need be, to lay down their lives in any great cause that appeals to their higher nature, should spare a little time to watch the recruiting of the Salvation Army for the Indian mission field. The delicate dressmaker and the sturdy puddler, the young people raised in the densest layer of English commonplace, under the stimulus of an appeal to the instincts of self-sacrifice, and of their duty to their brethren, abandon home, friends, kindred, and go forth to walk barefoot through India at a beggar's pittance until they can pick up suffiecient words of the unfamiliar tongue to deliver to these dusky strangers the message of their Gospel. Certain disease awaits them, cruel privations, and probably an early death. But they shrink not. A race whose members are capable of such devotion cannot be regarded as hopeless, from the point of those who seek to rouse among the most enlightened a consuming passion for their country's good.

But how can it be done? As everything else of a like nature has been done since the world began—by the foolishness of preaching. And here again let Mr. Carlyle speak:—

"There is no church, sayest thou? The voice of prophecy has gone dumb? This is even what I dispute: but in any case hast thou not still preaching enough? A preaching friar settles himself in every village and builds a pulpit which he calls newspaper. Therefrom he preaches what most momentous doctrines is in him for man's salvation; and dost not thou listen and believe? Look well; thou seest everywhere a new clergy of the mendicant order, some barefooted, some almost barebacked, fashion itself into shape, and teach and preach zealously enough for copper alms and the love of God."

It is to these friars that we must look for the revival of civic faith which will save the English speaking race. For other hope of salvation from untutored democracy, demoralized by bosses and wirepullers weighted with the burdens of state and distracted by its own clamor, wants and needs, it is difficult to see.

That which we really wish to found is in very truth a civic church, every member of which should zealously, as much as it lay within him, preach the true faith, and endeavor to make it operative in the hearts and heads of its neighbors. Were such a church founded it would be as a great voice sounding out over sea and land the summons to all men to think seriously and soberly of the public life in which they are called to fill a part.   Visible in many ways is the decadence of the press.   The mentor of the young democracy has abandoned philosophy, and stuffs the ears of its Telemachus with descriptions of Calypso's petticoats and the latest scandals from the Court.   All the more need, then, that there should be a voice which, like that of the muezzin from the eastern minaret, would summon the faithful to the duties imposed by their belief.

A recent writer, who vainly struggled towards this ideal, has said:—
" We are told that the temporal welfare of man, and the salvation of the state, are ideals too meagre to arouse the enthusiasm which exults in self-sacrifice.   It needs eternity, say some, to stimulate men to action in time.   But as there is no eternity for the state, how then is patriotism possible?   Have not hundreds and thousands of men and women gladly marched to death for ideas to be realized solely on this side of the grave?   The decay of an active faith in the reality of the other world has no doubt paralyzed the spring of much human endeavor, and often left a great expanse of humanity practically waste so far as relates to the practical cultivation of the self-sacrificing virtues.   We go into this waste land to possess it.   It is capable of being made to flourish, as of old, under the stimulating radiance of a great ideal and the diligent and intelligent culture of those who have the capacity for direction.   If we could enlist in the active service of man as many men and women, in proportion to the number of those who are outside the churches, as any church or chapel will enlist in self-sacrificing labor for the young, the poor, and the afflicted, then indeed, results would be achieved of which, at present, we hardly venture even to dream.   But it is in this that lies our hope of doing effective work for the regeneration and salvation of mankind."

This, it may be said, involves a religious idea, and when religion is introduced harmonious co-operation is impossible. That was so once; it will not always be the case, for, as we said recently in the *Universal Review*:—"A new Catholicity has dawned upon the world.   All religions are now recognized as essentially Divine.   They represent the different angles at which man looks at God.   All have something to teach us—how to make the common man more like God.   The true religion is that which makes men most like Christ.   And what is the ideal which Christ translated into a realized life?   For practical purposes this: To take trouble to do good to others.   A simple formula, but the rudimentary and essential truth of the whole Christian religion.   To take trouble is to sacrifice time.   All time is a portion of life.   To lay down one's life for the brethren—which is sometimes literally the duty of the citizen who is called to die for his fellows—is the constant and daily duty demanded by all the thousand-and-one practical sacrifices which duty and affection call upon us to make for men.

As the result of the publication of the foregoing appeal and the subsequent agitation of the subject through the *Review* was the formation of associations or federations of workers for the public good in various

cities in England and Scotland. None of these associations, however, called themselves churches. The
name of church is unpopular with the unchurched
masses. And the application of the term to associations, including atheists, horrified many orthodox Christians. Cardinal Manning wrote me shortly before he
died: " Call it anything but a church and I am with
you with all my heart. Call it a church and not one of
my people will lift a finger to help you." Mr. Price
Hughes, of the Methodist body, was even more vehe-
ment than the Cardinal in denouncing my attempt to
restore the great word which has been degraded into
the label of ecclesiastical coteries to its original purpose
describing the union of all who love for the service of
all who suffer. In some towns the name preferred was
Civic Centre; in others, the Social Questions Union;
and again others preferred the title An Association for
Improving the Condition of the People. In Chicago
the name preferred has been that of the Civic Federation. The name is immaterial, but I still hold that the
conception of the church universal and militant conveys
better the idea which the Civic Federation is established
to realize than any other yet invented by the wit of man.
The Church was the machinery Christ devised for saving the world by self-sacrificing love.

What is wanted is a civic center which will genera-
lize for the benefit of all the results obtained by isolated
workers. The first desideratum is to obtain a man or
woman who can look at the community as a whole, and
who will resolve that he or she, as the case may be,
will never rest until the whole community is brought
up to the standard of the most advanced societies. Such
a determined worker has the nucleus of the Civic
Church under his own hat; but, of course, if he is to
succeed in his enterprise he must endeavor by hook or
by crook to get into existence some federation of the
moral and religious forces which would be recognized by
the community as having authority to speak in the

name and with the experience of the Civic Church. The work will of necessity be tentative and slow. Nor do I dream of evolving an ideal collective Humanitarian Episcopate on democratic lines all at once. But if the idea is once well grasped by the right man or woman, it will grow. The necessities of mankind will foster it, and all the forces of civilization and of religion will work for the establishment of the Civic Church.*

*See Appendix D.

CHAPTER II.

"LEAD US NOT INTO TEMPTATION!"

What would Christ do if he came to Chicago? **Surely** he would endeavor to help to fulfil His own prayer.

"Lead us not into temptation" is not a prayer which is regarded with much respect in the city administration of Chicago. It would be more accurate to say that the whole system from bottom to top has been constructed on the principle that it is a good thing to lead aldermen and officials into temptation on every possible occasion.

To prove this it is only necessary to refer to the unrestricted liberty which is given to a snap vote of the majority of the alderman to dispose of the common property of the city without any check excepting the mayor's veto which is nugatory in case the majority in the council exceeds two-thirds. Another instance is the position of the assessors. An honest assessor cannot meet his expenses whereas a man need not be very dishonest to make $100,000 during his term of office. If the aldermen and the assessors are to be kept from picking and selling they must be removed from temptation. It is not fair to human nature to expose it to a stress and strain to which it has proved manifestly unequal.

There is no reason in the nature of things why aldermen, for instance, should be exposed to that temptation. The Australian ballot has done much to purify American elections from the scandalous abuses which prevailed when the ward politician was tempted by endless opportunities to stuff ballot boxes and to poll repeaters. If the City Council of Chicago would not be above taking another hint from English-speaking men under the Union Jack they might remove much of the temptation to boodle which at present is altogether too strong to be resisted by the average alderman.

An ordinance of the city of Chicago conferring a franchise upon a company for the supply of gas, corresponds to a private act of Parliament and it is both interesting and instructive to compare the precautions which are taken in England against such scandals as that which disgrace the city council with the rough and tumble methods which prevail in Chicago. The situation which prevails in Chicago is not unlike that which exists in an English city which is supplied with gas by a private company.

No private bill is passed in England until it has been dealt with in quasi-judicial fashion by two impartial committees one selected from the Commons and the other from the House of Lords. Inexorably standing orders prevent any possibility of rushing the measure through the legislature without due consideration and ample opportunity being afforded to all sides to be heard before an impartial tribune of their own selection.

Compare this with the hitty-missy, hugger-mugger fashion in which the recent boodle Gas ordinance was dealt with by the City Council. Somebody, nobody knows who, it may have been a man of straw, as mythical as John Doe or Richard Roe, thrusts a piece of paper into the hands of an alderman and asks him to bring this proposal as an ordinance before the attention of the City Council. This ordinance may affect adversely millions of dollars invested under the sanction of the Council under previous ordinances. It would certainly have affected for the worse all the conditions of existence in Chicago for years to come if it had been carried out. It decided once for all in a manner prejudicial to the interests of the citizens, the price that they were to pay for all time to come for artificial light. This reckless and criminal proposal without any preliminaries is introduced into the Council, and then, without any opportunity being afforded for proving either the need of such an ordinance or of defending the *bona fides* of its promoters, this measure is thrust by a fine brute majority through the City Council in a single sitting. The existing gas company had no opportunity of being heard in their own defense. The representatives of other interests vitally concerned in the case were never consulted; but at a single sitting, after a wrangle which could not be dignified by the name debate, a scratch majority, secured, it is universally believed, by out-and-out bribery of the grossest kind, passed the ordinance into law, and law it would have been but for the veto of the Mayor. No amount of standing orders and regulations can make rogues into honest men; but a very simple proposition, entirely in harmony with the principles of the American constitution and the charter of the city of Chicago, would remove three-fourths of the temptation before which the aldermen succumb. No man in his senses would dream of suggesting that the elaborate and cumbrous machinery of English private legislation should be transplanted to this western soil, but ordinary common sense would suggest that in every case where an ordinance was introduced, affecting either public or private interests, some adequate caution should be taken to prevent the prostitution of legislation for the purposes of blackmail.

It would not be difficult, for instance, to adopt so much of the principles of English private bill legislation as to insist that before any ordinance was introduced it should be submitted to the corporation counsel, say, one month before it was read before the City Council, and that he should stop its further progress until the promotors had done three things. First, to furnish full information as to what they proposed to do, when they proposed to begin and finish, and how they were going to find the money. Secondly, to fully inform the local public of the proposed ordinance by means of advertisement, and to give notice to all persons whose property was affected or whose interests were endangered by the ordinance. Thirdly, to deposit with the City Treasurer, say, 10 per cent of the total sum which they propose to spend should they receive their franchise. Some such system would be simple, convenient and easily worked. After the ordinance had been introduced into the Council and had received the approval of a majority of the aldermen it might be referred to a quasi-judicial committee of four disinterested persons nomi-nated, say, two by the Mayor and two by the city council, who would be instructed to take evidence as to the proposed scheme, to hear everything that could be said against it by those whose interests it adversely affected, and to report back to the council as to whether or not it was to the public interest that the ordinance should pass. The final vote of the whole council on the ordinance as passed or amended by the committee could still remain as at present subject to the Mayor's veto, which can only be over ridden by a majority of two-thirds. To adopt such a procedure would involve no fresh legislation, and would establish no new precedent at variance with constitutional practice. It would on the other hand give invested capital security which it does not possess at present against wild cat legislation, and the sand bagger and black mailer would find three-fourths of their business disappear. As to the aldermen it would in every case be a veritable answer to the petition "Lead us not into temptation." From a boodle point of view the post of an alderman would hardly be worth having.

That brings me to another consideration, namely, whether it would not be wiser and more economical in the long run to pay the alderman $5,000 a year rather than to leave them as at present to sacrifice millions of the property of the city in order that they may levy an illicit toll upon the plunder which they convey to pred-atory corporations. $5,000 a year would at least remove the temptation of picking and stealing from the alderman. At present they are paid three dollars a sitting of the Council. This takes no account of the much more arduous sittings in committees. As a matter of fact the $156 a year hardly supplies the alderman with drink money. In England no representative in Parliament or any municipality is paid for his services. The result is that a very heavy money fine is virtually imposed upon the most public spirited citizens who devote their time to the service of the community. They have to pay their election expenses to begin with, and as long as they represent the people they have to neglect their own business and sacrifice often half of their working time in the unpaid service of the people. Hence, among the English democracy there is a growing feeling in favor of the payment of members, not only on the ground of justice but in order that the community may be able to command the services of its ablest members without regard to the question whether or not they are sufficiently wealthy to stand the racket of election expenses and the loss on neglected business. In Chicago, considering that the wealthier classes, who alone can afford to serve the city for nothing, refuse to take any part in the city government, there is a great deal to be said in favor of paying the aldermen respectably if we expect them to live honestly. At present the aldermen regard themselves as morally justified in recouping the losses incurred in getting elected or in devoting their time to the public business by levying black mail on all those who are asking the people for franchises. And until the wealthier classes can be induced to come into politics, I fail to see any way out of it short of the adequate remuneration of the aldermen.

With regard to the assessors and also to the assessed any attempt to realize our Lord's prayer to lead them not into temptation, but to deliver them from evil would necessitate a radical revision of the whole system of assessment. At the present moment assessments are based upon a lie, and the whole superstructure is honeycombed through and through with dishonesty and perjury. The arbitrary power of assessment given to elected officials whose hopes of continuance in office depend entirely upon propitiating those whose property they assess would make thieves of archangels, and the assessors in the three towns of Chicago are not arch-angels. The result is that it is assumed that they are not honest and that they will take advantage of their positions to make money. The basis of a true system of assessment is very simple. Whether it is a matter of realty or personalty there exists an automatic method of assessment that lies ready at hand. Why not make every citizen his own assessor? The city might accept as final the sworn statement of each of its citizens as to the value of his possessions subject to the distinctly understood proviso that they might at any time be con-demned or appropriated at the figure at which the owner assessed them. By this means no citizen would dare to assess his property much below its real value. If he did so he would simply invite the condemnation of his own property for the benefit of the city. The law in that case instead of leading citizens into the tempta-tion of making false statements in order to dodge the taxes would practically tend to deliver them from the evil of inadequate assessment by holding over them *in terrorem* the possibility of having to sacrifice their goods and their real estate in return for an inadequate sum. Of course, provision might be made for heirlooms and for some exceptional cases in which the sentimental value could not rightly be appraised for assessment pur-poses, and which at the same time it might be very cruel to condemn. But as a broad general principle, every man his own assessor, under penalty of ex-pro-priation at his own figures is a sound one, and would enormously simplify the question of assessment.

Another great department of public administration in Chicago which stands in very serious need of being delivered from evil is that belonging to justice and the police. Law should be impartial and just. In Chicago it is neither one nor the other. The administration of the law should be resolute, and merciful, but whatever punishment is allotted should be enforced with the same calm unswerving regularity which distinguishes the revolution of the planets. Almost every principle of sound jurisprudence is violated every day in the justices' courts, both civil and criminal, in Chicago. Justices nominated for political considerations and swayed more or less shamelessly by partisan feelings set before the lawless members of the community a shameful object lesson in injustice and corruption. I do not mean for a moment to assert that the justice in any Chicago court would sentence an innocent man for a bribe, or that for so many dollars down he would deliver the guilty. But there is hardly a court in Chicago where a prisoner who has a political pull is not tolerably sure of escaping punishment, unless, of course, his crime has been too flagrant or too sensational for it to be safe for him to be liberated after the usual fashion.* But take the case of an ordinary offender. That man, if he stands in with an alderman or the owner of an alderman can almost always escape scotfree. For the sake of appearances he will be fined but before the court rises his fine will be suspended indefinitely—that is it will be remitted. The practice of imposing fines and then suspending them is one which leads many justices into

---

*At a meeting of the Sunset Club held March 31, 1892, Mr. W. S. Forrest read a paper based on his personal experience as a lawyer in the courts of the city of Chicago or rather of Cook County in which Chicago is situated. In the course of that paper he said: "There are wrongs in the administration of criminal law in Cook County, wrongs against the accused, wrongs against society, wrongs against the letter and spirit of the Constitution of the state. What are some of these wrongs? The rich and powerful are seldom indicted and never tried, well, hardly ever. The Criminal Court of Cook County exists only to punish the poor and the vulgar. Manslaughter is committed by corporations with impunity—Men are convicted who are innocent. Even in ordinary trials the forms of law are frequently set aside and the rules of evidence ignored."

Gen. Stiles who followed Mr. Forrest confirmed his statement, and strengthened it. He said: "Brother Forrest complains that no rich merchants are ever convicted. Don't forget to mention that no prominent criminals are ever convicted. No prominent gambler is convicted. Three convictions would send him to the penitentiary, and they take mighty good care at the States Attorney's office that no second conviction shall ever be had against an open, notorious and leading gambler in the city. No prominent confidence man is convicted. A man who kills another in a prominent saloon is hardly ever tried, never convicted and never was his worthless neck stretched at the end of a halter. The People must wake up. I don't exactly want them to form a vigilance committee, but to go so almighty close to it that you can hardly tell the difference. Run out the riff raff, the gamblers, the men who live upon the honest toil of others. Put a stop to the frauds at elections. Run out of office men who are there only for the boodle that is in it. Do this and you will soon have a better order of things, and unless you do it yourselves no reform can be accomplished." "Sunset Club Year Book 1891-2," pp. 170, 181.

temptation. It makes easy the way by which he is lead step by step to be a mere tool of party politicians. An appreciable step would be taken towards delivering the justice from the evil course into which he has fallen if he were compelled to make a monthly return of all fines which he has imposed and the fines which he has suspended, specifying in every case the reason for such suspension. It is an old saying that the progress of civilization may be measured by the extent to which the authority of impartial law supersedes arbitrary will of the individual in the judicial administration. Judging by the justices' courts Chicago is still in the state of barbarism. Justice there in too many cases is the measure of the justice's foot modified by the conflicting influences of antagonistic political pulls. The evil is as great in civil as in criminal courts. if not greater. A distinguished lawer quoted by the *Chicago Herald*, Feb. 26th, says:

The petty court or "justice shop" system in Chicago and Cook County is the most iniquitous method that human ingenuity could have devised to oppress the poor, harass the financially distressed and annoy victims of spite and enmity. It is a reflection upon the fair fame of the city and a disgrace to the bar that such a condition of things should continue to exist.

The *Herald* commenting on these remarks says:

That the present system of administering justice in petty cases is a disgrace to the judicial system of this city is known to everybody, and is so patent to all that countless efforts have been made to remedy the evils which it produces. The fundamental element of the evil, that is, the system itself, being based upon a constitutional provision, cannot be changed without an amendment to the constitution.

That is usually the case in Chicago. Whenever you find a very unmistakable manifestation of the Devil, you are certain to find him entrenched behind the Constitution of the State of Illinois.

If any change is to be made justices should be paid by salaries instead of as at present partly by salaries and partly by fees. The practice of giving the justices the interest of a solid silver dollar in every person whom they pull, or in every case they hear, is a crying shame which has been denounced times without number but it remains today as yesterday the same. The temptation which leads police to make raids in order that they may net a sufficient harvest of dollars from the luckless captives of these arbitrary razzias is one into which the justices should not be led.

These are a few of the more salient instances of maladministration of justice in which Chicago is distinctly below the level of any European town. There are plenty of evils which the city shares with other cities in the Old World. The bureau of justice is an excellent and well meaning institution but unfortunately it has not the funds to enable it to discharge the duties of the poor man's lawyer. Some day possibly just as the physicians in the community consider themselves honored by being allowed to practice for nothing in the city or county hospital so that day may come when the same standard of society may prevail among the legal profession, and the leading lawyers in the community may consider it a distinction to be allowed to practice without fees in the cases of the poor.*

The last class of persons whom I shall consider as subjected to temptations from which they might be delivered by the same Christian and rational system is the police. At present it is almost impossible for the policeman to resist the temptation to supplement his salary by bribes. It may be taken as a general rule that whenever a law exists in the statute book that is not enforced that law is the source of pecuniary profit to all persons charged with the enforcement of the law.

---

*Speaking on this subject at a meeting of the Sunset Club March 31, 1892, Mr. Joseph B. David said: "As one who has had a somewhat extended experience in the practice of criminal law in this county for the past seven years, I wish to say a word or two on the subject under discussion. No man who is tried in the Criminal Court of Cook County, who is without means to hire able lawyers, can get a fair trial. The law of this state provides that when a man accused of crime is too poor to hire a lawyer the court shall appoint counsel to conduct his defense. What happens? A man who has just been admitted to the bar, who never tried a case in his life before, whose only knowledge of criminal law is gathered from a few months reading of text-books, such a man is appointed to cope with able counsel such as the States Attorney and his distinguished assistants. The result is inevitable. The trial is a farce—a parody on justice."

Whether it be gamblers, or prostitutes, keepers of opium joints, or any other offender against the municipal ordinances nothing is more certain than that they have to pay for their immunity from prosecution by more or less political blackmailing levied by the police. The remedy for this can only be sought by bringing the written law into closer relation with that which can be actually enforced. A law ideally good may become the source of endless corruption when it is applied to a community that is really bad. It may be, for instance, considered an excellent thing that every house of prostitution, and every opium joint, and every gaming hell should be outlawed, and authority given to every member of the police force to suppress them whenever he finds them; but in communities where prostitution, opium smoking and gambling are deeply rooted the responsibility for the initiative in suppressing these evils should not rest upon individual policemen. It ought either to be placed under the responsible authority of neighboring citizens or of some body other than the officials charged with the execution of the law. To leave the initiative to the patrolmen is simply to expose them to a temptation to levy blackmail to which in most cases they succumb. If, for instance, no house could be raided on the initiative of a private constable, and if in other cases the law could only be put in motion either by a citizen's committee or by local residents the power to levy blackmail, and therefore the temptation to receive it would largely disappear. The greater the power the policemen have of exercising option in favor of or against the offenders the more increase of corruption. The ideal police service is that in which the policeman should have no law to enforce excepting laws which he must enforce or be responsible for their non-enforcement. At present in Chicago the policeman is nominally expected to enforce an endless mulplicity of ordinances which are openly set at nought by thousands of citizens every day, and every non-executed ordinance affords an opening for official blackmail.

These evils and many others which might be described are admitted to exist by every observant citizen in Chicago. All the preaching in the world would fail to help our Lord to realize his own prayer in relation to those offenses. But what preaching cannot do, what the personal religion of the individual would be powerless to effect, civic religion practically applied by the election of honest men would assuredly accomplish. If then our churches and our Christians mean what they say when they pray " Lead us not into temptation, but deliver us from evil," is it not obvious that it is their Christian duty to go into politics and stay there until they have done something to help to fulfill their own prayers?

Obvious though it may appear to us, it is unfortunately the reverse of obvious to many good men. This winter at the Willard Hall in the Woman's Temple a " trophy " was produced in the shape of a confirmed drunkard who had found salvation through conversion. " Friends," said this brand plucked from the burning, " I have been wonderfully delivered by the grace of God from the bondage of sin and Satan. All my life long I have been devoted to whisky and politics. Now, thanks be to God for his redeeming mercy, I am delivered from both." There is small prospect of the redemption of the city when the first thought of the redeemed is to leave whisky in undisputed possession of politics.

CHAPTER III.

CASTING OUT DEVILS.

They greatly err who imagine that the doctrine of diabolical possession is an exploded superstition. Not only individuals but communities are often the victims of this unhallowed appropriation by the Powers of Evil of that which was designed as the temple of the Holy Spirit. As in Judea in olden time the casting out of devils was one of the most manifest signs of the power of the Messiah, so to day if He were to appear amongst us in Chicago He would doubtless signalize His divine presence and power in a similar fashion.

Chicago like other cities is possessed by a host of unclean spirits, whose name is Legion for they are many. There are several, however, which can be distinguished sufficiently to be named and described. These I will now proceed to enumerate with some brief suggestions as to their exorcism.

First and foremost, Plutocracy. I came to America to see what Mr. Carnegie described as the Triumph of Democracy. I found instead the Evolution of Plutocracy. The new tyranny which is being installed behind the convenient mask of republican form is likely to cure itself by its own excess. Compound interest which if left undisturbed will concentrate the wealth of the world in the hands of a corporal's guard of multi-billion-aires has already destroyed the distinctive glory of the American Republic. Nearly half of the once independent proprietors of their own holdings are now tenants of these usurers without tenant's rights.

According to the lastest Government statistics, we possess sixty billions of wealth. Nine per cent of the families own 71 per cent of this, leaving but 29 per cent to the remaining 91 per cent of the families. The 9

per cent is composed of two classes: rich and million-
airs. Of the latter there are 4,074 families. They average three million dollars each. They constitute only
three one-hundredths of 1 per cent of the whole number
of families, while they own 20 per cent of the wealth.
That is, they own nearly as much as the 11,593,887
families.

The process of accumulation goes on irresistibly.
The snow ball gathers as it grows. Even spendthrifts
and prodigals cannot dissipate the unearned increment
of their millions which multiply while they sleep. The
millionaire is developing into the billionaire, and the
end is not yet. The transformation is hidden from the
multitude because the coming despot eschews the tawdry
tinsel of the crown, and liberty is believed to be as safe
as well, let us say, as the populace of Rome believed
the republic to be when Julius Caesar refused the
imperial purple. But everywhere the money power has
the people by the throat. Whether it is the pawnbroker
down the levee, charging ten per cent. per month
interest upon the pledges of the poor, or the millionaire,
negotiating with newspapers for the abandonment of
the Interstate Commerce Act, the spectacle is the same.
The poor man is the servant of the rich, and at present
stands in some danger of becoming his slave.

Plutocracy in America even more than in England, to
which I have already compared it, recalls Victor Hugo's
memorable description of the octopus. Victor Hugo
was a great artist in words and he described the octopus
from life. Had he described it from his observation of
plutocracy in America he would not have altered a
single sentence. This description of this spectral
phantom of the deep, the devil fish, with its eight huge
arms, with its four hundred pustules that cut and suck
like a cupping glass, this loathly horror of vampire-
death lurking in ocean caves to seize the limb and drain
the life of the unwary fisherman, is only too true to life
as many an unfortunate will recognize.

It winds around its victim, covering him and enveloping him in its slimy folds. . . . It is a spider in its shape, a chameleon in its rapid changes of hue. When angry it becomes purple. Its most disgusting characteristic is its impalpability. Its slimy folds strangle; its very touch paralyzes. It looks like a mass of scorbutic gangrened flesh; it is a hideous picture of loathsome disease. Once fixed you cannot tear it away. It clings closely to its prey. How does it do so? By creating a vacuum. . . . It is a pneumatic machine that attacks you. You are struggling with a void which possesses eight antennae. No scratches, no bites, but an indescribable suffocation. The terrible wretch grins upon you by a thousand foul mouths. The hydra incorporates itself with the man, and the man with the hydra. You become one and the same. The hideous dream is in your bosom. The devil fish draws you into its system. He drags you to him and into him; bound helplessly, glued where you stand, utterly powerless, you are gradually emptied into a loathsome receptacle, which is the monster himself. . . . The devil fish is a hypocrite.

Nothing can be more hypocritical than the way in which plutocracy disguises its designs, until its victim is well within its reach. It has already flung its all devouring tentacles round almost every institution in the United States. Some it has devoured, others it is preparing to engulf. Among the latter that which most excites my sympathy and dismay is the last refuge of independent criticism in the domain of sociological study. I refer to the universities. Among the younger university professors in America there are many who have devoted themselves to a life long study of the sociological phenomena. They know and appreciate the advantages of municipal monopolies as opposed to the monopoly of the predatory rich. They have been most of them in the old world, and they have learned the lessons which the most progressive of the municipalities of the Old World have to teach the cities of the new. They are devoted to the cause of labor and of social progress. They write and teach the necessity of dealing with the problems of labor in a sympathetic spirit, of making the municipality the ideal employer and of leveling up all other employers to the municipal level. They are in favor of everything or nearly everything that I have advocated in this book, for municipal gas, municipal water, municipal street cars, municipal telephones and in short for the municipalization of all the monopolies of service. Nowhere in the world will you find more thoughtful and fearless exponents of the new economics than in the American universities. Contrasted with the servile subjugation in which most of the slaves of the press are kept by their plutocratic owners, the university is as an oasis in the desert, a fresh green spot in the midst of an arid waste of sand. How long will this oasis be permitted to continue? I am afraid that when the battle becomes hotter, and the hosts now being arrayed against each other grapple in the struggle for life and death, it will go hard with these teachers of truth. For the endowment of the universities is one of the fashionable pastimes of the American millionaire. Vanderbilt has given his name to a university in the South, and Rockefeller—the story of whose Standard Oil Trust will some day be given to the public in all its infamy of detail, and continental grandeur of rapacity, by some Zola of reality who will discover in it one of the most interesting episodes in all history—is the great patron of the University of Chicago. There is hardly a university in the country which has not either received large sums from millionaires or which does not live from day to day in the hope of receiving large sums from millionaires. Universities like every other institution in the country are "on the make," and just as the modern Herod becomes a pew holder and gags John the Baptist by starving him out of the pulpit, a much more efficacious method than the ax of the executioner, so the predatory rich have intrenched themselves in the citadels of the American universities.

I heard a story the other day which is significant of much. A well known millionaire who was one of the trustees of an eastern university met at one of the university functions a professor to whom he freely expressed his opinion that it was a very good thing that there were half a million men out of work in the United

States. By such a condition of affairs the laboring men could be kept down. The professor shocked by the cynicism of the avowal strongly controverted the millionaire's view unmindful of the fact that the millionaire was a trustee of the university.

Shortly after the professor ventured to publish an article in which he formulated the right of the laboring man to be shielded from being dismissed at the mere caprice of his employer. This article was made sufficient cause to compel him to leave the university. He was not dismissed, but strong representations were made by the millionaire in question to his fellow trustees that this professor must be cleared out. The board, like Pilate, was loath to yield to the pressure of the modern Caiaphas, but ultimately the professor, for peace's sake, resigned his post and accepted another in a state university in the west which he still holds. A vacancy occurred quite recently in his old university and it was mooted that it might be well to invite the professor to return. But the suggestion was immediately negatived. The millionaire would have no such pestilent fellow about his place.

Another instance also came to my notice quite recently. One of the younger professors who had taken a very energetic and honorable part in the agitation for the municipal ownership of the monopolies of service, was warned by the representative of a great trust, that he had better take care what he was doing. Articles which he had published had attracted the attention of the combine and they were considerably alarmed at the effect which they had upon their invested capital. He told his friend quite frankly that if he continued in his present course they would have to down him. He regretted it very much but he said "there is no doubt it is a financial necessity and we shall have to down you" for the trusts and corporations have a curious knack of using even the phrases of the Camorra and other associations of assassins. Not, of course, that the

Professor was to be assassinated. I have been assured that the predatory rich do not shrink even from using the sandbag and the revolver — of course by deputies. That, however, is not a very usual method. They prefer to starve a man out. It costs less and does not make so much scandal. Under these circumstances it is not surprising that the professor feels that a Damocles sword is hanging over his head. If these things are done in the green tree what will be done in the dry? It remains to be seen whether the university which should be before everything else the home of free and independent thought is to be subjected as completely by the money power as the City Council of Chicago or the newspaper press of America. For the sake of the American people and the evolution of society in the United States I sincerely hope that the various faculties charged with the control of higher education in the republic, may stand to their guns and may prove themselves proof alike against the menace and the bribes of the plutocrats.

To check this stealthy but rapid encroachment on popular liberty, and to cast out this demon, is the task which lies before American patriots at the close of this century. Of one demon it was said this kind goeth out by prayer and fasting, and it is so with plutocracy. Of fasting we have had but a foretaste. When to that is added enough prayerful, earnest wrestling with the Throne of Grace as leads the men who pray to vote as they pray, the way of escape will appear. But there must be more fasting and more prayer than there has yet been if the grasp of the Octopus with its myriad arms is to be loosened from the throat of the republic. At present the plutocrat is supreme because the democracy is divided and apathetic. Nor has "the sense of power from boundless suffering wrung" yet given the masses of the despoiled courage to resent their wrongs. Here in Chicago the first obvious step is to insist upon the readjustment of the burden of taxation so that wealth may no longer shift its share upon the shoulders of the poor. The next is to resume as rapidly as possible all the franchises and other sources of revenue which have been stolen from the people by corrupting their representatives and to peremptorily veto all further appropriation of the wealth of the many for the profit of the few. When the democracy is disciplined enough and has established sufficient confidence in its leaders to do these two things, it may safely be trusted to discover ways and means to carry out the rest of the programme of its emancipation.

The second devil which today needs exorcism is one I did not expect to find in a civilized and progressive country.

We rid ourselves of it so long ago in the old country that it was startling to find that it had simply migrated to the New World. Of all the folklore tales of Europe the most horrible is that of the Vampire of the Levant. The vampire is the reanimated corpse of an evil doer which is doomed to leave the tomb and return to the living in order that with livid lips he shall draw in the life blood from the veins of his sleeping friends. In the A. P. A., that strange association for the protection of American citizens which seems to have within its ranks far more Canadians and Orangemen from Ulster and Glasgow than native-born citizens of the United States, always reminds me of that restless vampire of southeastern Europe. No-Popery fanaticism died fifty years ago in England. We imagined it dead and buried. But here is the vampire thing making night hideous by revisiting the pale glimpses of the moon in western America. It is the same old demon, with its familiar hoof and horns and tail, scaring the old women of both sexes with the bogey of impending massacre and of the domination of sixty millions by six. To avert the menaced St. Bartholomew the Protestant Mayor of Toledo and many of the A. P. A.'s in that city laid in a stock of Winchester rifles, a fact of which the public only recently became aware owing to the reluctance or inability of these doughty champions to pay for their guns after they had been delivered. Ridicule ought to be the best means for exorcising this belated survival of antiquated bigotry. To lay a vampire the Greeks say it is necessary to drive long nails into the quivering carcass of the Dead-Alive. When the last nail is driven home the vampire walks no more. There are several nails of hard fact and solid sense which intelligent and patriotic citizens should drive up to the head into the A. P. A. The first is that this is a land of liberty, where the whole armed force at the disposal of the authorities will be used to protect freedom of speech even when it is as much abused as it sometimes is by A. P. A. lecturers. And the Catholics of all men should be foremost in demanding that no mob shall be allowed to interfere in their name with the utterances of their enemies. The second is the fact that this anti-Catholic propaganda is chiefly the work of non-Americans who, finding no field for the reception of their pernicious nonsense in Cardinal Manning's country, are endeavoring to palm off upon the New World the cast-off trumpery for which we have no more use on our side of the water. But the third and by far the most effective nail in the coffin of this propaganda of distrust, malice and all uncharitableness is to refuse absolutely to batten upon the bones of the martyrs of the sixteenth and seventeenth centuries, and to insist constantly upon the immense and but little recognized services which the Catholic Church is rendering to humanity and to civilization here and now. To hate your brother who is doing Christ's work here in Chicago because his great-great-grandfather burned your great-great-granduncle three centuries since in Europe is hardly rational and not at all Christian. This devil, however, will disappear, like the materialized spectres of the seance room, if you simply turn on the light.

After Plutocracy and Religious Intolerance, there is

the devil of Intemperance. In Chicago there is said to be sixty millions of dollars spent every year in intoxicants. The victims of strong drink are to be found in the Olympian heights where the millionaires dwell and in the humblest homes. Dr. Keeley is curing thousands of the craving for drink, and by his success has paved the way for numbers of rivals. But to cast the demon of intemperance out of individuals is not enough. There is the community to be considered, what is to be done with the saloon?

In Chicago the question was one of the most hotly debated of all those on which I touched. What I said to the prohibitionist was simply this: " Prohibit where you can and where you cannot prohibit do as much as you can in that direction. But remember that the saloon is not to be got rid of by swearing at it. The true policy is to recognize the need to which it ministers and to put something better in its place."

Nothing but harm can come from a foolish refusal to look the facts in the face. And the facts which the prohibitionists ignore is that with all its faults the saloon is ministering to many great wants of the citizens which the church ignore. In many neighborhoods the saloon is the only parlor and the only club of the working people. It is their solitary place of recreation. They shelter therein the wet and cold, they meet their friends there, and read the papers. Chicago is abominably ill supplied with lavatories and similar conveniences. The saloon is the only place where a poor man can wash his face outside his own house, and the only substitute there is for the retiring rooms which every city should establish as necessary conveniences. Bad as the saloon is it holds the field and deserves to hold it until there is at least one temperance saloon in every precinct. There are 800 precincts and 7,000 saloons. But in all Chicago there are not seventy temperance resorts such as the Teetotums of London, the cafés of Liverpool and the coffee parlors and cocoa palaces of many English towns. Until the temperance people put something better in the place of the saloon, the saloon will never be got rid of.

Failing the wholesale extirpation of the saloon can nothing be done to exorcise the worse evils which attend the sale of drink? I' am too keenly sensible of the miseries of intemperance to dare to advise that nothing should be tried until everything can be accomplished. The evil is too terrible such for fooling as this.

No remarks of mine excited more general discussion or evoked stronger dissent than a passing observation I made at the Central Music Hall Conference in November concerning the saloons. It was made the theme of much animadversion in the temperance press and on the temperance platform. Suppose there are three saloons. Grant that they are all diabolic because all sell intoxicants, and you have only two prohibitionist votes, what are you to do?* If you insist on closing them all, you will close none, for two men cannot outvote three. But suppose that while all the saloons are strongholds of Satan because they sell beer, No. 1 is a clean, well conducted place to which, excepting for the

---

* An important decision in the Indiana Supreme Court, as to the nuisance of saloons, which suggests a possibility of getting rid of the saloons even when they have a majority was pronounced in December 1893. The facts are as follows (summarized from the *Chicago Tribune*, December 24):—An Indianapolis woman owned a house on a residence street of that city. There were no saloons in the neighborhood. The owner of the adjoining lot built a store on it and started a saloon there. He did this against the united protest of the people in the neighborhood. The authorities said that they could not refuse to grant him a license, because the law, there as here, is that a man who has "a good moral character" and pays the license money is entitled to a license.

Thereupon the woman brought suit for damages, alleging that the saloon was a nuisance and that it hurt the rental and selling value of her property. The defendant claimed that he was licensed pursuant to law, and as long as he did not keep a disorderly place he was not amenable to any law; if neighboring property was damaged it was something for which he was not responsible. The lower court found for the defendant, and so did the Supreme Court at first, but on a rehearing reversed itself, and decided in favor of the plaintiff.

The court holds now that while the Legislature has the right to license saloons, the saloon business is an immoral one and is licensed in order that the citizen may have some protection against the evils from the unrestrained sale of liquor. It could not be assumed that it was the intention of the Legislature to place the sale of spirits above the rights of the citizen and make him endure a nuisance and submit to loss for the benefit of the saloonkeeper. Hence the court says in conclusion:

If the saloon causes property to depreciate in value it is a nuisance within the law and can be abated. Not only that, but the person who operates the saloon is liable in damages to the injured party and the measure of damages is the measure of injury to the property.

sale of drink, no objection can be taken; No. 2 runs a gaming hell and No 3 runs both a gaming hell and a house of prostitution. Here two prohibitionists are confronted with three saloons, possessed respectively by one, two and three devils. Why not ally yourselves with No. 1 to vote No. 2 and No. 3 out of existence? "No covenant with hell?" Well, the result of that policy of refusing to use a single barrelled devil of the good saloon to cast out the double and triple barrelled devils of gaming and prostitution and drink is that all three will go on running and you are responsible for that.

Some criticism was offered chiefly on the grounds that such a policy would give a monopoly to No. 1. To which my reply is make him pay for it, and if you are wise enough make him your paid agent, for I am as I have been since 1873, a sworn advocate of the Norwegian system of dealing with the license question. To avoid monopoly municipalize the saloon! This, however, by the way.

The argument has also been used that this would involve the municipalizing or the licensing at least of the house of ill-fame. But that is absurd. There is a distinction as wide as the poles between the saloon and the brothel. No one in his senses can assert that to drink a glass of beer is a mortal sin, whereas every Christian recognizes that a house of ill-fame exists expressly and solely in order to facilitate direct breaches of the moral law. Of course those who do hold that it is a mortal sin to drink a glass of beer under any circumstances are quite right in refusing to license saloons or to accept any responsibility for their existance. But all who admit that the drinking of beer although terribly liable to abuse may be indulged in without sin are bound to do what they can to control the supply and minimize the evils of the traffic. That is why I have sometimes said that the ideal church would run a saloon. For if the sale of drink where it

cannot be prohibited is so dangerous a business, it
ought to be in the hands of the very salt of the earth.
It takes a very elect saint to make a saloon a means of
grace.   A man good enough to be a minister, may fall
far short of the ideal standard required for the saloon
business.   And as the church was founded to produce
saints for the world's salvation it is right that the church
should see to it that if the saloon is to exist it should
be in the hands of men who will not make it a curse and
a scourge to the community.*

The temperance element expected that the city would go dry at the
municipal election and made no more than a perfunctory effort to get
out the vote.   The liquor men, on the other hand, put a large amount
of money into their campaign and won the city for license, to the surprise of everybody.   The temperance element was chagrined.   And
in this novel and perhaps effective way they will harass their opponents.

They will fit up one of the largest stores in the heart of the city as
a saloon.   This they will stock with the best liquors and beers of all
brands.   An efficient business man will be put in charge, and behind
the counter will be a dozen expert drink mixers.   Prices will be as
follows : Mixed drinks and fine wines, 5 cents; liquors, plain, 3 cents;
beer, 2 cents; ponies, 1 cent.   Bottled goods will be sold at cost, and
no profits will be expected from sales, except sufficient to pay for the
running expenses, as the rent, fixtures, advertising, and license fee
will be paid for by subscription.

In this way the promoters hope to draw enough customers from the
other saloons to ruin their business.   This may be the more easily
effected as all who take out licenses have to pay $2,000 each May 1, and
it takes considerable time to get the equivalent back in ordinary business.   The trade is extremely lucrative here.   The law limits the
number of licenses to one to every 1,000 inhabitants, which gives
Haverhill twenty-seven liquor shops, but as all the neighboring cities
and towns connected by electric roads regularly vote no license the
trade here supplies a population of 100,000 persons.   The projectors
have $1,400 already subscribed toward the saloon.

During my stay in Chicago, Mayor Eustis of Minneap-
olis passed through the city on his way to New York.
Before I was aware that he had arrived he had departed.
But the previous day I read in the papers the following

---

* A Chicago paper published a special telegram dated Haverhill, Massachusetts,
Dec. 23, describing a curious development of temperance activity in the heart of a
prohibition district.   I wrote to Haverhill but I have received no reply; the story
may be an invention.   I quoted, however, as indicating a possible use of the competitive principle for the destruction of the vested interest of the saloonkeeper
which may be more useful in England than in Chicago.

interesting expression of opinion in an interview with Mayor Eustis:

"We are operating under the Stead plan of local government," said he, "and strange to say we adopted the policy before we ever heard of Stead or his ideas. By conferences with the liquor dealers' associations we have succeeded in closing up all tough saloons and stopped robberies and fights that had taken place in them every day. In this way all thieves, swindlers and thugs have been driven from town. Ministers took offense because I refused to close the back doors of saloons on Sunday. I believe men will drink on Sunday if they wish, and if one door be closed another will be opened. I preferred to employ the saloon-keepers as allies in trying to bring about a decent government. How I have succeeded may be seen from the police court records. One year will develop statistics to show the correctness or error of my position."

I wrote at once to the mayor asking him for further information, and he was good enough to write me a long and most interesting letter which is a most valuable contribution to the solution of a very knotty problem. The best way of fighting the saloon is to put something better in its place. It is a great delusion to imagine that the need of social centers or public rooms is only confined to laboring men. The modern club of the middle and upper classes show that the need is felt by them and not even the conveniences of the American hotels are sufficient to meet the needs of the situation. Hotels and clubs have alike one great disadvantage, they are both places in which treating goes on as a matter of course. If intemperance is to be successfully exorcised provision must be made for supplying a meeting place without drink. An admirable example of what can be done in this way is supplied by the Commerce Club, in the Auditorium Building. This institution has no bar but it has all the other conveniences of an ordinary club with the additional advantage that it can be used by both sexes.

A number of such institutions with moderate terms— the subscription to the Commerce Club is only $20 for resident and $12 for non-residents, while $100 secures a life membership—scattered about the city would have a wholesome effect. Having used the Commerce Club every day for months I gladly testify to the fact that it is the most convenient place I have ever seen in any city. It is a model of what such an institution should be.

The exorcising of the gaming fiend so far as public gaming hells go is easier than that of dealing with other vices which perplex the moral reformer. The experience of Europe suffices to prove that the public gaming house can be suppressed by law without any difficulty. The experience of Chicago from the 6th of January to the 12th of February shows that open gaming can be suppressed by the mere fiat of the Mayor. That every gaming house in Chicago is not shut up tight at this moment is due to those who are charged with the enforcement of the law. The law itself leaves nothing to be desired on the score of stringency.

There is practically unanimity on the part of the respectable and decent people, that open gaming houses are an evil, this is admitted as frankly by the newspapers as it is by preachers, nor is it only journalists and ministers who have expressed a clear opinion on the subject.

Last December the grand jury in Mr. Justice Brentano's court investigated the subject, drew up a report which concluded with a very emphatic condemnation of the system and a practical proposal for dealing with the evil. The following is the closing passage of that report.

This conflicting testimony from officials charged with the responsible duty of enforcing the laws of the state and ordinances of the city wisely enacted for the purpose of protecting the persons, property and morals of the people from the vicious and criminal classes so closely associated with gambling, together with evidence of several other subordinates, who confessed to honest efforts to earn their salaries by preventing "crap," "brace" and "copper" operations (terms not fully understood by all the grand jurors), led us unanimously to the conclusion that there is collusion between the police force of the city and the gamblers so general and wide that its "devil fish" tentacles reach to a large portion of the police force. In a community claiming the concomitants of civilization there ought to be sufficient moral and legal power to locate the head center of official collusion with gambling and smite it to the death. While any portion of the police force is under suspicion of this conspiracy—a "combine" which hesitates not at the crime of perjury—no citizen can feel a sense of security in life or property; and inasmuch as grand juries of the regular panel have as much as they can do, or more, with the regular docket cases, we suggest the calling of a special grand jury for the sole purpose of considering the subject of gambling and the relation of the city police thereto, as herein set forth.

We have, therefore, a very favorable condition of things. The law is all right; public opinion is all right; the Mayor wishes to do everything he can to suppress it; and Chief Brennan's orders are all right, whatever they may be worth. The grand jury which has reported on the subject so emphatically declares that there ought to be sufficient moral power to locate the head sinner of official collusion with the gambler and smite him to the death; and further, the grand jury has indicated the way in which this can be done, viz., by the calling of a special grand jury for the sole purpose of considering the subject. The state's attorney or any judge on the bench can act upon this recommendation. Judge Brentano, upon whom would naturally devolve the calling of such a grand jury, has been engaged with the trial of Prendergast so long that he has not had time to look into the matter. He stated, however, that it was his opinion that,

The report reveals a state of affairs that should be investigated without delay, and if the regular juries cannot find time to do it no time should be lost in calling twenty-three men who can devote their entire time to an honest inquiry into a matter that so much concerns the public welfare.

What, then, is still needed in order to put the machinery of the law in motion? Here we have some help from an unexpected quarter. The late Carter Harrison in defending his policy made a notable speech which may well be taken into account by all those who are interested in this question. He said:

Those who have so vigorously cried out for its extermination have failed to suggest any possible or practicable plan by which the desired end can be accomplished, and they forget that every effort at its annihilation has been a dismal failure. * * * Considering what the results had been, I came to the conclusion, on becoming Mayor, that the evil must be kept within proper bounds and restrictions. More than that, I determined to restrict these houses to the central portion of the city, where they could be closely watched and kept in check. By this course of procedure I had in view the easy and unrestricted entrance of either the police, to detect sharp practices by the gamblers, keep minors out and find any crooked persons who might seek its enchantments, or of business men, who might desire to see whether an employe was squandering money surreptitiously taken from their funds. By such a course as I have thus outlined I have had the endorsement of a large number of citizens and the results have been far better than they would have been under different conditions. Under the apparent rigid rule in vogue in 1873 there were in the city forty-four gambling establishments and twenty odd bunko places; in 1877 over thirty gambling-houses and a dozen or more bunko-rooms, while during 1888 there have not been seventeen of the former and not a single bunko room. The present state of affairs here is due to restrictions, and while a great number of complaints came to my office shortly after my inauguration, there have been not more than a half dozen within the past eighteen months. The plan of keeping these places in the heart of the city enables the police officers to learn where brace boxes are played upon unsuspecting victims. Such houses are promptly dealt with. Those that run are put upon their good behavior; minors are excluded, and those who must play protected from the tricks of dealers, and games of a character calculated to attract the man of small means entirely prevented.

After having laid down his position and stated the ground upon which he defended it he then proceeded to suggest the natural and proper course to be taken by those who have differed from him, if they had the courage of their convictions and were determined to have their way.

I am not defending gambling *per se*, but if I am wrong in my position in dealing with it from a practical standpoint, the people have their remedy. They can appeal to an authority higher than mine, and strange it is that such citizens and newspapers as have assailed me have not also directed their batteries toward that authority. Those who think my plan not the best have a state law under which any one so disposed can take his hand in suppressing gambling. I fear, however, that Mr. Lincoln was not mistaken when he said that "statutory enactments can't turn a calf's tail into a third hind leg." The fireside, the lyceum and the well-stocked public library will do more than laws to suppress social evils.

That is to say, Mr. Harrison points to the same remedy which Rev. O. P. Gifford referred to in his speech at Willard Hall. Under the law of the State of Illinois it is quite possible for any association of citizens, or for any individual to swear in police for a special purpose to enforce any law which may be violated, and to employ these police to raid the gambling houses and prosecute the gamblers under the law of the State of Illinois. There is no necessity of doing this on a very extensive scale. If one prominent gaming house were raided and its proprietors prosecuted, not once, but twice or thrice in succession—until they had qualified for Joliet—that would settle matters. Gamblers do not mind in the least being fined; they have a strong objection to being sent to the Penitentiary. After a second or third conviction they would be sent to prison and when once it was well understood that every leading gambler in the town would be taken in turn and prosecuted with the utmost rigor of the law until his career is terminated by incarceration, Mr. Hopkins would be able to realize his pious wish for the suppression of public gambling and the city would be rid of one of its most conspicuous plagues.

Of course, this work should be undertaken by the constituted authorities, but if the constituted authorities fail in their duty, as they have habitually done in Chicago, then the duty of action would devolve upon the committee of the Federation charged with moral questions, of which committee, by the by, the chairman is none other than the Rev. O. P. Gifford.

The open air gaming hell which is carried on on the public race tracks—a much more difficult question, owing to the element of innocent amusement that enters into it—and the "respectable" speculation which is but another term for the gambling on the Board of Trade—equally difficult from the element of business which pervades it—are much more insoluble problems. But the fact that it is difficult or impossible to deal with racing is no reason why so simple and obvious measures as the closing of public hells should not be carried out. The machinery is there, the law is clear, and all that is necessary is for some one to put it in operation, who has a steady hand, cool head and resolute heart.

The Social Evil usually so called is one of those problems which confront the administrator in every land and which are satisfactorily solved in none. In Chicago it is not greater than elsewhere, and in some respects it is manifestly reduced to smaller proportions.

There is very little street walking in the ordinary sense of soliciting on the streets in Chicago. I went about the town at all times of the night and in many of the thoroughfares which have the worst reputation in this respect, and I had nothing to complain of. This result, however, is obtained by practically sacrificing the liberty of the single woman in the streets of Chicago at night. A woman sauntering or gossiping with a friend in the streets of Chicago at night is liable to be arrested by the police, in virtue of no ordinance, for the law is singularly weak, but in virtue of the high and singular power with which every police officer in Chicago seems to be invested to arrest anybody without the slightest risk of penalty for false imprisonment, at least when the person arrested is a woman. No corroborative evidence ever seems to be asked for on the charge of molestation which is alleged against the street walker by her captor. The rule enforced in London police courts is that a woman shall not be arrested for molestation and annoyance unless the person molested and annoyed will appear against her. This rule does not prevail in Chicago. Street walkers are outside the law and the question as to whether a woman is a street walker or not, is decided according to the arbitrary caprice of the policeman. He has only to swear that he has seen her soliciting. No other testimony is required. The woman may deny the accusation as much as she pleases. It is only her word against the policeman's, and he can, as a rule, obtain a brother officer to swear to anything that he pleases. The habit of levying black mail is almost universal. On Wabash avenue the officers "pinch," to use the technical term, girls regularly unless they pay up regularly. "Pony up or we will run you in," is the formula which secures the requisite backsheesh to the officers of the law. A woman in thriving bnsiness will pay up $10 to the policeman, while those who are not doing so well are allowed to compound for $2 or $3 as the case may be. Refusal to pay simply lands the unfortunate in the police cell every time she puts her face outside the door. One very bad case on Wabash avenue was one in which a girl had quarrelled with the police. She refused to give them their black mail, was arrested on one occasion when going to a drugstore. Shortly afterwards they broke into her house and said that if they could not get her on the street they would take her in her home.

In all great cities it is the same. Where arbitrary power of arrest is given to the policeman, and no confirmatory evidence is required by the justices in convicting those whom they accuse, the street walker proves a great revenue to the policeman. I have been disillusioned as to American freedom. There is much more freedom in London than in Chicago, and any girl, say a typewriter or a work girl, can go from one end of London to the other at any hour of the night, with much less chance of molestation by policemen or by other people, than she can go through Chicago. Victor Hugo said truly, long ago, that it was a delusion to believe that slavery had vanished from the earth. It still exists, he said, only they call it prostitution. These women are as much slaves of the police as was any negro on a cotton plantation before the war. The idea that a prostitute has as much right to be treated with justice as any other human being, is a conception that has not yet dawned upon the mind of the average man. The day upon which immoral men are subjected to the same arbitrary authority, without a hope of redress or chance of escape, that these women are subjected to, would see the beginning of a revolt. But women are weak, and there are few who dare to plead for the prostitute. It is a bad way to reform men, or women, either, by denying them justice and sacrificing their liberty. Chastity is a good thing, and purity of life, but these things are not more holy than the right of all human beings to liberty and to justice; nor will you in the long run promote purity by trampling justice under foot. To make women the chattels of the administration as is done in France, or whether it is a system of arbitrary arrest tempered by black mail as in Chicago, does not moralize the women, but it does demoralize the administration. *

What then can be done? The first thing to decide is, what cannot be done. One thing is impossible, and that is to yield for a single moment to that temptation of the devil which is ever whispered in the ears of the authorities when they are confronted with this question. Regulation in the European sense, apart from its hideous immorality and cynical violation of every principle of right is absolutely futile from the standpoint of health which is the plea usually put forward in its defense. A system against which the womanhood and the moral sense of the manhood of the world are in hot revolt is not likely to find much favor in the western world. Any system of official license and registration is virtually an authorization of vice by the state. It is as if the constituted authorities were to certify for the use of the citizens a number of women guaranteed healthy by the certificate of some state

---

* It has been reserved for Mayor Weir of Lincoln, Nebraska, to take the lead in a repressive campaign directed not against the unfortunate women but against their customers. After taking every precaution that adequate accommodation was provided for all women on the town in public institutions if they wished to abandon their present life, he gave six weeks notice of his determination to root up the traffic in vice. On the 1st of March the name of every man found entering a house of ill fame or gambling house was noted by the police. They were instructed to take pains to obtain their real names, and the order significantly continued "it does not matter if the arrests occur every day or oftener." The order was issued to break up and destroy this alleged business, and the mayor assured the police that he would support them to the last extremity in the performance of its duty. "I will under no circumstances," says the Mayor, "concur in the custom of fining the woman alone, believing that all prostitutes male and female should be dealt with exactly alike." The names of all men entering houses of ill fame will be publicly exposed at the police station for general inspection. All owners of property rented for immoral purposes will be prosecuted.

surgeon. "This is the way, walk ye in it" would be written up over the broad and easy way which leads to the house of debauchery. The system or no system of irregular arbitrary license by black mail which prevails in Chicago at present with all its faults, is immeasurably better than any attempt to legalize or to give the imprimateur of the state or of the city to the practice of prostitution. This system in the garrison towns in England has been shattered by the uprising of all that was best in the English people. The agitation against it is hot and strong on all parts of the continent. To introduce the system of compulsory surgical examination while it may secure the health of a faction it tends directly to increase the disease among the women who elude the register. In Paris where the system has been in existence the longest, the administration admits that for one woman who is licensed and periodically examined in a licensed house there are ten who ply their calling clandestinely. The only way of combatting venereal disease is to take it at the outset when it can be cured instead of allowing it to continue until it assumes a more aggravated form, when it is almost incurable and dangerously contagious. Hence from the hygienic point of view the great object is to tempt sufferers from this malady to seek medical assistance at the earliest possible moment. This is directly hindered by trying to subject these women to a periodical examination which they detest and which makes them the bondslave of the police doctors. Besides no system of regulation and examination can ever succeed when it is applied only to one sex. The immediate consequence of any system of state regulation or municipal authorization for houses of debauchery is to teach every citizen that vice is necessary and lawful and to encourage the delusion that freedom from disease is guaranteed to debauchees by the government. The law then becomes a schoolmaster to lead men to the brothel,

In Cleveland, where Chief Director Pollner has on his own mandate, introduced a system of regular medical inspection and police registration, the girls trade upon the fact and assure hesitating men that they are all right because they have the official certificate at home. One of them, while I was there showed me a whole bundle of duly signed copies of the original certificates which have to be filed every week in the Director's office. What then must be done?

Common sense would suggest that the entrance to the profession should be narrowed and made as difficult as possible, while the exit from it should be made broad, easy and accessible to all the unfortunate victims of the system. This is exactly the opposite to the course which at present prevails.

Sexual incontinence is not a crime, and should not be treated as such. It is a sin which should be left to the moralist, and the Christian teacher. It only comes within the lash of the law when it becomes the source of disorder and public scandal, and actual crime. If this principle were recognized, many of the greatest difficulties would disappear. An immoral woman who plies her vocation, so as to make no scandal and create no nuisance should no more be subjected to police surveillance, to say nothing of arrest, than the immoral man who takes pleasure in a dissolute life. The case is different when the woman converts herself into a peripatetic nuisance, or makes the house a moral cesspool, so that it infects the neighborhood. In that case she should be proceeded against as a nuisance and her neighbors should take prompt action against such a center of contagion being established in the midst of their young people. Even then the greatest care should be taken against arbitrary and vindictive measure in which justice is violated under the plea of protection for morality. These people forget that it is a greater immorality to prostitute justice than to follow the calling of a prostitute. The girls for the most part are victims rather than the accomplices of the criminals and should not be interfered with. It is the keepers, and the landlords of such houses, who should be prosecuted when prosecution is deemed advisable; and in every case when they are proved to be guilty they should be sent to jail and the house broken up. The present system of arbitrary pulling is simply a regulation system under the mask of arbitrary arrest. Those who make a traffic in vice by exploiting their fellow creatures, the procurers, the souteneurs and the "macs" are the worst parasites of the vicious system, and should be severely dealt with instead of being allowed, as at present, to escape scotfree.

A lady who has devoted much time to the subject, and who has had practical experience in the work of reclaiming and rescuing the unfortunates, called upon me soon after my arrival in Chicago to urge upon me the importance of more vigorous action in this matter. The Anchorage mission, an admirable institution established close to the sunken district of Fourth Avenue does a good and noble work. So does the Refuge for Fallen Women which is one of the most remarkable institutions of its kind in the country. But they are inadequate. The Home of the Good Shepherd is another institution which is doing excellent work. But these three do not do more than touch the fringe of the question. My friend wrote me as follows-

I wish to see established over the city a series of seven graded homes.

1ST HOME.—For pure girls found in hospitals, depots, worn out clerks, etc., where if they desire they could be trained into service for this field.

2ND HOME.—For those who come in after their first offence. There is so much need of this, they have no refuge now.

3RD HOME.—For those who have lived the life, either as kept women or madames, or those who have frequented houses of shame.

4TH.—A home for the workers, chapel school and work rooms of many kinds, type writing, music, drawing, painting, dress making, book keeping, or any other thing a woman can do credit to or develope a *taste for* Care being taken, no woman is where she does not fit, misapplied people cause much of the confusion in life to my thought.

5TH.—Maternity home. Mothers living here with little ones.

Children born here and cared for afterwards.   Kindergarten, kitchen garten etc., etc.

6TH HOME.—For women addicted to drink.

7TH.—A home where old sinners can come and die—*with a Saviour* —and hospital in which these women can help much and in making themselves useful, they will be more content.

The women able to work should receive wages, kept for them in a bank of our own, as it were, and after a few years, strong in the physical and spiritual with a sum of money at their command, they could go out from us citizens, able, having been taught their trade, to build up a business of their own.   Desirable, that this should be done in our city, than the one in which they have been living and known in sin.

All that is needed to start this home *at once* is *the money*. God grant it may soon come.   I am looking alone to Him for it, and I *firmly believe* it will be given, and you can see the benefit of having a preventive home in connection with the others.   No girl coming from the neighborhood would receive any stigma, no one knowing from which she came, it would be no disadvantage to the pure girl, as those homes would be perfectly distinct and what greater honor could be conferred on any woman, than to be educated for this field in the vineyard.

When Mr. Carter Harrison ordered all the women to leave State street, and concentrate on Fourth Avenue and Clark street, he effectively destroyed the value of all decent property in the neighborhood. If such a policy is pursued in the future, the owners who have property in the condemned district should be compensated otherwise they are driven to the alternative of either closing their property or of entering the business of brothel keeping. The Japanese alone have carried this policy out to its full logical extent. There are prostitute quarters in Japanese cities which are the Fourth Avenues magnified. Should such a policy be adopted, it would be well to adopt it with our eyes open, giving due regard to the interests of the neighbors and with adequate security for the escape of the inmates. It is possible to establish such a quarter, brilliantly lighted and constantly patroled by police matrons, who would have power to suppress any house which would be proved to have debauched innocent girls, or to have admitted any inmates without first sending them to a good woman to dissuade them from the life into which they were entering. This could be done. It would be better than the present system, which has the disadvantage of establishing a prostitute quarter without the safeguards which might be secured where the Japanese system is logically carried out. For my own part I prefer the scattering system, but this is too large a subject to discuss here.

All these measures, however, are but palliatives, the real exorcism must be accomplished by raising the standard of morality until it will be regarded as shameful for a man to be unchaste as it is now for a woman, and in the promotion of everything which tends to give men and women more points of contact. Any advance that is made in the direction of the emancipation of woman tends to reduce the physical relation to its proper subordinate position. Nor does this in any way imply the ignoring of the important part which that relation occupies in society. Unless civilization is a mistake, and Christianity a delusion, monogamy is the ideal towards which our race is tending. In the future, adultery and fornication will be regarded as almost as inconceivable as incest. Every step towards this tends to exalt the conjugal relation and at the same time to extend the possibilities of friendship between the sexes.

Hitherto I have confined myself to discussing the exorcising of evil spirits which are vices rather than crimes. But the criminal demon must not escape attention, he is the superlative degree of human crookedness. To cast him out is the task which the police and magistrates have continually before them and there is no truce in that eternal warfare. But there are one or two things which might be done with advantage in Chicago. The first is to cease manufacturing criminals. That is much more practical and easier withal than to reclaim them after they are manufactured. Chicago manufactures her criminals in two ways: first, by the absence of any arrangement for dealing with incipient criminality in the child; secondly, in the lack of any adequate arrangements for reclaiming the idle tramp, or of preventing the gravitation into bumdom of the unemployed workingman, and thirdly, by the scandalous abuses which prevail in her police courts.

An admirable little book written by my friend, Mr. Waugh, the Hon. Director of the Society for the Prevention of Cruelty to Children was published in England some fifteen or twenty years ago. It was entitled "The Jail Cradle, and Who Rocks it," and constituted such a damning indictment against sending children to herd with criminals, that the practice of sending juvenile offenders to jail has almost ceased, with advantage to society and to. the children themselves. New South Wales, and some of the Australian colonies have gone further than any other countries, in the protection of the juvenile offender from the influence of other criminals.   If New South Wales is at the head of the scale Chicago lies very near the bottom. Police magistrates, journalists and every other authority, have deplored the practice of accustoming children before they are in their teens with the police station and the cells in the Bridewell.   There is very little reverence for children in Chicago.   Messenger boys not more than fourteen years of age, go in and out of the police cells every hour of the night gaining an intimacy with the drunken and debased classes, which can hardly be said to tend towards edification.   Mere lads of the same age, make a regular tour through the houses of ill-fame, selling newspapers on Fourth Avenue, nor is it thought that it is undesirable that such young children should be introduced so early to the abominations of a great city.   As for the waifs and strays, if it were not for Mr. Daniels, the indefatigable superintendent of the mission of State street, I do not know what would become of them.   This mission is one of the most admirable charities in the city; and it is housed in a way which would be a disgrace to a third rate country town. Mr. Daniels has set his heart upon the building on the Lake front, where there could be established a department dealing entirely with the juvenile offender so that he would be removed altogether from contact with elder criminals. His scheme, which is well thought out and carefully planned, would supply a court for all offenders whose youth would entitle them to special consideration, but he would use the greater part of the building as the headquarters of his busy boys. Mr. Daniels has made a business success of the Waif's Mission. He has taken the riff-raff of the streets and trained them in habits of industry and thrift, and made them earn their own living. This is done under every conceivable difficulty; wretched accommodation, lack of support, in fact, lack of everything except what is supplied by Mr. Daniel's own indomitable will and loving heart. He is ready, if he is provided with adequate housing for his lads to ask for no further contribution. He would make the institution self-supporting and rid the town of the shame and disgrace of the manufacture of juvenile criminals. I sincerely hope that the philanthropy of Chicago will see that Mr. Daniel's prayer does not go unanswered.

Criminals are also manufactured by neglecting the tramp. If no adequate provision is made for relieving the necessities of the penniless and destitute, they will beg and be supported by the conscience of the community in doing so. But begging is only one shade better than stealing, and the habit of mendicancy leads naturally to actual thieving.

There is no excuse for a city like Chicago in which the elementary necessities of sanitation and of street cleaning are so poorly attended to for refusing to provide a labor test for the tramp. It is in the winter when the tramp plague is the most formidable in the towns and at that time there is work for 10,000 men on the streets and the allies of the city. There is work enough to be done, it is only a question as to whether the tramps will be allowed an opportunity of working at useful labor for their rations instead of prowling round the city, infesting every street and alley and rapidly degenerating into the semi-criminal condition of professional bum.

CHAPTER IV.

THE BROTHERHOOD OF LABOR.

It was an old jug, and withal much worse for wear. It had lost its handle and its sides were seamed with many a flaw, but still it held the water and that sufficed. Nor did the speakers in the Trades and Labor Assembly of Chicago, object to use its contents because of its forbidding and even repulsive exterior. For the battered old gallon jug stood on the table all worn and frayed with much pounding of the gavel, at which sits the chairman of the Parliament of Associated Labor in Chicago, and the water which it contains refreshes the unionist orators when they are dry and parched by their own fiery eloquence. For the water is there all the same and thirsty men are not particular about the jug.

Which jug is a parable of the relations which ought to exist, but which at present do not, between the labor unions of America and the organized Christian churches of the continent. The labor unions look askance at the church as it exists and is organized today. If they do not say with the French Republicanism, "Clericalisme—voila l'ennemi!" they say much the same thing—American style. They have got no use for the church, they say. It has no handle by which they can use it to help labor. It is seamed and flawed with numberless imperfections. So they will have nothing to do with it; and they don't. Not five per cent of the members of labor unions in Chicago, I was assured on my first visit to the Trades and Labor Assembly, ever darken the doors of a place of worship. Such unionists as are churchmen are chiefly Catholic.

The result is what might be expected. The labor unions are suffering from the lack of the support which

389

the church could give them, and the church is vaguely
and painfully conscious that it is not ministering to those
who need her most.   And all because of the prejudice
against the battered and ugly old jug which, nevertheless, is the vessel that contains the water of life.
    By water of life I do not mean what many labor men
think is religion, which is as they would put it, the
mere obtaining of passports duly vised and countersigned by certificated sky pilots for admission to the
celestial regions after death.   I mean the help which
they need on earth to enable them to realize their ideals
here and now.   I mean the strength which would
enable them to redress grievances, to elect just judges,
to amend unjust constitutions and generally to deliver
them from the bondage under which they are laboring.   I mean the friendly sympathy that would, for
instance, secure them places in which to meet and liberal
support both in the moral backing and in the financial
help of which they stand in sore need.   And I mean
more than any of these things, more than all of them put
together, a reinforcement of the moral sentiment among
the unionists themselves, a restoration of confidence of
man in man which is almost eaten out by the all-
pervading worship of smart money making, and as
the result of this the discovery of leaders among
their own ranks whom they would not hesitate to
trust with uncounted gold.   Unionists in Chicago
and in America lack many things, but this above
all.   For they, like other men have forgotten
God, and have learned to distrust men.   There is as
much envy, malice and all uncharitableness among
them as among any other class in the community.
They distrust each other, malign their leaders and are
more singularly lacking in enthusiastic devotion to
their chiefs than any body of men I have ever met.
    I do not for a moment believe what I hear on every
side as to the universal dishonesty of everybody whose
name I mention. But this readiness to hurl the reproach

of dishonesty against every labor leader by the men who follow them shows that the rank and file is suffering from what might be expected from the divorce between labor and the church. The divorce has gone much further here than in the old country. In England most of the labor leaders even if they have quit church going bear the stamp of their early training in church and Sunday school. Some of them, notably those who more or less ostentatiously repudiate Christianity, are as stalwart as puritans in everything but the ordinances. And as a result English trades unionists and the labor movement in the old country has the advantage of half a dozen leaders, whose personal character is unimpeachable and whose record is as stainless as that of the highest and noblest in the land. There may be many such men in America but they have not succeeded as yet in securing the same general recognition even among their own class, let alone in the community at large. That seems to me the greatest weakness of the labor movement in America.

Distrust and lack of faith are due to lack of character on one side or the other. It is only the honest man who believes in the honesty of men. Those who are certain all men are thieves but see the reflection of their own inner soul in the mirror of their neighbor's faces. But whatever the cause and wherever lies the secret of this lack of confidence, it is a fatal bar to any real progress. If in the heat of the fight you have to keep squinting over your shoulder to see that your officer is not picking your pocket, you stand a very poor chance of victory. The labor movement suffers and will suffer more from these indirect consequences of the worship of the dollar among its own members than from the tyranny of Mammon in all its trusts and corporations.

I never realized so clearly before the eternal truth of the saying that, "by faith ye are saved," as when I was confronted with the consequences of the lack of faith. Not faith in formulas, but faith in the divine in man,

of so much at least of the divine in man as will lead
him to keep his word, to stand to his guns, and to
keep his hands from picking and stealing.   That elementary indispensable, irreducible quantum of faith
seems to be more lacking in Chicago than in London.
Faith has perished among the people and as a result
they are handed over helpless and hopeless to be trodden under foot by the strong.

Long centuries of oppression during which all the
resources of England were employed to foment distrust
and destroy the confidence of the Irish in each other
have produced their natural results in Ireland and
here, where the Irish element is strong, the fatal heritage brought across the seas has lost none of its evil
power.   But that would not be sufficient to account for
this deep ingrained conviction that if you elect your most
trusted comrade to office he will in a few months be as
corrupt as the rest, that every man is more or less ''on
the make'' and that the more you trust a man the more
certain it is that he will sell you when he gets an opportunity and that you will get left.   No brotherhood of
labor or of anything else is possible until this fundamental lack of faith is replaced by that more generous
confidence of man in man which is the basis of every
good thing.

" Do your neighbor as he would do you—if he gets the
chance," the Chicago version of the Golden Rule is not
working out well for the laboring man.   In so far as he
has substituted for this the older version he has succeeded in bettering his condition.   The Cigar Makers
Union, for instance, which is one of the strongest in the
country with a reserve fund of half a million in the
bank has gone through these hard times without having
to submit to wage reductions and that without having
recourse to strikes.   The Lumbershovers' Union on a
smaller scale has been, and is, very successful.   Of
course no amount of confidence in each other will enable
men to keep up prices against a falling market, but it

minimizes the loss and enables them to tide over bad times. "A brother that is helped by a brother is like a strong city." It may have its reverses but the strong city stands.

The unions of Chicago have done good, noble service to the cause of labor this winter. They undertook at the outset to provide for the relief of all the unemployed of their own number and on the whole this promise has been honorably kept. There are 297 unions in Chicago with 100,000 members representing a population of 400,-000. Very few of these unionists have come upon the fund raised by public charity. The sum which the unions have distributed to their unemployed members, this winter in Chicago, probably exceeded all the money subscribed by the rest of the community for the relief of distress. Exact statistics are lacking but the facts speak for themselves.

The more thoroughly organized unions, especially those connected with the building trade which have a separate council or federation of their own have succeeded in securing the eight hours day without legislation and until the recent bad times they maintained a high standard of wages. Wages, however, have tumbled in some cases very heavily and what is much worse to bear, the work itself is not to be had. The aristocracy of labor in Chicago is apt to imitate other aristocracies and having obtained its own comforts to leave its less fortunate brethren to get along as best they can. This lack of a realizing sense of human brotherhood, combined with the deep underlying conviction of almost all unionists that if any wider movement is promoted outside their own immediate trade it is in order that some "skate" or boodler may get something out of it, paralyzes the labor party in Chicago as elsewhere in America.

The labor movement in America seems to me to be about where the English labor movements stood nearly thirty years since. The unions are still to a certain extent outlawed. They have no allies and many enemies. They have no representatives in City Councils,* in state legislatures or in the Federal Congress. The newspapers, almost without exception, are against them. Among the churches they have some sympathy but little support. They are hampered, as we were not, by the fetters of written constitutions.

These are the consequences to labor of the divorce between the unions and the churches. The results to the churches are not less disastrous. They have lost the confidence of the leaders of the labor movement. The local unions regard them with suspicion, and in some cases with positive dislike that is a barrier to doing any good work. A well known minister, in Chicago, told me a curious instance of how this operates. He is a doctor of divinity and he recently made a tour round the world. On his return he was asked by a member of a Milwaukee labor union to give them an illustrated lecture about his travels. The union approved of the invitation believing that he was a medical man. Before the lecture was delivered they discovered that he was a doctor not of medicine but of divinity. They immediately cancelled the invitation with only one dissensient and the lecture was declared off. To preach and teach in the face of such prejudice as this is somewhat difficult work. The result is that as the unionists don't attend church while their employers do, the ministers naturally and inevitably tune their music to their audience.†

---

* See Appendix F, "What London County Council has done for labor.'

† The Lutherans, of Oshkosh, honestly believe that labor unions are contrary to the law of God and in February all unionists were expelled from the south side Lutheran church in that town. Admission to membership was refused to the son of an officer in the church because he was a member of a labor union. The arguments used by the minister in question are somewhat archaic. "We Lutherans are against labor and trade unions, because their principles, endeavors and proceedings are against God's commandments. Their principles, endeavorings and proceedings are evidently against the order which God has put in the fourth commandment. In this commandment God has drawn the line of difference between the employer and the employed, parents and children, masters and servants. If the workman does not come to the employer with decent requests or desires, but with firm demands, taking the control of the business into his hand, he removes the bars which God has put between master and servant; in fact, he makes himself the master of the business. It is the duty of father and husband to care for their families. If they do not do this, if they rather go on a strike, they sin against the word of God, neglecting the duties imposed upon them in the fourth and sixth com-

The wealthy pew holder, the liberal supporter of church funds becomes as potent in the church as he is elsewhere, and so the breach is made worse. The net effect of it is that the church cannot fulfil her divine mission.

All that I have done or tried to do in Chicago resulted from my conviction that no good worth speaking of will be done in Chicago or elsewhere which does not bring together again into a firm fighting alliance the forces of organized labor and the forces of organized Christianity. When on my first Sunday in Chicago I was asked to address the Trades and Labor Assembly, I was earnestly cautioned against saying a word about religion. "If you say anything about God or the church or religion they will hiss you off the platform. This crowd takes no stock in these things." I listened and wondered. But when my turn came to speak I could not refrain from telling them that the first condition of social emancipation was a hearty alliance between the church and labor. "You don't take much stock in churches I am told," and the audience assented heartily. "Don't take stock in them," I continued, "if you don't believe in them, but it is fatuous folly on your part to refuse to use them for all they are worth to attain your own ends and to promote the regeneration of society." The ice was broken. They didn't hiss. "The boys stood it," said a journalist who was present, and from that day I never lost an opportunity of pleading for the recognition of the need which each of these two great factors has of the other.

---

mandments. It is the will of God; laid down in the seventh and ninth commandments, 'That we may not craftily seek to get our neighbor's money, goods, inheritance or house, nor obtain it by a show of right;' nor by oppresion or extortion. But this is done if the unions meet their employers with firm demands, threatening with strikes and carrying out the same. It is well known how many a strike is the cause of sins against the fifth commandment. The eighth commandment is sinned against by calling nonunion men 'scabs' and abusing them in different ways. According to the tenth commandment we should urge our neighbor's servants 'to stay and do their duty.' Union men on the contrary alienate the servants from their employer by telling him whom he has to or whom he has not to employ. The members of this union have to pledge themselves not to divulge the proceedings of this union to any person not a member of the same. The Bible says: 'Woe unto them that seek deep to hide their counsel from the Lord, and their works are in the dark, and they say: Who seeth us and who knoweth us?'"

"No practical solution of this question will ever be found without the assistance of religion and the church." That is the dictum of the Pope in his famous encyclical, and it has been and is the burden of all that I have said or what I have to say. Labor parched and thirsty will yet overcome its prejudice against the chipped old ungainly jug that contains the living water of helpful sympathy and effective support. It was the chasm between the unions and the churches organized as Mr. Pomeroy told the Labor Federation by "the Great Master Mechanic, and his immortal twelve walking delegates," one that is impossible to bridge. There is every disposition on the part of the better men on both sides to join hands for helpful mutual service. The ministers of religion for the first time in the history of Chicago sent an influential deputation of their number to bid welcome to the American Federation of Labor when it held its annual meeting in the city last December, and the act was hailed on both sides as a harbinger of better days to come. Nor has labor on its part been indifferent. At the Central Music Hall conference in November the chair was taken by Mr. M. H. Madden, president of the Illinois Federation of Labor, who in an eloquent opening speech made an earnest appeal to the churches to clasp hands with labor and to do something for God and humanity. "We yearn," he said, "for the co-operation in the work of doing good and alleviating suffering."

At Milwaukee, under the auspices of an energetic young Methodist minister a church and labor social union has been formed, which was inaugurated by an address by a well known labor leader who had not darkened the doors of a church for a quarter of a century until he came by invitation to occupy the pulpit and explain why the working classes were not within its pale. In Chicago the retail clerks union through their able and indefatigable representative, Mr. L. T. O'Brien, appealed to the Ministerial Federation for their assistance on securing the passing of an ordinance giving the clerks in the stores the boon of Sunday closing. Nor were the ministers slow to respond. The ordinance was approved by the judiciary committee, and it is expected it will be passed by the council.

One of the most remarkable of all the evidences of the altered spirit of the labor men has been afforded by the formation of a church in the identical building where four months ago I was told I should be hooted off the platform if I so much as mentioned religion. "The Modern Church" was founded by Mr. Pomeroy, Mr. O'Brien and other leading labor unionists on modern principles in response to a challenge thrown out by Dr. Harper of the University of Chicago at a social gathering of Congregationalists, where a labor leader had severely denounced the church for her indifference to the interests of labor. " Why not organize a church of your own?" said Dr. Harper. " So we will " responded the labor men, and "The Modern Church" was the result.

It met for the first time, on Sunday afternoon, February 11, in the Bricklayer's Hall, which is occupied by the Trades and Labor Assembly on alternate Sundays. The church therefore meets once a fortnight. Its salient features as defined by its founders are " free seats, no collection, no dogma."

It is the intention of the committees in charge to have a different preacher each time and to see that every creed has its representative. In course of time they hope this will cause the labor people to think differently of preachers, and preachers to change their opinion of the labor people.

As yet "the Modern Church" has not progressed so far as to build itself a local habitation and is perforce content to accept the hospitality of the Temple of Labor. But if it makes headway it intends to have its own building.*

* The following extract from the programme of the founders will be read with interest: The most radical departures from established church construction are to be observed in the plan proposed for the home of the "Modern Church." It will be not only a place of worship but a pleasant lounging place where the members may find any recreation they desire. It will be an educational institution, and

The church was opened by the Rev. J. Lloyd Jones, the Unitarian who defined it as a church whose cornerstone was sympathy, and declared that its object was to make here in Chicago a new Holy Land. The second meeting, held February 25, was devoted to a discussion between Mr. Pomeroy on the one hand and the Rev. Mr. Burch on the other as to the relation between the church and labor. The hall was crowded by an attentive audience which remained for two and a half hours following the debate with the deepest interest. Both agreed that the time had come for more hearty co-operation between the two, but they differed as to who was to blame. Both speakers were capable and earnest but the most eloquent passage in the speeches was that in which Mr. Pomeroy in his impeachment of the organized church referred to the character of Jesus. He said:

I am pleased to have my friend know that the labor people have cheered the name of Christ, that carpenter of Judea, the sweet pathos of whose life has softened the stone in the bosoms of men, whose teachings have made the world better beyond measure; Christ, whose fraternity was as broad as eternity, and as immeasurable as is space, whose mission among men was to teach them brotherly love; Christ, whose name is the synonym of fellowship, whose lessons were love, whose words were love, whose every act was fathered by His mighty love and pity for the poor, the weak, the persecuted and the helpless —love for every man, woman, child and beast of the field. Christ, the halo of whose glory makes the sunshine dim, the magic of whose name calls the evil hand to halt; Christ, whose church was the world, whose pulpit was the breasts of men; Christ whose religion was humanity. No wonder the sons and daughters of toil cheer His name. Nor can you separate Christ and His church. His church, I say; for His church is within the inner temples of the pulsating hearts of the people of the world, and in listening to His sermons they forget those of the "salaried soothsayer."

---

from the pulpit rostrum university extension lectures will be given, debates on every topic of any interest whatsoever will be held, and musical and other entertainments given. The central idea in the club-house arrangement will be to keep men away from saloons and other bad resorts. In furthering this object the basement will be given up to a set of baths, a bowling alley and a fine gymnasium. On the ground flour will be a large amusement hall, billiard and pool tables, checkers, dominos and other games, and stands for the sale of cigars, light temperance drinks, and lunches. A library will be installed in one corner. This floor will be a general lounging place where men may read, smoke, or enjoy themselves as they see fit. On the floor above will be the auditorium proper, church, lecture hall and theatre combined.

It was in full accordance with the spirit of this declaration that Mr. Pomeroy concluded his speech by an impassioned appeal to the churches to produce a new Peter the Hermit who would preach a new crusade for the redemption not of the holy sepulchre but of the desecrated temple of humanity. " Peter," said Mr. Pomeroy " must come from the churches. We want their help and they will not follow Peter of our raising." A notable declaration from one who in this same speech eulogized Tom Paine's writings as the only revelation accepted by the American workman.

Mr. Pomeroy is a Kentuckian, of some education and wide reading with a natural genius and magnetic power which stood in small need of book training. He is in many respects the most remarkable personality in the camp of labor at Chicago. His address of welcome to the Federation of Labor was unique. His position—idolized by some, detested by others, and distrusted by most —is exceptional. It might be made commanding. All that he needs to attain to any position for good to which he might care to aspire is the command of the confidence of his fellows. On the day when Mr. Pomeroy is trusted in America as John Burns, for example, is trusted in England, the labor men will not need to look further for their leader.

There is ample need tor the advent of a Peter the Hermit if the social crisis in America is not to culminate in bloodshed. The working people without allies have given no hostages to fortune and have no visible reason for refraining from violence. It is true that violence will injure them in the long run far more than it can help them, but like all men who suffer and who are weak they think more of the immediate winning of a strike by knocking a few ' 'scabs" on the head than of the permanent loss which such violence inflicts upon their cause. The fact that large numbers of labor men are at this moment in what in England we call the Broadhead stage of development, Broadhead being the secretary of the Sheffield cutlers union, who use to hire men to kill and maim scabs or black-legs, simply proves that they are more or less outlawed.

If they were within the pale, if they had churches to back them, and newspapers to plead for them, and courts to do them justice and their own trusted represent-atives on the bench and in Congress to see fair play, they would have long ere this emerged from the stage of incipient Thuggee in which many of them dwell. As they have no church to help them they clutch the revolver, and in default of an impartial judge to appeal to on the bench, they fetch the "scab" a clout over the head with a sandbag or a club. Every time they do this they supply Mr. Carnegie and others with plausible justi-fication for the use of Pinkertons and of Gatling guns, and public opinion even among those who are most sympathetic is driven over to reinforce the enemies of labor.

What American labor needs is (1) a definite prac-tical programme—not a wild cat scheme for inau-gurating the millenium by passing a resolution and appointing a committee, (2) honest and capable leaders, and (3) a policy of making allies with all who will help labor to elect to city councils, to state legislatures, the bench and congress honest men first and foremost. Infinitely better in the interest of labor itself to send an honest capitalist to congress or to Springfield rather than a dishonest laborer who is simply in the market for the dishonest capitalist who prefers to buy his legis-lators ready made. Honesty is a jewel of price. With-out honesty political life is simply a den of thieves in which justice and right are sold at auction to the highest bidder.

The policy of electing labor men to office is excellent, if labor men can be found to subscribe to pay their representatives. Here it is that the universal distrust, bred from want of confidence in character and the loss of faith in the very possibility of disinterested service, hamstrings the labor movement. Until labor men learn to trust each other, and are worthy of trust, their cause is under a curse and can never prosper. It can only writhe like a wounded snake occasionally inflicting injury upon its enemies but never doing any real permanent good for itself.

The alliance with the churches can best be secured by appealing to their help for definite practical reforms. Take for instance the question of the emancipation of labor from the seven days a week. On this point the churches ought surely to be solid with the unions. In a kind of a way they are. But even here in Chicago, they are still half asleep on this subject. Instead of eagerly volunteering to help the clerks in their crusade against the open Sunday store, they have for the most part needed to be coaxed and entreated and worried into action. A still more promising field is now opening before them. The attack upon the statutory limitation of child labor under the guise of a technical question of its constitutional legality ought to bring the churches into line with the unions not merely on this question, but on the broader question of constitutional revision.

Mr. Pomeroy has directly challenged the ministers to take issue on this question. He said:

Is the church the protector of women and children? Let us see. A society of wealthy manufacturers has recently been formed to purchase a verdict from the state supreme court declaring that most just law unconstitutional. They have retained the strongest legal firm in the state to handle their case. Here the lines of contest are plainly drawn. On the one side wealth and legal craft, seeking the re-enslavement of women and children. On the other the labor organizations saying "hold your hand! with all you. money, all your lawyers, with all the past record of that supreme court against us, we say hold!" Where is the church in this controversy? How many sermons have been hurled from the pulpit against this threatened infamy, this huckstering of childhood, this immolation of feeble women on the altar of greed? "By their works shall ye know them." Who are the members of this soulless manufacturers' association? Prominent pillars of the church—men whose consciences are as hard as their marrow bones are soft I charge the church as being tacitly guilty of complicity in this premeditated crime. The church has guilty knowledge of this most damnable scheme, and forgets to call down damnation upon the heads of the men who conceived it.

What has the church to say to this? And what has the church to say to the demand that will assuredly follow a ruling by the court that the law is unconstitutional for a revision of the constitution? Legislative restrictions which even the most reactionary, hard hearted capitalist in England admits to be indispensable for the protection of labor are unconstitutional according to the State of Illinois. That constitution makes a fetish of freedom of contract and immolates before this idol victims whom British law would have long since rescued. The lawyer of the Manufacturers Association in explaining why he regards the Factory Act as unlawful said:

It denies to both employer and employee freedom of contract. The Supreme Court of this state has held somewhat similar legislation unconstitutional. It declared the truck law illegal, also the mining statute, which provided that miners should be paid by actual weight, equally invalid.

The simple fact of the matter is that from the point of view of the working man and the working woman if the State of Illinois could be suddenly placed under the Acts of Parliament passed by the British legislature they would attain at one stroke almost all the reforms for which they are now clamoring in vain.

The need of an indissoluble union between labor and the church which was proclaimed as the great need of the age by the present pope will if recognized and worked out practically, offer the best chance of securing the reunion and the revivification of American Christianity. There is only one saving faith, says Prof. Briggs, but "nowhere in the world is the Christian Church so torn to pieces by denominationalism as in America." If there is to be a Universal Church it will have to be based on the ministry of service, and the more practical that service the more insignificant will seem all speculative points of theological difference. The natural result of this new departure will be a breaking down of the barriers which sectarian theology has built up between Christians of different rites and creeds. When you are concerned solely upon hoisting an invisible soul into an impalpable heaven, you may without sense of shame or of guilt refuse the co-operation of all who do not see eye to eye with you about the Immaculate Conception or the Procession of the Holy Spirit. But when it comes to be a question of hauling a half-drowned donkey out of a mudhole in which he is in danger of suffocating, there is not a bigot in any of the churches but would feel condemned before God and man if he let that donkey drown rather than take his place at the windlass side by side with a heretic and a schismatic. And the more the church sticks to the outward and visible works of charity and philanthropy, the more anti-Christian will seem to be the spirit of exclusion and excommunication which destroys Christian power.

The church cannot do better service to labor than by helping labor to help itself. The time is perhaps coming when under the inspiration of religious enthusiasm, we may see the problem of the unemployed solved by the establishment of a great Brotherhood of Labor, which would utilize in co-operative industry at ration rates, the unemployed labor of the nation. There is plenty of work to be done and plenty of workers, only too anxious to do it. Who shall bring those together whose separation spells starvation? Anything can be done if you can get men to trust each other. Nothing if trust is absent. The organization of labor camps for the unemployed, where a workless worker could pawn his future earnings in return for rations and shelter, might be carried out by such a brotherhood if men were honest. There is money in that scheme of a labor pawn-broker which will be realized by somebody some day—as Mr. Farnsworth has been endeavoring in vain to point out all this winter—and it would be well that its profits should accrue to associated labor. In like manner the issue of local inconvertible paper currency in the shape of labor certificates against material work into which the labor has been put which is advocated by Mr. DeBar-

nardi in his "Trials and Triumph of Labor," might be
carried out with advantage, if men but trusted each
other as brothers should.

Faith not only can move mountains.   It can earn dollars.   Without it even the securing of the dollar seems to
be becoming more and more difficult.

If we had but a more real faith we should have more
practical religion.   Chicago has been somewhat interested by a series of discourses in which Dr. Harper,
president of the University, has been expounding week
by week the generally accepted theories as to the more
or less poetical or mythical nature of the narrative in
the first chapter of Genesis.   Hence much perturbation
among many good souls inside the church, and a more
or less languid curiosity on the part of those who are
without to see whether anything will happen.   The
alarm is quite unnecessary, and the public interest
might well be devoted to something more practical.   The real religious issue before the city is not
whether Cain killed Abel, but whether rascals compared
with whom Cain was a gentleman, are to be allowed to
continue to sit as aldermen in the City Council.

Either the whole gist of the teaching of the Old Testament Scriptures was misleading, or the silence of pulpit upon the moral and social issues of the election is a
practical negation of the church's belief in the inspiration of the sacred books, infinitely more serious than
the speculations of the scholars as to the conflicting
theories of their dates and origins.   It does not matter much to John Jones in the Rookery whether a
real Cain did or did not kill a real Abel.   It
does matter a very great deal to John Jones whether the
condemnation pronounced upon the man who asked,
"Am I my brother's keeper?" expressed the inner
thought of the Eternal Lawgiver.   Ministers and
priests who at this juncture drone away with their
homilies and their platitudes, without one vital-
izing word of inspiration and of guidance to their

flocks, may not be bad men. They are simply blind.

"Humanity," said Heine, "yearns after more solid food than the symbolic blood and flesh of the Eucharist. Humanity smiles compassionately at the ideals of its youth, that have failed in realization in spite of all its painful attempts, and it grows manfully practical. Humanity in our day worships a system of earthly utility; it has serious thoughts about establishing itself in citizen prosperity, about a reasonably ordered household, about securing comfort for its old age."

What a change has come over the whole aspect of Christendom since the century begun! The modern spirit—of which Heine was the exponent—which was then in fierce feud with the church, has ended by triumphing over its old adversary, and changing the standpoint from which it contemplates the affairs of men. This life is no longer merely the ante-chamber of eternity. We are no longer mere pilgrims through a wilderness to a heavenly city, which rises on the other side of the waters of the river of death. We have become, on the contrary, citizens of the kingdom of God on earth, charged with the duty of transforming the world and regenerating human society. "Thy kingdom come, thy will be done on earth as it is in heaven." The human spirit, which in the early ages, affrighted by the bestiality and cruelties of Imperial Rome, could find no resting place, even for its imagination, on this side the grave, now sees the waters subside, the tops of the mountains appear, and the dove already bears the olive branch to the window of our social ark.

CHAPTER V.

WHO IS MY NEIGHBOR?

One afternoon in February an unknown visitor announced himself at the Commerce Club. On going out to see who he might be I came upon a little Irishman who introduced himself as one who was a man about fifty and lived in Custom House place. " I am all alone in the world," he said, "am getting on in years, and I should like very much to make the acquaintance of some people, especially of some good women, who are in a somewhat better social position than myself. I have neither man nor woman friend to whom I can tell my troubles or with whom I can have any conversation. The only people with whom I can speak are those in my own rank in life. They shift and move about and cannot help me if I get into trouble, and I feel as if it would be a good thing to be able to go, now and then at least, and have a friendly talk with somebody who would take an interest in me. So," he said, " I have called upon you. Do you think you could help me? You see," he said plaintively, " I don't see why I should be condemned for wishing to know people who are higher up in the world than myself. I noticed the other day that Chauncy M. Depew has been over to Europe and has been received by the Pope. Now, Mr. Depew is as much below the Pope as I am below Mr. Depew, yet if I should go and call upon Mr. Depew I should be treated as a tramp and should never be allowed to get a word with him. It is a little lonely for a workman who has got along in years, and I often think if I could only tell my troubles now and then to a good friend I should feel like another man. I should feel twice as much energy as I have. I am so lonely all alone in Custom House place."

The plaintive little Irishman set me thinking. How

many must there be in every great city who are more
or less inarticulately echoing the complaint of this forlorn and lonely carpenter. They are alone in the world
—alone in a great city. They have all the aspirations
of a human being to be in healthy sympathetic relations
with the rest of their kind. Educated men and refined
and sympathetic women, in so far as they are educated
and refined, represent a capacity for human intercourse
which the uneducated and inarticulate can hardly be
said to possess. What that carpenter wanted was not
money. He indignantly disclaimed any desire for money
for which he, indeed, stood in no need. It was not
charity that can be expressed in dollars, but the much
rarer and more valuable charity of friendship and sympathy that he craved.

It is a sad enough thing to contemplate the number
of the destitute of this world's goods; after all it is not
so sad as to see that other host of the lonely and forlorn. Persons who seem to be orphaned of the uni-
verse and who never go to sleep without feeling somewhat of the bitterness of the third Richard's anguished
cry, "There is no creature loves me, and if I die no one
will pity me." It was said of old time that the Lord
setteth the desolate in families, but our modern civilization masses them together not in families but in blocks, in
hordes regimented only for industrial work. That process is the reverse of divine. Every human being, man
or woman, in so far as they are human and not animals,
have tendrils of the heart which are perpetually yearn-
ing to clasp and to cling to their fellow-creatures. Sometimes cruel disappointments early in life, or bitter periods
in later years, sear these tendrils as with hot iron, and
the man or woman, instead of being a living vine, full
of the grace of life, and of the tender and delicate sympathies and associations which blossom so freely in the
heydey of youth, becomes but dry and withered stick.
Useful, perhaps, but living no more.

If Christ came to Chicago it seems to me that there are

few objects that would more command his sympathy
and secure his help than efforts to restore the sense of
brotherhood to man and to reconstitute the human
family on a basis adjusted to modern life.

In the doing of this work the Christian Churches are
doing a good deal. Not so much as they might do and
will do when once they have grasped the social obligations of the Christian faith. But they are probably
doing more than any other institution that can be
named. The Young Men's Christian Association, the
Young Women's Christian Association, the Christian
Endeavor Societies, the Epworth League, the King's
Daughters and other associations are all efforts in the
right direction. And after a time it is to be hoped that
they will make practical efforts to see how far it is possible for them to secure the advantage of federated
co-operation without losing the strength which comes
from a firm, narrow foothold upon a single principle.
The time is surely coming, however, when something
more must be done to knit together the caste and class
severed units of the city's population into a homogeneous whole, in which the strong should bear the burdens
of the weak and where the rich and poor could meet
together as a first step towards recognizing that the
Lord is the maker of them all. The lesson of the Incarnation needs to be taken into the hearts and worked
into the lives of all of us. That is to say, the Word
must be made flesh, and if your fellow-man is to be
helped he can best be helped by making him your
neighbor. You have got to come unto him to lift him
up, and it is vain to think that the great, submerged,
toiling multitude can be substantially assisted to a
higher and more human life if their higher and more
humane fellows remove themselves apart. When Christ
came to save the world He did not do it from some con-
tiguous star from which messages of love and mercy
could be securely conveyed by some missionary angels
to a miserable, sin-smarting world. He did just the op-

posite. He came right down and lived as a man among
men; among the artisans of Nazareth, with the fishermen of Galilee, and then finished His course without a
place to lay his head among the homeless wanderers of
Judea. As He did then, would He not do now if He came
to Chicago? That is to say, if His object was to redeem
the least of these, His brethren, who live in Halsted
street and in Little Hell or down the levee, He would
take up his quarters where His brethren and sisters
could be within talking range, and where He could see
them from day to day, hear their troubles, heal their
sicknesses and minister to them from the store of His
divine compassion.

If so, then Miss Addams was right in going to Hull
House, where, with her friends she for some five years has
been endeavoring to help the people by the redeeming
grace of good neighborliness. Hull House is one of
the best institutions in Chicago. Not merely because
of the humanitarian influences which it radiates around
the district in which it stands, but because it will become a training ground and nursery for multitudes of
similar institutions speedily to spring up in all the
great cities of America. What the monastery of St.
Bernard was to the Cistertians, what the original Brotherhood of St. Francis was to the Franciscan order, so
Hull House will be to the brotherhoods and sisterhoods
or helpers and neighbors, who in increasing numbers
will take up their residence in the midst of the crowded
and desolate quarters of our over-crowded cities. Only
by this means can we hope to reconstruct the human
family, and restore something approaching to a microcosm of a healthy organization in every precinct of the
city. Mere propinquity counts for a great deal in
human affairs. The healthy natural community is that
of a small country town or village in which every one
knows his neighbor, and where all the necessary
ingredients for a happy, intelligent and public-spirited
municipal life exist in due proportion. Within a single

square mile you will find ministers of religion, the lawyer, the doctor, the laborer and the business man all within stone's throw of the blacksmith and the carpenter. Such a community constitutes a unit of which each human life forms a part where public opinion is powerful, and where the influence of the best members can be immediately brought to bear upon the worst. But there are square miles in Chicago from which the cultured and the wealthy and the well to do flee as if from the plague. Whole quarters are left to be crowded with the poor and the ignorant who become sodden together in houses where the only civilizing light is the bull's eye of the policeman's lantern. My chief hope for our great cities is that the increasing number of intelligent, warm-hearted people will establish neighborly friendship with the crowded precincts which at present are almost as unknown to them as the territory of Timbuctoo. If in every one of the eight hundred odd precincts into which Chicago is divided, there were but one educated man or woman who had leisure to devote, say one hour a day to making friends with the people of that precinct, a great step would be taken towards civilizing the city. Each of the eight hundred helpers would be like a living filament linking on the precinct in which he or she spent an hour a day with the wealthier and more favored circle in which the other twenty-three hours of their daily life was spent. Hull House is one of the best illustrations of what can be done by intelligent and sustained effort in this direction. The pioneer of this system of settlement was probably Toynbee Hall in the East of London, but Toynbee Hall is a very much less humane institution, and by no means so beneficent in its multifarious activities. The University settlement in Bethnal Green is on a much larger scale than Hull House, but it is much more of a polytechnic or democratic people's palace, than a settlement in the strict sense of the word. Mansfield Hall, founded by the Congregationalists in London, is more on the lines of Hull House.   There are similar institutions in both New York and Boston, but of all those that I have seen in the old country Hull House seems to me best because it is most helpful.   This, perhaps, is due to the fact that a woman, with a woman's instinct of natural motherliness is at the head of Hull House, whereas the other institutions are all more or less under the supervision of men.   Whatever is the cause, Miss Addams and her associates have good reason to thank God, and take courage when they contemplate the work they have done in the last five years, and the prospect now opening before them of a still wider field of usefulness.   For they have realized the ideal settlement of which many have dreamed, but which they alone have brought into life.   Hull House has avoided the Scylla of denominational narrowness, and at the same time has not less dexterously steered passed the Charybdis of the luke-warmness and apathetic indifference which are the bane of much undenominational effort.   A High Church movement or a Catholic sisterhood or a branch of the Salvation Army may generate more enthusiasm, but they insist upon confining it to the straight and narrow channels of their conception of orthodoxy.   On the other hand institutions which are maintained by those who are Laodacean in matters of theology, are too often very tepid in their humanitarianism.   Very broad people are very seldom as earnest as they are broad.   Human enthusiasm seems to be like a volume of water in a river, if you confine it to a mill race, it is powerful enough to work the most powerful machinery, but if you spread it out over a wide, shallow bed, it has not sufficient force to drive a single wheel.   Hull House has been enthusiastic without being intolerant, and broad without losing the fervour of its humanitarian zeal.   Therein Miss Addams has done good work.   She has been the subject of considerable criticism, not to say denunciation, among the stricter devotees of cast iron creeds, but she has bravely stuck to her guns. and vindicated her position, not by arguments, but by quietly and constantly endeavoring to live the life and do the deeds of Christ. What is wanted is a multiplication of Hull Houses all over the city. Some, of course, will be founded by denominationalists and sectarians on denominational and sectarian lines, and of all of them I can only say that every one must wish them God speed in the name of the Lord. It is a thousand times better that Christ should be preached in this practical way, even if He preached of envyings and strife. But these dogmatic partition walls are wearing very thin, and justice and righteousness, and the weightier matters of the law, which, being interpreted, mean honesty, cleanliness, and brotherly kindness are becoming more and more recognized as of infinitely greater importance than the tithe of ecclesiastical mint and anise and cumin, to which the scribes and pharisees in every age attach such exaggerated importance. In southern Chicago, in the neighborhood of the stock yards, a new settlement has been founded in the last month or two, in connection with the University, with the co-operation of a company of kindergartners, who are entering upon their residential movement in the best spirits, with practical heads and kindly hearts. The only fault about Hull House is that it has been too successful, and has increased and extended to such an extent, that solitary individuals who might be disposed to attempt something of a residential helpership, may shrink back aghast at the thought of having to found an institution with all the adjuncts and paraphernalia which have sprung into existence around Miss Addams' original venture. Let them not be afraid. If they can do but one thing let them do that, and do not shrink from doing the duty of today from any fear that your strength may not be equal to the duty of tomorrow. In this matter I am disposed to look most of all to individual effort, but a great impetus would be given to this work if the churches in various districts could practically combine to found a residential settlement in the most neglected precincts.   There is great advantage in a union of churches, because when half a dozen churches have to work together, the necessity for co-operation prevents any undue insistence upon the sectarianism of any one of the associated churches.   Once let us get the people thoroughly well satisfied that we have not even begun to enable the masses to realize Christ until we have got one Christlike man or one Christlike woman living within five minutes' walk of his door step, and a great deal of the light of the life of God will penetrate into the heart of darkest Chicago.

Yielding to many and pressing applications from those who have sought information about Hull House, Miss Addams has at last been good enough to publish a brief statement or outline sketch of the work which is being done at that social settlement.   Hull House has entered upon the fifth year of its existence with a residential membership of eighteen, thirteen of whom have been in residence longer than six months.   The settlement began with two ladies, who believed that "social intercourse could best express the growing sense of the economic unity of society."   They simply went to Hull House, 335 South Halsted Street, and lived there in the Nineteenth Ward, which returns Alderman Powers to the Council.   Miss Addams was attracted to it by the fact that it was so forlorn and desolate.   She says :

> In a ward where there is no initiative among the citizens the idea underlying our self-government breaks down.   The streets are inexpressibly dirty, the number of schools inadequate, factory legislation unenforced, the street lighting bad, the paving miserable and altogether lacking in the alleys and smaller streets, and the stables defy all laws of sanitation.   Hundreds of houses are unconnected with the street's sewer.   There are seven churches and two missions in the ward; all of these are small and somewhat struggling save the large Catholic church on the west boundary.   Out of these nine religious centers there are but three in which the service is habitually conducted in English.

It was her conviction that this ward and similar God-forsaken regions could not be saved by mere political activity. They could only be saved by applied Christianity working out into the social sphere. But who was to apply this Christianity? Miss Addams believed that among the mass of unemployed people of culture there was a reserve battalion of the Lord of Hosts which might be brought into the field. She says:

> We have in America a fast-growing number of cultivated young people who have no recognized outlet for their active faculties. The impulse to share the lives of the poor and desire to make social service, irrespective of propaganda, express the spirit of Christ, is as old as Christianity itself. That Christianity has to be revealed and embodied in the line of social progress is a corollary to the simple proposition that man's action is found in his social relationships in the way in which he connects with his fellows; that his motives for action are the zeal and affection with which he regards his fellows.

When she settled in Hull House she did not know exactly what line of development experience would suggest. She was content to wait and see how things framed themselves. She began by living among the people, visiting them and asking her neighbors to call as friends and guests. They responded to her invitation so willingly that Hull House has 2,000 visitors a week. These guests of hers formed the first class of what is now a regular system of College Extension courses with 250 enrolled members, with twenty-five teachers, mostly college-bred men and women, some of whom have taught continuously for three years, and all of whom give their services free. The only charge made is fifty cents per student to cover cost of prospectuses, etc. Here is a week's diary of these classes and reading parties:

Day.	Hour.	Subject.	Day.	Hour.	Subject.
Mon.	4.	Pedagogics, or how to teach Science.	Tues.	5.	Reading in English Literature.
	7.	Latin, Elementary.		7.	Arithmetic.
	7.	Drawing.		7.	Emerson.
	7.30,	Gymnastics (women).		7.30,	Gymnastics (women).
	8.	Latin Reading.		7.30,	English and Letter Writing.
	8.	History of Art (Early Italian).		7.30,	Cooking.

Day.	Hour.	Subject.	Day.	Hour.	Subject.
Tues.	8.	English Poetry, Arnold and Clough.	Fri.	7.	German, Elementary.
	8.	Book-keeping.		7.	Algebra.
	8.30,	Delsarte.		7.	American History.
	8.30,	English Composition		7.	Drawing.
Wed.	3.30,	Cooking.		7.	Physiology.
	7.	Shakespeare, Othello.		8.	German Reading.
	7.30,	Gymnastics (men).		8.	French, Advanced.
	8.	Dante (Purgatorio).		8.	French, Elementary.
Thurs.	4.	Biology, with Laboratory.	Sat.	8.	Geometry.
				7.	Chemistry.
	7.	German Needlework.		7.30,	Gymnastics (women).
	7.	Singing.		8.	Bohemian Literature
	8.30,	Reading, Lang's Odyssey.		8.	Electricity.
				8.	Physics.
				8.30,	Dancing Class.

In addition to these regular courses there are three University Extension courses. The Students' Association is divided into Literary, Dramatic, Musical and Debating sections, each of which gives an entertainment once a month, which is always followed by an informal dance in the gymnasium. Twice a year there are exhibitions of pictures, small but select. No pictures are admitted to the walls of Hull House but those helpful to the life of mind and soul, and much of the influence of the House is traceable to the harmony and reasonableness of the message of the walls. On Sundays there are meetings of choral societies and a free concert in the gymnasium. A branch of the Public Library is established in Hull House, with a reading room attached. The first public bath in the city was established last year on Hull House property. It has seventeen shower baths and one swimming bath.

Situated as it is in the midst of the sweat shop district of Chicago, its residents have been the central nucleus of the anti-sweating agitation in Illinois. It was largely owing to Hull House that the Factory Inspection Law of 1893 was passed, and it owes what efficiency it possesses to Hull House influence, both in framing it and in its administration, for one of its residents, Mrs. Kelley, is Inspector of Factories in the State of Illinois.

Hull House breeds clubs. The Jane Club occupies five flats, for it is a co-operative boarding club for young working women. It now numbers fifty members and is entirely self-supporting and self-managing, without either matron or outside control. The members pay $3 a week, which covers rent, service, food, heat and light. The furnishing and first month's rent were supplied by Hull House. An Eight-Hour Club of women meets twice a month at Hull House. The Working People's Social Science Club meets every week. The Arnold Toynbee Club meets once a month. The Chicago Question Club meets every Sunday in the art gallery. The Nineteenth Ward Improvement Club, which has standing committees on street cleaning, etc., meets once a fortnight.

In connection with this Improvement Club, a co-operative association has been formed which has just started a co-operative coal yard. The Hull House Woman's Club consists of fifty of the ablest and most active women in the ward. They visit the sick, relieve the poor, look after the inspection of streets and alleys and keep in active touch with all the reform movements of the city. Every Friday evening there is a social reception for Germans. Two hours are spent in singing, reading, games, etc., with occasional coffee drinking and entertainment. The Hull House Men's Club has 150 members, and has a reception once a month. The Lincoln Club is a debating society which meets once a month with a Social Club of young women. They have also at Hull House three clubs for boys and four for girls. The latter are the School Girls', the Pansy, the Story Telling and the Kindergarten. One club had a consecutive course of legends and tales of chivalry. One boy, after· a number of Charlemagne stories, flung himself half crying from the house and said that "there was no good in coming any more now that Prince Roland was

dead ! "   The Shamrock Club is a mixed club of boys
and girls.   In the children's dining room dinners are
served on five-cent tickets to children who attend school in
the neighborhood.   A class of 120 Italian children meets
in the gymnasium every Monday afternoon, where a
superintendent and fifteen teachers instruct the little
foreigners in the mystery of sewing and dressmaking.
Cooking and natural history classes are also in full
swing.   Every year Hull House takes 500 children for
a day in the country, and all last year Hull House secured the use of a vacant lot, rent free, for a children's
playground, which was filled with swings and sandheaps
and was immensely appreciated.

For the youngest of all, Hull House has a creche,
where mothers can leave their little ones for five cents a
day.   The walls are hung with large photographs of
Raphael's Madonnas, and there are also casts from Don-
atello and Della Robbia.   The children talk in a familiar way to the babies on the wall ; sometimes climbing
upon the chairs to kiss them.   The babies vary in number from thirty to fifty.

The latest addition to Hull House is a coffee house,
built like an old English inn, with a coffee and lunch
room, a New England kitchen, a gymnasium with
shower baths, and a men's club room filled with billiard
and card tables.   The coffee house is open from 6 a. m.
to 11 p. m., every day, Sundays included.   The New
England kitchen supplies cooked food, well cooked, for
home consumption ; coffee, soup and stews are delivered
piping hot, every day at noon, to the neighboring factories.   Five cents will buy a pint of soup or coffee and
two rolls.   Hot lunches at ten cents were supplied last
winter to the unemployed.

There is a public dispensary open from 3 to 4 and from
7 to 8 every day.   It is hoped to put this on a mutual
benefit plan.   A physician resides in Hull House, and a
nurse from the Visiting Nurses' Association.   There is a
Labor Bureau in connection with the House.

No public appeal for funds has ever been made, but the money comes. The residents give their lives to the work and they are esteemed worthy of support. No rent is paid for Hull House, or to adjacent lots on which friends of the House have put up needed buildings. All superintendence and teaching is given free. Residents pay for their board and lodging, what just covers the cost, which is arrived at by calculating all expenses as if they were incurred by a co-operative club, under the direction of a house committee. Such is a very brief, bald and inadequate survey of the social settlement.

But no mere catalogizing of the institutions which have blossomed into being from the parent stem of Hull House can give any idea of the gracious and blessed influence which Miss Addams and her residents diffuse throughout as squalid, and as mean a precinct as is to be found in Chicago. You need to live in the district to understand. But even a casual visitor can catch a glimpse of it as he hears the continual ringing of the door bell and sees Miss Addams, pale and weary, but indomitable to the last, answering with ready helpfulness to every appeal from without. Now it is a sick infant that wants doctoring, then it is someone out of work who wants a recommendation; a third ring brings someone in danger of eviction, and before they have cleared out someone else comes in with a tale of petty tyranny. For Miss Addams, like the name of the Lord, is a strong tower, and not the righteous only but all the forlorn and miserable in the neighborhood feel that if they can but run into that stronghold they are safe. From early morn till late at night these good and gracious women, strong sisters of the poor, by the potent influence of their own example, show their neighbors how to bear one another's burdens, and so fulfil the law of Christ.

CHAPTER VI.

IN THE TWENTIETH CENTURY.

Chicago was *en fete.* It was a bright June morning between the hours of six and seven o'clock, but already there were many signs that something unwonted was in the air. Groups were gathered together at places of vantage, while the decorators were putting the final touches to the triumphal arches. Streets were being festooned with flags and everywhere were to be seen the signs of an approaching festival. *

It was in the twentieth century. The population of the city was between three and four millions. Although it was more than ever a city of magnificent distances, the population was more compact, due to the more general utilization of lofty buildings for purposes of co-operative housekeeping. A great impetus had been given to the city by the construction of the oceanic canal which made Chicago the greatest seaport of the world. The Atlantic steamers now plowed their way direct from Europe to Lake Michigan. Their constant arrival and departure added fresh elements to the various phases of the life of the capital of America, for all rivalry to Chicago as the capital had disappeared at the dawn of the twentieth century. Even New York no longer dreamed of contesting the supremacy of the younger city. The workmen were putting the finishing touches to the mag-

---

* I thought it was better to adopt the historico-prophetic method of treating this subject instead of making a schedule of suggestions as to what might be done towards making Chicago the ideal city of the world. Unlike most writers who enter the field of imaginary prediction, I have endeavored scrupulously to confine myself to the practical In describing Chicago as it might be in the twentieth century, I have refrained from coloring the picture by introducing any element that is not well within the grasp of her citizens, if only they would give their minds to the task of obtaining it. The majority of the changes wrought in the social economy of the city have been realized piece-meal elsewhere ; it now remains for the Chicago of to-day to unite all the best things which exist in other cities and combine them in the great ideal Chicago of the twentieth century.

nificent series of state buildings which were reproducing in marble the architectural glories of the World's Fair, in order to provide accommodation for the Federal Government which was shortly to be transferred from Washington to the continental center.

Chicago's ascendancy was even more marked in social and municipal affairs than in the realm of commerce and the play of politics. For Chicago had become the ideal city of the world. The changes had begun about the middle of the last decade of the nineteenth century. The great impulse, born of the World's Fair, led the citizens to decide, when the White City had gone up in flames, that their black city should be transformed according to the best thought of the world's greatest thinkers. The great civic revival, which had liberated an hitherto unutilized moral force in that direction, brought into existence what in an ecclesiastical age would have been called a religious order, but which in this age was simply the appearance of a body of men and women who were known as "helpers." They dedicated themselves to the service of the city, as the followers of Loyola dedicated themselves to the service of the Church. It was the first time that an order or a society of consecrated souls dedicated to the redemption of the municipal and social system who undertook the task of civic regeneration with the same self-sacrificing zeal which Xavier showed in Asia, Livingstone in Africa and Judson in Burmah. The civic revival had another effect more potent still in bringing about the transformation. Before that time the administration of the city had been entirely in the hands of one moiety of the citizens; the other, the home-making portion, was jealously excluded from all share in the rights and duties of citizenship. As a result the civic administration was almost brutally lacking in all the amenities of life. It became evident that if the city had to be remodeled on the ideal of the family, woman must not only be permitted, but even compelled, to take a full and fair share with man in all civic work.

The result of this infusion of the more refined and cultured and graceful element into municipal work was everywhere apparent.

Side by side with this civic revival came a new and great re-enforcement from the side of material development. The construction of the drainage canal, by which the waters of Lake Michigan and the great arterial system of the Mississippi Valley were connected, enabled Chicago to utilize the inert force of Lake Michigan in the same way in which Niagara was long ago harnessed for industrial purposes. Immense turbines, worked by the descending volume of the surplus water of the lake, generated electricity which, when transmitted to the city by cables, supplied all the power necessary to drive all the machinery in the city. The tapping of this great reservoir of costless power corresponded with the great moral and social upheaval which, following the civic revival, enabled citizens to accomplish many things which otherwise would have been beyond their reach.

The City Council did not allow the monopolies of service to pass into the hands of private corporations. Every such source of power and of wealth was jealously preserved for the benefit of the city.

The sky was singularly bright and clear; hardly a wreath of smoke was visible over the great expanse of roofs which spread north, south and west as far as the eye could reach, for the day of smoke was almost a thing of the past. When the gas trust was broken up, and the city entered upon the supply of gas, the low prices which followed, together with its more general introduction into the houses of the citizens, led to its adoption as fuel. Every facility possible was made for this change. One of the first ordinances passed by the City Council in the twentieth century was a stringent decree drafted by Thomas J. Morgan, then Corporation Counsel,

---

*At the great pottery works of Doulton, Lambeth, London, England, the five-minute rule is rigidly enforced, a policeman being on duty to note the time. Prosecution and fine follow if the five minutes' grace is exceeded.

rendering anyone liable to imprisonment in the Bride-well if from his chimney smoke was seen to appear for more than five minutes at a time.

A great deal of heating, however, was done by the municipality direct. A central furnace in each block, fitted with the latest improvements, enabled the municipality to provide heat at a fixed charge for every room in the block. In this climate heat is as much a necessity as water, and at the City Hall the Heat Department had long been recognized as an indispensable part of the municipal machinery. The discontinuance of coal fires greatly reduced the difficulty of garbage. The unsightly garbage boxes which used to be such an eyesore to the city had long ago disappeared. Early every morning the refuse of the city was collected by a body of scavengers in the municipal service, who carted it away before seven in the morning.*

The garbage so collected was taken to the heat generating furnaces, where the bulk of it, after it had been sorted, was used as fuel.† Tin cans and similar unburnable rubbish was picked out, and everything was rescued that could be utilized.‡

Those who had not visited Chicago since the World's Fair, would have been startled by the appearance of the streets. All wood pavement for the sidewalks had disappeared, but the changes in the roadway were greater still. In the heart of the city the pavement was of asphalt, washed every morning and thoroughly cleaned before business commenced. The more frequented thoroughfares outside the heart of the city were paved

*This may seem rather early, but such a municipal regulation is enforced in many of the old cities of the Old World, notably in Rouen, where all refuse from the houses must be removed during the night or early in the morning. Every householder has a portable garbage pail into which the refuse of the house is placed over night and removed in the morning. By 7 o'clock the refuse of the whole town has been cleared away.

†The utilization of garbage for fuel in order to generate heat and steam is practically carried out in the town of Rochdale, Lancashire, England, where the only fuel used for the municipal boilers, employed in utilizing the sewage, is the refuse of the city.

‡Few people have any idea of the value of the city refuse. Whole colonies in Paris exist entirely from the findings of the rag pickers. Chicago has hitherto not recognized this, and has gone so far as to pay a man $35,000 to accept a monopoly, which in other cities would have been a source of revenue.

with wooden blocks and these also were swept and washed every day by an efficient staff. All streets were paved.*

Before the universal paving of the streets was introduced, provision was made for the construction of a vast system of underground communication which is carried to a greater extent in Chicago than anywhere else in the world. Under every thoroughfare there runs a steel-lined tunnel in which are laid the pipes, tubes and wires necessary for the supply of the needs of the city. In this underground subway, which was built so as to be accessible at all times, the gas, water, hot air, pneumatic tubes, telegraph and telephone wires and the electric light cables are so arranged that repairs can be carried on at all times without tearing up the streets or the interruption of the traffic. This was immensely facilitated by the city's acquiring all the monopolies of service.

One of the first effects of the civic revival was the acceptance of the doctrine that as it was ridiculous for private corporations to own the roadway of the streets so it was wrong for them to own either street railways, gas, telephone or telegraph systems. One by one, as the franchises fell in or as they were forfeited for non-user or mis-user, all these monopolies came into the hands of the city. For accommodation of their pipes, wires and mains, and for the convenience of the citizens, the subway was constructed. This was not the only use that had been made of underground communication. When the old ruin formerly known as the Post Office was demolished, the site was utilized for a central underground terminal from which lines radiated to all parts of the city and communicated with all the railway depots. The

---

*In Chicago in 1892 of 2,900 miles of streets in the city only 900 were paved. Of sidewalks 3,356 were of wood and 547 of stone. No attempt was made to sweep the streets from day to day. Even when the street cleaning department had the free service of the unemployed brigade of 3,000 men, hundreds of miles of streets were never cleaned at all. In Paris a municipal force of 3,000 men sufficed to clean the whole city from end to end every day. But in France street cleaning ranked as a virtue, and even the main roads in the country were swept from end to end, a practice which was much appreciated by bicyclists.

street railways were free within the city limits. This plan was adopted in order to reduce the congestion of the population near the center of the town. To induce the citizen to give up half an hour in the morning and evening in traveling backward and forward to his place of business, it was held that the least that could be done to equalize matters was to allow him free transit. The cars were operated by electricity from underground conductors. As no fares had to be collected a single driver was sufficient for each car. They were under perfect control. For the barbarous and dangerous rail of olden times was substituted the groove slot rail, laid level with the roadway, so that it was possible to drive across the tracks without a perceptible jar.

Chicago was the center of 100,000 miles of railway, some 3,000 miles of which lay within the city itself. Grade crossings had long disappeared and the only memorial which remains to commemorate the annual massacre of the early day was a fine monument of Mayor Hopkins, erected at the former crossing at Sixteenth Street, where more people had been killed by the railroads than had been slaughtered in the massacre of the garrison of Fort Dearborn.

The subway was divided into two divisions, down the center of which passed the footway for workmen and inspectors. The gas and water mains lay on the left, while the right was devoted to electric cables and telegraph and telephone wires.

The pneumatic tube system had been in use for some time. The construction of the subways led to the universal adoption of this convenience of life. The development of the system was very rapid. It began with the despatch of pneumatagrams, following the example of Paris. Then a larger tube was introduced, and all letters and post cards were dispatched from the central office to the branches in this manner. They were looking forward to a still further development, when parcels and newspapers would also be so dispatched, but as this would have necessitated an enlargement of the subway there was some hesitation in undertaking so great a task.

Great as were the changes which had taken place in the city, those on the Lake Front were still more remarkable. The land had been thrust forward into the lake as far as the breakwater, but due care had been taken to preserve open water for boating, bathing and landscape purposes. The whole of the Lake Front was laid out as a lovely park, half land and half water. The wonderful effect which had been achieved by the landscape gardeners who laid out the World's Fair had been reproduced here on an even more extended scale. There were more wooded islands and picturesque promontories on the Lake Front, while winding lakes afforded ample field for innumerable gondolas which gemmed at nightfall like fireflies the surface of the illuminated water. Another breakwater had been constructed outside the reclaimed land and it surrounded the city like an atoll does a Pacific island. The boating clubs, which had become so remarkable a feature of Chicago, found ample space for exercise; while a harbor, well protected against the storms, gave shelter to the yachts, which on regattas and holidays covered the great extent of the lake with their white-winged sails. The Manufactures Building, or all that was left of it after the last great fire at Jackson Park, had been brought down to the Lake Front and established as the first of a series of half a dozen People's Palaces which were one of the most conspicuous features of Chicago. The Home of the Waifs and Strays had been built on the site of the Battery, which had so long been an eyesore and had been demolished as a nuisance. At intervals along the Lake Front were bathing establishments, similar to those which abound on the Seine and Rhine, the presence of the breakwater rendering their erection along the shore of the lake possible.

The People's Institute, of which the Manufactures Building was the pioneer, formed the center of the Democratic university system of Chicago.

There were also polytechnics in connection with these institutes, the first of which had been started in connection with the Van Buren and Oakley Streets People's Institute in 1895. In each of these institutes were meeting rooms, concert, reading and news rooms and all the social adjuncts which made Mr. Quinton Hogg's polytechnic in London so valuable an agent of social progress. Every ward of the city had its institute and every precinct its Hull House outpost. Hull House had gradually extended its borders until it had become the greatest social center of the city. It had its affiliates in every one of the two thousand precincts, who were living among the people, sharing their life and constantly interchanging their experience for the purpose of bringing the help of all to the aid of each.

The saloon had practically disappeared, and so, very largely, had the drug store. Under the changed conditions of life, with the absence of wear and tear, overwork and the anxiety about the loss of work, improved cooking, and the careful training in the laws of health which was given to everyone in the public schools, the demand for medicine had shrunk so much that corner lots were no longer in demand for drug stores. As fast as they fell vacant the municipality entered into possession and established what was known as the New Saloon, which in a very short time drove the old saloon entirely out of the field. The ground floors of these saloons were fitted up like the admirable cafés of Liverpool, with provision for light refreshments and beverages. The supply of food and drink, however, was but a fractional part of the functions of the New Saloon. Upstairs the rooms were fitted up much as the Commerce Club in the Auditorium Building was in 1894, with the addition of a circulating library, and billiard table. Lavatories and all other conveniences of the kind were provided free, the library and reading room were also free, but the customers paid for their refreshments. There was no interdict on the sale of beer and light wine, but it was the policy of the administration to discourage the sale of intoxicants so far as it was possible to do so without interfering with the liberty of the citizen to choose his beverage.*

The churches had undergone the same beneficent transformation which had taken place in the saloon. To begin with, there was now a Church of Chicago which included as its effective members all the religious organizations. When Archbishop Ireland, afterwards Cardinal, succeeded Archbishop Feehan, a wonderful change came over the churches of Chicago. The Cardinal speedily achieved for himself on the shores of Lake Michigan the same position which Cardinal Manning used to enjoy on the banks of the Thames. His primacy was acknowledged with enthusiasm by men of all creeds and of none. He had most trouble at first with his own people, but after a time they also began to see that the ideal of the Catholic Church could only be realized by widening the conception of Catholicism. The germ of the Federation of the Ministers of Religion which had begun in the year of the World's Fair was developed under his influence, and before long the Church of Chicago was organized with the Cardinal Archbishop at its head as Chairman. The Rev. Jenkin Lloyd Jones, the Unitarian, was the first Vice-President. Then was introduced for the first time a systematic districting of the city. This is now carried on so effectively that there is not one man, woman or child in the whole city who can suffer an accident or receive injury, but that it could be acertained in one moment, which of the churches must be called upon to take charge of the case. The Church of God in Chicago has only one belief, and that is to do what Christ would have done if He were confronted with the problems with which they have to deal. The principle of centralized administra-

*This suggestion of the municipal saloon is well within the pale of practical achievement. The experience of the Aerated Bread Company, in London, and the Coffee Palaces, in Liverpool, proves that nothing pays better than a well-conducted place of refreshment and place of call which can be used equally by both sexes. The new saloon when it is established would be a source of revenue to the city and not a charge upon its finances.

tion, with local responsibility and close intercommunication, has been adopted in the service of the Church. If any spiritual or moral evil occurs in one district, the whole of the massed forces of the associated churches can be depended upon to assist in its removal.   Under this system, no district is left without the appliances of the civilization or of the means of grace.   The churches have thus undergone a great change, and each is the center of the locality in which it stands.   The minister every morning sits, with one or more assistants, to hear complaints, to listen to the distressed, to give counsel and to compose the difficulties of his parishioners.   It is the new and modernized confessional, adapted to the endless diversities of life, in the complex civilization of the twentieth century.   The church buildings are open all day and they are gradually being transformed into picture galleries and museums of sculpture, commemorating all that is best in the world of human reverence and gratitude.*

Besides this, every church was also a reading room, while all the class rooms were placed at the service of students who wished for a privacy which they could not find in the boarding house or at home.   In the working class districts every church was also a concert room at the dinner hour.   Nothing could be more remarkable than to see the church edifices crowded with grimy, brawny workmen eating out of their dinner pails and listening to organ recitals and vocal and instrumental music.

Chicago, which long ago achieved the foremost position in musical America, had not lost ground.   The seed sown by Mr. Thomas and Mr. Tomlins had borne good fruit, and no privilege was more coveted by the

---

* If this seems strange to some who are accustomed to the scandalous spectacle of a church costing $100,000 locked up from week end to week end, and only opened a few hours on Sunday, presumably for the worship of God, they may be reminded that in Southern Europe the churches do fulfil this function.   They are the only picture gallery of the poor man; there he can find his wax statuary figures and learn something of architecture and the liberal arts.

singing classes in the public schools than to be allowed
to sing at the midday concerts for the people.*

The schools had also undergone a great and memorable change. The post of Superintendent was regarded
as the most important in the city after those of the
Mayor, the Chairman of the Civic Federation, the President of Hull House and the Chairman of the Church of
Chicago. He was a highly trained university man who
had had practical experience in public school work. He
had a staff selected from the brightest and best teachers, under the direction of a board whose duty it was
to be perpetually on the road visiting all other cities
for the purpose of getting pointers and picking up ideas
for the schools in Chicago. Under their stimulating
influence a great change had been brought about.
Half of the teaching was done in the open air and by
means of the natural object lessons with which the city
abounded. The idea suggested by the German, the
Austrian and the Irish villages had been taken up, and in
Chicago there could be found, in the public parks, typical
specimens of the buildings and scenery of the countries
which had contributed of their most adventurous sons to
the city of Chicago. Geography was studied as it is in
various German and Swiss towns, by taking the children
out into the country and making them draw maps and
sketch what they saw. Natural History was not taught
with cut-and-dried specimens in cases, but by contact with
the living nature which surrounds us. A great improve-
men had been made in providing every school room
with adequate playgrounds. At first the roofs were
utilized for this purpose, but soon it came to be regarded
as a public disgrace if the children were not provided
with convenient playgrounds at the street level. Every
vacant lot in the city was taken possession of and converted into a playground until such time as the owner
thought fit to build upon it. By this means the vacant

* The experiment of having midday concerts for working people was tried on
a small scale at the City Temple in London with remarkable success.

lots which used to so disfigure the city were utilized for the service of the children.

One of the first things which was rendered possible by the union of the Church of Chicago was the possibility of having religious teaching in the public schools. The Church was broad enough and wise enough to draw up a system of religious teaching to which all could subscribe. The teaching everywhere became more practical. Special attention was paid to cooking. The French *chef* who was at the head of the Culinary Department of the Education Board was at first in despair, but after a few years he comforted himself with the belief that, in the course of another generation, every woman in Chicago would be able to cook as well as if she had been born in France and had had the training of a French home.

After the Superintendent of Schools, the most important official in the town was the Chief of Police. His position, of all others, was perhaps the most coveted. The same feeling which leads the scions of the first families in Europe to aspire to commissions in the army or navy, in the twentieth century led the youth of the city to aspire to positions in the Police and Fire Departments. As these positions could only be secured by service in the ranks, there was great competition for the position of patrolmen. Entrance was by competitive examination, and for these examinations, the sons of the most cultured and of the wealthiest citizens entered most eagerly. Hence it was not at all strange to see the son of a millionaire in the patrolman's helmet, superintending the traffic at Madison and La Salle Streets, while others would do patrol duty before their own mansions. This raised the standard of the police force and "on the word of a patrolman" came to be regarded as equivalent to the old phrase "on the word of a gentleman," or "on the honor of an officer." Pupils who had attained special distinction at the public schools were sometimes, as a great reward, granted entrance into the police force without undergoing the preliminary examinations; but with that exception the rule of admission by competitive examination was enforced. The police force was largely composed of women. The experiment begun by the Municipal Order League when police matrons were appointed had led to the adoption of a female police. This change resulted in raising the moral tone of the force and facilitated the dealing with the social evil, and with all matters relating to the welfare and custody of the children. The functions of the police had become greatly extended until from mere thief-catchers they had become the indispensable servants of the administration in almost every department of life.

The school buildings were utilized as covered-in playgrounds of evenings by the younger children, and as gymnasiums by the elder; while many of the class rooms were used for the purpose of social intercourse by the inhabitants of the neighborhood.*

Another great change which had come over the town was the increased attention which was paid to recreation. There was a circus in every park, and a theater in every ward. Both circus and theater were under the direct control of the municipality. The circuses were a source of perpetual stimulus to the physical training of the youth of the city. In the gymnasium which were connected with every school in the city, the achievements of the athletes of the circus were a constant inspiration both to boys and girls, and the Board of Education specially granted free admission to the circuses to such pupils as had distinguished themselves in their physical training. This applied to both sexes, the circus being one of the institutions which afford women with practical object lessons as to

---

* This is no more than what is done in London and several other towns. The London School Board allows the use of its finest school buildings during the week to the Happy Evenings Association, which uses them for playgrounds for the young children, and the Recreative Evenings Association, which utilizes them for gymnasiums, concerts and other means of social intercourse and entertainment.

the fact that they are not made of porcelain, but that
they can, with training, make as much of their limbs as
if they had been born of the other sex.

Another institution which was established for the
mingled purpose of amusement and education was the
Zoological Garden. There were three such gardens in
Chicago. No lesson was given in natural history unless
it was accompanied by a visit to the animals, which
were lodged in cages fitted up so as to resemble as
closely as possible their native habitat.*

But it was the theater which was the greatest re-enforcement of all the moral forces of the city. The
dramatic instinct, so strongly rooted in every human
breast, instead of being repressed, was developed and
relied upon as a special means of cultivating the mind
and reaching the heart of the population, and especially
of the scholars. Every school and every Sunday School
had its own dramatic society, and it was a proud day for
the pious parent when her daughter was permitted to
make her debut on the boards of the municipal theater.
As the stage was recruited from the best citizens and the
ablest scholars, the standard of its morality was at least
as high as that prevailing in the Sunday School and the
church choir. Any ward without its municipal theater
was regarded as being in a state of spiritual destitution
which called for the prayers of the churches, and their
immediate assistance to supply the want.†

This work in Chicago began by a relative of Mrs.
Potter Palmer who had been studying in Germany and
who came back to Chicago full of the idea of starting a
town theater. Happening one day to look in at the
Park Theater, in order to contrast the stage of

---

*The Jardin des Plantes in Paris is a zoological and botanical garden to which
all citizens have free access. Most of the German cities have zoological gardens
for the instruction and amusement of their citizens.

† No one who has been to Oberammergau and seen the way in which a population of two or three thousand peasants can supply a whole dramatic troupe,
capable of playing not merely the "Passion Play," but most of the classical
dramas of their native land, can doubt that in the theater, rightly conducted, lies
the most potent instrument of popular education which human hands have yet
grasped.

Chicago with what he had seen in his university town in Germany, he was unutterably disgusted by the vulgarity and the obscenity of the play and the orgies of debauchery which followed the performance. As a result, he decided to make a beginning then and there. Calling upon the Mayor he laid facts before him. This led to the summary closing of the theater and the forfeiture of the license. He then formed a syndicate which decided to supersede the old farrago of brutality and indecency by a first-class variety entertainment. He decided to begin on a small scale and made a tour both of America and of Europe in order to ascertain what could be best done in order to obtain popular amusement that would amuse without degrading. When he returned he brought with him assistance which enabled him to make the Park Theater the most popular institution in Chicago. Its success led to the improvement of the standard of popular entertainments in other quarters, and after a time the syndicate felt strong enough to undertake the regular drama. From that time their progress was rapid. The church co-operated heartily and at last, at the suggestion of the Civic Federation, the City Council took the matter in hand. There was no pedantry about the entertainments. Man is a creature who needs to be amused, and amusement must be supplied to him in his own sphere with an upward tendency. This was recognized to the full, and in the seafaring quarters the entertainments were of a very free and easy nature. It was held that where the need was greatest, there must the means of grace be the most abundant; and it was a sight for the gods and men to see Archbishop Ireland presiding over an entertainment in the Sailor's Home where jolly tars, the hornpipe and the fiddlers, were playing as merrily as ever they did in any popular resort ungraced by the presence of a dignitary of the Church.

The means for supplying these appliances of civilization were furnished with less strain upon the resources of the citizens than was felt under the old system. This was partly due to the action of some public-spirited millionaires, and also by the immense resources of revenue provided by the municipalization of the monopolies of service. Great markets were established in which the producers of the necessaries of life were able to sell directly to the consumer without the interference of the middleman. This of course is no more than what is done in every center of civilization in Europe, but Chicago went one better, as it has been her custom to do. The way was opened up by the action of Mr. Marshall Field and Mr. Leiter, who decided that as they had made a sufficient number of millions in their great stores it would be an interesting social experiment if they were to hand them over to the city. The City Council had long been composed of the best citizens in Chicago, who administered its affairs with efficiency and probity. The two great stores of Marshall Field & Co. and Siegel, Cooper & Co., passed into the hands of the City Council, fully stocked and with an adequate capital for carrying on the business. Other millionaires followed this example and soon the city found itself in the possession of income enough to carry out the realization of most of its ideals.

I referred to the fact that the skyscrapers had been built for the purpose of co-operative housekeeping. The first of these was established by the municipality for the housing of the employes of Siegel, Cooper & Co., after it passed into their hands. No one was compelled to live there unless they pleased, but the advantages were found to be so great and so much above what could be obtained elsewhere that it was soon filled. The cook, for instance, was a first-class French *chef,* and there was also in connection with it a large library with reading rooms, concert rooms, etc. There were also established, in connection with these co-operative homes, branch establishments in the country, which in summer time were always crowded. The roads were so good that there was nothing to prevent the employes from cycling backwards and forwards to their place of business and their summer retreat. Cycling, I may add, has come into almost universal use both for men and women, with great advantages to themselves, and in the distribution of population. In these great homes domestic service became a profession. The cooks and the housemaids in the co-operative homes had at least the social position of a stenographer or a retail clerk. They worked in relays, and after they had finished they were as free to go and come as any clerk in an office or store.

The hours of labor generally had been adjusted to the eight-hour standard, with an immense gain to family life and without diminishing the economic value of the day's labor. Child labor was strictly forbidden, and the spectacle of a child of twelve or thirteen working in a store was so unusual as to lead to an immediate summons to the police. A labor bank had been established where those who were temporarily out of work could pawn themselves on security of their future labor, and a system of co-operative distribution among workers had been established on the basis of labor certificates which, within a small area and among friends and neighbors, facilitated exchange and dispensed with the costly service of the middleman. When employment was slack and periods of depression came, exact information was obtained as to the number of the unemployed and provision made for the utilization of their labor in the service of public improvement. Men could always work for their rations, and an unemployed man was considered as a wicked waste of a valuable asset of the community. The Church of Chicago in this followed the example of the Latter Day Saints, who have from the first regarded the organization of labor and the employment of the unemployed as one of the first of religious duties.*

* Few persons interested me more during my stay in Chicago than George Q. Cannon, of the Latter Day Saints, whom I met at the Auditorium Hotel on his way through the country. I had a long talk with him on the subject of the organization of labor and the relieving of the workless worker, which forms so important a

All pawnbrokers had disappeared and their places were taken up by popular banks of deposit managed by the municipality. Instead of paying ten per cent per month as was the case under the old system, the depositors did not pay more than ten per cent a year, and the municipal pawn shop, like the municipal saloon, more than paid its running expenses. The poor were relieved upon very different principles than what had formerly prevailed. The poorhouse at Dunning, to which at the end of the nineteenth century the helpless and forlorn were dispatched by the slowest trains that crawled over the iron way, in order to be packed together in a crowded building, is a thing of the past. The change was made not so much for the sake of the poor as in order to give better opportunity to their neighbors to visit them. After grave discussion and long consideration the Church of Chicago decided that with the poorhouse at Dunning, this means of grace was too far removed from the Christians of Chicago. It was necessary for their own souls that they should visit the sick and the afflicted, and the homes of the oppressed. As they could not find time to go down to Dunning the poor must be brought closer to them and established at their doors. Hence instead of one huge mass of overgrown pauperism, there were a multitude of citizens' almshouses, where the poor people were established within easy range of their neighbors. The churches took special charge of these institutions, maintained their efficiency and supplied the visitors. The responsibility of the churches for the moral and social well-being of the community was sharply recognized, and for any failure were taken to account promptly.

In the midst of all the preparations which were going on, on this bright June day, one church was conspicuous for the absence of any adornment. It was draped in black;

feature of American polity. President Cannon's ideas upon polygamy are detestable enough, but as a captain ot industry, if I were an unemployed man I would rather look to him than to most of the Christian bishops with whom I have had any acquaintance.

and the reason why this church stood out in solitary gloom amid its gay and decorated neighbors was because of the birth of an illegitimate child in the block for which it had accepted responsibility to the Church of Chicago. Such a scandal, it was held, could not have occurred if the local church had done its duty. As the church had not been able to prove that it had done all that it might have done to have remedied the evil from which this seduction sprang it was doomed to wear penitential garb on this day of public rejoicing.

Medical service was provided free for all the citizens. The reason for making this municipal change was because it was held that disease in most cases arose from conditions for which the individual was not responsible, and that it was often traceable directly to the neglect of the city authorites. It was thought only just that if the individual citizen had to bear the pain and risk of death resulting from his illness, the least the city could do was to give him a free doctor and free drugs. The convalescent system of Chicago was the wonder of the world. Mr. George M. Pullman on his retirement from business had handed over three-quarters of his immense wealth to be employed in conveying convalescents and consumptives by Pullman cars to regions where their recovery would be expedited. Floating hotels in the summer season surrounded by a small flotilla of pleasure craft were anchored off the more beautiful and shelter spots of the lake, where, in the midst of air and water, the patients made a much more rapid recovery than was possible on land.

Disease, however, had been much improved owing to the improved cooking which had been brought about by the combined agency of the public schools and of Mr. Kohlsaat's bakery. Mr. Kohlsaat, when he devoted himself exclusively to the editorship of the *Inter Ocean*, had followed the example of Mr. Marshall Field, and handed over his bakery to the city to be utilized for the purpose of experimenting in supplying well-cooked food at a

minimum cost. The result was so successful that the
Civic Restaurant became a kind of Cooks' University.
The menu was always published the day in advance,
and householders and their cooks could come down and
take lessons in the preparing of the delicate dishes with
which the Civic *Chef* made cooking almost a fine art.

It was not cooking alone which had become a fine art.
The much-neglected art of hospitality, especially civic
hospitality, had been revived. Nothing in the traditions
of the Lord Mayor of London or the Syndic of Florence
could rival the hospitality of the Mayors of Chicago.
They entertained as a matter of course every distinguished visitor who arrived on the American continent.
This notable innovation was begun in the first mayoralty
of Mrs. Potter Palmer, which made the year 1900
memorable in the history of America. Nor was it only
at banquets that they displayed their hospitality. Gala
performances, operatic, dramatic and musical, were provided for their guests, while all the citizens regarded it
as an honor to keep open house for the entertainment
of the stranger, for open house was not confined to
distinguished strangers. The millionaires no longer
kept their treasures of art to themselves and a select
circle of friends. The same generous rule which prevails in the Old World was accepted here. On visiting
days the poorest citizen in Chicago could drink his fill
of beauty in the picture galleries of the richest millionaire on Prairie Avenue. A citizen who possessed valuable pictures and excluded the citizens from seeing them
was regarded as virtually a thief, and when due representation had been made and made in vain, was boy-
cotted by his neighbors and excommunicated by the
Church.

Owing to the general introduction of taller buildings
in the residential quarters, great spaces had been cleared
and devoted to parks and recreation grounds. Each
nationality had its own playing ground, in which it pursued its national sports. The streets were planted with

shade trees and provided with seats. Fountains played in all the public places and in winter time the squares were converted into winter gardens where artificial warmth enabled the citizens to enjoy the music and the society which in summer time they found in the parks. Every citizen was supplied every week with the official gazette of the city, by which everyone was kept informed as to the movement of the civic life.

Pageants were numerous and splendid. On Mayor's Day the procession which filed through the city cast the civic pageants of the Lord Mayors of London far in the shade. But that was only one of the half a dozen which brightened the civic life of Chicago. Chicago Day was a great popular *fete.* Bands played, processions moved through the streets, all gay with flowers and bunting, all those who had deserved best of the city were decorated and the day finished with a grand display of fireworks. The whole world was ransacked for hints how to beautify and enliven these *fetes.* The *Fete Dieu* of Southern Europe supplied many hints which enabled the Master of Ceremonies to decorate the streets of the city with a wealth of beauty the like of which was never seen in the Windy City in the olden times. The great aquatic *fete* which took place at the annual regatta was another ceremonial which it was worth coming to Chicago to see.

Enough has been said to indicate the scope and range of civic life which has made Chicago the ideal city of the world. Meanwhile the sun had risen high in the heavens and the first notes of the national anthem were heard mingled with the sounds of many voices, and the cheering of the crowd that was mustered thickly round the magnificent palace which had taken the place of the old City Hall. As far as the eye could see the streets were gay with flags and bright with arches. An expectant crowd lined the sidewalks waiting for the approach of a procession. Bells were ringing and now and again from the Lake Front could be heard the deep boom of the salute of the men-of-war lying off the harbor. Pres-

ently an advance corps of cavalry trotted down the street
in front of the procession.   The notes of German music
filled the air and the smart uniforms of the Imperial escort excited universal admiration as they swept by.
Presently, surrounded by a brilliant staff, there rode down
the street a resolute soldier, with an imperial presence,
saluting as he ackowledged the cheers of the enthusiastic people.   It was the German Emperor on his way to
the City Hall to be presented with the freedom of the
city of Chicago, which had been voted to him on his
first visit to the American Continent, to which he had
come expressly in order to see for himself the ideal city
of the world.

CHAPTER VII.

A CLOSING WORD.

If Christ came to Chicago what would He wish me to do?

That is the question with which I hope every reader will close this book. Nor is the answer difficult or far to seek.

For what He would have you to do is to follow in His footsteps and be a Christ to those among whom you live, in the family, in the workshop, in the city and in the state.

Be a Christ. The more you disbelieve in Christianity as it is caricatured, the more earnestly should you labor to live the life and to manifest the love and, if need be, to die the death of Jesus of Nazareth.

Even if you doubt whether He ever really lived, God Incarnate in mortal flesh, the more imperative is your duty to endeavor so far as you can, to realize in your own person that supreme embodiment of Love, in order that now, if never before, there may be on earth a Messiah of God who is Love among men who are perishing for want of love.

Be a Christ!—everything is summed up in that.

What Christ would do if He came to Chicago in these last days and were living in your circumstances, even so do you; and do it not once or twice in moments of spiritual ecstacy or of moral enthusiasm, but do it all the time.

Each day's duties at home or at work, every friend whom you love, every acquaintance which you form, every occasion where a duty confronts you and every opportunity where you can manifest love by word or deed or look—there and then you can be a Christ. If you are selfish and unloving, then instead of being God's Messiah to your fellow men you are shutting out God from a portion of His own world.

Whenever you give up yourself—your time, which is a part of your life; your thought, which is a part of your mind; your love, which is a part of your soul—to serve others, you are, so far as that sacrifice goes, manifesting God's Love to man. For God is Love and His service is sacrifice of self in helping others.

His commandment is exceeding broad. As I have attempted to show in the previous pages, it applies especially to a great field of human service, with which many imagine religion has nothing to do. A religion which has nothing to do with any human effort is not religion. For religion is the life of man going out of himself to unite itself to the life of other men so that they may all be one in Love, which is God.

The New Redemption for which the world has long been waiting wearily is nigh at hand. The old forms having served their turn and done their work are passing away. They hinder where they ought to help, and fail to interpret the full orbed revelation of the will of God toward us in all its bearings upon the social, political and national life of man.

"A new commandment give I unto you, that you love one another," is still, alas, a new commandment in a world that is more or less avowedly dominated by the doctrine of Cain. The New Redemption will come when that new commandment has cast out the Evil Spirit, the Prince of this world, whose watchword is, "Each man for himself and the devil take the hindmost." For it was the hindmost whom Christ came to save.

For this New Redemption for which the world waits, there must come a new Catholicity, transforming and widening and redeeming the old. The new religion, which is but the primitive essence of the oldest of all religions, has but one formula—Be a Christ! The new church which is already dimly becoming conscious of its own existence, under all kinds of ecclesiastical and dogmatic and agnostic concealments, is not less broad. What is the Church? It is the Union of all who Love in the Service of all who Suffer.

Are you willing to help? If Christ came to your city would He find you ready? If so you will not have long to wait. For the least of these, My brethren, are a numerous tribe, and an hour will not pass after you close this book before your readiness will be put to the test. And Christ will then see in your case, "How the men, My brethren, believe in Me."

THE END.

BLACK LIST.

OCCUPIERS, OWNERS AND TAX-PAYERS OF PROPERTY USED FOR IMMORAL PURPOSES.

No.	Street.	Description.	Keeper.	Owner.	Taxes Paid By
423	Clark St.	Saloon	....	Annie M. Howard	Jacob Franks, 163 Clark-st.
429	"	Saloon and assignation house.	Joe Moll	Sidney A. Kent	A. E. Kent.
435	"	Saloon and assignation house.	C. F. Kinnucan.	Albert E. Kent.	
441	"	House of ill-fame	Carrie Watson	Caroline V. Watson	Caroline Watson.
443	"	"	Kitty Plant	No record	S. Hofman, 744 W. Monroe-st.
445	"	"	Daisy Plant	No record	
447	"	"	Miss Lulu	Jenney Lehr	Mrs. M. Myer.
449	"	"		Andrew Iuerotte	Mrs. R. Iuerotte, 457 S. Clark-st.
451	"	"	May Blank	Samuel Hofman	S. Hofman, 744 W. Monroe-st.
459	"	Saloon		Andrew Iuerotte	Mrs. R. Iuerotte, 457 S. Clark-st.
463	"	House of ill-fame	Miss Lillie	Philo C. Hildreth	Philo C. Hildreth, 523 N.Weber-st., Colorado Springs, Col.
467	"	"	Cora Clark	Annie C. Soloman. Grace M. Cheney. Blg., Le Grand O'. Dell. Deed in trust to Thos. H. Bliss.	Grace M. Cheney, 453 Washington-bl.
469	"	Saloon			Bliss & Hanscomb.
471	"	House of ill-fame	Jennie Moore.	Anna A. Cheney.	W. W. Strong, 436 Washing'n-bl.
471½	"	"	Thos. May	Rosa Foster.	Rosa Foster, 685 W. Indiana-st.
473	"	"	Jessie Wilson.	Est., Hannah Meyer Lease, W. T. Adams.	W. T. Adams, 125 La Salle-st.
477	"	Saloon and house of ill-fame		Livi Winsberg	T. H. Schintz, 81 Clark-st.
477½	"	"	F. Whittaker	C. E. Robinson est.	
479	"	"	Wm. Reidy		
481	"	"	J. Finley		
481½	"	House of ill-fame	Ada Dick	William Short	Knight & Marshall.
483	"	Saloon and house of ill-fame		Sarai B. & Hariet Port.	Wm. Port, 5046 State-st.
495	"	"	Adolph Miller	Bldg., W. M. Jenks.	J. Lafe. Curtis, 69 Dearborn-st.
497	"	"	Joe Moll	Lease, L. Friedberg.	

No.	Description	Occupant	Owner	Owner address
499 Clark St.	Saloon	Frank Gary	C. E. Robinson estate.	T. H. Schintz, 81 Clark-st.
501 "	Saloon and house of ill-fame " "	French Georgie	Julius Berndt	Julius Berndt, 3232 Vernon-av.
507 "	Saloon	Jimmie's Place.	C. E. Robinson estate.	T. H. Schintz, 81 Clark-st.
509 "	House of ill-fame			C. L. Jenks, 100 Washington-st.
511 "	" "	Maud Gillian	Louise Mackway	Marian Mackway, 508 Belden-av
511½	" "	Belle Gireoux		E. Mackway, 930 Chi. Op. Hse.
513	" "	Miss Gerbold		Louise Mackway, 16 Kendall-st.
513½		Miss Maggie.		
515 "	Saloon and house of ill-fame " "		C. E. Robinson estate.	T. H. Schintz, 81 Clark-st.
517 "	" "		Gerado Nugliore.	
519 "	" "		Gerado Nugliore. V. Di Stefano	Gerado Nugliore, 519 Clark-st.
523 "	Saloon and house of ill-fame " "	Marcus & Leis.	Herman H. Gage, sold to A. Gage.	
525 "				
527 "	Saloon and house of ill-fame " "	H. Johm.	C. E. Robinson estate.	T. H. Schintz, 81 Clark-st,
529 "				
531 "	Saloon and house of ill-fame " "	{ M. Hilderbrand.	Roger Plant, Jr	Roger Plant, 531 S. Clark-st.
533 "	House of ill-fame below level of street. A den of thieves.		{ Roger Plant, Jr .... Lse., M. Hilderbrand	May Hilderbrand, Santa Monica California.
535 "	" " "	Clifford Moody.	Edwin O. Gale, Sr. }	Churchill C. Clarke, Hotel Metropole.
537 "	" "	Jennie Love.	Edwin O. Gale, Sr. }	Churchill C. Clarke, Hotel Metropole.
539 "	" "	Belle Taylor.		
541 "	Saloon and house of ill-fame	Miss Davis.	Ambolena Jones et al }	A. M. Wells, Quincy, Ill.
547 "	Saloon (below street)		Martha E. Buckingham }	C. L. Jenks, 100 Washington-st.
549 "	House of ill-fame, 2d floor.	{ Lena Christianson.	Eva C. Reker........	Eva C. Reker, 5124 Halsted-st.
549 "	Saloon (below street)			
553			No record ...	No record.

No.	Street.	Description.	Keeper.	Owner.	Taxes Paid by
555	Clark St....	House of ill-fame and den of colored thieves.	Sallie White (a notorious thief).	C. E. Robinson estate.	T. H. Schintz, 81 Clark-st.
561	"	House of ill-fame....	Miss Amanda N. Campbell	Bldg, W. M. Jenks.	J. Lafe. Curtis, 69 Dearborn-st.
54	Taylor St...	House of ill-fame....	Mrs. Jordan	Lse., L. Friedberg..	
52	"				
51	"	Saloon and house of ill-fame.	A. Prato.....	Chancellor L. Jenks.	Chancellor L. Jenks.*
53	Cust. H. Pl. (Fourth Ave.)	Saloon	Roger Plant		
76		Saloon	J. Monahan...	Isaac Atkinson estate.	Mead & Co.
78	"	House of ill-fame....	Miss Davis..	C. E. Robinson estate.	T. H. Schintz, 81 Clark-st.
80	"	"	MaggieMoore		
82	"	"	Mrs. Mitchell	Samuel L. Alexander.	S. L. Alexander, 905 Jackson-bl.
84	"	"	Mrs. Ellison		
86	"	Saloon.... Gambling den, 2d floor.	C. C. Salvator A. J. Scott...	Mary L. & Andrew J. Scott.....	Mary L. & Andrew J. Scott, 86 Custom House-pl.
88	"	House of ill-fame....	J. Goodrich...	Jennie Tompkins, sold to E. Lowery.	
90	"	"	Ida Moss....	Mrs. Emily Barkers..	Mrs. E. Barkers,1332 Wash'n-bl.
92	"	"	Jennie Letang.	E. Alice Miller..	E. A. Miller, 6218 Michigan-av.
94	"	"	Blanch D'Ory.	Jennie Phillips..	Eugenia Phillips, 13 W. Park-av.
110	"	"	Nellie Dillon.	Fred R. Otis... Olliver Tillingast...	F. R. Otis, 236 State-st.
112	"	"	Madam Theo.	Annie Conway....	E. A. Cummings & Co.
114	"	"	Nellie Dihville.	Mary O'Day....	Mary O'Day, 132 Dearborn-st.
122	"	"	E. Ritchie...	E. Ritchie....	E. Ritchie, 122 Custom Hse.-pl.
124	"	"	Miss Monroe...	Abraham Wilkins...	Abraham Wilkins, 124 4th-av.
126	"	"	Miss Shakes...	Chas. A. Roggio	Chas. A. Roggio,3219 S. Park-av.
128	"	"	Miss Andrea.	Lot 21, blk. 125, add to Town of South Chicago......	
130	"	"	Belle Smith...	Bernard Mahon	Bernard Mahon, 1355 State-st.
132	"	"	Mad. Cloquette.	V.Fields,138-40C.H.P.	J. W. Thomas, 144 Clark-st.
134	"	House of ill-fame....	Lucy Celorime.	Dora Goldstine......	Stein Bros.

* Mr. Chancellor L. Jenks wishes me to deny that he owns any property that is used as a house of prostitution.

No.	Street	Character	Keeper	Owner	Owner's address / Remarks
138 } 140 }	Cust. H. Pl. (Fourth Ave.)	House of ill-fame	Vina Fields	John G. Mott	John G. Mott, 206 LaSalle-st.
	"	"	Vina Fields	Sarah O'Hanna	D.W. Mitchell, 45 Macalister-pl.
142	"	"	Mary Hastings	Zyulica Mercier	P. Brown, 126 Dearborn-st.
144	"	"	Mad. Andrea	No Record	P. S. Kelley, 21&22,506 State-st.
146	"	"	Miss Ritta	Catherine Hull	Cath. Hull, 61st & Tenth-av.
148	"	"	Miss Masker	Chas. Metyner	C. Metyner, 112 Harrison-st.
150	"	"	Miss Masker	Gastain Ailara	Barnes & Parish.
152	"	"	Madame Flora	Jane Barnet	J. Barnet, 152 Custom H. Pl.
154	"	"	Madame Flora	Jno B. Grossett	Estate of Mary Kelsey, by G. S. Newbury, 164 LaSalle-st.
156	"	"	Madame Flora	Chas. D. W. Crocker	Mrs. C. D. Crocker, 3131 Forest-av.
158	"	"	Mme. Carmen	Chas. Metyner	Chas Metyner, 112 Harrison-st.
160	"	"	Margueritta	Morris Eisenberg	M. Eisenberg, 96 E. 40th-st.
164	"	"	Miss Lillie	Morris Eisenberg	M. Eisenberg, 96 E. 40th-st.
168	"	{ Saloon and Assignation house }	Geo. Bower	Morris Eisenberg	Louis Batee, 400 Dearborn-st.
131	"	House of ill-fame	Lizzie Payton	No Record	Joel Bigelow, 2449 Prairie-av.
133	"	"	Miss J. Clyde. } EmmaHarper }	No Record	
137	"	"	Clara Ferris	Han. W. Jennings. } Leased to L. Olcese. }	Louis Olcese, 111 S. Water-st.*
141	"	"	Minnie White	W. C. S. R. R. Co	W. C. S. R. R. Co.
176	"	"	May Willard	Geo. Heath	W. Wood, 827 Op. H.
178	"	"	Dora Lyons	Mary A. Monroe	M. A. Monroe, 184 Cus. H. Pl.
180	"	"	M. A. Monroe	Jane S. Haven	Jane S. Haven, 184 Cus. H. Pl.
182	"	" (col)	Mrs. Morris	Mary A. Monroe	M. A. Monroe, 184 Cus. H. Pl.
117	Plymouth Pl	House of ill-fame	Zoe Owens	Jno. B. Baxter	Jno. B. Baxter, Moreland, Ill.
119 } 125 } 127 }	"	"	Mary Woodson	Mrs. E. W. Knights	C. S. McCoy, 608 Tacoma Bdg.

Anchorage Mission for Fallen Women.

* Mr. Olcese informs me that these premises are held under a lease which expressly provides they shall not be used for any immoral or illegal purpose or in contravention of the ordinances of Chicago or the statutes of Illinois. Neither he nor his agent had ever visited the premises since the lease was granted. "Acting upon information acquired since receiving your communication, I have this day instructed my attorney to cancel the lease and institute proper proceedings to obtain possession of the premises."

449

No.	Street.	Description.	Keeper.	Owner.	Taxes Paid by
145	Plymouth Pl	House of ill-fame	Josie Burnham	Gataina Ailara	Barnes & Parish.
153	"	"	Miss Frankie	A. E. Kent	A. E. Kent.
173	"	"	Nellie Michell	Sophie Miller	H. Miller, 58 Evergreen-av.
175	"	"	Mrs. H. Skinner	A. E. Kent	A. E. Kent.
177	"	"	Dora Claflin	Mrs. Bertha Pollak	Mrs. B. Pollak, 2714 Indiana-av.
181	"	"	Eva Little	John Koch	John Koch, 385 Evanston-av.
183	"	"	Annie Huff	Rudolph Weber	Mrs. H. Weber, 451 State-st.
189	"	"	Ollie Prosser	Catherine Buckley	W. Buckley, 5300 Lexington-av.
191	"	"	Mrs. Parker	B. & P. Mahone	B. & P. Mahone, 1355 State-st.
193	"	"	S. Washington	Edward Fox	Sold to R. Fuller.
197	"	"	Colored Prostitutes.	C. S. Frank.	
205 to 213	"	"	Colored Prostitutes.	A. T. & S. F. R. R No. 205-7-9-13, A. T. S. F. R. R., 211 Jno. Johnson, Jr.	A. T. & S. Fe R. R. Co.
215 to 223	"	"	Colored Prostitutes.	No. 215, F. Knoepfle. Nos. 217-18 & 221, no record. C. S. French. No. 223, A.T.&S.F.R.	
225	"	"	Nannie Powers.		
227	"	"	Nannie Powers.		
2006	Dearborn St.	House of ill-fame	Cora Campbell	Kate Hastings	G. W. Crawford, 1444 Unity blg.
2014	"	"	Nellie Tuttle	Emanuel Pilser	E. Pilser, 34 Randolph-st.
2016	"	"	Clara Dinnick	Mary J. Robbins	M. J. Robbins, 2016 Dearborn-st.
2018	"	"	May Wilson	C. E. Robinson estate	T. H. Schintz, 81 Clark-st.
2020	"	"	Minnie Ross		
2024	"	"	E. Ritchie	E. Ritchie	Bayley & Waldo, Borden blk.
2034	"	"	Mrs. C. Hastings	Jennie B. Walker	D. F. Flannery, 100 Wash't'n-st.
2108	"	"	Ellen Sherman	No record	S. Chadwick, 3010 Wabash-av.
2110	"	"	L. Manning	John J. DeLacy, 2222 Dearborn-st.	Clara Weber, 2913 Dearborn-st.
2112	"	"	Ollie Lavan		J. J. DeLacy, 2222 Dearborn-st.
2116	"	"	Jessie Martin	Matt. Melwery, et al	Libby P. Hardy, 3123 Rhodes-av.
2118	"	"	Madame Lulu	Emma Leronx	Emma Leronx, 2124 Dearb'n-st.
2120	"	"		No record	Sold to W. H. Johnson.
2124	"	"	Annie Honore	Emma Leronx	Emma Leronx, 2124 Dearb'n-st.

No.	Street		Keeper	Mrs. Cath. A. Duffey.	Mrs. C. A. Duffey, 2109 Dearb'n-st.
2109	Dearborn St.	House of ill-fame	Mrs. King } Mrs. Hatfield		
2113	"	"	Mrs. Johnson	James A. Ryan	Jas. A. Ryan, 469 S. Clark-st.
2119	"	"	May Myers	Olof Rudbeck } Cornelia A. Miller	D. F. Crilly, 167 Dearborn-st.
2121	"	"	Mrs. Slater	Mrs. P. A. Stanton	Mrs. Stanton, 2121 Dearborn-st.
2127	"	"	Clara Hudson	Lucretia Brennan	L. Brennan, 2127 Dearborn-st.
2129	"	"	Emma Rose	C. E. Robinson estate	T. H. Schintz, 81 Clark-st.
2131	"	"	Mrs. Allen	Ellen Williams	E. Williams, 2131 Dearborn-st.
2133	"	"	M. Blanchard	J. F. Primky	W. H. Wilson, 209 36 LaSalle-st.
2108	Armour Ave.	"	Mrs. S. Stewart	Jos. Lavin	D. J. Hamilton, 11 Reaper blk.
2106	"	"	Miss Robinson	No record	C. D. Doran, 2107 Clark-st.
2117	"	"	Maggie Jones (col)	No record	A. Ponsely, 2117 Armour-av.
2115	"	"	Madame Brown	Mary F. Wells	T. H. Schintz, 81 Clark-st.
2111	"	"	Miss Lulu	No record	Dan Scott, 3647 Armour-av.
2107	"	"	Allon White	No record	S. Chadwick, 3010 Wabash-av.
2103	"	"	Grace St. Clair	No record	J. H. Lyman, 2103 Armour-av.
2028	"	"	Millie Stern	Harriet F. Storey	J. M. Cliver, 84 LaSalle-st.
2026	"	"	Minnie Shima (Jap)	John E. Oehman	John E. Oehman, 2247 Wentworth-av.
2022	"	"	Nellie Woods		
2014	"	"	Kate Edwards	Edward J. Fisher	Edward J. Fisher, 2015 Clark-st.
2008	"	"	Fannie	Arthur Meyer	J. Thomas, 2006 Armour-av.
2031 } 2033	"	"	Edwards	Wm. E. Wicker	W. J. Maynard by E. Goodrich & Co., 125 LaSalle-st.
2029	"	"	May Harrison	Nettie Maynard	
2027	"	"	Minnie Harlan	John D. Ryan	John D. Ryan, 469 S. Clark-st.
2017	"	"	Lizzie Crane	No record	F. Heldebrand, 2026 Dearborn-st.
2015	"	"	Irene Oakland	C. E. Robinson estate	T. H. Schintz, 81 Clark-st
2011	"	"	Mrs. Wilson		
2009	"	"	Miss Stewart	Catherine Norton	Catherine Foley, 2007 Armour-av.
2007	"	"	Miss Rogers }		

451

It is only just to remember that persons who pay taxes as agents for property have often no means of controlling the disposition of that property. It is also well to state that in many cases the owners of the houses are only owners of the ground on which the houses stand, with next to no power of control over the tenants of the houses built on their land. In other cases they have inherited the property and do not know what to do with it.

It is possible to cancel a lease under the law of the State of Illinois if the tenant uses the premises for immoral purposes, but the difficulty of obtaining legal evidence sufficient to convict is an obstacle in the way of speedy and effective action.

STATE OF ILLINOIS, } ss
CHICAGO, COUNTY OF COOK. }

NORMAN A. LEES, being first duly sworn, deposes and says that the annexed sheets attached to and forming part of this affidavit, have been compiled by him, and that the description of the property duly numbered and tabulated thereon, is to the best of his belief true.   NORMAN A. LEES.

Subscribed and sworn to before me, a Justice of the Peace, for the Town of South Chicago, County of Cook, State of Illinois, this 3d day of January, A. D. 1894.
                                        D. J. LYON, Justice of the Peace.

The foregoing list, as will be seen, does not attempt to include all the houses used for this purpose in Chicago. The field is too wide. I selected two districts, Armour Avenue and the Levee, and instructed a detective and police reporter to make an exhaustive return of the houses used for purposes of prostitution in those districts. When he had done so, I sent another person around to check his information as to names, etc. I then submitted the return so obtained to a competent real estate agent, with instructions to obtain from the official records the name of the owner and the name and address of the tax-payer. In order to avoid any mistake or injustice, inadvertently committed through an error in the returns, I sent notice in the following form to all the tax-payers named in the list.

M.............................   January 12, 1894.

Sir : I find your name in a return prepared for me as paying taxes on premises situate.......................on behalf of the owner.............................

As these premises are described on affidavit in the same return as being openly used as a House of Prostitution. in contravention of Articles 1602—5 of the Municipal Code, I write to ask whether you are aware of the fact, or whether you have any explanations to offer, or corrections to make, before I publish the said list of owners of Houses of Ill Fame in the book on Chicago which I am preparing for the press.   I am your obedient servant,
                                        WILLIAM T. STEAD.

One of the tax-payers informed me that I had rendered myself liable to fine and imprisonment by the mere fact of issuing this circular. It may be so, but I think it would not have been just to have risked including any name in the list without giving ample opportunity for correction and explanation. The list is as precedes, after emendations made in consequence of the issue of this circular.

The foregoing list of houses of ill fame, their keepers, owners, agents, etc., has only been compiled after a very careful inquiry into the matter by a fully competent investigator and a real estate expert. Owing, however, to the constant change of residence on the one hand, and the frequent sale of property on the other, it may not be exactly correct when it meets the eye of the reader. The list *was* correct on Jan. 1st of this year (1894), and it therefore fulfills the purpose for which it was compiled.

Chapter 38, Section 97, of the Criminal Code of the State of Illinois, says :

Whoever keeps or maintains a house of ill fame or place for the practice of prostitution or lewdness, or whoever patronizes the same, or lets any house, room, or other premises for any such purpose, or shall keep a common, ill-governed and disorderly house, to the encouragement of idleness, gaming, drinking, fornication or other misbehavior, shall be fined not exceeding $200. * * * * And whoever shall lease to another any house, room, or other premises, in whole or in part, for any of the uses or purposes finable under this section, or knowingly permits the same to be so used or occupied, shall be fined not exceeding $200, and the house or premises so leased, occupied or used, shall be held liable for and may be sold for any judgment obtained under this section. * * * *

EXTRACT FROM MUNICIPAL CODE OF CHICAGO.

No person shall keep or maintain or be an inmate of, or in any way connected with or in any way contribute to the support of any house of ill fame or assignation, under a penalty of not less than ten dollars for each offense, and the further penalty of one hundred dollars for every twenty-four hours such person shall keep or maintain said house after the first conviction, or after any such person shall have been ordered by any member of the police force to discontinue the same.

Every person found in any house of ill fame or assignation, shall be considered an inmate within the meaning of Section 1602 of this Article.

Every house of ill fame or house of assignation, where men and women resort for the purpose of prostitution, is hereby ordered to be a nuisance.

APPENDIX B.

THE CHICAGO CENTRAL RELIEF ASSOCIATION.

The following are particulars of the Constitution and Objects of the Central Relief Association, formed in December at a conference summoned by the Civic Federation:

President—T. W. Harvey.
Vice-Chairman Executive Committee—C. S. H. Mixer.
Treasurer—Lyman J. Gage.
Chairman Finance Committee—John J. Mitchell.
Auditor—Andrew McLeish.

The Executive Committee is composed exclusively of the chairmen of the various Standing Committees, as follows :

On Finance—J. J. Mitchell.
On City, County and State Relations—Alderman Madden.
On Provisions of Supplies in Food, Fuel, etc. and Storage—C. S. H. Mixer.
On Distribution of Supplies in Kind—Otis S. Favor.
On Transportation—R. A. Waller.
On Shelter of Men—D. J. Harris.
On Shelter and Employment of Women—Dr. Sarah H. Stevenson.
On Hospitals and Homes—Mrs. Potter Palmer.
On Children's Homes—Mrs. J. M. Flower.
On Medical Aid—Dr. Frank S. Johnson.
On Visitation—Professor C. R. Henderson and Professor A. W. Small, Vice Chairman.
On Organization and Co-operation with Charitable Institutions—T. W. Harvey.
On Co-operation with Social Organizations and Clubs—John W. Brooks, Jr.
On Co-operation with Churches and Religious Organizations—P. F. Pettibone.
On Publications and Press—R. A. Waller.
On Auditing—A. McLeish.
On Legal Action—H. B. Hurd.

To the Public: All who give money to men on the streets or at the door are doing harm. They are increasing pauperism, and doing a wrong to the individual and to the State.

Do not give tickets that will entitle the recipient to food or lodging without investigation, or without an equivalent in work.

It is just as harmful to give food, shelter or clothing to the unworthy as it is to give them money, since the one as well as the other gives support to lazy and dishonest people.

Give only such tickets as are provided by reputable institutions, and which refer families or single persons to the various institutions where their case will be investigated, work provided for those who are able, hospitals for those who are sick; fuel, food or money to families who are in distress.

Most of the following institutions issue such tickets either to their members or to the public at large, viz.:

The County Agent, No. 107 South Clinton Street, who cares for permanent paupers or families in which there is no probability of their bettering their condition.

The Chicago Relief and Aid Society, that investigates and cares for families who are usually self-supporting, at its central office, Nos. 51 and 53 La Salle Street, and its various branch offices, as follows: No. 420 Lincoln Avenue, No. 1105 Milwaukee avenue, No. 529 West Monroe Street, No. 317 West Polk Street, No. 380 South Halsted Street, No. 3101 Wabash Avenue, No. 5433 Lake Avenue, No. 395 North Clark Street. Work for married men at their woodyard.

The United Hebrew Charities, No. 223 Twenty-Sixth Street, that relieve suffering and prevent pauperism among the Jewish poor of the city.

The German Relief and Aid Society, at No. 49 La Salle Street, that gives aid to Germans who have been in the city less than three years.

St. Andrew's Society, at No. 1341 Fulton Street, that relieves all deserving Scotchmen.

St. George's Society, at No. 195 Washington Street, grants relief to persons of English parentage.

Danish Relief Society, No. 249 West Chicago Avenue, assists worthy Danish people.

Polish National Alliance, No. 574 Noble Street. This is a National organization holding beneficiary funds, and for the present emergency a general relief committee has been formed, which gives food, fuel and money for rent, to worthy resident Polish families.

Scandinavian Relief Society, at No. 133 North Peoria Street, that aids Swedish, Norwegian and Danish worthy poor. They give relief in the form of provisions and lodgings.

Norwegian Society, corner Peoria and Indiana Streets, that gives immediate temporary relief to all Norwegians.

Bohemian Society, No. 776 West Twelfth Street, that aids all worthy Bohemians. The society has visitors and all worthy cases receive food, coal and clothing, but no money.

Swiss Benevolent Society, No. 49 La Salle Street, to assist indigent Swiss people with pecuniary relief or hospital care.

Soldiers' Home in Chicago, Nos. 51 and 53 La Salle Street, devotes the income from its investments toward relieving indigent soldiers, their widows and children.

The G. A. R., that gives relief to needy soldiers and their widows.

The Brotherhood Employment Bureau, at No. 37 Michigan Street, that gives work to able-bodied men.

The St. Vincent de Paul Society, which has a bureau of relief in every Catholic parish in the city.

The Visiting Nurses' Association, Room 1116 Masonic Temple, furnishes nurses and promotes cleanliness and procures proper care for the sick.

The Young Women's Christian Association, with their various homes and offices, as follows: Home, No. 228 Michigan avenue; transient homes, No. 367 Jackson Boulevard, No. 3528 Wentworth Avenue, No. 6307 Stewart Boulevard; Rosalie Court Home, No. 583 Rosalie Court; employment bureau, No. 243 Wabash Avenue; travelers' aid department, Englewood branch.

Woman's Club Emergency Bureau, Room 29 Athenæum Building, gets situations and gives work and shelter to women.

Minnetonka Workingwoman's Home, No. 21 South Peoria Street, which is a home for self-supporting women, $2.50 per week.

Home for Friendless, No. 1920 Wabash Avenue, free for women and children.

St. Joseph's Home for the Friendless (Catholic), free and pay, No. 409 South May Street.

Home of Providence for Unemployed Girls, Calumet Avenue and Twenty-Sixth Street, Catholic, free and pay.

Adelphia Industrial Home, Austin, Ill., for girls, free.

Workingwoman's Home, No. 529 Monroe Street, free and pay.

Anchorage Mission, No. 125 Plymouth Place, free, for women.

W. C. T. U. Home, No. 870 West Madison Street.

Woman's Shelter, corner Polk and Halsted Streets.

Chicago Exchange for Woman's Work, No. 130 Wabash Avenue, provides a depot for the reception and sale of any marketable article which a woman can make in her own home, or any valuable article which her necessities oblige her to dispose of.

Masonic, Odd Fellows, and other brotherhood organizations care for their own members.

The various free dispensaries, of which there are twenty-two in the city.

Bureau of Justice to assist in securing legal protection against injustice for those who are unable to protect themselves.

For information concerning applicants for relief of which you are in doubt as to the proper reference, apply to No. 82 Market Street, to the Central Relief Association.

For information concerning the work of societies doing relief work in Chicago apply to the Central Relief Association, No. 1015 The Rookery. They refer to all the various institutions to which any applicant may properly belong. They are now preparing an alphabetical list by names and street numbers, in which all those who are receiving aid will be recorded, and which can be examined by any citizen who desires to know what any society may be doing, thereby preventing fraud and duplication, and also furthering the work of properly aiding the worthy poor.

There are many hospitals and homes which are known to our citizens generally, for men, women and children, and there are various reformatory institutions of which information may be had at the office of the Central Relief Association, No. 1015 Rookery Building.

Information concerning other relief societies will be published as soon as the committee on co-operation have the facts ready for publication.

By order of Executive Committee.

T. W. HARVEY, Chairman.

APPENDIX C.

SOME CURIOSITIES OF CHICAGO ASSESSMENTS.

The present system of assessing real and personal property in Chicago has been denounced as scandalous and unjust, iniquitous and contrary to sound policy by the Mayor of Chicago, by successive Comptrollers, and by the Finance Committee of the City Council. It has been vehemently assailed by the Chicago *Times*, which has published a series of articles commenting in the strongest terms upon the injustice and the disparity of the taxes levied upon the poor property owner, who pays through the nose while his rich neighbor goes comparatively scot free. The facts, however, are so startling and the figures so strong that it is impossible to frame a statement which is more damning than a few extracts from the tax books. In order to see how things stood I instructed a real estate agent to go through the official returns and extract from them the assessments of real and personal property made in the cases of most prominent people in Chicago, including the millionaires, the aldermen, the members of the Civic Federation and the newspapers, etc. I also instructed him to obtain the assessments of the more notable buildings in the city, and for the purpose of comparison to obtain the assessed value of various smaller premises owned by wage workers and others. The returns which he has made will be scrutinized with keen interest in Chicago, and they will afford much matter for curious comment elsewhere. The returns would have been much more complete if it would have been possible to have employed a real estate valuer to have made a really fair valuation, but this is difficult, especially in the case of personalty. I could not send a valuer into the stables of a millionaire, nor could I introduce a competent assessor into the domesticities of Mr. Yerkes. There seems to be no reason to doubt the general correctness of the statement that taking the city all around the assessed value is only one-eighth of the real value. The owners of small houses are often assessed at one-fourth, one-third, and even one-half of their real value, while the owners of the mansions and the sky-scrapers escape with one-tenth, one-twentieth, or even one-thirtieth of their real value. The following is a table of some of the curiosities of Chicago assessments. Personalty to the amount of $500 to $1,000 is exempt from taxation.

SOME CURIOSITIES.

Owners, Clinton J. Warren and Adolphus W. Maltby, Lots 82, 83, 86, 87, 90, 91, 94, 95, 98, except east 49 feet of lots 91, 94, 95 and 98, Burton's subdivision of lot 14, Boonson's addition to Chicago. $95,000.

"Plaza." Seven-story apartment. South-east corner Clark and North Avenue. 1892 assessed value $10,000. Taxes paid, $982.80. 1893 assessed value $30,060.

U. S. Brewing Co. (4824 Cook Street.) 1893 returned personal property at $50.00.

Union Rendering Company, Stockyards. 1893 returned the following personal property : 25 horses, $250; 11 wagons, $110; one safe, $15.00. Total $390.

Four-story brick building, Milwaukee and North Avenue. (Stores below and hall on top.) Worth at least $20,000, assessed in 1893 at $1,830, or one-eleventh. Owned by Joseph Sokup, formerly West Town Assessor.

West Chicago Street Railroad Company personalty is assessed at $275,000.

Chicago City Railway Company is assessed $260,000 for personalty. 180 horses assessed at $8,000; 500 cars, at $50,000; machinery, etc., at $100,000, and money at $100,000.

North Chicago Street Railroad Company returns $65,500 personalty, of which the following are some of the items ; 200 horses, $2,800 ; 220 cars, $20,000 ; machinery, $25,000.

ALDERMEN.

Ward.		Personal.
1st.	John J. Coughlin, 145 E. Madison-st	Nothing.
	Louis I. Epstean, 113 E. Randolph-st	"
2d.	Daniel J. Horan, 169 Eighteenth-st	"
	Martin Best, 1429 Michigan-av	"
3d.	Edward Marrener, 3227 Groveland-av	"
	Eli Smith, 3147 Vernon-av	$100.00
4th.	John W. Hepburn, 3633 Ellis-av	Nothing.
	Martin B. Madden, 3563 Forest-av	"
5th.	John Vogt, 448 Twenty-sixth-st	"
	Patrick J. Wall, 605 Twenty-seventh-st	"
6th.	Henry Stuckart, 2519 Archer-av., 3 horses, $300; 3 cows, $400	$800.00
	Thomas Reed, 2500 Main-st	Nothing.
7th.	John A. Cook, 624 S. Halsted-st	"
	William J. O'Neill, 547 S. Halsted-st	"
8th.	William Loeffler, 369 Johnson-st	"
	Martin Morrison, 362 Blue Island-av	"
9th.	Frederick Rohde, 278 Washburne-av	"
	Joseph E. Bidwell, 736 W. Twelfth-st	"
10th.	Charles C. Schumacher, 266 Blue Island-av	"
	John F. Dorman, 971 Twenty-second-st	"
11th.	George B. Swift, 52 Loomis-st	"
	William D. Kent, 450 W. Congress-st	"
12th.	Robert L. Martin, 719 W. Van Buren-st	$200.00
	James L. Campbell, 99 DeKalb-st	Nothing.
13th.	Charles F. Swigart, 280 Park-av	"
	Martin Knowles, 337 Walnut-st	"
14th.	James Keats, 225 W. Chicago-av	"
	William L. Kamerling, 339 Glenwood-av	"
15th.	James Reddick, 143 Perry-av	"
	Michael Ryan, 601 W. North-av	"
16th.	Peter J. Ellert, 482 N. Ashland-av	
	Stanley H. Kunz, 685 W. North-av	Nothing.
17th.	J. N. Mulvihill, 118 Austin-av	"
	Stephen M. Gosselin, 182 N. Green-st	"
18th.	William F. Mahony, 74 Center-av	"
	John J. Brennan, 15 S. Carpenter-st	"
19th.	John Powers, 243 S. Canal and 170 Madison-sts., saloons	"
	Thomas Gallagher, 256 S. Halsted-st	"

Ward.		Personal.
20th.	Albert Potthoff, 97 Willow-st.................................	Nothing.
	Otto Hage, 185 Southport-av..............................	"
21st.	Joseph H. Ernst, 271 E. North-av.........................	"
	John McGillen, 967 N. Halsted-st.........................	"
22d.	Arnold Tripp, 596 Dearborn-av............................	
	Edward Muelhoeffer, 112 Clybourn-av....................	$200.00
23d.	John A. Larson, 305 N. Wells-st...........................	Nothing.
	William J. Kelly, 168 Oak-st..............................	"
24th.	Louis L. Wadsworth, 252 Michigan-st....................	$100.00
	Zara C. Peck, 238 E. Huron..............................	Nothing.
25th.	Austin O. Sexton, 1457 Wrightwood-av..................	"
	Albert H. Kleinecke, 914 Racine-av......................	"
26th.	Henry N. Lutter, Perry-av. and Wellington-st...........	"
	William Finkler, 843 Perry-av............................	"
27th.	Frederick F. Hanssen, 15 W. Huron-st...................	"
	M. J. Conway, Hermosa.................................	"
28th.	Daniel W. Ackerman.....................................	Nothing.
	Thomas Sayle..	"
29th.	Robert Mulcahy, 4335 Wentworth-av.....................	"
	Thomas Carey, 4304 S. Wood-st..........................	"
30th.	John F. Kenny, 5205 State-st.............................	"
	John W. Utesch, 4836 S. Ashland-av.....................	"
31st.	Edwin J. Noble, 6621 Harvard-st.........................	"
	James L. Francis, 7757 Sherman-st.......................	"
32d.	James R. Mann, 334 Oakwood-bd.........................	$100.00
	William R. Kerr, 5126 Washington-av....................	$200.00
33d.	Cyrus H. Howell, 7828 Edwards-av.......................	$ 50.00
	George H. Shepherd, 9151 Commercial-av................	Nothing.
34th.	John A. Bartine, Roseland................................	"
	John O'Neill, 5900 Wabash-av............................	"

Sixty-eight Aldermen, $1,700. Average personal property, $26.

THE MONOPOLIES.

The Railroads (1892).....................................	$16,698,589
City Railway Co., (1893).................................	1,350,000
West Chicago Railway Co., (1893)........................	1,000,000
North Chicago Railway Co., (1893).......................	500,000
Chicago Gas Light and Coke Company....................	700,000
Consumers Gas Company.................................	250,000
People's Gas Light and Coke Company...................	250,000
Hyde Park Gas Company.................................	5,000
Lake Gas Company.......................................	5,000
Telephone Company......................................	2,100,000

THE NEWSPAPERS.

Name.	Personalty. 1893.	Realty 1892.	Taxes on Realty.
Record and Daily News......................	$15,000	$ 8,700	$ 742.
Herald.....................................	18,000	49,800	4,250
Tribune....................................	18,000	35,000	2,987
Inter Ocean...............................	11,000	76,000	6,486
Times......................................	......	7,500	......
Evening Post..............................	7,500	25,200	2,150
Evening Journal...........................	7,000	12,000	1,024
Mail.......................................	2,600	......	......
Dispatch...................................	300	......	......
Staats Zeitung.............................	6,000	32,400	2,765

NAME.	HORSES.		CAR-RIAGES.		PIANOS.		TOTAL.		TAXES ON REALTY, 1892.
	No.	Value.	No.	Value.	No.	Value.	Personal. 1893.	Realty. 1892.	
NEWSPAPER PROPRIETORS—EDITORS.									
Joseph Medill, 101 Cass-st.............	2	$200	2	$500	1	$100	$2,600	$11,130	$1,093
H. H. Kohlsaat, 2978 Prairie-ave......	3	60	1	30	..	.....	1,500	13,760	1,174
Wm. Penn Nixon, 743 N. Clark-st....	..	....	..	....	..	.....	300	....	......
*Carter H. Harrison. 231 Ashland-bd..	2	50	2	50	1	25	300	30,000	2,695
J. W. Scott, 184 Pine-st.................	..	....	..	....	1	100	300	....	......
John R. Walsh, 2133 Calumet-av.......	1	20	1	30	1	50	1,000	9,800	836
Victor F. Lawson, 317 La Salle-av....	..	....	..	....	1	100	300		
R. W. Patterson, Astor-st & Burton-pl.	..	....	..	....	..	.....	Nothing.	....	......
MILLIONAIRES AND OTHERS.									
Marshall Field, 1905 Prairie-ave......	6	$120	6	180	1	180	20,000	....	......
Marshall Field, Jr., 1919 Prairie-av...	2	40	2	60	..	.....	2,000	....	......
P. D. Armour, 2115 Prairie-av.........	..	....	..	....	..	.....	5,000		
G. M. Pullman, 1729 Prairie-av	10	200	6	180	1	150	12,000	36,000	3,072
Potter Palmer, 100 Lake Shore-dr.....	10	600	6	600	1	125	15,000	51,220	5,033
H. N. Higinbotham, 2838 Michigan-av	10	200	5	150	2	100	2,000	32,420	2,767
J. W. Doane, 1827 Prairie-av.........	5	100	5	140	1	150	10,000		
Mrs. Wm. Armour, 2017 Prairie-av....	4	100	3	100	1	50	7,500	12,500	1,066
*C. H. McCormick, 321 Huron-st.....	1	50	2	200	..	....	10,650	42,580	4,184
C. T. Yerkes, 3201 Michigan-av.......	2	300	1	1,000	1	1,700	4,000		
Lambert Tree, 94 Cass-st..............	3	300	2	300	1	100	2,000	27,910	2,742
Edward S. Isham, 1 Tower-pl.........	5	250	2	250	..	....	2,000	13,450	1,321
Wm. G. Hibbard, 1701 Prairie-av	..	....	..	....	..	....	2,500		
C. M. Henderson, 1816 Prairie-av.....	6	120	2	60	..	....	8,000	11,900	1,015
T. W. Harvey, 1702 Prairie-av.........	2	40	2	60	..	....	3,000	17,680	1,508
*Frank'n MacVeagh,103LakeShore-dr	5	500	4	1,000	1	200	2,500	16,750	1,646
O. W. Potter, 130 Lake Shore-dr......	..	....	..	....	..	....	1,500	12,030	1,182
Volney C. Turner, 112 Lake Shore-dr.	..	....	..	....	..	....	2,500	15,900	1,562
E. W. Blatchford, 375 La Salle-av....	2	200	2	200	1	200	3,300	20,280	1.903
Lyman J. Gage, 470 N. State-st.......	..	....	..	....	1	100	1,000	9,610	944
Henry Keith, 3360 Prairie-av...........	..	....	..	....	..	....	100		
W. W. Kimball, 1801 Prairie-av.......	..	....	..	....	..	....	2,100	....	......
Elbridge G. Keith, 1900 Prairie-av....	..	....	..	....	.	....	3,000	....	......
Edson Keith, 1906 Prairie-av.........	..	....	..	....	.	....	4,000	....	......
Mrs. C. P. Kellogg, 1923 Prairie-av...	..	....	..	....	.	....	4,000	....	......
Fernando Jones, 1834 Prairie-av......	..	....	..	....	.	....	1,200	....	......
Mrs. H. O. Stone, 2035 Prairie-av....	2	40	3	90	1	40	1,100	....	......
S. W. Allerton, 1936 Prairie-av.......	5	150	5	150	1	50	8,000	41,600	3,550
Chas. D. Hamill, 2126 Prairie-av......	..	....	..	....	..	....	2,250	7,620	650
Henry C. Rew, 2619 Prairie-av........	..	....	3	100	..	....	1,500	7,500	640
Noble B. Judah, 2701 Prairie-av......	..	....	..	....	..	....	300	3,660	312
Marvin Hughitt, 2828 Prairie-av......	2	100	1	100	..	....	300	5,500	469
John G. Shortall, 1600 Prairie-av......	..	....	..	....	..	....	2,000	5,300	452
P. E. Studebaker, 1612 Prairie-av.....	4	40	3	90	1	50	1,500	4,050	345
Granger Farwell, 1623 Prairie-av.....	..	....	..	....	.	....	Nothing.	3,040	259
Mrs. Wirt Dexter, 1721 Prairie-av.....	3	60	3	90	1	50	3,750	1,350	1,152
Richard T. Crane, 2541 Michigan-av..	5	250	3	150	1	100	3,000	22,900	1,954
Warren Springer, 1635 Prairie-av......	..	....	..	....	..	....	Nothing.	4,550	388
John Mason Loomis, 55 Lake Shore-dr	6	300	6	300	1	100	2,500	9,980	980
Henry J. Willing, 110 Rush-st	..	....	..	....	1	200	2,000	8,870	871
Henry W. Bishop, 167 Rush-st........	..	....	..	....	1	100	600	3,420	336
†John P. Hopkins, 2813 Calumet-av...	..	....	..	....	1	20	150	....	......
Hempstead Washburne, 154 Astor-st..	2	100	2	100	..	500	500	2,800	275
Dewitt C. Cregier, 418 Chicago-av.....	..	....	..	....	..	....	Nothing.	1,180	115
*Judge C. C. Kohlsaat, 239 Ashland-av	..	....	..	....	..	....	200	3,400	305
Richard Prendergast, 534 Jackson-bd	..	....	..	....	..	.....	Nothing.	1,320	118

NAME.	HORSES.		CARRIAGES.		PIANOS.		TOTAL.		TAXES ON REALTY, 1892.
	No.	Value.	No.	Value.	No.	Value.	Personal. 1893.	Realty. 1892.	
*Judge R. Tuthill, 532 W. Jackson-bl..	..	....	..	....	1	50	100	......	......
*Charles H. Case, 201 Ashland-av.....	2	50	2	50	1	25	500	9,100	817
*Wm. A. Pinkerton, 196 Ashland-av..	2	50	2	50	1	50	400	4,400	395
Mrs. Owsley, 245 Ashland-av.........	..	....	..	....	..	....	200	9,000	808
*George R. Davis, 692 Washington-bd	1	25	1	25	1	25	100	2,520	226
J. B. Hobbs, 343 La Salle-av...........	1	50	1	50	1	100	550	3,900	383
Robert Lindblom, 678 La Salle-av							600	......	......
Malcolm McNeill, 448 La Salle-av....	3	90	2	80	1	30	400	4,140	406
Harry Rubens, 581 La Salle-av........	..	....	..	....	..	....	Nothing.	2,140	210
John DeKoven, 402 Dearborn-av......	5	200	2	100	1	50	950	8,170	802
A. A. Munger, 308 E. Ohio-st..........	..	....	..	....	..	....	Nothing.	2,100	206
John M. Smyth, 300 W. Adams-st.....	..	....	..	....	..	....	Nothing.	4,250	382
Peter Schuttler, 289 W. Adams-st.....	..	....	..	....	..	....	Nothing.	23,900	2,147
Carrie V. Watson, 441 S. Clark-st.....	4	500	2	700	2	300	4,000	4,300	367
Vina Fields, 138 Custom House-pl.....	..	....	..	....	4	200	400	......	......
*J. J. Badenoch, 391 W. Randolph-st..	4	100	2	50	..	....	200	......	......
*W. P. Rend, 153 Ashland-av..........	2	100	1	100	..	....	500	......	......
Louis Wolff, 1319 Washington-bd.....	3	75	2	50	1	50	500	......	......
*Daniel W. Mills, 1510 Washington-bd	4	100	2	100	1	50	350	......	......
‡L. Z. Leiter, 4 Tower-pl.............	2	100	3	150	..	....	1,000	......	......

*Returned personal property.
†In the name of Mary Hopkins.
‡In the name of Joseph Leiter.
Potter Palmer returns 5 watches, $100; one billiard table, $100; one sewing machine, $25.
E. W. Blatchford returns gold and silver worth $300, diamonds worth $400.
John Mason Loomis returned gold and silver worth $100, diamonds worth $200, one sewing machine, $10.
John DeKoven returned 2 watches worth $100.
Henry J. Willing returned gold and silver to the amount of $200, and diamonds valued at $600.
Lyman J. Gage has one watch, $100, gold and silver, $100, and diamonds, $100.

SKYSCRAPERS.

Building.	Assessed.	Equalized.	Taxes.	Paid by.	Per Cent.
Masonic Temple $284,700		$350.181	$24,299	Masonic Temple Assoc.	1-13
Tacoma Building...... 93,000		114,390	7,987	Wirt de Walker.........	1-14
Unity Building........ 161,800		199,014	13,809	John W. Lachard (Agt.)	1-14
Auditorium Building.. 305,500		375,765	26,074	Chicago Auditorium Co.	1-14
Siegel, Cooper & Co... 254,000		312,420	21,678	{ L. Z. Leiter and Siegel, Cooper & Co........... }	1-14
Monadnock Building.. 300,500		368,615	25,647	Owen F. Aldis..........	1-14
Palmer House......... 40,000					

THE RICH AND THE POOR.

The following comparative figures are extracted from the *Chicago Times*, which has addressed itself to this subject with great energy and perseverance :

	Actual Value.	Assessed Value.	Per Cent.
Pullman Building, Michigan-av. and Adams-st.........$1,200,000		$ 85,000	1-14
Title and Trust Building, 100 Washington-st............ 1,500,000		158,000	1-10
Ashland Block, Clark and Randolph-sts................ 1,800,000		153,000	1-8
Woman's Temple, Monroe and LaSalle-sts 1,800,000		230,000	1-8
Chamber of Commerce Bldg, LaSalle and Wash'gn-sts. 2,225,000		225,000	1-10

	Actual Value.	Assessed Value.	Per Cent.
Hartford Building, Madison and Dearborn-sts.........	$1,000,000	$110,000	1-9
Rand-McNally Building, Adams and Quincy-sts........	1,600,000	160,000	1-10
Rookery Building, LaSalle and Adams-sts..............	1,600,000	200,000	1-8
Security Building, Fifth-av. and Madison-st............	750,000	75,800	1-10
Manhattan Building, 307-321 Dearborn-st	1,800,000	90,000	1-20
Monon Building, 320-326 Dearborn-st	800,000	37,700	1-21
Edward Morgan's cottage, 3141 Dearborn-st............	1,700	527	1-2
W. J. Miesler's store, 587 Sedgwick-st	3,500	1,109	1-3
Mathias Boesen's building, 300 Mohawk-st.............	4,500	1,100	1-4
C. E. Carlstrom's building, 190 Milton-av..............	1,600	400	1-4
James McCombie's store, Twenty-fifth and State-sts....	2,500	1,743	3-5
R. W. Lemke's building, 167 Wells-st...................	4,000	900	1-4
P. D. Lynch's residence, W. 47th and Monroe-sts.......	2,000	500	1-4
Fred G. Libke's shop, 248 Milwaukee-av	2,200	1,100	1-2
David Kahn's store, 114 Chicago-av....................	8,000	2,000	1-4
F. A. Ruck's store, 273 Wells-st.......................	7,200	1,800	1-4
M. McNulty's residence, 138 Seminary-av..............	2,000	517	1-4
C. L. Young's residence, 613 Melrose-st................	4,000	1,600	2-5
Robert Berndt's building...............................	2,000	1,050	1-2

THE FAIR SELLING VALUE OF COOK COUNTY.

Statement of property assessed for the year 1892 in Cook County (including the city of Chicago), as returned to the Auditor's office:

Description.	No.	Value.	Average.
Horses..	37,216	$879,335	$ 23.63
Cattle..	35,303	241,852	6.85
Mules and asses......................................	245	4,588	18.73
Sheep..	1,453	1,479	1.02
Hogs...	7,674	8,616	1.12
Steam engines including boilers....................	563	156,410	277.82
Fire and burglar proof safes........................	432	15,885	36.77
Billiard, pigeonhole, etc., tables	169	5,074	30.02
Carriages and wagons	25,068	586,474	23.40
Watches and clocks.................................	5,989	28,113	4.69
Sewing and knitting machines	4,266	24,326	5.70
Pianos	11,066	373,896	23.79
Melodeons and organs	439	4,510	10.27
Franchises.	10	50,463	6.30
Annuities and royalties	......	....	5.04
Patent rights	......	....	......
Steamboats, sailing vessels	239	52,010	217.61
Materials and manufacturing articles,............			1,157,743
Manufacturers' tools, implements and machinery......................			1,181,838
Agricultural tools, implements and machinery..........................			61,911
Gold and silver plate and plated ware.			16,460
Diamonds and jewelry			21,000
Moneys of bank, banker, broker, etc...................................			1,097,755
Credits of bank, broker, etc			8,200
Moneys of other than banker, etc.......................................			970,129
Credits of other than banker, etc.......................................			123,605
Bonds and stocks..			6,670
Shares of capital stock of companies not of this State			500
Pawnbroker's property..			5,350
Property of corporations not before enumerated			1,776,213
Bridge property...			710
Property of saloons and eating houses..................................			15,625
Household and office furniture...			3,090,975
Investments in real estate and improvements thereon...................			14,845
Grain of all kinds..			2,625
Shares of stock of State and National banks			5,903,550
All other property..			489,123
Total value of unenumerated property.................................			27,974,158
Total value of personal property			30,407,189

REAL ESTATE—LANDS

	Number of Acres.	Value.	Average Value per Acre.
Improved	362,729	$7,777,776	$21 44
Unimproved	97,040	6,702,363	69.07

REAL ESTATE—TOWN AND CITY LOTS.

Description.	No. of Lots.	Value.	Average Value.
Improved town and city lots	167,094	$126,394,249	$756.43
Unimproved lots	470,822	31,052,151	66.00

APPENDIX D.

THE FEDERATION OF MINISTERS OF RELIGION.

The Executive Committee of the Federation of the Ministers of Religion in Chicago is one of the many signs indicating a desire on the part of the ministers to exercise a more effective influence upon the affairs of the city by means of co-operative action. The question as to whether or not the Ministers of Religion could come together as a body had been discussed, but it was not until the 11th of December that any actual step was taken towards bringing the subject to a test. On that day I summoned a conference in the Willard Hall for the purpose, which was defined as follows : "To take counsel as to the best means of convincing the masses that the Church of God is the agency which can best help them to redress their grievances and realize their aspirations for a better social condition." A copy of the circular summoning the conference was sent to every minister of religion designated as such in the Chicago directory. The conference thus summoned was influentially attended, and after a meeting lasting about two hours, it was resolved to form a committee representing the churches of all denominations to convey the greetings of the Ministers of Religion to the American Federation of Labor, which was then meeting in Chicago. The same committee was also instructed to attend the conference summoned by the American Federation to discuss the question of the relief of the unemployed. This committee was to report to the adjourned conference which was held a week later. The representatives named by the conference attended the Federation of Labor and expressed their hearty sympathy with the object of the labor unions. They were very courteously received by the President, and there was a feeling on both sides that the visit was timely and useful. The committee also attended the conference summoned by the Civic Federation, at which the Central Relief Association was founded.

On December 18, the adjourned conference met in order to discuss the question as to how the Church of God in Chicago could best be organized as a unit for the relief of the poor and for the realization in Chicago of the prayer: "Thy will be done on earth as it is in Heaven." Accompanying the circular summoning the conference there was appended a schedule of information which it was suggested would facilitate the work of the conference if it were filled in by each minister of religion.

As a number of inquiries have been made as to this schedule, it may be well to reprint it here.

Ward No....   Precinct No....

IF THE CHURCH OF CHICAGO WERE ORGANIZED AS A UNIT.

I would undertake to be responsible in the name of my church and congregation for the district lying between........on the north, and........on the south, and between........on the east, and........on the west.

Estimated population..... ; of above....are church goers, and....non-English speaking.

Our church building seats....persons, and is occupied....days in the week. We have....rooms available for social or civic service, seating....persons. Of these.... are occupied....days in the week.

We have....enrolled members of above.   ....are engaged more or less actively in church work. In the Sunday School....children are on the books and....teachers, with an average attendance of......

In connection with our church we have the following branches of social work in progress:

Temperance..
Purity...
Economics...
Civic Duties...
Education..
Philanthropy ....
Music..
Sanitation...
Recreation...

The capital invested in our church buildings, etc . is about................Dollars and we raise annually for all purposes..............Dollars.

In the district for which my church is responsible, the following are among the influences detrimental to the social welfare: We have....places of business open on Sunday, which deprive....employes of their weekly rest from labor.

We have....saloons and houses for the sale of intoxicants. Of these....are of average character, ...are bad, and....are very bad.

We have....notorious houses of ill fame, containing....inmates. There are... massage houses with....inmates, and....other resorts maintained for purposes of immorality.

We have....gaming houses and....resorts of betting men.

We have....sweating shops, or factories, where....men,....women and... children work in conditions of labor which render it impossible for them to be either happy, healthy or human.

Among the agencies of service in the district in all of which my church is more or less actively interested are the following :

Police station with....policemen,....schools with... scholars,....school attendance officers and....teachers,....playgrounds for children.....covered playrooms, ...Happy Evenings Associations,....gymnasia....Recreative Evenings Associations for youths,....technical classes,....cooking classes,....university extension lectures,....public reading room,....people's institutes,....temperance saloons, ... drinking fountains,....temperance societies,....night refuges,....good lodging houses,....labor registries,....labor unions' offices,....thrift agencies,....relief agencies,....maternity homes,....homes for deserted children,....societies for crippled and blind,....hospitals,....convalescent homes.....sick nurses.....visitors of sick,....fresh air fund,....flower mission,....early closing associations,....Sunday rest associations,....societies for prevention of cruelty to animals.

(Signed)...Minister.
        Address................................ ....
        Of the...Church
        Address...
                ....

DENOMINATION...

The attempt was nearly shipwrecked by objections taken to the admission of Catholics, Jews and Unitarians. Were they Ministers of Religion? What was Religion? I answered, "Pure religion and undefiled before our God and Father is this, to visit the fatherless and widows in their affliction, and to keep himself unspotted from the world."

The objectors collapsed, and after a somewhat desultory discussion a committee of organization was appointed with instructions to meet as soon as possible and to report what should be done, both in relation to the relief of the poor, and for the effective realization of the force of the Church of God in the cause of righteousness. This committee decided to put itself in communication with the Relief Association, and to undertake what could be done in the way of districting the city, and organizing a house to house visitation which was necessitated by existing distress. They further determined to constitute an Executive Committee which would represent all denominations, including the Catholics and the Jews, for the purpose of carrying out the rest of the programme. This Executive Committee, which met for the first time on January 15, had before it the question of securing one day's rest in seven for the Retail Clerks. Mr. O'Brien of the Retail Clerks' Association attended and made a statement, calling attention to the extent to which the action of three individuals in the various districts of the town impeded the closing of stores in the evening, and also made a statement as to the reasons which induced the Retail Clerks to appeal to the City Council for the purpose of securing legal protection for one day's rest in seven. The Rev. Jenkin Lloyd Jones was appointed to see the Chairman of the Judiciary Committee, to which the ordinance had been referred by the Council. On January 22, the committee met and passed a resolution assuring Mayor Hopkins of the support of the churches if his administration would keep the gaming houses closed. On January 29, it was decided to hold a conference at some future date at the Willard Hall, for the purpose of uniting all the churches in the campaign for honesty and pure government at the aldermanic elections.

The Executive Committee represents all the churches, as will be seen from the following list:

Baptist—Rev. O. P. Gifford, D. D., 4543 Greenwood Avenue.
Independent—Prof. David Swing, D. D., 66 Lake Shore Drive.
Jewish—Rabbi Emil G. Hirsch, D. D., 3612 Grand Boulevard.
Reformed Episcopal—Bishop Samuel Fallows, D. D., 967 West Monroe Street.
Unitarian—Rev. Jenkin Lloyd Jones, D. D., 3939 Langley Avenue.
Episcopal—Rev. Floyd Tomkins, D. D., 310 Superior St.
Methodist—Rev. Arthur Edwards, D. D., 57 Washington Street.
Rev. R. S. Martin, D. D., 142 Locust Street.
Prof. A. W. Small, Ph. D., Chicago University.
Prof. Graham Taylor, D. D., West Side Theological Seminary.
Lutheran—Prof. R. F. Weidner, D. D., 1311 Sheffield Avenue.
Presbyterian—Rev. J. G. Inglis, D. D., 6518 Woodlawn Park.
Congregational—Rev. J. G. Johnson, D. D., 7 Ritchie Place.
Rev. R. A. Torrey, D. D., Moody's Bible Institute.
Presbyterian—Rev. Thomas C. Hall, D. D., 425 North State Street.
WM. A. BURCH, Secretary, Argyle Park.

But before long it is hoped that a Catholic priest may be found who will be willing to serve side by side with his brethren outside the Roman fire in the interest of the city.

It was not intended to have any elaborate organization but it was proposed that the committee should meet fortnightly and on occasion when questions arose of sufficient importance they would summon all the Ministers of Religion in Chicago to a conference to concert action and to consider what should be done.

The task of organizing the ministers of religion as a whole has been made in several towns in the United Kingdom and has been partially successful in some towns in the United States. One of the earliest efforts made in the United Kingdom was made at Newcastle-on-Tyne and in Liverpool, where representative conferences were called consisting of representatives of all the churches for purposes of discussing such questions as gambling, the social evil, drunkenness, the treatment of the poor and so forth. In England the concerted action of ministers of religion has been for the most part upon less broad lines than those laid down in Chicago. In Bradford, Birmingham, Halifax and Leeds, and other similar towns where the ministers have met together and have undertaken a house to house visitation for the purpose of making a census of church attendants and a list of all children of school age in the Sunday Schools, there has been an attempt to exclude the Unitarians and neither the Catholics nor the Episcopalians have taken part in the work. It is thought possible that in Chicago where the differences are not so marked as in the Old World ministers of all religions and all creeds may unite in common effort in order to survey the city as a whole from the point of view of the Church of God in order to ascertain what districts remain to be occupied and what work there is which they can better undertake collectively than otherwise.

The questions raised at the Central Music Hall meeting seem to have made a deep impression upon one of the papers, where it least might have been expected. The *Chicago Mail* ever since the Music Hall meetings has been publishing articles more or less avowedly suggested by the discussion on that occasion. Its first series was in reference to the vices of the city to which reference has been made in the text of this book. The second was an attempt to ascertain the amount of capital locked up in church buildings in Chicago, the number of church members and the total annual revenue raised by them from all sources. The *Mail* set out with a thesis of its own to prove, its object being to impress upon the minds of the public that the millions sunk in church property were more or less wasted and that the amount spent in running the churches of Chicago was far in excess of what was justifiable considering the hardship of the times and the ideal poverty of primitive Christianity. Suppose, said the *Mail*, with all reverence and love, the Man of Nazareth were to come to Chicago to-day and survey the work of the churches, what would He think of it all? The leaven seems to be working although in strange places. We may not agree with all the answers made to the question but the fact that it is being asked on all sides is a hopeful sign for the future spiritual and social life of Chicago.

The following is a table summarizing the results of the *Mail's* uncritical inquiry :

DENOMINATIONS.	Number of Members.	Church Expenses.	Missions, etc.	Value of Property.
Congregational..................	10,890	$103,328	$168,623	$1,069,500
Methodist Episcopal..................	15,703	170,824	38,205	2,378,600
Presbyterian......................	12,941	267,637	107,071	1,910,000
Episcopal	23,247	357,907	47,351	3,000,000
Baptist	12,228	178,072	41,971	1,233,000
Universalist	900	39,200	1,750	256,000
Unitarian	1,200	34,000	2,000	485,000
Jewish.............................	1,115	82,000	49,700	435,000
Reformed Episcopal	1,108	23,530	9,364	231.000
Lutheran	58,000	188,500	....	1,550,000
Outside Lutheran	50,000	85,000	....	1,000,000
Roman Catholic......................	500,000	635.900	....	9,220,000
Total	687,341	$2,055,897	$466,035	$22,679,100

APPENDIX E.

THE CIVIC FEDERATION OF CHICAGO.

At the Conference which I held in Central Music Hall in November, 1893, I had an opportunity of setting forth the idea of a Civic Church or Federation of all good citizens, in the hearing of a large and representative audience. After some discussion it was unanimously decided to choose a committee of nominators who should call together a representative committee of leading citizens for the purpose of discussing the question with a view to action. That committee was chosen and in due course of time it evolved the body known as the Civic Federation of Chicago.

The following is the Chronology of the foundation of the Civic Federation of Chicago, the text of the Constitution and the names of the members and officers:

Nov. 12, 1893.—Formation of Civic Federation suggested and approved at meeting at Central Music Hall and committee of nominators of a temporary committee of inquiry appointed: Mr. T. W. Harvey (Business), Miss Addams (Philanthropy), Rev. Dr. Thomas (Religion), Professor Bemis (Education), and Mr. O'Brien (Labor.)

Nov. 17. —The following was the form of notice sent out by T. W. Harvey, as the Chairman of the Committee of Nomination, to those nominated to serve on the Joint Executive Committee:

The committee named at the Central Music Hall meeting Sunday night to appoint an Executive Committee to take in charge the establishment of the proposed Civic Federation in this city, begs leave to inform you of your appointment as a member of the committee.

The object of this organization, briefly and in general terms, is the concentration into one potential, non-political, non-sectarian center all the forces that are now laboring to advance our municipal, philanthropic, industrial and religious interests, and to accomplish all that is possible towards energizing and giving effect to the public conscience of Chicago.

It is not expected to accomplish all this in one day, but all great movements must have a beginning, and a consultation with a great many of our leading citizens of all classes who desire to see Chicago one of the best governed, the healthiest and cleanest city in this country, leads us to believe that now is the time to begin. Especially do we believe it opportune that such a movement should begin while our people are yet filled with the new ideas, new ambitions and inspirations drawn from the great Exposition and its most valuable adjunct, the World's Congresses. An early acceptance of this appointment is earnestly desired.

Dec. —Committee nominates a provisional committee.
First meeting at the Palmer House.
Conference summoned on the condition of unemployed.
Central Relief Association formed.
Jan. —Committee appointed on organization, Judge Collins, Dr. Hirsch, Prof. Small and Mr. Easley.
Feb. 3, 1894.—Civic Federation incorporated at Springfield.

INCORPORATORS.

T. W. Harvey,	J. J. McGrath,	Lyman J. Gage,
A. C. Bartlett,	Ada C. Sweet,	M. J. Carroll,
Bertha H. Palmer,	Emil G. Hirsch,	O. P. Gifford,
James W. Scott,	L. C. Collins,	Jane Addams,
Sarah Hackett Stevenson,	F. MacVeagh,	W. P. Nixon.

CONSTITUTION.

The text of the Constitution of the Federation is as follows :

Name—This corporation shall be called The Civic Federation of Chicago.
Purpose—The purpose of this Federation shall be :
1. The concentration into one potential, non-political, non-sectarian center of all the forces that are now laboring to advance our municipal, philanthropic, industrial and moral interests, and to accomplish all that is possible towards energizing and giving effect to the public conscience of Chicago.
2. To serve as a medium of acquaintance and sympathy between persons who reside in the different parts of the city, who pursue different vocations, who are by birth of different nationalities, who profess different creeds or no creed, who for any of these reasons are unknown to each other, who nevertheless have similar interests in the well being of Chicago and who agree in the wish to promote every kind of municipal welfare.
3. To place municipal administration on a purely business basis, by securing the utmost practicable separation of municipal issues from state and national politics.
Methods—The means employed by the Federation will be investigation, publication, agitation and organization, together with the exercise of every moral influence needed to carry into effect the purpose of the Federation.

MANAGEMENT OF THE FEDERATION.

Management—There shall be a central council, consisting of one hundred members, the Mayor of Chicago being ex-officio a member. The incorporators shall constitute the council until the first annual meeting. At the first annual meeting the incorporators shall appoint ninety-nine councilors, to be divided by lot into three equal groups, the same to hold office for one, two and three years respectively. At each subsequent annual meeting the vacancies in the council, occasioned by the expiration of terms of office, shall be filled by vote of the remaining council.
The membership of the central council may be increased by the addition of one delegate from each ward organization. As soon as practicable, branch ward organizations shall be formed, and each of these branches may elect annually a representative to the council, to serve one year. The council shall elect annually from its own members the board of trustees, to consist of a president, two vice-presidents, a secretary, a treasurer, a legal adviser, a general organizer and eight other members. The Board of Trustees shall also be the executive committee of the council. The officers of the Board of Trustees shall be the officers of the council. They shall hold office for one year, or until their successors have qualified.

DIVISIONS INTO DEPARTMENTS.

Departments—The work of the Federation shall be divided into the following departments :
Municipal.
Philanthropic.
Industrial.
Educational and Social.
Moral Reform.

Departments may be subdivided as the council may from time to time determine.

Amendments—The purpose and methods herein indicated may be modified or extended, as occasion may demand, by a two-thirds vote of those present at any regularly called meeting of the council.

Branch Organization—Twenty-five or more citizens, who are residents of a ward in which there is no branch organization, may at any time form a branch of the Federation. No organization shall be deemed a ward branch of the Federation until it has been recognized as such by the council. Said council shall always have power to pass upon the regularity and good faith of any ward organization, and upon the qualifications of any person claiming to represent, or be a candidate of, or a delegate from such an organization. There shall not be more than one ward organization in any ward, but there may be as many precinct councils as the ward may deem expedient to authorize in its respective precincts.

Feb. 5, 1894.—First meeting of the council at the Palmer House.

Feb. 15.   —Meeting of Council at Commerce Club to elect officers.

OFFICERS.

President—Lyman J. Gage.
First Vice-President—Mrs. Potter Palmer.
Second Vice-President—J. J. McGrath.
Secretary—R. M. Easley.
Treasurer—E. S. Dreyer.

Trustees—J. J. Linehan, M. J. Carroll, T. W. Harvey, L. C. Collins, Jane Addams, Ada C. Sweet, Dr. Sarah Hackett Stevenson, Franklin MacVeagh, G. E. Adams, E. B. Butler.

In the absence of President Lyman J. Gage Mrs. Potter Palmer, First Vice-President of the Civic Federation, called a meeting of the trustees on February 20, at the Palmer House, to appoint the standing committees required by the by-laws of the Federation :

Political—L. C. Collins, John J. McGrath, E. S. Dreyer, John F. Scanlan, George E. Adams, J. W. Ela, Victor F. Lawson, Franklin Mac-Veagh, R. W. Patterson, Jr., Wm. Penn Nixon, Carter Harrison, Slason Thompson, J. W. Scott, A. C. Hesing. The seven representatives of the press in the Federation will also be asked to co-operate with all the department committees.

Ways and Means—T. W. Harvey, Arthur Ryerson, George E. Adams, Wm. Penn Nixon, E. S. Dreyer, Z. S. Holbrook, A. C. Honore, E. B. Butler, J. Irving Pearce.

Municipal—Professor John Gray, W. A. Giles, W. J. Onahan, Marshall Field, Professor E. W. Bemis, M. J. Carroll, Ada C. Sweet, Mrs. H. W. Duncanson, J. W. Ela.

Industrial—James J. Linehan, M. H. Madden, August Jacobson, Mrs. Potter Palmer, Mrs. Charles Henrotin, W. J. Niestadt, Frank Sweeney, Jane Addams, Dr. H. W. Thomas.

Philanthropic—Mrs. J. M. Flower, T. W. Harvey, Professor Albion W. Small, Professor Graham Taylor, J. J. Ryan, Mrs. W. J. Chalmers, H. N. Higinbotham, Dr. Sarah H. Stevenson, C. S. H. Mixer.

Morals—Rev. O. P. Gifford, Edwin D. Wheelock, Cyrus H. McCormick, L. T. O'Brien, H. H. Van Meter, Rev. Frank M. Bristol, Rev. M. C. Ranseen, Rev. Floyd Tomkins, Dr. Arthur Edwards.

Educational and Social—Mrs. H. M. Wilmarth, Mrs. Marion F. Washburn, John McLaren, Emil G. Hirsch, William C. Ames, M. R. Grady, G. Fred Rush, Professor Bamberger, Bishop Fallows.

By vote Mrs. Palmer was requested to call a special meeting of the general council of one hundred for Tuesday evening, February 27, to receive the recommendation of the committee on political action, and to decide how the Federation can be the most effective in the coming campaign.

LIST OF MEMBERS OF THE FEDERATION UP TO FEBRUARY.

Geo. R. Peck..611 Monadnock.
Frank Sweeney.....................................Commerce Building.
John J. McGrath, Pres't Trades Assembly.394 South Paulina Street.
L. T. O'Brien......................................214 Washington Boulevard.
M. J. Carroll......................................148 Monroe Street.
T. J. Griffin ....177 North Lawndale Avenue.
Frank Kidd...185 Barclay Street.
M. H. Madden, Pres't State Fed. of Labor .86 Eda Street.
Dr. Sarah Hackett Stevenson............322 North State Street.
Mrs. Marion Foster Washburn.............555 West Jackson Street.
T. W. Harvey ....825 Rookery.
Lyman J. Gage.....................................First National Bank.
J. Irving Pearce...................................Proprietor Sherman House.
Franklin MacVeagh.............................Lake and Wabash Avenue.
Rev. E. G. Hirsch.................................3612 Grand Boulevard.
Rev. O. P. Gifford................................4543 Greenwood Avenue.
Mrs. W. J. Chalmers.............................234 Ashland Bonlevard.
Bishop Fallows....................................967 West Monroe Street.
Rev. Jenkin Lloyd Jones................3939 Langley Avenue.
W. J. Niestadt.....................................14 Tell Place.
Rev. Dr. Thomas..................................536 West Monroe Street.
Prof. Edward W. Bemis ....Chicago University.
Prof. Albion Small...............................Chicago University.
R. M. Easley..Inter Ocean.
J. W. Scott ....Chicago Herald.
Melville E. Stone................................Globe National Bank.
Dr. Bayard Holmes ....36 Washington Street, Room 914.
A. C. Hesing.......................................Pres't Staats Zeitung Co.
Prof. R. D. Sheppard...........................Northwestern University, Evanston, Ill.
Prof. Graham Taylor ....Chicago Theological Seminary.
Mrs. J. M. Flower.................................Ontario House.
Mrs. Potter Palmer...............................100 Lake Shore Drive.
Mrs. Charles Henrotin..........................Walton Flats, Walton Place.
Miss Ada Sweet....................................175 Dearborn Street, Room 82.
Miss Jane Addams................................335 South Halsted Street.
John J. Mitchell...................................Illinois Trust and Savings Bank.
Rev. P. J. Muldoon...............................311 Superior Street.
Wm. Penn Nixon..................................Inter Ocean.
Mrs. Henry Wade Rogers......................Evanston, Ill.
C. S. H. Mixer......................................Woodruff Hotel.
A. C. Bartlett.......................................32 Lake Street.
Prof. Gray..Northwestern University, Evanston, Ill.
Judge L. C. Collins..............................Rookery.
Azel F. Hatch.......................................Title and Trust Bdg., 100 Washington St.
Wm. Crear...263 South Washtenaw Avenue.
J. J. Ryan, Pres't Building Trades Council.199 Randolph Street.
M. R. Grady...478 Marshfield Avenue.
John Anderson.....................................185 North Peoria Street.
L. W. Kadlec.......................................179 West 12th Street.
Lloyd G. Wheeler.................................119 Dearborn Street.
Mr. Barnett..184 Dearborn Street.
Edwin D. Wheelock..............................99 Washington Street.
W. H. Tatge...79 Dearborn Street, Room 644.
Charles J. Holmes................................91 Dearborn Street, Room 601.
Rev. M. C. Ranseen..............................B79 West Huron Street.
Rev. T. F. Cashman..............................658 West Jackson Street.
Rev. E. D. Kelly..................................West 12th Street, corner May Street.

E. F. Rennacker.................................185 West Madison Street.
Mrs. H. M. Wilmarth.......................Auditorium Annex.
C. A. Mair.......................................169 Jackson Street, Room 212.
Mrs. G. W. Huddleston ....903 West Adams Street.
Mrs. Celia Parker Wooley..................Geneva, Ill.
Mrs. Henry L. Frank........................1608 Prairie Avenue.
Mrs. Henry Solomon........................4060 Lake Avenue.
Mrs. H. W. Duncanson ....190 Warren Avenue.
Miss Hattie A. Shinn........................115 Monroe Street.
W. J. Onahan..................................37 Macalister Place.
John F. Scanlan...............................Postoffice Building.
Z. S. Holbrook................................475 Dearborn Avenue.
E. B. Butler ....230 Adams Street.
John H. Hamline............................The Temple, Room 500.
Wm. Vocke ....520 LaSalle Avenue.
Luther L. Mills..............................122 LaSalle Street.
John W. Ela ....1331 Unity Building.
Dr. W. R. Harper. ....University of Chicago.
Henry Wade Rogers ....Northwestern University, Evanston, Ill.
O. S. A. Sprague ....2700 Prairie Avenue.
Chas. L. Raymond..........................2239 Calumet Avenue.
H. N. Higinbotham ....29th Street and Michigan Avenue.
A. C. Honore.................................2103 Michigan Avenue.
Prof. Bamberger.............................Jewish Manual Training School.
C. U. Gordon................................115 Dearborn Street.
Arthur Ryerson..............................59 Bellevue Place.
Rev. J. H. Barrows.........................2957 Indiana Avenue.
Rev. F. W. Gunsaulus......................Armour Avenue and 33d Street.
Rev. Frank Bristol ....Evanston, Ill.
Rev. Floyd Tomkins ....310 Superior Street.
Dr. Arthur Edwards........................2816 Indiana Avenue.
Augustus Jacobson ....1416—100 Washington Street.
Geo. E. Adams...............................The Temple, Room 914.
E. S. Dreyer..................................99 Dearborn Street.
Willis G. Jackson ....59 Dearborn Street, Room 403.
F. M. Atwood................................Clark, N. W. Corner Madison Street.
A. H. Revell..................................Wabash Avenue.
John McLaren................................2 Franklin Street.
Cyrus H. McCormick, Jr...................329 Wabash Avenue.
Marshall Field...............................Washington Street & Wabash Avenue.
Phillip Henrici................................175 Madison Street.
H. H. Van Meter...... ....21 Groveland Park.
Wm. C. Hollister............................148 Monroe Street.

The Federation was organized in accordance with ideas of leading citizens irrespective of party. Considerable difference of opinion prevailed as to the best method of constituting such an organization, but the principle of Tammany Hall ultimately prevailed. That principle is organization from above downwards instead of what naturally seems to an Englishman the natural organization from the bottom upwards.

Tammany Hall, however, is undoubtedly an organization distinctly American. It has at least vindicated its capacity to survive and it is probably, notwithstanding some temporary reverses, one of the most powerful political organizations in the United States.

Down the levee on Clark Street there is to be found a saloon keeper who for twenty years was a Tammany captain in New York. He keeps a saloon and a house of ill fame in Chicago, but he still keeps up his connection in New York, where he is the proprietor of a house of ill-fame, which will entitle him, no doubt, should he return to the East, to resume his political captaincy in the ranks under the command of Boss Croker. I saw him the night after Dr. Parkhurst had scored his first great success over the politicians of New York. The ex-Tammany Captain shook his head when I asked him what he thought of Dr. Parkhurst's campaign. He had no use for Dr. Parkhurst. For a time, he thought, he might advertise himself, which was no doubt his object, but after that everything would go on as before. The one permanent institution in New York was Tammany.

I asked him to explain its secret. "Suppose," said I, "that I am a newly arrived citizen in your precinct, and come to you and wish to join Tammany, what would be required of me?"

"Sir," said he, "before anything would be required of you we would find out all about you. I would size you up and then after I had formed my own judgment I would send two or three trusty men to find out all about you. Find out, for instance, whether you really meant to work and serve Tammany or whether you were only getting in to find out all about it. If the inquiries were satisfactory then you would be admitted to the ranks of Tammany and would stand in with the rest."

"What should I have to do?"

"Your first duty," said he, "would be to vote the Tammany ticket whenever an election was on, and then to hustle around and make every other person whom you could get hold of vote the same ticket."

"And what would I get for my trouble?" I asked.

"Nothing," said he, "unless you needed it. I was twenty years captain and I never got anything for myself, but if you needed anything you would get whatever was going. It might be a job that would give you employment under the city, it might be a pull that you might have with the aldermen in case you got into trouble, whatever it was you would be entitled to your share. If you get into trouble, Tammany will help you out. If you are out of a job Tammany will see that you have the first chance at whatever is going. It is a great power, is Tammany. Whether it is with the police, or in the court or in the City Hall you will find Tammany men everywhere and they will stick together. There is nothing sticks so tight as Tammany."

Therein, no doubt, this worthy ex-captain revealed the secret of Tammany's success. Tammany is a brotherhood. Tammany men stick together, and help each other.

Their members may be corrupt, their methods indefensible, but the question for Chicago is whether or not the Civic Federation can organize a brotherhood that will work as hard to make Chicago the ideal city of the world as Tammany has been successful in organizing a party which practically holds New York in the hollow of its hand. In other words, are there as many men and women in Chicago who will work as hard for the Kingdom of the Lord in Chicago as there are men who will work for the rule of Tammany in New York?

Tammany has not only organization; it has spoils and power. Power the City Federation may have and will have if its operations are directed with energy and discretion, but there are no spoils. Still, if anything is to be done in practical politics the sinews of war must not be wanting. Many of the members of the Federation are wealthy enough to meet the running expenses of such an organization. But if the Federation is to root itself deeply in every ward in the city it will have to democratize its finances.

There are many persons who wish well to the work of political and social reform in the city who cannot render much active service, but who would be able and willing to contribute say a dime a week for the coming of the Kingdom. If there are 10,000 men and women in Chicago who are sufficiently in earnest about the regeneration of the city to subscribe the cost of a cigar a week for the attainment of their ideal the war chest of the Civic Federation would be able to command $50,000 a year. With that sum a great deal might be done.

APPENDIX F.

WHAT THE LONDON COUNTY COUNCIL HAS DONE FOR LABOR.

The following brief outline of the way in which the labor unions of London have used the London City Council for the purpose of improving the condition of the wage-earners may not be without interest to the unionists of Chicago. By means of a hearty working alliance with the non-conformist churches and the temperance and other societies, the trades unions of London succeeded in 1889 in electing a majority of representatives on the Council, pledged to do what they could to improve the condition of labor in London. John Burns, the engineer, who was the hero of the great dock strike, was elected as a representative of labor to the Council, and from the first sittings his genius, his eloquence and business capacity, his absolute honesty and transparent sincerity, made him one of the most influential members. The labor policy of the London Council was largely dictated by him, and it has become a model for the most democratic municipalities in the kingdom.

The following is a brief summary of what the London County Council, under the leadership of John Burns, has succeeding in doing for labor :

"Fair" wages established in all cases.

Sub-letting and sub-contracting abolished except for work that contractors could not do in ordinary manner.

Practical clerk of works employed in each case where work of any trade is undertaken.

A maximum week of fifty-four hours established.

No man to work more than six days.

Where continuous working goes on, and two twelve-hour shifts were the rule, three shifts of eight hours are now observed.

Overtime abolished,

Contract labor abolished.

In works of maintenance connected with parks, bridges, highways, all classes of men—such as painters, laborers, engineers, scavengers, carpenters, etc.—employed direct.

Firemen, extra holidays.

Pensions are now granted to all retiring employes instead of as formerly only to the higher officials. The wages of the employes of the Council have been raised by $250,000 a year.

All the foregoing relates to what the Council has done when it directly employs labor. The police force in London is not under the control of the Council. Neither are the school teachers; they are controlled by a School Board, not by the Council. None of the employes of the London Council are engaged for political reasons, nor are any dismissed on account of politics. But, not reckoning the police and the teachers, the London Council is one of the largest employers of labor in the kingdom. It sets an example in insisting upon human conditions of service for its workmen and in doing so has done an incalculable amount of good.

But, great as this is, it is less far-reaching than the action which the Council took in deciding that no contracts shall be let to contractors who keep sweat shops or refuse to concede to their workmen the union rates of wages and hours of labor. This step was taken in 1889 when the following resolution was passed which struck at the root of the system which had previously prevailed of accepting the lowest tender without any regard to the conditions which the contractors exacted from their workmen:

That the Council shall require from any persons formally tendering for any contract to the Council a declaration that they will pay such rate of wages and observe such hours of labor as are generally accepted as fair in their trade, and in the event of any charges to the contrary being established against them, the tender should not be accepted.

Mr. H. M. Massingham, one of the ablest of English journalists, writing in the *Daily Chronicle* upon this charter of London labor, says:

Here, then, was a direct blow at the sweating system, at which the pulpit, the press, and politicians had been hammering blows for half a century without ever substantially impairing its direful sway. In other words, the great moral problem of the treatment of labor was placed in the hands of the workmen's organizations as the only bodies capable of guaranteeing a righteous system. The Council's resolution has been carried out with unflinching sternness, and its result has been to mitigate in favor of the workers of London the whole system of accepting the lowest tender. Under it the employer who cuts his estimate for public work in the hope of sweating his profit out of ill-paid and ill-organized labor finds to-day his occupation gone. Linked with this reform was another of equal importance. The Council decided that it would be impossible to allow the contractor to slip out of his engagements to his workmen by letting out his business to another man. They therefore decided to forbid sub-letting and sub-contracting, save in those cases where work lay outside the ordinary scope of the contractor's trade. This regulation has not only been laid down, but enforced; and one fine of £500 was inflicted as a warning, which it has not been found necessary to repeat. The petty sweating jobmaster has thus been eliminated, for the good of every creature except himself.

In other directions the same beneficent spirit is manifested. It has established bands in the parks, laid out and beautified hundreds of acres of common lands, has made playgrounds for children and has enormously raised the standard of the music hall entertainments in London. It has established a municipal lodging house for single men, and is steadily working to acquire possession of the street railways, the water and gas works, and the markets, in order that it may use all these monopolies of service to cheapen the cost of living for the poor, and to remove the obstacles which at present stand in the way of their leading a human life. The policy of the Council has been strongly in favor of temperance. The chairman of the Council is a strong temperance man, and the majority of the members are deadly enemies of the saloon. I need hardly say that no saloon keeper was brought forward on either side as a candidate at the last election, nor if any had been would he have had the remotest chance of being elected. If these things can be done in London, why cannot they be done in Chicago by the labor unions acting together with the other moral and religious forces of the town?

Other Books By Chicago Historical Bookworks

surrection Mary: A Ghost Story. By Kenan Heise
Buddy Wojcik, an almost 100 year-old patient at Peoria State Hospital, had a secret
d he was about to reveal it: he had danced with Resurrection Mary, a ghost.
Softcover $10.95

e Cliff Dwellers: The History of a Chicago Cultural Institution. By Henry Regnery.
This book spans the history of the club from its auspicious behinnings to the present.
Hardcover $20.00

llinger: A Short and Violent Life. By Robert Cromie and Joseph Pinkston. (1962)
print.
Classic biography of an extraordinary American folk hero and bankrobber.
Softcover $10.95

talogue of the WPA Writers' Program Publications: September, 1941. By the WPA
riters' Program. (1941) Reprint.
A catalogue listing more than 1,000 WPA books, plays, pamphlets, etc.
Softcover $ 7.50

Bibliography of Illinois, Chicago, and Environs. By the WPA Writers' Program. (1937)
print.
A guide to literature and materials prior to 1937 on the state of Illinois, the city of
icago, and its suburbs.
Softcover $15.00

e Chicagoization of America: 1893-1917. By Kenan Heise.
scinating evidence of Chicago's profound cultural and moral impact on the rest of the
ited States between the World's Columbian Exposition and World War I.
Softcover $12.95

eck List of Chicago Ante-Fire Imprints: 1851-1871. By the WPA Writers' Program.
938) Reprint.
Bibliography of 1,880 books and pamphlets printed in Chicago in the 20 years before
e Chicago Fire.
Spiral-bound $35.00

phonse: A Play Based on the Words of Al Capone. By Kenan Heise.
Contemporary newspapers and the transcript of the trial of Al Capone contributed
e material from which this play was written.
Softcover $ 6.95

e Cost of Something for Nothing. By John Peter Altgeld. (1903) Reprint.
Strong words from the man whom Darrow called "one of the most sincere and
voted friends of humanity this country has ever produced."
Hardcover, D.J. $ 9.95